A General Theory of Entrepreneurship

The Individual–Opportunity Nexus

Scott Shane

Case Western Reserve University

NEW HORIZONS IN ENTREPRENEURSHIP

Edward Elgar

Cheltenham, UK • Northampton, MA, USA

Published by
Edward Elgar Publishing Limited
Glensanda House
Montpellier Parade
Cheltenham
Glos GL50 1UA
UK

Edward Elgar Publishing, Inc.
136 West Street
Suite 202
Northampton
Massachusetts 01060
USA

A catalogue record for this book
is available from the British Library

Library of Congress Cataloging in Publication Data
Shane, Scott Andrew, 1964–
    A general theory of entrepreneurship : the individual–opportunity nexus / Scott Shane.
        p. cm. — (New horizons in entrepreneurship series)
    1. Entrepreneurship. I. Title. II. Series.

    HB615.S477 2003
    338'.04—dc21

ISBN 1 84376 382 6 (cased)
Printed and bound in Great Britain by MPG Books Ltd, Bodmin, Cornwall

A General Theory of Entrepreneurship

NEW HORIZONS IN ENTREPRENEURSHIP

Series Editor: Sankaran Venkataraman
Darden Graduate School of Business Administration,
University of Virginia

This important series is designed to make a significant contribution to the development of Entrepreneurship Studies. As this field has expanded dramatically in recent years, the series will provide an invaluable forum for the publication of high-quality works of scholarship and show the diversity of issues and practices around the world.

The main emphasis of the series is on the development and application of new and original ideas in Entrepreneurship. Global in its approach, it includes some of the best theoretical and empirical work with contributions to fundamental principles, rigorous evaluations of existing concepts and competing theories, historical surveys and future visions. Titles include original monographs, edited collections, and texts.

Contents

Figures

Boxes

Foreword

Although the study of entrepreneurial opportunities – their origins, nature and evolution – should form the core of the field of entrepreneurship, it has been a relatively neglected topic. Finally, we have a book that fills this much needed gap in the literature.

Professor Scott Shane provides a deep and comprehensive discussion of the individual–opportunity nexus in entrepreneurship. Eschewing the usual approaches of either focusing exclusively on the individuals and their motivations and actions or focusing exclusively, almost always *ex-post*, on the economic potential of opportunities, Shane fixes his gaze squarely on the nexus of the individual and the opportunity. It is this nexus that I believe is the building block for a better understanding of the entrepreneurial phenomenon.

A remarkable feature of Shane's work is its breadth of discussion. Shane surveys a vast literature, from economics to psychology and from sociology to management as he builds a compelling framework of the individual–opportunity nexus. He alternates dexterously between the phenomenon and theoretical discipline, always striking a good balance between the two and never falling into the trap of becoming either phenomenon-centric or discipline-centric. Nor does he stop at theoretical frameworks alone. You will find rich and compelling evidence to back up the arguments in the book.

Shane's work will certainly be provocative because he takes at least two positions which will evoke considerable debate in the field. First, Shane firmly believes that entrepreneurial opportunities exist independent of the actors in a system. In Shane's view, every price, every invention, every bit of information already engenders within itself opportunities for the creation of new ends. However, human creativity and some idiosyncratic conditions have to exist for the *objective* opportunity to be brought to life. The reason *specific* individuals are required in a world of objective opportunities, in Shane's view, is because opportunities themselves lack agency. A human being is required to provide this agency so that when *a market can come to be, it will come to be*. This explicitly *discovery* view of entrepreneurship is in marked contrast to an alternate view emerging in the literature, namely, the *creative* view. According to the creative view, opportunities do not exist in any objective form, but are merely a social construction. I foresee a vigorous debate, perhaps even central to the development of the field, on this issue.

Second, Shane also firmly believes that individuals, and not groups or firms, discover entrepreneurial opportunities. Since discovery is a cognitive process, it is meaningless to talk about a cognitive process as a collective act. The collective process is meaningful only in discussions of execution and exploitation, but not in the discovery process itself. Both of these arguments run counter to recent developments in the literature on entrepreneurship. Shane's ideas and arguments will certainly provoke a healthy debate about our underlying assumptions and arguments about the entrepreneurial phenomenon. I say, let the debates begin!

I am pleased to introduce the Edward Elgar series _New Horizons in Entrepreneurship_. I am further pleased to be able to publish Scott Shane's provocative book as a first in the series. The purpose of this series is to publish the best thinking about the nature and role of entrepreneurship in business. The books in this series are aimed at three audiences: entrepreneurship and management scholars, teachers of entrepreneurship and management, and reflective practitioners.

Sankaran Venkataraman
Series Editor

Acknowledgements

Writing a book, even a sole authored one, requires the work of large numbers of people. This book is no exception. While many people have made this book possible, the most important of them has been my colleague and mentor, S. Venkataraman. Venkat helped with this book in almost too many ways to list. As my dissertation advisor, his ideas and approach to entrepreneurship research have shaped my thinking over the past 13 years. His 1997 article 'The distinctive domain of entrepreneurship' in *Advances in Entrepreneurship, Firm Emergence, and Growth*, first proposed the individual–opportunity nexus as a lens to examine entrepreneurship, and dramatically altered my thinking about this topic, leading to many of the ideas presented in this book. Our co-authorship of 'The promise of entrepreneurship as a field of research' in *Academy of Management Review* provided the basic framework for this book.

Over the years, I also have been fortunate to have several additional collaborators who have taught me a great deal about entrepreneurship. Although there have been many, four have been particularly important in helping to shape the ideas in this book. Dan Cable and I have collaborated on several papers on new venture finance over the past six years. Chapter 8 of this book is very much an outgrowth of my work with Dan. Frederic Delmar has been my collaborator on a series of empirical studies of the new firm formation process, examining a random sample of newly formed Swedish firms. My discussions with Frederic, both in person and via email, have greatly sharpened my thinking about many of the ideas presented here. Jon Eckhardt was a collaborator on two conceptual articles that greatly expanded the individual–opportunity nexus as outlined in my *Academy of Management Review* article with Venkat. Jon's probing and challenging questions helped me to significantly expand on many of the key ideas in my earlier work on this topic. In particular, many of the ideas in Chapters 2 and 3 of this book would not have been possible without my collaboration with Jon over the past several years. Bill Gartner and I wrote an article together in the early 1990s that helped to shape my thinking about the role of institutional factors in entrepreneurship. Moreover, Bill's tireless efforts to convince me of the importance of the entrepreneurial process finally led me to pay attention to that topic, a recognition that greatly spurred my understanding of the field and made it possible for me to write Chapter 10 of this book.

During my earliest years as a researcher, I benefited greatly from the support and encouragement of Ian MacMillan. Not only did Mac support me financially through the Ph.D. program in Management at Wharton, but also he kept me from quitting the program when I wasn't doing well. To the extent that my scholarly work has any impact on the field of entrepreneurship, people should attribute a large portion of that impact to Mac's efforts to keep me in academia. Without him, I would not be a professor today.

Several other colleagues also need to be acknowledged as work with them led to many of the ideas and research in this book: Pierre Azoulay, Robert Baron, Chris Collins, Maw Der Foo, Dante DiGregorio, Riitta Katila, Rakesh Khurana, Ed Locke, Atul Nerkar, Wes Sine and Toby Stuart. In addition, several other colleagues have helped me over the years by discussing many of my ideas about entrepreneurship: Bob Baum, Terry Blum, Per Davidsson, Brent Goldfarb, David Kirsch, Rudy Lamone, Ed Roberts, Saras Sarasvathy, Scott Stern, Rama Velamuri and Eric Von Hippel.

I also owe a debt of gratitude to the participants in the one-week intensive Ph.D. seminar in entrepreneurship that I have run at the University of Maryland over the past two years. There is nothing like presenting your ideas to a bunch of highly trained and critical Ph.D. students to lead you to discover the errors and omissions in your work and lead you to correct them.

Several people did me a tremendous service in reading and commenting on an earlier draft of this book. Frederic Delmar not only read the book, but also gave me detailed and extensive comments that allowed me to greatly improve the final version of the manuscript before publication. Robert Baron read the entire manuscript and gave me extensive comments on Chapter 5, which greatly improved that chapter. Bill Gartner, Chuck Allen and Pat Maggitti also read through the entire book and gave feedback. My research assistant, Stephanie Materese, checked references, tables, quotations, grammar and style, and caught numerous errors that I would otherwise have missed.

Lastly, I have to thank my daughter, Hannah, for being such a good baby that I could concentrate on finishing this book in the first few months of her life. I also have to thank my wife, Lynne, for encouraging me to write this book and then spending countless hours talking to me about the academic field of entrepreneurship, when I am sure that she would have rather discussed just about anything else. Moreover, I cannot thank Lynne enough for supporting me through writing this book by getting everything ready for Hannah, and then by doing more than her fair share of Hannah care so that I could get this book out to the publisher.

1. Introduction

A visitor from another planet who came to earth for the first time would think that entrepreneurship was one of the best-understood subjects examined by business school academics. Almost every explanation for business and, for that matter, capitalism itself, relies on entrepreneurship as a cornerstone. Moreover, huge numbers of people around the world engage in entrepreneurial activity. Estimates of the number of people in the United States who take part in founding a firm every year reach roughly one million people, or 4 per cent of the US labor force (Aldrich, 1999; Reynolds and White, 1997). This number is larger than the number of people having children or getting married in a given year (Reynolds, 1997). As a result, at any given point in time, business owners account for approximately 13 per cent of all non-agricultural employees, a fraction comparable to the percentage of the private sector labor force that is unionized (Hamilton, 2000). Furthermore, entrepreneurship contributes heavily to job growth, with new firm births estimated to account for one quarter of gross job growth in the United States (Reynolds and White, 1997).

The level of interest in entrepreneurship among business school students is also extremely high. Every university campus, it seems, has a wealth of courses about how to start and finance new businesses. Most institutions, if not all, have business plan competitions that provide student and faculty entrepreneurs with prize money to start new companies that, everyone hopes, will revolutionize some industry and make all associated with it fabulously wealthy. Several universities have even started formal venture capital funds to finance the development of student and faculty run businesses, and more still run incubators for new businesses.

On top of all of this is the community of scholars who teach students how to found successful new companies. This field has grown at a prodigious rate in recent years. The academic field of entrepreneurship now supports no fewer than 15 scholarly journals. In the business school field of management alone, approximately 10 per cent of all professors consider entrepreneurship their primary or secondary area of affiliation. As a result, every year, several thousand scholarly articles about entrepreneurship are produced.

Given the level of interest devoted to entrepreneurship in the economy, and among academics at business schools, one would think that researchers would have deep insights into understanding this phenomenon. However, those who look closely at academic investigations of entrepreneurship realize that scholarly understanding of this field is actually quite limited. Unlike its sister fields of accounting, marketing, finance, organizational behavior and strategic management, entrepreneurship is rather poorly explained by academics. Much of what passes for evidence is often unconvincing. Moreover, the pieces of knowledge are fragmentary, unlinked by an overarching framework or explanation, giving a very descriptive feel to the academic understanding that does exist.

As a result, our collective knowledge about entrepreneurial opportunities; the people who pursue them; the skills and strategies used to organize and exploit opportunities; and the environmental conditions favorable to this activity is so limited that even academics frequently resort to anecdotes as explanation. Simply put, academia has no coherent conceptual framework for entrepreneurship and has offered virtually no systematic efforts to assemble the fragmentary pieces of knowledge about this phenomenon in one place.

THE PROBLEMS WITH PRIOR RESEARCH

A central premise of this book is that the failure of academics to offer a coherent conceptual framework for entrepreneurship has resulted from a tendency of researchers to look at only one part of entrepreneurial process – the characteristics of the entrepreneurs themselves, the opportunities to which they respond, their strategies, their resource acquisition or their organizing processes – without consideration for whether the explanations that they offer have any explanatory power for, or even relationship to, the other parts of the entrepreneurial process examined by other researchers.

Perhaps the largest part of this problem lies with the division of the field of entrepreneurship into two camps: those who want the field of entrepreneurship to focus exclusively on individuals and those who want the field of entrepreneurship to focus exclusively on external forces. A large number of entrepreneurship researchers have sought to explain the entrepreneurial phenomenon by identifying those members of society who could be considered 'entrepreneurial individuals'. In general, this school of thought has focused on explaining entrepreneurship as a function of core human attributes, such as willingness to bear uncertainty (Khilstrom and Laffont, 1979), tolerance for ambiguity (Schere, 1982), or need for achievement (McClelland, 1961) which differentiate entrepreneurs from the rest of society. Unfortunately, this approach has proved largely unsuccessful (Gartner, 1990), perhaps because entrepreneurial activity is episodic. Because people engage in entrepreneurial behavior only at particular points in time, and in response to specific situations, it is impossible to account for entrepreneurship solely by examining factors that should influence all human action in the same way all of the time (Carroll and Mosakowski, 1987).

Another group of researchers has sought to explain entrepreneurship by reference to the environment in which entrepreneurs have been found. In general, this school of thought has sought to identify situations in which entrepreneurial activity, often measured as new firm formation, is more likely to occur. Key situational factors that have been argued to lead to entrepreneurial activity have included competence-destroying technological change (Tushman and Anderson, 1986), industry dynamics (Hannan and Freeman, 1987), and market structure (Acs and Audretsch, 1990). Unfortunately, this approach, too, has failed to provide an adequate explanation for entrepreneurship, largely because it does not consider human agency (Shane and Khurana, 2001). Entrepreneurship is a self-directed activity that does not occur spontaneously from the presence of technological or industrial change. Rather, it requires the action of individuals who identify and pursue opportunities. No amount of investigation of the environment alone can provide a complete explanation for entrepreneurship.

The division of the field into these different camps has stymied the development of the field of entrepreneurship. By focusing on only one aspect of the entrepreneurial process, most researchers fail to provide a comprehensive explanation of the phenomenon. Not only does this approach hinder the development of a general theoretical framework for entrepreneurship, it also leads to a diversion of scholarly attention away from real questions towards largely academic debates. For example, the field of entrepreneurship has devoted disproportionate attention to scholarly efforts by one set of scholars to show that individual differences have little effect on entrepreneurship, and another set of scholars to defend their focus on individual characteristics. We would know much more about entrepreneurship had both sets of scholars directed their attention toward the investigation of specific hypotheses about entrepreneurial activity rather than toward each other's intellectual position.

Neither the environment-centric nor the individual-centric approach toward entrepreneurship is more 'correct' than the other. Both probably explain equal amounts of the variance in entrepreneurial activity. Moreover, even if scholars were to find that one approach explained slightly more variance than the other, such a discovery would be of little intellectual and practical importance. The phenomenon of entrepreneurship cannot be explained either by environmental forces or by individual factors in the absence of the other. Therefore, the scholarly field of entrepreneurship would be much better off if academics devoted more energy toward the development of a comprehensive framework for entrepreneurship that incorporated the effects of individuals, as well as the effects of opportunities and the institutional and industry environment in which the pursuit of opportunity occurs, than on attempts to prove the superiority of one perspective over another.

THE PURPOSE OF THIS BOOK

The purpose of this book is to offer an overarching conceptual framework for entrepreneurship that explains the different parts of the entrepreneurial process in a coherent way. Rather than focusing on only one part of the entrepreneurial process – such as the characteristics of the entrepreneurs themselves; the opportunities to which they respond; their strategies; their acquisition of resources; or their organizing processes – without consideration for whether the explanations that offered have any explanatory power for, or even relationship to, other parts of the entrepreneurial process, the perspective outlined here provides an overarching framework for the field.

As a general framework for the field of entrepreneurship, I offer the individual–opportunity nexus (Eckhardt and Shane, 2003; Shane and Venkataraman, 2000; Venkataraman, 1997). This framework examines the characteristics of opportunities; the individuals who discover and exploit them; the processes of resource acquisition and organizing; and the strategies used to exploit and protect the profits from those efforts.

In the book, I make a conscious effort to explain the different parts of the entrepreneurial process by adhering to the same basic assumptions of the nexus framework (which I will discuss below). The book also outlines the relationships between the different parts of the entrepreneurial process so that readers can see the process as a related whole, rather than as unrelated fragments.

Lastly, the book provides both the arguments for particular patterns, and the empirical evidence collected to date about that dimension of entrepreneurship, so that readers can judge for themselves what dimensions of the phenomenon have truly been explained and what dimensions have only been suggested. To do this, I review the existing literature on entrepreneurship to show the relationship between the conceptual arguments made in that literature and the parts of the individual–opportunity nexus or to provide empirical evidence that is consistent with one of the propositions that emerge from the nexus perspective.

A Definition of Entrepreneurship

To provide a conceptual framework for something, a researcher must first define it and put some boundaries around it. Therefore, I begin by defining entrepreneurship.

Entrepreneurship is an activity that involves the discovery, evaluation and exploitation of opportunities to introduce new goods and services, ways of organizing, markets, processes, and raw materials through organizing efforts that previously had not existed (Venkataraman, 1997; Shane and Venkataraman, 2000). Given this definition, the academic field of entrepreneurship incorporates, in its domain, explanations for why, when and how entrepreneurial opportunities exist; the sources of those opportunities and the forms that they take; the processes of opportunity discovery and evaluation; the acquisition of resources for the exploitation of these opportunities; the act of opportunity exploitation; why, when, and how some individuals and not others discover, evaluate, gather resources for and exploit opportunities; the strategies used to pursue opportunities; and the organizing efforts to exploit them (Shane and Venkataraman, 2000).

While this definition is a useful conceptual definition for entrepreneurship, it is also very difficult to operationalize in empirical research. Because this book reviews empirical research on the topic of entrepreneurship, I also discuss two major operational definitions of entrepreneurship used in the empirical research reviewed in this book: new firm formation and self employment. To keep the operational definitions clear throughout the book, I refer to the specific operational definition used by the authors when discussing a particular piece of empirical research. I define *self employment* as performing work for personal profit rather than for wages paid by others (Le, 1999). The studies on self employment reviewed here can include situations in which the self employed person incorporates a business and employs others, as well as situations in which these things do not occur. The second operational definition of entrepreneurship discussed in this book is the *founding of a new business*, which is defined as the forming of a business venture or not-for-profit organization that previously was not in existence.

This book also examines the relationship between different dimensions of entrepreneurship and several measures of performance at entrepreneurial activities – survival, growth, profitability and experiencing an initial public offering. Therefore, below I define each of the performance measures that are reviewed and explain why they are useful dimensions on which to evaluate efforts to exploit opportunity.

The first operational measure of performance discussed in this book is *survival*, which I define as the continuation of the entrepreneurial effort. Survival is an important measure of entrepreneurial performance because very few entrepreneurial efforts survive. Aldrich (1999) estimates that half of all entrepreneurs fail to complete their organizing efforts. Moreover, approximately 750 000 new businesses are founded and fail every year in the United States (Bhide, 2000), with 40 per cent of the new businesses failing to survive one year (Taylor, 1999), 64 per cent failing to survive five years (Kirchhoff, 1994), 75 per cent failing to survive eight years (Kirchhoff and Phillips, 1989), and 88 per cent failing to survive 19 years (Kirchhoff, 1994).

The second operational measure of entrepreneurial performance discussed in this book is growth, which I define as an increase in the new venture's employment or sales. When I discuss specific empirical research on growth, I define whether the specific measure used in the research was growth in sales or growth in employment.

Growth is an important dimension of new venture performance because it, too, is rare. Fewer than 10 per cent of new organizations ever grow on any dimension, and fewer than 4 per cent of new organizations add more than 100 employees during their lifetimes (Duncan and Handler, 1994). Moreover, growth is important because most new ventures start very small for a variety of reasons that I will explain in Chapter 9. Therefore, to differentiate high and low performing entrepreneurial efforts, one must capture the improvement over time in the condition of the effort to exploit the entrepreneurial opportunity, which growth does.

The third operational measure of entrepreneurial performance discussed in this book is profit (or income), which is defined as the surplus of revenues over costs. This operational definition of performance best captures the concept of entrepreneurial profit discussed in the theoretical literature. In addition, profit is a valuable measure of entrepreneurial performance because it is a rare, but desirable, outcome of entrepreneurial activity. For instance, Schiller and Crewson (1997) found that only 8 per cent of self employed women and 21 per cent of self employed men have self employment income above the median for their cohort in any year, and fewer still do this in more than one year.

The fourth operational measure of entrepreneurial performance discussed in this book is the achievement of an initial public offering, which is defined as the sale of stock to the public. While this definition of performance does not map closely on the concept of entrepreneurial profit, or any other measure described in the theoretical literature, it does capture the idea of significant performance of an entrepreneurial venture. As a result, it is useful at measuring the outcome of Schumpeterian (1934) types of entrepreneurial efforts. Therefore, I examine this dimension of entrepreneurial performance along with the other measures.

Some Necessary Conditions

The definition of entrepreneurship presented above imposes several necessary conditions on a conceptual framework to explain the entrepreneurial phenomenon. I present these assumptions here to make them clear to the reader before introducing the conceptual framework underlying the book. First, entrepreneurship requires the existence of opportunities, or situations in which people believe that they can use new means–ends frameworks to recombine resources to generate profit (Shane, 2000). While people's perceptions influence the discovery, evaluation and exploitation of opportunities, I will argue (in Chapter 2) that opportunities have an objective component that does not exist solely in the mind of the entrepreneur. Therefore, entrepreneurship cannot be only a fixed attribute of certain people, but rather must involve their reaction to the existence of opportunities for profit.

Second, entrepreneurship requires differences between people. Specifically, entrepreneurship requires the preferential access to or ability to recognize information about opportunities, both of which vary across people. The existence of individual differences is central to the approach to entrepreneurship outlined in this book. In the absence of variation across people, everyone would recognize and act upon all opportunities, making it impossible for any one person to gain access to resources at a price at which recombination could yield a profit. Resource owners would recognize the same opportunities as entrepreneurs and simply would be unwilling to sell resources to the entrepreneur at a price that made the opportunity profitable for the entrepreneur.

Moreover, entrepreneurship requires a decision by a person to act upon an opportunity because opportunities themselves lack agency. Unlike many environmentally oriented explanations for entrepreneurship (for example, Aldrich, 1990; Carroll and Hannan, 2000), this book explains that opportunities do not spontaneously result in exploitation. Rather, they are exploited only when a human being acts. Therefore, variation among people in their willingness or ability to act influences the entrepreneurial process.

Third, risk bearing is a necessary part of the entrepreneurial process. The exploitation of opportunity is, by definition, uncertain. The information necessary to determine whether a particular effort to exploit an opportunity will be profitable cannot be known with certainty at the time that the opportunity is identified because that information does not come into existence until the entrepreneur pursues the opportunity. The pursuit of opportunity, itself, determines whether demand exists, whether the entrepreneur can compete with others, whether the value chain can be created, and so on (Arrow, 1974a; Venkataraman, 1997). Therefore, those engaged in the entrepreneurial process cannot know with certainty that their plan for recombining resources will result in a profit and not a loss at the time they make a decision to act, forcing the entrepreneur to bear risk in the entrepreneurial process.

Fourth, the entrepreneurial process requires organizing. By organizing, I do not mean that the entrepreneurial process requires the creation of a new firm. While founding a new firm is one way to organize an opportunity, the use of market mechanisms (for example, licensing) is another.

However, whether the entrepreneurial process results in the founding of a new firm or the use of market mechanisms, it does require the creation of a new way of exploiting the opportunity (organizing) that did not previously exist. When prices fail to allocate resources adequately (for reasons I will discuss in Chapter 3), people cannot make decisions by optimizing within existing means–ends frameworks and must formulate new means–ends frameworks. The new means–ends frameworks lead the entrepreneur to come up with a way to organize the exploitation of the opportunity that she has identified. The fact that the entrepreneur exploits an opportunity to recombine resources, and attempts to sell that recombination at a profit means that some mechanism for organizing the resources in a way that had not been done before is a necessary condition of entrepreneurship.

Fifth, the entrepreneurial process requires some form of innovation. By innovation, I do not mean that all entrepreneurial efforts require the grand Schumpeterian (1934) innovations that result in new combinations that spur creative destruction. As I explain in Chapter 2, the entrepreneurial process can involve a type of innovation that is much milder, such as placing a restaurant on a different corner of an intersection from existing restaurants, or using different recipes or employees in a new restaurant in the same location as an old one. Researchers (for example, Shane and Venkataraman, 2000; Venkataraman, 1997) have pointed out that this milder form of innovation is often associated with Kirznerian (1997), rather than Schumpeterian, entrepreneurial opportunities.

However, even Kirznerian opportunities involve innovation. By definition, entrepreneurship cannot involve the perfect imitation of what has been done before. The simple fact that it involves the recombination of resources into a new form according to the judgment of the entrepreneur means that entrepreneurship involves some innovative activity.

Some Things Not Assumed

While the framework presented in this book makes several assumptions, it also does not require certain assumptions present in other explanations for entrepreneurship. First, new organizing efforts do not *require* the creation of new firms to exploit opportunities. A firm is a legal entity, and people do not need to create new legal entities when they organize. Organizing can exist without the formation of a new legal entity, as is the case when a group of traders is formed to smuggle goods into a country. Moreover, the entrepreneur can use market mechanisms, such as licensing, to exploit opportunities; there are times when organizing a market mechanism is a better approach than organizing a firm (Amit, Glosten and Muller, 1993; Casson, 1982; Shane and Venkataraman, 2000). For example, many entrepreneurs in biotechnology license their new technologies to established pharmaceutical firms rather than develop new firms because the pharmaceutical firms' assets in marketing and distribution make licensing to them a much better approach than building the value chain of a new firm from scratch. In Chapter 10, I will address this issue directly when I discuss the process of organizing, and the use of markets as opposed to hierarchies, as a mode of opportunity exploitation.

Second, an entrepreneurial effort does not have to be undertaken by a single entrepreneur alone. Rather, more than one person can undertake a given entrepreneurial effort, either simultaneously or sequentially. For example, the person who discovers an opportunity can sell it to another person. In addition, the discoverer of the opportunity can obtain the assistance of other people in the resource assembly or exploitation parts of the entrepreneurial process. The relaxation of the assumption that a single person has to undertake all parts of the entrepreneurial process alone is important because it makes the individual–opportunity nexus approach discussed in this book different from person-centric approaches to entrepreneurship. Person-centric approaches, which explain entrepreneurship by reference to particular types of people, have to assume that those people with key entrepreneurial attributes engage in the entire entrepreneurial process.

Third, successful outcomes are not a necessary condition of entrepreneurship. Although many researchers approach entrepreneurship with a backward lens, searching for the factors that explain success at this activity, success is far from a necessary condition. In fact, the modal outcome of the entrepreneurial process is the founding of a failed firm. As a result, success at entrepreneurship might be explained by actions taken in ways contrary to the norm. This is not to say that there are not performance effects of entrepreneurial actions. Rather, it is to say that entrepreneurship is rarely successfully undertaken.

Fourth, the factors that explain one part of the entrepreneurial process do not have to explain other parts. For example, people who are high in independence may be more likely than those low in independence to exploit entrepreneurial opportunities, but they may not be better at forming strategies that capture the returns to that activity.

In fact, success at entrepreneurial activities may be explained by taking actions that are rare for entrepreneurs to take. For example, Bhide (2000) found that the *Inc* 500 firms, the fastest growing private firms in the United States, tended not to be started in the most popular industries for start-ups. This pattern suggests that certain industries might be very popular for entrepreneurship, but, because of their popularity, they may not be very good choices for entrepreneurs.

The Central Premise

The central premise of this book is that entrepreneurship can be explained by considering the nexus of enterprising individuals and valuable opportunities (Shane and Venkataraman, 2000; Eckhardt and Shane, forthcoming; Venkataraman, 1997), and by using that nexus to understand the processes of discovery and exploitation of opportunities; the acquisition of resources; entrepreneurial strategy; and the organizing process.

The conceptual framework that underlies this book is quite straightforward. Because the economy operates in a continual state of disequilibrium and change, situations arise in which people can transform resources into a form (new goods and services, new ways of organizing, new methods of production, new markets or new materials) that they believe will have greater value than their cost to create (Venkataraman, 1997). The entrepreneurial process begins with the perception of the existence of opportunities, or situations in which resources can be recombined at a potential profit. Alert individuals, called entrepreneurs, discover these opportunities, and develop ideas for how to pursue them, including the development of a product or service that will be provided to customers. These individuals then obtain resources, design organizations or other modes of opportunity exploitation, and develop a strategy to exploit the opportunity.

As Figure 1.1 indicates, the entrepreneurial process involves the identification and evaluation of opportunity; the decision whether or not to exploit it; the efforts to obtain resources; the process for organizing those resources into a new combination; and the development of a strategy for the new venture. These different activities are all influenced by individual-, industry- and institution-level factors.

AN INTERDISCIPLINARY APPROACH

Readers will note that any effort to provide a conceptual framework for entrepreneurship seems to require an interdisciplinary approach. The domains of psychology, sociology and economics all seem to provide insight into a piece of the puzzle, but none seem to explain the phenomenon completely. In fact, many classical researchers of entrepreneurship, like Knight (1921) and Schumpeter (1934), viewed entrepreneurship in just this way. These authors saw the economic framework of entrepreneurship as demanding certain characteristics of entrepreneurs best explained by psychology and sociology.

Although the vogue in business schools today seems to be for scholars to explain phenomena from the perspective of a single social science discipline, this book follows in the tradition of classical writers on entrepreneurship and deliberately takes an interdisciplinary perspective. As a result, readers will find this book very different from works written about entrepreneurship by economists, historians, political scientists, psychologists or sociologists. The book's focus is not on testing theories of entrepreneurship from a particular disciplinary perspective, but instead seeks to use work from the fields of psychology, economics, organization theory, finance, strategy, technology management and public policy to create a conceptual framework for entrepreneurship and provide supporting empirical evidence for that framework.

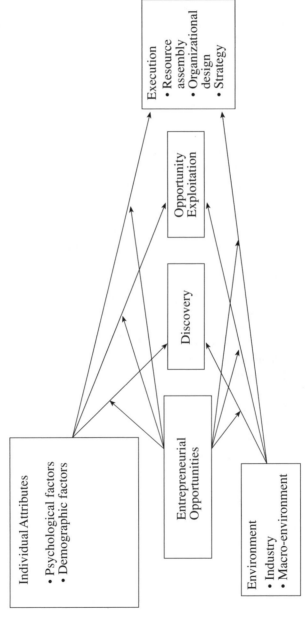

Figure 1.1   A model of the entrepreneurial process

THE STRUCTURE OF THE BOOK

This book has a very simple structure. As Figure 1.2 shows, the book starts with the assumption that entrepreneurial activity is directional and ordered, though it is accepting of the possibility of feedback loops and non-linearity. The order in which entrepreneurial activity occurs is as follows: before opportunities are identified, sources of opportunities must lead them to exist. To be evaluated and a decision made to exploit opportunities, these opportunities must be identified. For resources to be assembled, the decision must have been made to exploit the opportunity. For the resources to be recombined into a new form (the organizing process), the resources must have been assembled. For the entrepreneur's approach to exploitation to be organized into a new entity, the entrepreneur must have a strategy, either implicit or explicit, to exploit the opportunity. For performance to occur, the effort to exploit the opportunity must have been organized into a new entity. For ease of exposition, the chapters of the book follow this directional process.

Chapter 2 provides a detailed explanation of the role of opportunities in entrepreneurship, one of the main components in the perspective described in this book. This chapter examines three important dimensions of entrepreneurial opportunities. First, it summarizes the two major perspectives on the existence of opportunities: The Schumpeterian (1934) and Kirznerian (1973) perspectives. Second, this chapter discusses three major sources of entrepreneurial opportunity: technological change, political/regulatory change and social/demographic change. Third, Chapter 2 discusses the different forms that entrepreneurial opportunities take, including new products or services, new ways of organizing, new raw materials, new markets and new production processes (Schumpeter, 1934).

It is one thing for opportunities to exist and another for them to be discovered. Chapter 3 explores the process of opportunity discovery. It explains why the price system cannot always allocate resources, and shows how entrepreneurial decision-making overcomes limitations to the price system. In addition, Chapter 3 discusses the role of individual-level variation in the discovery process. This chapter explains how idiosyncratic life experiences, search processes and social

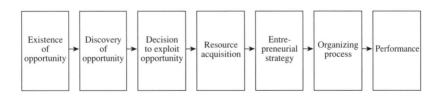

Figure 1.2   The direction of the entrepreneurial process

ties provide some people with access to information about opportunities before that information is generally available. The chapter also explains that people differ in their ability to recognize opportunity because they have different prior stocks of knowledge. Prior knowledge provides an absorptive capacity that facilitates the acquisition of additional information about markets, technologies and production processes, which, in turn, enhances the ability to formulate new means–ends frameworks (Cohen and Levinthal, 1990). Finally, this chapter explains how differences in people's cognitive processes influence their ability to identify the new means–ends frameworks necessary for opportunity discovery.

Chapter 4 discusses non-psychological individual-level differences that influence the tendency of people to exploit entrepreneurial opportunities. This chapter explains that people exploit opportunities when they believe that the value of opportunities exceeds their opportunity cost of alternative activity, plus a premium for bearing illiquidity and uncertainty (Venkataraman, 1997). The person's education and experience influence the expected value of the outcome of opportunity exploitation and therefore influence the decision to exploit. Moreover, a person's social ties and social status influence the exploitation process.

Chapter 5 considers the body of research that explores how psychological characteristics influence the likelihood that a person will exploit an entrepreneurial opportunity. Because the value of an opportunity can be non-monetary (desire to be one's own boss, need to express one's achievement motive and so on) and because the evaluation of uncertainty or outcomes can be affected by psychological characteristics such as risk preference or optimism, opportunity exploitation is also a function of a person's psychological make-up.

However, people do not make decisions about the exploitation of opportunities in a vacuum. The industry context influences their willingness and ability to found new firms in order to exploit entrepreneurial opportunities. Chapter 6 discusses the arguments for and empirical evidence in support of five major perspectives on industry-level differences on the exploitation of entrepreneurial opportunities through firm formation: knowledge conditions, demand conditions, industry life cycles, appropriability conditions and industry structure.

Chapter 7 examines the effect of the institutional environment on the decision of people to exploit opportunities. Focusing on three major dimensions of the institutional environment – the economic environment, the political system and the cultural context – this chapter explores how the context in which the entrepreneur finds herself influences the exploitation of entrepreneurial opportunities.

To exploit her opportunity, an entrepreneur must gather resources from others and recombine them into a new form. Chapter 8 discusses the process of resource acquisition. In particular, this chapter discusses the effect of uncertainty about the value of the entrepreneur's conjecture and the significant information asymmetry that exists between entrepreneurs and resource providers, both of which are necessary conditions of the entrepreneurial process (Venkataraman, 1997). The chapter explains how these factors impose several conditions on the resource acquisition process, including self-financing, contract structure, pre- and post-investment tools, the exploitation of social capital, entrepreneurial behavior and signaling efforts.

Chapter 9 examines the strategies used by entrepreneurs to exploit opportunities. If entrepreneurial opportunities are exploited successfully, the profit that ensues is transitory for several reasons. First, the sources of change that triggered the existence of opportunities themselves change, closing up opportunities that once existed. Second, the actions taken by the entrepreneur to exploit the opportunity disseminate information about how to exploit the opportunity successfully. As a result, other people can imitate the entrepreneur's approach to exploiting the opportunity and capture some of the profit for themselves. Moreover, resource providers re-price the resources that they provide to entrepreneurs to capture some of the value of the opportunity for themselves. As a result, entrepreneurs take actions to preserve the value generated by successful opportunity exploitation. They use secrecy and causal ambiguity to preclude others from knowing about the opportunity and their method of exploiting it. In addition, they use scale, control of resources, legal barriers, reputation and innovation to keep others from exploiting the same opportunity, even if the others understand exactly how to do it. This chapter discusses the use of these tools, as well as strategies used by entrepreneurs to manage the information asymmetry and uncertainty that are fundamental to the entrepreneurial process.

To exploit an opportunity, the entrepreneur must organize the resources that she has acquired into a new combination. Chapter 10 discusses the process of organizing. This chapter examines several important issues. The first is the process by which organizations are designed. The chapter suggests that entrepreneurs design organizations through a dynamic process, not through optimal design mechanisms. The chapter then discusses the role of planning in the organizing process. Third, the chapter turns to the question of what mode of organizing will be used to exploit the opportunity. Contrary to the popular belief that entrepreneurial opportunities are always exploited through the formation for new firms, this chapter explains that entrepreneurs choose between markets and firms as a mode of opportunity exploitation. The last portion of this chapter describes the major elements of the organizing process.

Chapter 11 reviews the earlier chapters and provides some tentative conclusions about the individual–opportunity nexus framework on entrepreneurship. This chapter also discusses where future empirical research is necessary to confirm some of the arguments made in the book, that are not very strongly supported by existing evidence.

THE RESEARCH UNDERLYING THE BOOK

This book is the result of over ten years of scholarly research into entrepreneurship that was first initiated when I began the Ph.D. program in Management at the Wharton School of the University of Pennsylvania, and carried on through faculty stints at the DuPree College of Management at Georgia Institute of Technology, the Sloan School of Management at the Massachusetts Institute of Technology, and the Robert H. Smith School of Business at the University of Maryland.

The theory and findings that I describe in the chapters that follow are based on numerous different research projects conducted with many co-authors. One project, conducted with Lars Kolvereid at Bodo University in Norway, and Paul Westhead now at the University of Nottingham in the United Kingdom, sought to explore similarities and differences across countries in the effect of individual and environmental factors on the decisions of people to found firms. It also sought to explore the relationship between new firm strategy and environmental conditions on firm performance using data from a survey administered to a sample of 597 founders of new ventures in Norway, New Zealand and the United Kingdom.

A second project, which was my doctoral dissertation, was conducted with Ian MacMillan of the University of Pennsylvania and S. Venkataraman, now at the University of Virginia. This project explored the similarities and differences in how people from different national cultures championed new ventures, based on a survey of 4405 individuals from 43 organizations, from 68 nations.

A third project was conducted in part alone, and in part with my colleague Bill Gartner from the University of Southern California. This project looked at macro-level economic, social and psychological factors that influenced the rate of entrepreneurial activity in the United States from 1899 to 1988, using archival data.

A fourth project used data from the *Franchise Annual* and *Entrepreneur* Magazine to track 138 new business format franchisors established in 1983 over the first ten years of their lives; data from the *Sourcebook of Franchise Opportunities* to follow 157 new franchise systems established between 1981 and 1983 from 1984 to 1995; data from *The Sourcebook of Franchise Opportunities* on 2997 business format franchise systems operating in the United States between 1984 and 1996; data from *Entrepreneur* Magazine on the survival of 1292 new franchise systems established in the United States from 1979 to 1996; and data on the franchise offering circulars of 170 new franchise systems established in the early 1990s. This project, conducted in part alone and in part with Maw-Der Foo of the National University of Singapore and Pierre Azoulay of Columbia University, resulted in a series of articles that explained the effect of organization design and new venture strategy on the development of new firms.

A fifth project, conducted with Dan Cable of the University of North Carolina at Chapel Hill, examined a survey of 202 seed stage venture capitalists and business angels, as well as in-depth interviews with the entrepreneurs and financiers of 50 spin-offs from the Massachusetts Institute of Technology. This project sought to understand the venture finance decisions of early stage investors in new firms.

A sixth project, conducted both alone and with Rakesh Khurana of Harvard University, Toby Stuart of Columbia University and Riitta Katila of Stanford University, examined in-depth case studies of eight new ventures founded to exploit a single invention assigned to the Massachusetts Institute of Technology; explored the firm founding patents among the population of 1397 inventions assigned to the Massachusetts Institute of Technology between 1980 and 1996; examined the life histories of 134 companies founded to exploit inventions assigned to the Massachusetts Institute of Technology from 1980 to 1997; and examined efforts by new and established firms to commercialize 966 inventions licensed by the Massachusetts Institute of Technology from 1980 to 1996. The purpose of this project was to understand the opportunity discovery process; to explore individual differences that influence opportunity exploitation; to examine the effect of social relationships and business strategy on new venture finance and development; and to investigate the effect of industry conditions on the exploitation of opportunities through new firm formation.

A seventh project, conducted with Dante DiGregorio of the University of New Mexico and Wesley Sine of the University of Maryland examined the licensing and new firm formation activity out of the university technology licensing offices of 101 US universities from 1994 to 1998. This study examined the role of the external environment on opportunity exploitation.

An eighth project, conducted with Jon Eckhardt of the University of Wisconsin and Frederic Delmar of the Stockholm School of Economics, tracked 223 new Swedish ventures established in 1998 through the first 30 months of life. The purpose of this project was to explore the role of business planning in venture finance and organization design.

In addition to my empirical research projects, this book draws on my prior efforts to develop conceptual models of different aspects of the entrepreneurship process. One such project to explain entrepreneurial finance was conducted with Dan Cable of the University of North Carolina. Another project, conducted with S. Venkataraman of the University of Virginia, and extended with Jon Eckhardt, of the University of Wisconsin, sought to develop the general conceptual framework for entrepreneurship that provided the basis for this book. A third project sought to explain the psychological aspects of opportunity exploitation, and was conducted with Ed Locke of the University of Maryland and Chris Collins of Cornell University.

The book also draws heavily on the work of other scholars in the field of entrepreneurship. I make significant use of numerous published papers that I have read in scholarly journals or conference proceedings, as well as unpublished research that I have reviewed or have seen presented at conferences. Lastly, there is no doubt that the ideas in this book were spurred by discussions with Ph.D. students from a variety of universities who participated in the University of Maryland's intensive Ph.D. Seminar in Entrepreneurship, my academic colleagues, venture capitalists, angel investors, technology transfer officers and entrepreneurs.

In the next chapter, I explore the first piece of the puzzle that underlies the individual–opportunity nexus perspective on entrepreneurship. In that chapter, I explore the role of opportunities in a conceptual framework for entrepreneurship.

2. The role of opportunities

The examination of opportunities is a central, but largely overlooked aspect of entrepreneurship. As I explained in Chapter 1, entrepreneurship involves the nexus of entrepreneurial opportunities and enterprising individuals. This nexus indicates that opportunities are an important part of the entrepreneurial process. In fact, one of the key premises of this book is that variation in opportunities themselves can account for at least some of the observed patterns in entrepreneurial activity, by influencing the decisions by people to exploit opportunities and their performance at opportunity exploitation. In this chapter I discuss entrepreneurial opportunities.

I define an entrepreneurial opportunity as a situation in which a person can create a new means–ends framework for recombining resources that the entrepreneur *believes* will yield a profit. The main difference between an entrepreneurial opportunity and many other situations in which people seek profit is that an entrepreneurial opportunity requires the creation of a new means–ends framework rather than just optimizing within an old framework.

Readers should note that entrepreneurial opportunities are not necessarily profitable. Sometimes they can turn out to be unprofitable, as occurs when the conjectures about the profit from recombination turn out to be wrong. Because entrepreneurial opportunities are not always profitable, they should not be thought of as Ricardian, Schumpeterian or other kinds of rents. Such a view would require entrepreneurial opportunities always to be profitable.

Understanding entrepreneurial opportunities is important because the characteristics of an opportunity influence the entrepreneurial process. In particular, opportunities differ significantly in expected value. For example, research has shown that some industries consistently produce more valuable opportunities for new businesses than others. Eckhardt (2003) looked at the industry distribution of the *Inc* 500 companies (the fastest growing young private companies in the United States) and companies that had experienced an initial public offering (IPO), and found that some industries had a consistently higher percentage of start-up companies listed on the *Inc* 500 and that had experienced an initial public offering than other industries.

These data show that if a random entrepreneur started a business in certain industries and not in others, that person would be much more likely to have a very rapidly growing private or public company. Two explanations could potentially account for this observed data pattern, with the first being less plausible than the second. A purely person-centric approach to entrepreneurship would have to explain the variation across industries in the propensity of new firms that go public or appear on the *Inc* 500 list by arguing that some industries are more likely than others to attract people with the individual characteristics associated with entrepreneurial competence, such as education, risk-taking propensity, internal locus of control and so on. Moreover, because the industries generating *Inc* 500 and IPO companies vary significantly over time, those people with the characteristics associated with entrepreneurial competence would have to found firms in different industries at different points in time. For example, in 2002 people with entrepreneurial competence would have to start firms disproportionately in the biotechnology industry, but only a few years earlier, they would have needed to be over-represented in the Internet industry.

Because there is actually little evidence of such wide swings in the allocation of the individual characteristics associated with entrepreneurial competence across industries, we are left with a second, more plausible, explanation for industry-level variation in the proportion of IPO and high growth private firms. Industries differ in the entrepreneurial opportunities that they create, with some industries at some points in time being more fertile grounds for entrepreneurial activity than others.

I will leave a discussion of the relationship between specific industry characteristics and entrepreneurial opportunities until Chapter 6. For now, I only use these industry differences to illustrate the point that entrepreneurial opportunities vary significantly in their value and that understanding them is important in explaining entrepreneurial activity.

This chapter examines three important dimensions of entrepreneurial opportunities and their role in the entrepreneurial process. First, the chapter summarizes the two major perspectives on the existence and source of entrepreneurial opportunities: the Schumpeterian (1934) and Kirznerian (1973) perspectives. Second, the chapter examines three major sources of entrepreneurial opportunity: technological change, political/regulatory change and social/demographic change. Third, the chapter discusses the different forms that entrepreneurial opportunities take: new products or services, new ways of organizing, new raw materials, new markets and new production processes (Schumpeter, 1934).

KIRZNERIAN VS. SCHUMPETERIAN OPPORTUNITIES

Any explanation for entrepreneurial opportunities requires a discussion of where these opportunities come from. So why do situations emerge in which it is possible for a person to come up with a new means–ends framework for recombining resources? To date, the literature has offered two different explanations for these situations, the Kirznerian (1973) perspective and the Schumpeterian (1934) perspective, which Venkataraman (1997) termed the weak and strong form, respectively. In a nutshell, Kirzner (1973) and Schumpeter (1934) disagreed over whether the existence of entrepreneurial opportunities involves the introduction of new information or just differential access to existing information. Kirzner (1973, 1985, 1997) argued that the existence of opportunities requires only differential access to existing information. Kirzner (1973) explained that people use the information that they possess to form beliefs about the efficient use of resources. Because people's decision-making frameworks are not always accurate, they make errors when they make decisions, which, in turn, create shortages and surpluses (Gaglio and Katz, 2001). By responding to these shortages and surpluses, people can obtain resources, recombine them and sell the output in the hopes of making a profit (Shane and Venkataraman, 2000).

In contrast, Schumpeter (1934) believed that new information is important in explaining the existence of entrepreneurial opportunities. He argued that changes in technology, political forces, regulation, macro-economic factors and social trends create new information that entrepreneurs can use to figure out how to recombine resources into more valuable forms. By altering the equilibrium price for resources, these changes allow people with access to new information to purchase resources at low prices, recombine them into a more valuable form, and sell the output in the hopes of generating a profit (Schumpeter, 1934; Shane and Venkataraman, 2000).

While some researchers maintain that either the Schumpeterian or Kirznerian perspective explains the existence of entrepreneurial opportunities (Schumpeter, 1934; Kirzner, 1997), other researchers have begun to argue that the two perspectives represent different types of opportunities that can both be present in an economy at the same time (Shane and Venkataraman, 2000). The possibility that both Schumpeterian and Kirznerian opportunities are present in the economy, and that entrepreneurs identify and exploit both of them, brings up several very interesting implications for understanding entrepreneurship.

As Box 2.1 demonstrates, the two types of opportunity have different effects on economic activity. Schumpeterian opportunities result from disequilibrating forces, making Schumpeterian entrepreneurship a disequilibrating activity. In contrast, Kirznerian opportunities are the result of equilibrating forces, meaning that Kirznerian entrepreneurship brings the economy closer to equilibrium. Therefore, Kirznerian opportunities reinforce established ways of doing things, whereas Schumpeterian opportunities disrupt the existing system. This argument would suggest that most entrepreneurial opportunities are Kirznerian because most opportunities are constructive to established ways of doing things (Aldrich, 1999).

BOX 2.1   SCHUMPETERIAN VERSUS
KIRZNERIAN OPPORTUNITIES

Schumpeterian opportunities	*Kirznerian opportunities*
Disequilibrating	Equilibrating
Requires new information	Does not require new information
Very innovative	Less innovative
Rare	Common
Involves creation	Limited to discovery

Their disequilibrating nature should make Schumpeterian opportunities more valuable (as well as rarer) than Kirznerian opportunities. As a result, the wealth created from the exploitation of entrepreneurial opportunities should lie disproportionately with the exploitation of Schumpeterian opportunities. If investors are aware of these patterns, institutional arrangements to provide resources for entrepreneurial activity, such as venture capital, should be disproportionately represented among Schumpeterian opportunities. These factors would make the boundary conditions that explain Schumpeterian and Kirznerian opportunities quite different.

Moreover, the discovery, evaluation and exploitation of opportunities should differ between Schumpeterian and Kirznerian opportunities. Schumpeterian opportunities are innovative and break away from existing knowledge, while Kirznerian opportunities are not very innovative and replicate existing organizational forms. As a result, *ceteris paribus*, the risk associated with Schumpeterian opportunities should be higher than the risk associated with Kirznerian opportunities.

One implication of this line of reasoning is that the individual-level attributes necessary for the discovery and exploitation of opportunities, the processes of resource acquisition and organizing, and the strategies demanded by Schumpeterian opportunities are different from those demanded by Kirznerian opportunities. For example, the uniqueness of Schumpeterian opportunities makes the accumulation of evidence about opportunities difficult and hinders information aggregation. As a result, the exploitation of Schumpeterian opportunities requires people who are willing to make decisions on very little evidence. As I will explain in Chapter 5, making decisions on very little evidence is a characteristic of overconfident people (Bernardo and Welch, 2001). Therefore, overconfidence may be a more important individual attribute for Schumpeterian entrepreneurship than for Kirznerian entrepreneurship.

Similarly, the nature of Schumpeterian and Kirznerian opportunities might demand very different processes of opportunity identification. For example,

Kirznerian opportunities involve the recognition of opportunity largely through discovery processes, whereas Schumpeterian opportunities involve the creation of new knowledge, as well as its recognition (Aldrich, 1999). For this reason, large, established firms may invest in efforts to endogenize the discovery and exploitation of Schumpeterian opportunities (Schumpeter, 1942) much more than they do to endogenize Kirznerian opportunities. If this pattern were true, then the discovery and exploitation of Schumpeterian opportunities would lie much more with people inside large, established firms than is the case with Kirznerian opportunities.

THE SOURCES OF OPPORTUNITIES

To date, researchers have much more information about the sources of Schumpeterian opportunities than about Kirznerian opportunities. Part of the reason for this greater amount of information may be the potential value of Schumpeterian opportunities. However, another part of the reason may be that the sources of Kirznerian opportunities are idiosyncratic.

Kirznerian opportunities emerge because prior decision makers made errors or omissions that create surpluses and shortages. The idiosyncratic nature of these errors – they can occur at any time or in any place – makes it difficult for researchers to identify the source of these opportunities. For example, researchers might wonder why a vacancy in a storefront allowed for the introduction of a new restaurant where none had existed before. However, the specificity of the storefront vacancy makes it difficult to identify the sources of this opportunity. As a result, I can identify no research to date that has offered any more specific explanation for the source of Kirznerian opportunities than the fact that they emerge from the errors and omissions made by prior market participants, and I can find no empirical evidence about the sources of Kirznerian opportunities.

Much better explanation and empirical evidence exists for the sources of Schumpeterian opportunities. As I mentioned above, Schumpeterian opportunities are contingent on the introduction of new information that results in the creation of entrepreneurial opportunities that had not existed prior to the introduction of this information.

Some empirical evidence demonstrates the relationship between sources of Schumpeterian opportunities and the existence of those opportunities. For example, Bhide (2000) explained that about one half of the founders of *Inc* 500 companies (the 500 fastest growing private companies in the United States) that he interviewed indicated that they initiated their businesses in response to a specific change in technology, regulatory regime, fashion or other external factor.

This type of evidence suggests that identifying specific categories of sources of opportunity might be a useful activity for understanding entrepreneurship. For instance, it might be valuable to know if Schumpeterian opportunities tend to result more often from some sources of change than from others.

To compare sources of entrepreneurial opportunity, one first needs a typology of these sources. While a wide variety of different typologies could be offered (see Drucker, 1985 for an alternative example), I follow the lead of much of the entrepreneurship literature, and divide the sources of opportunity into three major groups: changes in technology, changes in politics and regulation, and changes in social and demographic factors. The sources of opportunity are summarized in Box 2.2.

BOX 2.2   THE SOURCES OF SCHUMPETERIAN OPPORTUNITIES

- Technological changes
- Political and regulatory changes
- Social and demographic changes

These three categories of sources of Schumpeterian opportunities have certain characteristics in common. Most notably, they introduce changes that alter the value of resources, thus upsetting the equilibrium price for resources and creating the potential for entrepreneurial profit. For example, the invention of the computer, an important technological change, created the opportunity to manufacture and sell microchips. The knowledge of this opportunity suggested that the materials used to make microchips, were mis-priced and could be profitably recombined into a new form. Similarly, the government's mandate of the use of car seats for infants, a regulatory change, created an opportunity for entrepreneurs to purchase idle factories and use them to make these devices for sale to consumers. Furthermore, the entry of women into the workforce in large numbers, a socio-demographic change, led to the dramatic growth in the need for prepared foods. As a result, an individual who recognized this opportunity before others could purchase the necessary raw materials and produce prepared foods to sell to consumers.

However, the three sources of opportunity also differ in important ways. In the subsections below, I review the explanations for why technological, political/regulatory, and social/demographic changes create opportunities, offer specific examples of these sources of opportunity, and review the empirical evidence for these examples. I look first at technological changes.

Technological Changes

Technological changes are an important source of entrepreneurial opportunity because they make it possible for people to allocate resources in different and potentially more productive ways (Casson, 1995). For example, before the invention of the Internet, people allocated resources to the use of facsimile, letter and telephone communication. However, electronic mail is a more productive mechanism for the transmission of certain kinds of information than these other types of communication. As a result, the invention of the Internet allowed people to create new resource combinations that exploited this technological change.

Some empirical evidence supports the argument that technological change is a source of entrepreneurial opportunity. Admittedly, this evidence is indirect because we cannot measure the existence of entrepreneurial opportunities and must use proxy measures instead. Two important proxy measures of the existence of entrepreneurial opportunities are the tendency of people to engage in self employment and the tendency of people to form firms. If technological change is a source of entrepreneurial opportunity, then rates of self employment and firm formation should increase in response to technological change.

The empirical literature supports this proposition. Blau (1987), for example, examined the self employment rate in the United States over a two-decade period and found that an increase in the rate of technological change led to an increase in the self employment rate. Similarly, Shane (1996) looked at the number of organizations per capita from 1899 to 1988 and found that the rate of technological change, measured as the annual number of new patents issued, had a positive effect on the number of organizations per capita in the economy in the subsequent year.

Other research demonstrates the role of technology as a source of opportunity by comparing the rate of technological change across industries. Klevorick *et al.* (1995) surveyed research and development managers in over 100 lines of business to evaluate the effect of technological change on the creation of entrepreneurial opportunities in their line of business. Arguing that technological change is a greater source of opportunity in some industries than in others, the authors showed that industries with closer ties to science have more entrepreneurial opportunities. These authors also showed that those industries with greater within-industry and extra-industry sources of technical advance, and greater sources of feedback from those advances, also have more entrepreneurial opportunities.

Moreover, these authors observed that the locus of opportunities differs across industries. In some industries, these opportunities lie outside the value chain, and are found in universities, government agencies and research laboratories. In other industries, these opportunities lie within the value chain and include firms, their suppliers and their customers (Klevorick *et al.*, 1995; Von Hippel, 1988).

A third stream of research has sought to examine which types of technological change are the greatest sources of entrepreneurial opportunity. Some researchers have argued that technological changes vary in magnitude and that larger technological changes are a greater source of opportunity than smaller technological changes. Larger technological changes provide a greater source of opportunity, the argument goes, because they create a larger change in productivity from recombining resources.

One empirical study provides support for this argument. Using citations to a patent as a measure of the magnitude of a technological change attributable to an invention, and the decision of someone to found a company as evidence of the presence of an entrepreneurial opportunity, Shane (2001a) examined the 1397 inventions patented by the Massachusetts Institute of Technology between 1980 and 1996. He found that more heavily cited patents were more likely to lead to firm formation than less heavily cited patents.

Political/Regulatory Changes

While technological change is an important source of entrepreneurial opportunity because it makes it possible for people to use resources in more productive ways, political and regulatory changes are also an important source of entrepreneurial opportunity. These changes make it possible for people to reallocate resources to new uses in ways that either are more profitable or that redistribute wealth from one member of society to another. For example, Sine and David (forthcoming) found that the US government's deregulation of the electric utility industry influenced the nature of entrepreneurial opportunities by changing the industry structure (Gioia, 1989), by creating new markets, and by changing the way profits were made (Sine *et al.*, 2001).

In addition, political and regulatory change is sometimes a source of entrepreneurial opportunity because the change makes possible more productive recombination of resources. The US government's deregulation of the telecommunications, airline, trucking, railroad and banking industries created opportunities for entrepreneurs to undertake more productive recombinations. Because regulations such as limits on intrastate banking, licensed entry into communications, and the regulation of trucking, block potential entrants, they allowed firms to engage in unproductive efforts to deter competition rather than productive efforts to innovate (Holmes and Schmitz, 2001). As a result, deregulation permitted the more productive recombination of resources than was present under regulation.

The empirical literature has examined the effects of both regulatory and political change on the existence of entrepreneurial opportunities. In the subsections below, I review this empirical evidence. I begin with political changes.

Political changes

Some empirical evidence supports the argument that political change is a source of entrepreneurial opportunity. Again, due to the non-observability of the construct of entrepreneurial opportunity, researchers have had to examine proxy measures. In general, they have proxied the existence of entrepreneurial opportunities by the creation of new firms. For example, Delacroix and Carroll (1983) examined the formation of Argentinean newspapers from 1800 to 1900, and Irish newspapers from 1800 to 1925, and found that there was a positive effect of political change on the rate of firm formation. Similarly, Carroll and Huo (1986) examined the formation of 2168 newspapers in the San Francisco Bay area from 1870 to 1980, and found that political change increased the firm formation rate. Moreover, the establishment of the Monetary Authority of Singapore led to the founding of a large number of commercial banks in Singapore (Carroll and Hannan, 2000). Lastly, many observers have noted that war creates new entrepreneurial opportunities by shifting upward the demand for military hardware.

However, just because political change is a source of entrepreneurial opportunity does not mean that new firms founded at times of political change will perform better than those founded at other times. While entrepreneurial opportunities might result from political change, that change might spur the entry of so many entrepreneurs that all of them perform worse than new ventures formed at other times. Moreover, the existence of entrepreneurial opportunity might be enhanced by political change, but the skills and abilities of entrepreneurs at exploitation might be hindered. As a result, political change might be a source of opportunity, but not a source of good entrepreneurial performance.

In fact, several studies have shown that political change *decreases* the survival of new ventures. Carroll and Delacroix (1982) found that newspapers founded during periods of political instability were more likely to die than those founded during stable periods. Similarly, Carroll and Huo (1986) found that local American newspapers tracked over a 125-year period showed higher failure rates if they were founded during a politically turbulent period.

At a more macro-level, McMillan and Woodruff (2002) examined the relationship between changing from a communist system and the growth in entrepreneurial activity. The authors explain that the distortions wrought by communism generated market opportunities which entrepreneurs entered to fill. In China, Russia and Poland, the profitability of these opportunities declined over a six-year period as entrepreneurs entered their respective markets to exploit these opportunities. The greater the distortions initially, the higher the average rate of profit, and the slower the rate of entrepreneurial entry, the more slowly the average rate of profit declined.

Regulatory changes

Some empirical evidence supports the argument that regulatory change is a source of entrepreneurial opportunity when the rate of new firm formation is used as the measure of the existence of opportunity. One set of studies demonstrates that deregulation *increases* the rate of firm formation. For example, both Kelly (1988) and Kelly and Amburgey (1991) found that the rate of airline formation in the United States increased after deregulation of the airline industry. Similarly, Barnett (1997) studied the founding rates of American breweries from 1633 until 1988, and observed that founding rates were significantly higher in the post-Prohibition period.

Another set of studies shows that increased regulation *reduces* the rate of firm formation. Examining data from the US Establishment and Enterprise Longitudinal Microdata File, which measured the number of new independent firms reported in 306 industries between 1976 and 1980, Dean and Brown (1995) found that new capital expenditures on pollution abatement in 1977 were negatively correlated with new firm entry into different manufacturing industries. Stuart and Sorenson (2002) examined the foundings of new biotechnology firms and found that initial public offerings and acquisitions of biotechnology firms located in the same metropolitan statistical area increased firm founding rates, but only when states did not enforce post-employment non-compete covenants. At a more macro-level, Dana (1990) compared the Caribbean Island nations of Saint Martin and Sint Maarten, and found that Saint Martin had a lower rate of business formation than its counterpart because it had more regulation.

However, increased government regulation does not always discourage firm formation, suggesting that the source of entrepreneurial opportunity is regulatory change, not deregulation. In general, regulations that support particular organizations are associated with an increased rate of formation of those organizations (Carroll and Hannan, 2000; Baum, 1996). For example, Hannan and Freeman (1989) found that the rate of formation of labor unions in the United States increased after the passage of the Wagner Act, which gave unions political protection, and fell after the Taft–Hartley Act, which rescinded some of those protections. Baum and Oliver (1991, 1992) found that increased efforts by regulators to monitor and certify day care centers in Toronto led to increases in the formation of those organizations. Aldrich *et al.* (1990) found that the National Industrial Recovery Act, which provided US government support for trade associations, increased the business trade association formation rate in the United States. Similarly, Dobbin and Dowd (1997) examined the formation of railroads in Massachusetts between 1825 and 1922, and found that pro-cartel government policies encouraged railroad formation, and antitrust legislation discouraged it.

Sometimes government regulation is a source of opportunity because it provides resources that increase demand or provide subsidies (Baum, 1996). These resources create opportunities to serve customers that could not be served without the government support. For example, Tucker *et al.* (1990) found that increases in government funding of social programs in Toronto between 1970 and 1982 led to an increase in the rate of formation of voluntary social service organizations. Examining licensed day care centers in Toronto between 1971 and 1989, Baum and Oliver (1992) found that the size of the city's budget for children's services had a positive effect on the rate of day care center formation. Feldman (2001) found that the rise of entrepreneurship in the Washington, DC area resulted, in part, from Federal government procurement policies to facilitate demand for information technology and biotechnology.

Similar patterns exist when the regulation exists at the organization, rather than the government, level of analysis. Using data on the rate of new firm formation to exploit university assigned intellectual property from different US universities from 1991 to 1998, DiGregorio and Shane (forthcoming) found that universities that adopted policies giving inventors a higher share of royalties discouraged inventors from founding firms (as opposed to licensing their technology to existing firms). Therefore, these institutions had lower start-up rates than other universities. In addition, they found that universities that adopted policies to take equity in firms founded to exploit the university's intellectual property had higher start-up rates than other universities because these policies reduced cash constraints on new firms that lacked cash flow from existing operations to finance the development of new technology.

Several macro-level studies also provide support for regulatory change as a source of entrepreneurial opportunity. Davidsson *et al.* (1994) examined the rate of new firm formation per member of the workforce-aged population across regions in Sweden from 1985 to 1989. They found a positive effect for government regulation that provided development support. Hart and Gudgin (1994) examined the rate of new manufacturing firm formation per 1000 manufacturing employees across 26 counties of Ireland from 1980 to 1990, and found a positive effect of the designation of an area as 'a development area'. Grant (1996) examined the annual percentage change in new business incorporations in the 48 contiguous US states from 1970 to 1985, and found that economic development policies had a positive effect on firm formation rates.

Socio-Demographic Changes

Social and demographic changes are an important source of entrepreneurial opportunity because they transfer information about ways for people to allocate resources in different and potentially more productive ways; because they create the potential for scale economies that are necessary for certain opportunities to exist; and because they generate additional demand. Three broad categories of socio-demographic forces have been documented as sources of entrepreneurial opportunities: urbanization, population dynamics and educational infrastructure.

Urbanization

Prior research has argued that urbanization is a source of entrepreneurial opportunity because entrepreneurship involves the identification of opportunities based on information transferred from other sources. Communication is greater in more densely populated areas, facilitating the transmission of information about opportunities in urban areas (Storey and Tether, 1998). In addition, urbanization increases the number of entrepreneurial role models, facilitating information transfer from observation (Bygrave and Minniti, 2000). Furthermore, urbanization is a source of opportunity because population density creates the potential for the scale economies that make certain opportunities possible.

Some empirical evidence supports the argument that urbanization is a source of entrepreneurial opportunity. Following the approach of using new firm formation as a proxy for the existence of entrepreneurial opportunity, several studies show that urbanization increases the level of entrepreneurial opportunity in a particular geographic location. For example, Barnett and Carroll (1993) found that the number of incorporated rural areas was correlated with the formation of independent telephone companies in Iowa from 1907 to 1942. Similarly, Barnett (1997) examined the rate of formation of Pennsylvania telephone companies from 1879 to 1934, and found that it was positively correlated with the percentage of population located in urban areas. Using US Small Business Administration data on per state business start-up rates for the 1978 to 1982 period, Dennis (1986) found that urbanization increased the start-up rate in a state.

At a more micro-level, similar results have been shown with self employment data. Schiller and Crewson (1997) examined data from the National Longitudinal Survey of Youth, which tracked 12 000 young people who were between 14 and 23 in 1979. Consistent with the idea that urbanization is a source of entrepreneurial opportunity, the authors found that being in an urban area increased the likelihood of entering self employment for men. Similarly, Boyd (1990) examined a Public Use Microdata sample of the 1980 US Census to explore the self employment of 21 290 African-Americans, and found that being located in the city center increased the probability that respondents would be self employed. Several studies also show that the rate of spin-offs from existing firms is higher in areas that are more densely populated (Garvin, 1983; Cooper, 1985).

Finally, data gathered at the country level also show that urbanization is a source of opportunity. Reynolds *et al.* (1994a) found that regional variation in both the number of firm births per 10 000 people and per 100 firms were positively correlated with population density in the region. Guesnier (1994) examined the rate of firm formation per 100 existing firms and 10 000 active workers across French regions from 1986 to 1991 and found a positive effect of population density. Audretsch and Fritsch (1994) examined the cross-region rate of firm formation per 100 existing firms and per 10 000 workers in Germany from 1986 to 1999, and found a positive effect of population density. Davidsson *et al.* (1994) examined the rate of new firm formation across regions in Sweden per member of the workforce-aged population from 1985 to 1989, and found a positive effect of population density. Keeble and Walker (1994) examined the spatial variation in firm formation per capita and per firm in the United Kingdom from 1980 to 1990, and found a positive effect for population density. All of these studies provide support for the idea that urbanization is a source of entrepreneurial opportunity.

Does this source of opportunity have any effect on the performance of new ventures? Although political change appears to be a source of opportunity that does not enhance the performance of new ventures, one might argue that urbanization, as a source of opportunity, should have a positive effect on performance. Two arguments could be made for this effect. First, the economies of scale that urbanization makes possible generate opportunities that do not exist in non-urbanized areas, and these opportunities are more valuable than other opportunities. Given the fixed cost of opportunity exploitation that results from the basic organizing process, opportunities that can be exploited at a larger scale are more profitable than other opportunities. Second, the greater communication about opportunities and the prevalence of role models allows people to learn about a greater variety of opportunities. This chance to examine and select from a larger pool of potential opportunities means that entrepreneurs in urban areas are choosing better opportunities, on average, leading to better outcomes.

The empirical evidence suggests that opportunities in urban areas tend to lead to better performing new ventures than opportunities in other areas. For example, Reynolds and White (1997) examined 2624 new firms founded in three US states in 1985. They found that those firms with high growth rates were more likely to be found in a metropolitan area or major center. Similarly, Reynolds (1993) examined representative samples of new firms in Pennsylvania in 1986 and Minnesota in 1987, and compared high performing firms (the 2 per cent of the sample that had sales growth greater than 100 per cent and annual sales greater than \$5 000 000 per year) with the rest of the sample of firms. He found that high growth firms were more likely than other firms to be located in urban areas.

Existing research on self employment also suggests that urbanization makes opportunities more profitable. For example, Evans and Leighton (1989) and Schiller and Crewson (1997) examined data from the National Longitudinal Survey and found that the earnings of the self employed were higher if they were located in urban areas. Both of these studies are consistent with the idea that urbanization is a source of relatively more valuable opportunities.

Population dynamics

Population dynamics are another source of entrepreneurial opportunity. In particular, research has shown that three dimensions of population dynamics are important: population size, population growth and population mobility. Population size is a source of opportunity because many opportunities face scale economies. As a result, the fixed cost necessary for the opportunity to occur is amortized over more demand in places with larger populations, making opportunities that would not exist in places with lesser population possible in places with greater population. Population growth is a source of opportunity both because population growth increases the likelihood that scale economies will be achieved, and because population growth generates demand growth. Demand growth encourages opportunity because the ability to recombine resources at a profit is higher when demand is higher simply because the number of people seeking a good or service is greater. Population mobility is a source of entrepreneurial opportunity because people transmit much of the tacit information that makes opportunities possible. By moving, people carry the information that makes opportunities possible from one location where an opportunity has been recognized and acted upon, to another location where it has not yet been recognized or exploited.

Population size Several pieces of empirical evidence support the argument that the magnitude of the population is a source of entrepreneurial opportunity when the existence of opportunity is proxied by new firm formation. For example, Davidsson *et al.* (1994) showed that the rate of new firm formation per member of the workforce-aged population across regions in Sweden from 1985 to 1989 was positively correlated with population size. Pennings (1982b) examined data on firm formation rates in plastics, telecommunication equipment and electronic components across 70 standard metropolitan statistical areas between 1967 and 1971 and between 1972 and 1975. He found a significant positive effect for population size on the rate of firm formation in the area. Carroll and Huo (1986) examined the formation of 2168 newspapers in the San Francisco Bay area from 1870 to 1980, and found that the size of the population had a positive effect on the firm formation rate. Sorenson and Audia (2000) examined firm formation in the footwear industry in the United States from 1940 to 1989, and found that the state population had a positive relationship with firm formation.

Population growth   Several pieces of empirical evidence also support the argument that population growth is a source of entrepreneurial opportunity. Guesnier (1994) examined the rate of firm formation per 100 existing firms and per 10 000 active workers from 1986 to 1991 across French regions, and found a positive effect of population growth. Audretsch and Fritsch (1994) examined the cross-region rate of firm formation per 100 existing firms and per 10 000 workers in Germany from 1986 to 1989, and found a positive effect of population growth. Davidsson *et al.* (1994) examined the rate of new firm formation across regions in Sweden from 1985 to 1989 per member of the workforce-aged population, and also found a positive effect of population growth. Keeble and Walker (1994) examined the spatial variation in firm formation per capita and per firm in the United Kingdom from 1980 to 1990, and found that population growth had a positive effect on firm formation rates.

Similar results have also been found across locations within countries. For example, Reynolds (1994a) looked at the rate of new firm birth across 382 labor market areas in the United States from 1986 to 1988, and found a positive effect of population growth.

Population mobility   Several pieces of empirical evidence support the argument that population mobility is a source of entrepreneurial opportunity. For example, Reynolds *et al.* (1994a) examined the cross-regional variation in firm birth rates for the mid-1980s in France, Germany, Italy, Sweden, the United States and the United Kingdom. They found that immigration to a region was positively correlated with firm births per 100 existing firms and per 10 000 people in five of the six nations. Examining the 1966 and the 1976 County Business Patterns data for Alabama, Schell and David (1981) found that the creation of new business units was positively related to migration as a percentage of the population. Pennings (1982a) examined the organizational birth frequencies across 70 standard metropolitan statistical areas for three industries from 1967 to 1975, and found that locations with more domestic migration had higher formation rates in all three industries. Lastly, Shane (1996) looked at the number of organizations per capita in the United States economy from 1899 to 1988 and found that immigration had a positive effect on this measure.

Educational infrastructure
Educational infrastructure is a source of entrepreneurial opportunity because educational institutions conduct scientific research that results in the creation of new knowledge that is the basis of many entrepreneurial opportunities. In

addition, educational institutions are a source of opportunity because they are important mechanisms to diffuse information, thereby facilitating the transmission of information that generates opportunities (Aldrich and Wiedenmeyer, 1993).

Several studies provide support for this argument. Bull and Winter (1991) examined INC magazine's measure of the new business birth rate for 129 communities in the United States in the late 1980s, and found that it was higher in locations that had a larger number of four-year colleges within 20 miles. Similarly, Pennings *et al.* (1982) examined the rate of organization formation in plastics, telecommunication and electronic components across 70 standard metropolitan statistical areas from 1967 to 1971 and from 1971 to 1975. They found that, in telecommunications and electronic components, the health and educational infrastructure had a significant positive effect on the rate of firm formation.

The most direct and persuasive evidence that education is a source of entrepreneurial opportunity comes from research on university technology start-ups. For example, Zucker *et al.* (1998) examined the rate of formation of biotechnology firms across 183 regions from 1976 to 1989. These authors found that both the number of star scientists and the number of top-quality universities in the area increased the stock and annual flow of biotechnology firms in the region. They also found that the number of university faculty members with federal support in the region increased the stock and annual flow of biotechnology firms in the region. Similarly, Stuart and Sorenson (2002) examined biotechnology firm founding rates and found a positive effect of the number of universities with biotech programs in the metropolitan statistical area; and Sine *et al.* (2002) found that more prestigious universities generate more licenses to their intellectual property than did other universities, controlling for the number of inventions that the different universities produce. These results strongly suggest that universities generate new knowledge from their high technology research and disseminate that knowledge to people in the community. This knowledge production creates entrepreneurial opportunities that do not exist in places where university research does not occur.

THE FORMS OF OPPORTUNITY

Another important question about entrepreneurial opportunities is the form that they take. In general, the entrepreneurship literature often views entrepreneurial opportunities as resource recombinations that result in new products or services. However, entrepreneurial opportunities could emerge in response to changes in many parts of the value chain. In fact, Schumpeter (1934) created a typology with five forms of opportunity, including new products or services, new geographical markets, new raw materials, new methods of production and new ways of organizing.

Examples of opportunities that take the form of a new product or service are new types of accounting software and new surgical devices. The Internet provides an example of an opportunity that takes the form of a new way of organizing, as it made possible the organization of economic activity without bricks and mortar locations. The introduction of snack crackers made of seaweed in the United States provides an example of an opportunity that takes the form of a new geographical market because this opportunity, which had existed before in Japan, had not existed in the United States. The discovery that oil is an excellent fuel is an example of an opportunity that takes the form of a new raw material. Finally, the assembly line and computer-aided drug discovery are examples of opportunities that take the form of new methods of production.

Despite the existence of Schumpeter's typology for almost 70 years, I can find evidence of only one study that has used this typology to empirically examine the forms that entrepreneurial opportunities take. Ruef (2002) examined attempts to found firms by 766 entrepreneurial teams that had at least one member who was an alumnus of Stanford Business School. He found that 56 per cent of the respondents sought to introduce a new product or service, 9 per cent sought to introduce a new production process, 85 per cent sought to enter a new market or market niche, and 43 per cent sought to introduce a new way of organizing supply or distribution. Unfortunately for the field, Ruef (2002) offers no information to explain this uneven distribution of forms that opportunities take.

Despite the relative lack of research that examines the different forms that entrepreneurial opportunity takes, I believe that such an examination would be valuable for several reasons. First, it would be useful to know if the different forms of entrepreneurial opportunity are equally common or if some forms are more common than others. If the distribution is uneven (as Ruef's study appears to suggest), researchers should explain why. Is this result a function of the industry, time period or location? Second, it would be useful to know if the types and sources of opportunities are related to the forms that they take. Are Kirznerian and Schumpeterian opportunities equally likely to take the form of products and services? Are technological, political/regulatory and social/demographic opportunities all equally likely to take the form of new market exploitation? Third, it would be useful to know if some types of opportunity are more valuable than others. For instance, are some forms of opportunity high risk and high return, while others are low risk and low return? Fourth, it would be useful to know if different types of opportunity influence different parts of the value chain with greater or lesser frequency. For example, do new raw materials transform the supply stage of the value chain, whereas new markets transform the marketing and distribution stage? Fifth, it would be valuable to know if the processes by which opportunities are discovered, evaluated and exploited are the same across all five forms of opportunity. For example, do people raise money, adopt strategies and implement organizational designs in the same way for new markets, new materials, new processes, new products and new ways of organizing?

SUMMARY

This chapter examined the role of entrepreneurial opportunities in the individual–opportunity perspective on entrepreneurship. The chapter first defined an entrepreneurial opportunity – a situation in which a person can create a new means–ends framework for recombining resources that she *believes* will yield a profit.

The chapter summarized the two major perspectives on entrepreneurial opportunities. The Kirznerian perspective holds that the existence of opportunities requires only differential views toward existing information. In contrast, the Schumpeterian perspective posits that new information is important to explaining the existence of entrepreneurial opportunities.

The chapter also examined three major sources of entrepreneurial opportunity: technological changes, political/regulatory changes and social/demographic changes. Technological changes are important sources of opportunity because the introduction of new solutions to problems makes it possible for people to allocate resources in different and potentially more productive ways. Political and regulatory changes are important sources of opportunity because they make it possible for people to re-allocate resources to new uses in ways that either are more profitable or redistribute wealth from one member of society to another. Social and demographic changes are also important sources of opportunity because they facilitate the creation and transmission of information about opportunities, increase demand and make possible opportunities that were otherwise not possible.

Lastly, this chapter pointed out that entrepreneurial opportunities do not always take the form of new products and services. It discussed the different forms that entrepreneurial opportunities take: new products or services, new ways of organizing, new raw materials, new markets and new production processes and suggested several ways that researchers could use a typology of forms of opportunity to provide a better explanation of entrepreneurship.

Having explained the role of opportunities in the individual–opportunity nexus, particularly the types, sources, and forms of entrepreneurial opportunity, I now turn to a discussion of the discovery of opportunity.

3. The discovery of entrepreneurial opportunities

In this chapter, I examine the discovery of entrepreneurial opportunities. The first section of the chapter examines the theoretical world in which entrepreneurial opportunities do not exist because the price system equilibrates supply and demand. By setting up the counterpoint of the price system, I can explain why this system cannot allocate resources for entrepreneurial opportunities, and make clear the nature of entrepreneurial decision-making. The second section of the chapter examines how people make decisions about entrepreneurial opportunities, focusing on how this decision-making process differs from the optimizing process that is used to make non-entrepreneurial decisions. The third section explores the role of individual differences in the discovery process.

THE PRICE SYSTEM

To understand the existence of entrepreneurship, it is best to begin with a theoretical world in which entrepreneurship does not need to exist and then examine the conditions under which that world breaks down. Textbook economic theory explains that the price system is valuable because prices contain all of the information from all participants in the economy needed to allocate resources (Hayek, 1945). Because prices in the textbook world contain all necessary information for resource allocation, people can make decisions about the allocation of resources through mechanical application of mathematical decision rules. People optimize the information contained in prices by selling when prices go up, and buying when prices go down, until the economy achieves equilibrium. When equilibrium is reached, people then have no reason to change their approach to buying or selling goods and services because no alternative allocation of resources is better than the alternative that is already in existence (Pearce, 1992).

Limits to the Price System

Unfortunately, prices do not always allocate resources effectively, imposing limits on the types of decisions that the price system can be used to make. For example, an inventor must make decisions about the use of resources in order to invent a new product. However, the entrepreneur cannot use the price of the new product to determine whether or not to acquire resources to invent it because information about the price of a new product cannot exist before its invention. Only after the inventor has developed the product and introduced it to the market place, can anyone know its price. Because information about prices is combined with information about quantity to determine the revenue earned from the exploitation of a product, the creation of the new product also occurs before information about revenues is available. Therefore, the decision to purchase and recombine resources to invent a new product cannot incorporate information about the price at which the new product will sell or the revenues that will be earned from its introduction. Therefore, prices and revenues for new products cannot determine the resource allocation decisions of the entrepreneur that lead her to acquire the resources to develop a new product.

In general, prices fail to provide the information necessary to use mathematical rules to allocate resources to create future goods and services through optimization for three reasons. First, prices contain only some of the information needed to serve markets. For the reasons outlined in the above paragraph, prices do not contain information on revenues and costs for future goods and services. Costs are never completely known until the product or service has been completed, and prices do not exist for markets that will only come into existence in the future. Even if prices might reveal the level at which customers are satisfied currently, the absence of contingent prices for future goods and services means that prices cannot reveal the level at which customers would be satisfied in the future (Arrow, 1974a). Therefore, people cannot use optimization to identify costs and revenues, and must estimate them through other means.

Second, prices do not provide information about a way of producing or organizing that requires a technology that does not yet exist. By definition, information on a technology that has not yet been created is not available to market participants. As a result, the advantages of unknown future technologies to producing or organizing are not incorporated in current prices, and appropriate future investment decisions in plant and equipment based on technologies not yet available cannot be made. For example, in the 19th century, entrepreneurs interested in ocean borne transportation could not effectively make decisions about investment in steamship technology before the steamship had been invented, nor could they adequately make investment decisions in sailboat technology based on prices in that market just before the steamship was invented.

Third, prices do not provide information about the actions of competitors in response to entrepreneurial entry. If prices fail to provide information about future revenues, costs, ways of producing and ways of organizing, they cannot provide information about the actions of others in response to these things.

Therefore, entrepreneurs make decisions about competitors through means other than optimizing on information contained in prices.

Even Hayek's (1945: 526) famous tin market example about the value of the price system shows that prices cannot be used to make decisions about entrepreneurial opportunities. Hayek wrote:

> assume that somewhere in the world a new opportunity for the use of some raw materials, say tin, has arisen, or that one of the sources of supply of tin has been eliminated. It does not matter … which of these two causes has made tin more scarce. All that the users of tin need to know is that some of the tin they used to consume is now more profitably employed elsewhere, and that in consequence they must economize tin.

However, prices do not provide any guide to entrepreneurs who would like to know if they should exploit entrepreneurial opportunities in the tin market. For an entrepreneur to exploit an opportunity in the tin market, she must formulate a plan to obtain tin and recombine it into a more valuable form. This decision requires the entrepreneur to make a conjecture about the cause of the tin scarcity. If the shortage results from a new use of tin, then she might formulate a new way to use the tin. If the entrepreneur's conjecture is correct, she will profit from a plan to purchase the tin and use it in the new way (Eckhardt and Shane, 2003). On the other hand, if the shortage results from an elimination of the source of supply, then this plan will not generate a profit because the entrepreneur will be unable to obtain tin. In this case, the key element in the entrepreneurial decision is not contained in prices. The key element lies in the entrepreneur's conjecture as to the cause of the price movement.

Figure 3.1 describes the entrepreneurial decision-making process. The existence of an entrepreneurial opportunity imposes limits on the use of prices to allocate resources. These limits lead to entrepreneurial decision-making, which either results in entrepreneurial profit or entrepreneurial loss. Having explained the existence of entrepreneurial opportunities in the last chapter and having just outlined the limits to the use of prices in the decision-making process, I now turn to an examination of how entrepreneurial decisions are made.

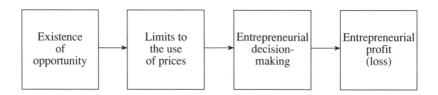

Figure 3.1   The entrepreneurial decision-making process

ENTREPRENEURIAL DECISION-MAKING

In economic theory, the relative efficiency of the market system means that people can use prices to make most decisions by optimizing (searching for the best solution) within known means–ends frameworks (existing parameters) (Harper, 1996). In situations that adhere to economic theory, the information required to make decisions is found in prices, allowing decisions to be made by using mathematical rules of optimization (Casson, 1982). However, what about situations in which the information necessary to make decisions is not contained in prices? How do people make decisions? Given that the necessary information is not contained in prices, it stands to reason that when entrepreneurial decision-making occurs, decisions about the allocation of resources are made by means other than optimizing within existing means–ends frameworks.

Several authors have described the process of making decisions about the allocation of resources by means other than optimizing within existing means–ends frameworks. Although known by a variety of different names, including 'judgmental decision making' (Casson, 1982, 1995), and 'effectuation' (Sarasvathy, 2001), entrepreneurial decision-making involves making non-optimizing decisions through the formation of new means–ends frameworks.

Non-Optimizing Decisions

Entrepreneurial decision-making is non-optimizing for three reasons. First, to optimize, prices and quantities in the future need to be known, which requires information about the future behavior of market participants to be represented in current prices (Arrow, 1974a). However, future information is only represented in current prices if futures markets exist. In most cases, the information that will lead to future action is not knowable in the present (Simon, 1955). Therefore, when people need to make decisions about future goods and services, they must make decisions before data on product demand, resource supply and production possibilities exist.

As Baumol (1993) explains, when people cannot know the range of options facing them or the consequences of those options, the calculation of an optimum within a given set of constraints is impossible. Therefore, entrepreneurs cannot make decisions about entrepreneurial opportunities by engaging in the mathematical process of optimizing on known prices and quantities but must, instead, exercise judgment about these parameters (Casson, 1995).

Second, even if the information necessary for future action were knowable in the present, market participants could not use it effectively. For future information to be usable, market participants would need to be able to overcome information problems. However, one cannot differentiate low effort or low quality from bad luck for novel, creative or unique activities, leading futures markets for entrepreneurial decisions to fail from information problems, such as moral hazard and adverse selection.

Third, to make entrepreneurial decisions, people must make decisions about resources on the basis of something other than the same price information that everyone else has and the same optimization rules that others are applying. If everyone applied the same decision rules to the same information as everyone else, they would come to the same conclusions about the value of resources. This situation would preclude people from obtaining resources and selling them to others for more than their cost to obtain. Therefore, for a person to identify an entrepreneurial opportunity – to identify a situation in which resources could be recombined and sold for more than they cost to obtain – all people must not all agree on the value of resources at a given point in time.

As I indicated above, under uncertain circumstances such as these, decision-making about resources cannot be a mechanistic process based on given prices (Wu, 1989). Rather, decision-making involves consideration of things other than prices through mechanisms other than optimizing.

New Means–Ends Frameworks

To formulate a conjecture that a profit is possible by buying, selling or transforming resources requires the perception of a new means–ends framework. A means–ends framework is a way of thinking about the relationship between actions and outcomes. Because prices do not contain all of the information necessary to make decisions about the value of resources, people develop different beliefs about the value of resources. That is, they develop new means–ends frameworks.

These new frameworks are formulated when something – such as information about prior errors in decision-making, knowledge of new demand or a technological invention – leads a person to believe that prices do not accurately represent the value of goods and services, and the potential exists to generate a better alternative to buying or selling resources than the one that currently exists. Therefore, a person's belief that they can come up with a new way to generate profit by recombining resources and selling the output for more than it costs to acquire or produce (a new means–ends framework), is central to making entrepreneurial decisions.

This new decision-making framework can result from the formulation of new means, ends, or means–ends relationships about products, raw materials, markets, or production or organizing methods. These frameworks can be triggered by a change that generates information about opportunities (Schumpeter, 1934) or because other market participants made errors in their decision-making, creating leads or lags, and shortages or surpluses (Kirzner, 1997). In all cases, the key characteristic is that the new framework leads people to believe that they could buy or sell goods or services, recombine them and sell the output at a profit (Schumpeter, 1934; Kirzner, 1997).

Entrepreneurs introduce new means–ends decision-making algorithms into the price system by using non price-based information to formulate new perceptions about the efficient allocation of resources. That is, the process involves the articulation of a new relationship between inputs and outputs that incorporates information not captured in prices. This new relationship is a proposition that resources can be obtained and transformed and the output sold in a way that will be profitable.

Judgmental Decision-Making

The creation of a new means-ends framework involves judgmental decision-making. For an entrepreneur to perceive an opportunity, she must believe that the value of resources must be higher than the cost of obtaining and transforming them (Casson, 1982). Moreover, all others must not share her opinion about the value of the resources (Wu, 1989). The possibility of entrepreneurial profit requires different beliefs about resources from those held by others because alternative beliefs are necessary to obtain the resources at a price that permits a profit (Shane and Venkataraman, 2000). Therefore, entrepreneurial decision-making means making judgmental decisions.

To exercise judgment by making different decisions from others, an entrepreneur must either possess different information than others or interpret the same information differently. As Casson (1982: 14) explained, 'The essence of entrepreneurship is being different – being different because one has a different perception of the situation.'

While the entrepreneur's information or interpretation can overlap to some extent with that of others, the lack of overlap is what encourages entrepreneurial decision-making. As Casson (1982: 120) explains,

> The greater the number of entrepreneurs searching in a given area, the lower the probability that any given one of them will be first to make a discovery. If each entrepreneur is basically as well equipped for search as the others, then his probability of obtaining a reward from search varies inversely with the number of entrepreneurs in the field (Casson, 1982: 120).

Therefore, entrepreneurial decision-making involves making decisions that require judgment at odds with the judgment of others.

The Importance of Creativity

When the parameters are not set and people must exercise judgment about them, decision-making also involves creativity. Similar to the way that a scientist or artist interprets the environment, the entrepreneur must create a new framework for valuing resources based on her beliefs about what will satisfy the market place, how competitors will act, or what the effect of a technological change will be (Wu, 1989). Because consumer preferences, technological change and other factors are uncertain, the entrepreneur is acting creatively to form opinions about assumptions that are as yet unproven. In essence, the entrepreneur is playing her hunches or exploiting her cognitions about better ways to do things or better things to do, rather than computing expected values. As a result, judgmental decisions differ from decisions in which people optimize scarce resources within existing parameters because entrepreneurial decision-making is a creative process (Gaglio and Katz, 2001).[1]

It is important to note that creativity can be important in entrepreneurial decision-making without negating the concept of opportunity discovery as described in much of the entrepreneurship literature and summarized below (Kirzner, 1997; Shane, 2000). That is, entrepreneurial decision-making can involve creativity even if opportunities exist as an objective reality because the identification of those opportunities requires the creation of a new means–ends framework.

I make this point because some researchers argue that opportunities are socially constructed in the minds of entrepreneurs and do not exist in objective form (for example, Gartner *et al.*, 1992). However, as the discussion of the sources of opportunity in Chapter 2 suggested, specific changes in technology, politics, regulation, demographics and social factors make entrepreneurial opportunities possible. Moreover, as I will explain in greater detail in Chapter 6, the high level of structural variation in opportunities across industries belies the idea that opportunities have no external component. As I will explain in that chapter, some industries at certain points in time have many more people founding new companies than other industries. Although it is possible that these industry-level differences have no objective basis, and that groups of people tend to socially construct certain types of opportunity at certain points in time or in certain industries, this explanation is less plausible than the explanation that the opportunities themselves are not completely socially constructed.

According to the nexus perspective, entrepreneurs respond to objective information about opportunities that varies over time and place (in particular, the information about technological, political/regulatory and social/demographic change described in Chapter 2, and the industry characteristics described in Chapter 6). As a result, the social construction of opportunities only takes place at the margin, with objective differences providing the basis for wide variations in opportunities across time and place.

In sum, the individual–opportunity nexus perspective described in this book argues that opportunities have an objective component, but that the process of discovery and exploitation requires creativity to formulate new means–ends frameworks to recombine resources. Moreover, the entrepreneur's perceptions and other individual attributes influence the discovery and exploitation of opportunities in ways that will be described below and in Chapters 4 and 5.

Popperian Conjectures

Making judgmental decisions is much more difficult than making decisions by optimizing within an existing means–ends framework because judgmental decision-making requires forming a causal argument about a future market (Arrow, 1974a; Venkataraman, 1997). This causal argument involves such things as identifying a problem that could be solved profitably, formulating some possible solutions to that problem, and selecting at least one solution (Harper, 1996).

The entrepreneur's new means–ends framework provides a causal explanation for why a profitable recombination is possible. For example, the entrepreneur might propose that the purchase and recombination of resources would be profitable because there are few alternatives to the entrepreneur's product; because the characteristics of the purchaser make her price inelastic; or because marketing strategies (such as, advertising) will increase the size or growth of demand (Harper, 1996).

Entrepreneurs do not have the information necessary to actually assess with certainty the correctness of their causal explanations.[2] Therefore, they make what can be considered Popperian conjectures (Hamilton and Harper, 1994) about such things as production process, alternative plans for plants and production capacity, the order in which organizing activities should take place, the inputs to be obtained, the relationship between costs and volume produced, and the cost structure of rivals (Harper, 1996). These conjectures are hypotheses in the entrepreneur's theory of the opportunity that subsequent empirical testing will support or reject.

Uncertain Decision Making

The entrepreneur's conjectures are necessarily uncertain. The correctness of an entrepreneur's conjecture cannot be known in advance of action because the accuracy of the conjecture depends on future events, such as consumer demand decisions or the ability to obtain resources (Knight, 1921). For example, suppose an entrepreneur believes that she can produce a new product. The entrepreneur makes a conjecture that demand for the product will exist and that she can sell the product for more than its cost of production. Because customers may be unable to foresee their demand for new products or services or even if those products or services will be useful to them (Christiansen and Bower, 1996), this conjecture may turn out to be false.

Shackle summarized the nature of the uncertainty of the entrepreneurial process. As he (1955: 81) explained,

> from that point in time when the decision is taken to commit some resources to a particular line of production, it is ... impossible for anyone to know precisely and for certain what will be the market exchange value of the end product at that future date when it will be ready. This situation is part of the essence of things.... In all production, because it takes time, there is ineradicable uncertainty.

Because entrepreneurs make real-time decisions under uncertainty, their judgment can be flawed and their conjectures may prove to be incorrect (Harper, 1996). For example, an entrepreneur might conjecture that consumers have unmet needs, which are actually met perfectly well by the products or services of existing firms. Alternatively, an entrepreneur might underestimate the cost of identifying the right consumers or of explaining to them that the new product or service solves their problem (Harper, 1996) and therefore not be able to serve the customers profitably.

Entrepreneurial Profit

Entrepreneurial profit is the difference between the *ex-post* value of a resource combination and the *ex-ante* cost of obtaining the resources and the cost of recombining them (Rumelt, 1987). Bearing uncertainty is a necessary condition for earning entrepreneurial profit. Absent uncertainty, entrepreneurial profit would be zero. If there were certainty about an opportunity, resource owners would know how much their resources would be worth to entrepreneurs in recombined form and therefore would sell resources to entrepreneurs at their recombined value, eliminating any entrepreneurial profit. Under uncertainty, however, the resources can be worth more than the resource owners thought. Therefore, if the entrepreneur believes or knows something that the resource owner does not, the resource owner will sell or lease her resources to the entrepreneur at a price low enough for the entrepreneur to earn a profit on her recombination. As a result, the entrepreneur earns a profit if she has better judgment than others about such things as production, new market opportunities, new ways of producing existing products, or new products that satisfy customer wants or needs (Wu, 1989).

Entrepreneurial profit is the reward that the entrepreneur earns for exercising judgment about a new means–ends framework. By substituting her own new decision-making framework for that of prices in the market, the entrepreneur bears risk about the accuracy of her judgment. By becoming a residual claimant on the proceeds of an effort to recombine resources, the entrepreneur receives the right to impose her production plan on the resources (Wu, 1989). She provides insurance to resource owners by obtaining their resources at a fixed price and bearing the uncertainty about whether they will be worth more recombined than they were in the form in which she obtained them. When the entrepreneur's conjectures prove correct, she earns an entrepreneurial profit, but when they prove incorrect, she incurs an entrepreneurial loss (Casson, 1982; Shane and Venkataraman, 2000). That is, entrepreneurial profit occurs because the entrepreneur had better judgment than the resource owners, and could obtain resources for less than they ultimately proved to be worth (Johnson, 1986).

THE ROLE OF INDIVIDUALS IN THE DISCOVERY OF OPPORTUNITIES

As I explained above, the discovery of an entrepreneurial opportunity requires the formulation of a new means–ends framework (Casson, 1982). As a result, the process of opportunity discovery is cognitive and cannot be a collective act. (At best, the initial discoverer of the opportunity can carry on discussions with others to refine the opportunity that she has already discovered.)[3] Therefore, individuals, not groups or firms, discover entrepreneurial opportunities.

This observation raises the question: why do some people, and not others, discover particular opportunities? The formulation of a conjecture is influenced by the possession of information or beliefs that lead a person to think a certain way about a means–ends framework. Because both beliefs and information are unevenly distributed across people, not everyone will recognize a given entre-preneurial opportunity (Shane, 2000). Research has explained that both psychological and non-psychological characteristics of people influence their tendency to discover entrepreneurial opportunities. I discuss both types of char-acteristics here.

In general, people discover opportunities that others do not identify for two reasons: first, they have better access to information about the existence of the opportunity. Second, they are better able than others to recognize opportunities, given the same amount of information about it, because they have superior cognitive capabilities (see Box 3.1).

Access to Information

Some people are more likely than other people to discover opportunities because they have information that the other people lack (Hayek, 1945; Kirzner, 1973). This information makes it possible for one person to know that an opportunity is present when others are simply ignorant of that situation.

**BOX 3.1   INDIVIDUAL DIFFERENCES AND THE
              DISCOVERY OF ENTREPRENEURIAL
              OPPORTUNITIES**

Access to information   *Opportunity recognition*

Life experiences   Absorptive capacity
Social networks   Intelligence
Search processes   Cognitive properties

Although the information that facilitates entrepreneurial discovery could be information about major scientific developments, it need not be. It could also be information about local demand or underutilized resources (Casson, 1982). Specific life experiences, such as one's job or daily life give people access to the information that others do not have (Venkataraman, 1997). These life experiences provide early access to information that others have made incomplete or inappropriate use of resources or that external shocks, such as technological changes or regulatory developments, are coming. For example, a person might know of a storefront becoming vacant because she is a real estate agent and has early access to information about retail vacancies. Therefore, even if other people have the same preferences as the real estate agent, the real estate agent has a greater likelihood of identifying an opportunity to put a clothing store in that location because she has more information or a better combination of information relevant to that opportunity than others have (Casson, 1982).

The literature has provided empirical evidence for three factors that influence the likelihood that people will gain early access to information valuable for recognizing opportunities: prior life experience, social network structure and information search. I discuss these three mechanisms for gaining access to information in the subsections below.

Life experience
Certain activities give preferential access to the knowledge necessary for opportunity discovery. In fact, earlier research has shown evidence of two aspects of life experience that increase the probability that people will discover opportunities: job function and variation in experiences.

Job function   A person's job function influences their likelihood of opportunity discovery. For example, chemists and physicists are more likely to start new technology companies than historians because their research gives them access to information about opportunities that others do not have (Freeman, 1982).

Among the types of jobs that provide privileged access to information that facilitates the discovery of opportunities, the most important may be research and development (Klepper and Sleeper, 2001). Because research and development creates new information that generates technological change, a major source of opportunity (Aldrich, 1999), people who work in research and development often know about opportunities for new technology ventures before people in other job functions (Freeman, 1982).

Marketing jobs also provide access to the information necessary for opportunity discovery (Klepper and Sleeper, 2001). Marketing people are often the first people to learn of customer preferences (Johnson, 1986) because customers often alert marketing personnel to shortages of supply or problems with existing products or services that provide the basis for identification of an opportunity or a method of exploiting it (Von Hippel, 1986).

Some empirical research has shown that a person's functional area of work influences their propensity to discover opportunities. For example, Roberts (1991a) compared scientists and engineers who became entrepreneurs to other scientists and engineers and found that the entrepreneurs had 32 times as many patents as non-entrepreneurs. He also found that non-entrepreneur scientists and engineers who had at some time been self employed had received more patents. Both of these findings suggest that people exposed to novel and valuable technical knowledge (both necessary conditions to receive a patent) are more likely to spot entrepreneurial opportunities than other people. Roberts (1991a) also found that the technical entrepreneurs were more likely than were other scientists and engineers to have been involved in development work rather than research at their prior employers. This finding suggests that, even within the area of research and development, the more applied area of development provides access to information that is better for the discovery of opportunity.

Variation in experience   Variation in life experience provides access to new information that helps people to discover opportunities. Discovery of opportunities is often like solving puzzles because a new piece of information is often the missing element necessary to see that an opportunity is present. Variation in experience increases the likelihood that a person will receive new information that will provide a missing piece in recognizing an opportunity (Romanelli and Schoonhoven, 2001) because people with a wide range of employment or living experience have access to more diverse information (Casson, 1995).

Because opportunity recognition is not observable, researchers have provided support for this argument by examining the relationship between variation in career experience, and firm founding or self employment. If the argument presented above is correct, then people with greater variation in employment experience should be more likely to discover entrepreneurial opportunities. In fact, this result is what the empirical research has shown. For example, using data from the National Longitudinal Survey, Evans and Leighton (1989) found that the probability of being self employed in 1981 was higher the more job changes that a person had had. Similarly, Dolton and Makepeace (1990) examined data on 4016 British people from the Survey of Graduates and Diplomates undertaken by the Department of Employment, and found that the number of jobs that a person had had since graduation increased the likelihood of self employment. Furthermore, Blanchflower and Oswald (1998) showed that the number of jobs held was positively correlated with self employment in the UK labor market.

A similar argument can be made for the access to new information that comes from geographic mobility. As Casson (1982) explained, people often learn about the entrepreneurial discoveries of others through participation in markets. Therefore, participation in more markets should increase the likelihood that a person will gain access to necessary information for opportunity discovery.

Several studies provide support for this argument. Delmar and Davidsson (2000) compared a random sample of 405 people who were in the process of starting a business with a randomly selected control group not starting a business and found that those in the process of starting a business were more geographically mobile than the control group. Similarly, Lerner and Hendeles (1993) surveyed 1530 Russian immigrants to Israel who arrived between 1989 and 1991, and found that those with greater residential mobility in Israel were more likely to become self employed.

Information search
A second explanation for why some people and not others gain access to information that facilitates the discovery of opportunity is that they are searching for that information. The logic of this argument is that people are more likely to find information that is useful to the discovery process through deliberate search than through random behavior.

Some empirical evidence suggests that those who search for information about entrepreneurial opportunities are more likely to discover opportunities than people who do not search for this information. For example, Gilad *et al.* (1989) surveyed 86 small business owners and 21 managers of small businesses in New Jersey and found that the entrepreneurs were more likely than the managers to search for profit in a new deal.

Arguing that people find opportunities when they search in places where others do not look, some researchers have posited that expert entrepreneurs will be more likely to search for opportunities in private, rather than public information. In support of this argument, Hills and Shrader (1998) surveyed 53 members of the Chicago area Entrepreneurship Hall of Fame (people they considered to be expert entrepreneurs) and compared them to a sample of 187 standard business owners collected from Dun and Bradstreet lists. They found that the members of the Hall of Fame were significantly less likely than the control group to identify their opportunities from public information sources such as trade publications, magazines and newspapers than from other sources. This study suggests that people will be more likely to find information useful to the discovery of entrepreneurial opportunities by searching for relevant private information than through random efforts, or efforts to examine public information.

Social ties

An important way that people gain access to information is through interaction with other people. Therefore, one of the ways that people gain access to information about entrepreneurial opportunities is through their social network. The structure of a person's social network will influence what information they receive, and the quality, quantity and speed of the receipt of that information. As a result, the social network should influence a person's access to information that facilitates the discovery of opportunities.

In particular, diverse social ties – or ties to a wide variety of people – should encourage access to information that facilitates opportunity discovery (Aldrich and Zimmer, 1986). Much of the important information for discovering opportunities – information about locations, potential markets, sources of capital, employees, ways to organize – is likely to be spread across a variety of people. Therefore, ties to a wide variety of people who all have some of this information, enhances opportunity discovery (Johansson, 2000). Moreover, diversity of the people with whom one has ties increases the probability that one will get non-redundant information because people gain little new information in more homogeneous networks (Aldrich, 1999). Thus, non-redundancy in social ties increases the likelihood that one will gain access to the right complement of information necessary for opportunity discovery.

Strong ties, or ties to people that one trusts, are also beneficial to opportunity discovery. Because strong ties are trustworthy, they provide people with information that the recipients believe to be accurate. Belief in the accuracy of information is important to opportunity discovery because the entrepreneur needs to gain access to, and synthesize, information before others. However, gaining access to information before others means that there are few ways to corroborate the accuracy of information. Therefore, the entrepreneur needs to know that the information she acts upon is valid (Casson, 1982).

Several studies have provided support for the arguments that social ties increase the likelihood that people will discover entrepreneurial opportunities. For example, Zimmer and Aldrich (1987) studied ethnic group self employment in three cities in England and found that most of the owners gathered information about entrepreneurial opportunities through social channels.

Two studies provide support for the idea that diverse social ties are important to opportunity discovery. Singh *et al.* (1999) surveyed 256 people who had started information technology consulting firms and found that entrepreneurs with more diverse ties were more likely to identify venture opportunities than entrepreneurs with less diverse ties. Kaish and Gilad (1991) compared 51 firm founders with 36 managers in a large financial services firm and discovered that the firm founders were less likely to use proximate sources of information and were more likely to use strangers to identify opportunities.

However, strong ties also appear to be important to the opportunity discovery process. Busenitz (1996) compared firm founders with managers in large organizations and found that entrepreneurs were more likely than managers to obtain information from people that they knew and trusted. Koller (1988) randomly sampled 82 firm founders from the telephone directory and found that 46 had their business idea suggested to them by a business associate, relative, or other social contact, demonstrating the importance of strong ties to the discovery process. In fact, in an in-depth qualitative study of seven entrepreneurs in rural Scotland, Jack and Anderson (2002) found that the embedding of the entrepreneurs in the social context in which they lived was what enabled the entrepreneurs to identify entrepreneurial opportunities.

Opportunity Recognition

In addition to the effects of access to information on opportunity discovery described above, researchers have argued that people are more likely to discover opportunities if they have a better ability than others to recognize opportunities in a given amount of information that they receive. Researchers have proposed two different factors that influence the ability to recognize opportunities in information: absorptive capacity and cognitive processes.

Absorptive capacity
People differ in their ability to recognize opportunities in information that they receive because they possess different prior information. Prior knowledge provides an absorptive capacity that facilitates the acquisition of additional information about markets, technologies and production processes, which enhances the ability to formulate new means–ends frameworks in response to new information (Cohen and Levinthal, 1990).

The knowledge that a person already possesses influences the tendency to discover entrepreneurial opportunities for two reasons. First, a person's existing stock of knowledge frames new information, thereby enhancing the ability to interpret it in a useful way (Yu, 2001; Shane, 2000). Second, people's stocks of information influence the ability to see solutions when they encounter problems that need to be solved (Yu, 2001). As a result, knowledge of an unmet market need, a technical problem, or a customer complaint all trigger the ability to formulate solutions (Venkataraman, 1997).

Prior research has examined two types of knowledge that enhance the absorptive capacity necessary for opportunity discovery: knowledge about markets and knowledge of how to serve them.

Knowledge about markets   Prior knowledge about markets makes it easier for people to recognize demand conditions, which facilitates the discovery of opportunity. As Shane (2000: 452) explains,

> new information about a technology might be complementary with prior information about how particular markets operated, leading to the discovery of entrepreneurial opportunity to require prior information about those markets. Important prior knowledge about markets might include information about supplier relationships, sales techniques, or capital equipment requirements that differ across markets (Von Hippel, 1988). For example, a person who had previously worked in a market as a customer, manufacturer, or supplier might possess information that is not publicly available about how a new technology might influence that market. This prior information enables him or her to discover an opportunity in which to use the new technology (Roberts, 1991a).

Several studies provide evidence that superior market knowledge facilitates opportunity discovery. For example, Shane (2000) examined eight cases of entrepreneurs who discovered entrepreneurial opportunities to exploit the same invention assigned to the Massachusetts Institute of Technology – Three Dimensional Printing. Examining the relationship between the particular opportunities discovered and the entrepreneurs' backgrounds, Shane (2000) found that prior knowledge of a particular market increased the likelihood of discovering an opportunity in that market.

In less direct studies than that of Shane (2000), Long (1982) and Boyd (1990) also provide evidence consistent with the effect of prior market knowledge on opportunity discovery. If prior market knowledge enhances opportunity discovery, people who have more experience in a particular market should be more likely to discover entrepreneurial opportunities in that market than people with less experience. Consistent with this proposition, Long (1982) showed that those born overseas, who have less local market knowledge than those born in the country, were less likely to be self employed. Similarly, using public use microdata samples of the 1980 US Census, Boyd (1990) found that Asians who had immigrated between 1975 and 1980 and between 1965 and 1974 were less likely to be self employed than Asians who immigrated before 1965.

Moreover, this argument also suggests that immigrants increase their likelihood of discovering entrepreneurial opportunities with the time that they have spent in their adoptive country (Aldrich and Waldinger, 1990). If one accepts self employment as a proxy for the discovery of entrepreneurial opportunity, several studies provide support for this argument. Evans (1984) found that the self employment of Third World female immigrants to Australia increased with residence in that country. Cobas (1986) surveyed a random sample of 220 Cubans living in San Juan and found that the length of time in Puerto Rico increased the probability of self employment. Sanders and Nee (1996) found that the more recent their immigration, the lower the likelihood of self employment for Chinese, Korean, Cuban, Mexican, Filipino and Puerto Rican immigrants in New York and Los Angeles for a sample drawn from census data on non-institutionalized civilians over 18 years of age. Borjas and Bronars (1989) also found consistent results, showing that, for Asian and Hispanic immigrants, self employment propensity increased with residence in the United States. Lastly, using a 1 per cent public use sample of the 1981 Australian census, Evans (1989) found that the probability of starting a business was higher the more years of Australian labor market experience and the fewer the years of foreign labor market experience that an immigrant had.

Furthermore, the knowledge of the market hypothesis for entrepreneurial discovery is supported by studies that show that immigrants exploit their differential knowledge of their own ethnic markets to discover opportunities. If market knowledge makes people more likely to discover entrepreneurial opportunities, then being located in an ethnic enclave should make immigrants more likely to be entrepreneurs. Consistent with this argument, Borjas (1986) found that immigrant Mexicans, Cubans and other Hispanics were significantly more likely to be self employed if they were in an ethnic enclave market (one with a high proportion of people of their background), even though there was no effect of this enclave on the self employment of native-born white people. Moreover, Evans (1989) found that the probability of starting a business increased with the size of the immigrant's ethnic group in that market.

Knowledge of how to serve markets Prior knowledge of how to serve markets also facilitates the discovery of entrepreneurial opportunity, by helping an individual to better determine the production or marketing gains from the introduction of a new product or service (Johnson, 1986). As Shane (2000) explained, a person is more likely to discover an entrepreneurial opportunity if she knows what product or services could be introduced, how these products or services could be produced or distributed, how a new material could be used in the production process, or what sources of supply are available. This information influences the entrepreneur's new means–ends framework, particularly, her beliefs about production and organization. Similarly, prior knowledge of customer needs or problems would increase the likelihood of opportunity discovery because such knowledge facilitates the understanding of how to solve customer problems in situations where the customer cannot articulate their needs or the solutions to them (Von Hippel, 1988; Roberts, 1991a).

Consistent with the idea that prior knowledge helps people to discover opportunities, research has shown that founders often start companies to make the same types of products or services that were made by their prior employers (Johnson, 1986; Klepper and Sleeper, 2001; Aldrich and Wiedenmayer, 1993). For example, Cooper and Dunkelberg (1987) examined data on new ventures founded by members of the National Federation of Independent Businesses, and found that 66 per cent of them were in the same or similar product line as their former employer. Similarly, Young and Francis (1991) found that 82 per cent of manufacturing firm founders they surveyed had worked in a company producing the same or a similar product to the one produced by their new venture. In fact, 40 per cent of Young and Francis's sample reported that their product was the same as their former company's product, and 26 per cent explained that they developed an original product from previous company experience.

Moreover, founders often serve the same customers as their previous employers. Johannisson (1988), for example, found that more than half of a sample of new Swedish firms served their prior employer's customers or the prior employer itself. Similarly, Cooper and Dunkelberg (1987) found that over 60 per cent of the entrepreneurs in their sample of new ventures founded by members of the National Federation of Independent Businesses reported serving the same or similar customers as their prior employer.

Furthermore, the approaches to exploiting an opportunity employed by entrepreneurs appear be related to those of the entrepreneurs' prior employers (Boeker, 1988; Klepper, 2001). In particular, several researchers have shown that the technologies employed by new ventures tended to be similar to those of the entrepreneurs' prior employers (Cooper, 1984; 1971), and the organizational forms and strategies that entrepreneurs establish tend to be correlated with those of the organizations where they used to work (Aldrich and Wiedenmayer, 1993).

Some empirical evidence even shows the direct impact of prior knowledge of how to serve markets on the discovery of opportunities. For example, Shane's (2000) investigation of eight cases of entrepreneurs who discovered entrepreneurial opportunities to exploit the invention of three dimensional printing demonstrated that prior knowledge of customer problems and ways to serve markets influenced the opportunities that the entrepreneurs identified. Similarly, in a study of 2994 firms that were started by members of the National Federation of Independent Businesses, Cooper et al. (1990) found that the respondent's prior job was the most common source of the new venture's business idea, reported by 43 per cent of the respondents.

While the evidence presented above indicates that people tend to discover their venture ideas from their prior employment, it leaves open the question of whether that tendency has any effect on the performance of their new ventures. On the one hand, entrepreneurs might be better off discovering business ideas that are not related to the activities of their prior employers because unrelated business ideas would minimize problems of establishing ownership of the ideas. On the other hand, entrepreneurs might be better off identifying business ideas that are related to the activities of their prior employers because that approach would allow them to make use of prior knowledge about how to serve markets in establishing the venture idea.

I could find only one empirical study that shed light on this question, and it suggested that identifying a business idea that is related to the activities of an entrepreneur's prior employer is performance enhancing for her new venture. Dunkelberg *et al.* (1987) surveyed 634 firms founded by members of the National Federation of Independent Businesses and compared those that had employment growth with those that had employment loss a year later. The authors found that those firms with employment growth rather than employment loss were significantly more likely than others to have identified their venture idea from a prior job.

Cognitive processes

Differences among people in cognitive processing also influence opportunity discovery because discovery requires people to formulate new means–ends frameworks in response to information that they receive. Sometimes calling this individual difference 'alertness to opportunity' (Kirzner, 1997), researchers have discussed how differences in cognitive processing influence people's ability to recognize opportunities. For example, Gaglio and Katz (2001) explain that some people are better than others at understanding causal links, categorizing information, seeing relationships and patterns in information, understanding how processes work, and evaluating assumptions and information accurately, all of which facilitate their ability to discover opportunity. In contrast, Sarasvathy *et al.* (1998) suggest that some people see opportunities that others miss because they categorize information differently, viewing a given piece of information as an indicator of an opportunity when others see it as an indicator of risk. Shackle (1982) identifies another aspect of cognitive processing that influences the discovery of entrepreneurial opportunity, differences in imagination. Other authors propose still other cognitive differences. To Schumpeter (1934) the greater ability to recognize opportunities is a function of a person's creativity, whereas to Knight (1921), it is a function of the person's intelligence and foresight. In the subsection below, I discuss the cognitive processes underlying the recognition of opportunity, focusing on four broad categories: intelligence, perceptive ability, creativity and not seeing risks.

Intelligence Knight (1921) argued that differences among people in their intellectual capacity would influence their likelihood of opportunity discovery. Because the entrepreneur must gather and process information to identify an entrepreneurial opportunity, a person's general intelligence should increase their ability to recognize opportunities inherent in the information with which they are confronted, as well as to formulate a conjecture about how to act upon it (Hebert and Link, 1988).

Four studies have examined whether intelligence influences opportunity discovery. The more direct of the studies examined the relationship between intelligence and self employment. Using the same longitudinal dataset, which explored a sample of Dutch people, and controlling for years of education (which had a significant negative effect when intelligence was measured), De Wit and Van Winden (1989) and De Wit (1993) both found that IQ scores, measured at age 12, had a positive and significant effect on self employment propensity later in life.

In a less direct test of the intelligence hypothesis, Busenitz (1996) compared 178 firm founders with managers in large organizations, and found that entrepreneurs were more likely than managers to get ideas for new businesses by thinking about them. Similarly, Gilad *et al.* (1989) surveyed 86 small business owners and 21 managers of small businesses in New Jersey and found that entrepreneurs spent more non-working hours thinking about business opportunities than did the managers. These studies support the idea that entrepreneurs have better cognitive capacity than non-entrepreneurs and therefore can identify opportunities by thinking about them.

If intelligence increases the likelihood of opportunity discovery, then people who are more intelligent might select from a greater variety of opportunities. As a result, more intelligent people might discover more valuable opportunities. In fact, two studies suggest that intelligence is correlated with the discovery of more valuable opportunities. Van Praag and Cramer (2001) explored data on a survey of 1763 elementary school children in the Dutch province of Noord-Brabant in 1952 that were surveyed again in 1983 and 1993. The authors compared the 258 who were ever self employed to the rest, using a structural model in which entrepreneurial talent was measured by the employment size of the firms created through self employment. They found that entrepreneurial talent was positively related to IQ measured at age 12. Similarly, Baum *et al.* (2000) examined the performance of 142 Canadian biotechnology firms founded between 1991 and 1996. They found that firms whose founders had master's degrees and Ph.D.'s at the time of founding had faster employment and revenue growth than the other new ventures in their sample.

Perceptive ability The fact that entrepreneurs need to perceive opportunities from the information that they receive suggests that entrepreneurs might have cognitive characteristics that give them superior perceptive ability relative to the rest of the population (Baron, forthcoming). In fact, Knight's (1921) view that entrepreneurship involves bearing uncertainty about the sales of output tomorrow using resources bought and recombined today, suggests that people who discover opportunities might have greater perceptive ability about the outcome of a future recombination of resources, a factor that he called 'foresight'. Using this idea of foresight, Bhide (2000) suggested that entrepreneurs might be better than the rest of society at attributing information to the correct sources.

Several studies support the idea that entrepreneurs have cognitive characteristics better suited to opportunity discovery than the rest of society. For example, Hills *et al.* (1999) surveyed 187 business owners in the Chicago area and found that using intuition or gut feelings rather than reliance on customer surveys to identify ideas was a significant predictor of the number of opportunities identified by the entrepreneurs. Hills and Shrader's (1998) comparison of members of the Chicago area Entrepreneurship Hall of Fame with a sample of typical business owners collected from Dun and Bradstreet lists showed that the members of the Entrepreneurship Hall of Fame were significantly more likely than the typical entrepreneurs to report that opportunity identification was a natural attribute that they possessed, and were significantly less likely to see the evaluation process as important to entrepreneurship.

More directly to the point, Roberts (1991a) examined 72 members of the MIT Enterprise Forum and the 128 Venture Group and found that the 48 who were firm founders at some point in their lives were more 'perceiving-oriented' than the others. Similarly, Mitchell *et al.* (2000) examined a convenience sample of 753 people in seven countries and compared those who were firm founders to those who were not. Arguing that firm founders have cognitive scripts that allow them to identify and use information that non-founders cannot see, these authors showed that cognitive scripts related to the ability to see opportunities differentiated firm founders from others.

Creativity   As I mentioned earlier in this chapter, people must formulate new means–ends relationships in response to information about a particular change or other people's prior decision-making errors to identify entrepreneurial opportunities (Shane and Venkataraman, 2000). Establishing a new means–ends framework involves imagination and creativity because it involves identifying, defining and structuring novel solutions to open-ended problems (Harper, 1996; Sarasvathy, 2001). As a result, several researchers have proposed that entrepreneurs have better ingenuity or creativity than the rest of the population (Schumpeter, 1934; Wu, 1989).

Some research supports this proposition. Fraboni and Saltstone (1990) compared 81 firm founders with 32 children of firm founders who were operating their family businesses. They found that the firm founders scored higher on the imagination component of the 16-factor personality scale. Robinson *et al.* (1991) compared 54 firm founders with 57 white-collar non-managers and found that the firm founders scored higher than non-founders on a scale of innovativeness. Bellu (1988) administered the Miner sentence completion scale to 70 firm founders and 77 managers and found the entre-preneurs higher than the managers on a scale measuring personal innovation.

Similar results have been found from studies conducted outside the United States. Sagie and Elizur (1999) compared 114 Dutch small business students to 171 general business students and found that the small business students had a greater preference than the other students for tasks involving inventive problem solving rather than following instructions. Hyrsky and Kangasharju (1998) surveyed 1479 Finns and found that firm founders were significantly higher than non-founders on innovation, as measured by the KAI scale. Lastly, Walsh and Anderson (1995) found similar results for a comparison of 51 Irish founders and 57 Irish non-founder managers.

The results are consistent when creativity was measured in place of innovation. Hull *et al.* (1980) surveyed 307 alumni of the University of Oregon, of which 57 were at least partial owners of a business, and found that the business owners scored higher on a creativity scale than the non-owners. (They also found that the creativity score was higher if the likelihood that a person would start a new business in the next three years was higher.) Caird (1991) compared 73 owner–managers of businesses to 189 teachers, nurses, clerical trainees, civil servants and lecturers and found that the entrepreneurs scored more highly than the others on a scale of creative tendency. Vesalainen and Pihkala (1999) surveyed a random sample of 2899 people in 16 municipalities in Sweden and asked them about the probability that they would start a venture in the next year, whether they were engaged in pre-start-up activities, and whether they were engaged in entrepreneurial studies. They found that a scale measuring creativity was positively correlated with all three measures. Lastly, firm founders also score more creatively than the general population in several studies that used Durham's GET test (Caird, 1991; Cromie and O'Donoghue, 1992).

Studies also indicate that people who intend to become entrepreneurs in the future appear to have the cognitive attributes that facilitate opportunity discovery. For example, Sexton and Bowman (1983) surveyed 401 students at Baylor University and found that entrepreneurial management majors were sig-nificantly lower on conformity, and significantly higher on innovation than non-business majors or non-entrepreneurship business majors. Sexton and Bowman (1984) administered a survey to another set of 41 business students, 43 entrepreneurship students and 51 non-business students, and found that the entrepreneurship students scored significantly higher than the other two groups on a scale of innovativeness. Similarly, Goldsmith and Kerr (1991) compared

34 entrepreneurship students to 24 other business students and found the entrepreneurship students higher on an innovation scale than the
non-entrepreneurship students. Koh (1996) surveyed 54 Hong Kong MBAs
about their inclination to start a business, and found that those who had a higher
innovativeness score were more likely to want to start their own businesses.

Research also suggests that the creativity that allows some entrepreneurs to
discover more opportunities than others also appears to help them to identify
more valuable opportunities. If one accepts the idea that entrepreneurs exploit
the best opportunities that they discover, then two studies provide support for
this relationship. Using data on 201 entrepreneurs who founded businesses
between 1990 and 1993, Utsch and Rauch (2000) found that employment and
profit growth of ventures increased with the founder's score on an innovativeness scale. Similarly, Thullar (2001) examined the average annual rate of
employment and sales growth for 58 Russian entrepreneurs who had participated in a training program four years earlier. He learned that the founder's
personal innovation was positively correlated with both the employment and
sales growth of their ventures.

Not seeing risks   Because entrepreneurship involves the formulation of a
conjecture about an opportunity in response to the receipt of some information,
many observers have argued that those who see opportunities, as opposed to
risks, in new information, should be more likely to discover entrepreneurial
opportunities.

Several studies support this proposition. Kaish and Gilad (1991) compared
51 firm founders with 36 managers in a large financial services firm and found
that the firm founders were more likely than the managers to pay attention to
risk cues, but less likely to pay attention to economic cues.

However, these risk cues do not deter entrepreneurs in the way that they deter
managers. Zietsma (1999) compared 52 technology firm founders with 22 senior
technology managers who had considered, but decided against founding firms.
These authors discovered that non-founders were significantly more likely to
mention that they saw risks in the technologies that they investigated than did
the founders. Similarly, Sarasvathy *et al.* (1998) asked successful entrepreneurs
and successful bankers to examine the same simulated venture – a computer
game about entrepreneurship. They showed that entrepreneurs identified fewer
risks and more opportunities than the bankers in exactly the same situation.

Perhaps the reason for the differences between entrepreneurs and non-entrepreneurs in the perception of opportunities is that self-efficacy encourages
people to recognize and exploit opportunities (a point to which I will return in
Chapter 5). Specifically, their strong self-efficacy leads some people to see
opportunities where others see risk. In support of this explanation, Krueger and
Dickson (1993a) gave 153 students a decision-making task and manipulated

their perception of self-efficacy. They found that when self-efficacy was increased, the students perceived more entrepreneurial opportunities in environmental changes than they did when self-efficacy was lowered.

SUMMARY

This chapter examined the process of entrepreneurial discovery and the individual-level differences that explain why some people and not others discover entrepreneurial opportunities. Entrepreneurial discovery occurs because the price system does not always allocate resources effectively. Prices contain only some of the information needed to serve markets. Moreover, prices do not provide information about a way of producing or organizing that requires a technology that does not yet exist. Furthermore, prices do not provide information about the actions of competitors in response to entrepreneurial entry.

When people use the price system to make decisions, they optimize within known means–ends frameworks using mathematical rules. However, when the price system cannot be used, people make decisions by means other than optimizing within existing means–ends frameworks. Entrepreneurial decisions are non-optimizing decisions because, to optimize, prices and quantities need to be known; market participants must be able to differentiate low effort or low quality from bad luck; and people must make decisions about resources on the basis of something other than the same information that everyone else has.

Entrepreneurial decisions are made by formulating new means–ends frameworks for the use of resources. New means–ends frameworks are created when something – such as information about previous errors in decision-making, knowledge of new demand, or a technological invention – leads a person to believe that prices do not accurately represent the value of goods and services, and that the potential exists to generate a better alternative to buying or selling resources than the current one.

The creation of a new means–ends framework involves judgmental decision-making. Because the exercise of judgment involves making different decisions from others, an entrepreneur must either possess different information than others or interpret the same information differently. As a result, entrepreneurial decision-making involves creativity.

Exercising judgment is much more difficult than making decisions by optimizing within existing means–ends frameworks because judgmental decision-making requires forming a causal argument about a future market for a good or service that does not yet exist. Because entrepreneurs do not have the information necessary to actually assess the correctness of their causal explanations with certainty, they make conjectures. These conjectures are necessarily uncertain because the correctness of an entrepreneur's conjecture cannot be known before future events occur.

Entrepreneurial profit is the difference between the *ex-post* value of a resource combination and the *ex-ante* cost of obtaining the resources. The entrepreneur earns a profit if she has better judgment than others about such things as production, new market opportunities, new ways of producing existing products, or new products that satisfy customer wants or needs.

Because the discovery of entrepreneurial opportunities requires the formulation of a conjecture based on information possessed by the entrepreneur, not everyone will recognize all entrepreneurial opportunities. Therefore, the field of entrepreneurship must explain why some people and not others discover those opportunities.

In general, people discover opportunities that others do not see for two reasons: First, they have better access to information about the existence of the opportunity. Three factors influence the likelihood that people will gain early access to information valuable for recognizing opportunities: previous life experience, social network structure and information search. Second, people are better able to identify opportunities than others if they can more easily recognize opportunities, given the same amount of information. Two factors influence the ability to recognize opportunities given a certain amount of information: absorptive capacity and cognitive processes. The most important aspects of absorptive capacity are prior knowledge about markets and prior knowledge about how to serve markets. The most important cognitive processes are intelligence, perceptive ability, creativity and not seeing risks.

Having explained the opportunity discovery process and the factors that influence which people discover opportunities, I now turn to explaining individual differences in the decisions of people to exploit opportunities.

NOTES

1. Sarasvathy (2001) illustrates this difference by analogy: a carpenter asked to build a desk to fit particular specifications would optimize, but a carpenter asked to build something out of wood using his tools would engage in entrepreneurial decision-making.
2. For example, entrepreneurs often engage in activities that ultimately prove to be unprofitable, as is apparent from the high correlation between entry and exit and the low level of success of entrepreneurial endeavors (Oxenfeldt, 1943).
3. Reynolds and White (1997) provide evidence, albeit indirect, that supports the argument that opportunity discovery is an individual-level process. In addition to the fact that approximately one-third of all new ventures are never exploited by a team, over 20 per cent of people who create a venture team to exploit their opportunity establish the team during the first month of their venture, and many more assemble their teams even later in the exploitation process. These patterns of team organizing suggest that many efforts by teams to exploit opportunities result from efforts by lead entrepreneurs who discover opportunities to subsequently assemble teams to pursue the opportunities that they have identified.

4. Individual differences and the decision to exploit

After an individual has discovered an opportunity, she must make a decision about whether or not to exploit it. Unlike many sociological explanations for entrepreneurship (for example, Carroll and Hannan, 2000), which tend to ignore the role of human agency in the decision to exploit opportunities, the individual–opportunity nexus underlying this book argues that individual differences, both psychological and demographic, exert a powerful influence over who exploits entrepreneurial opportunities and who does not.

I define individual differences as any type of variation among people, whether in their demographic characteristics, such as age or education, or in their psychological make-up, such as motivations, personalities, core self-evaluation or cognitive processing. Individual differences thus include things that are relatively stable over time, like personality, as well as things that change greatly over time, like cognitions. They incorporate things that can be learned, such as knowledge of markets, and things that cannot, like age.

The entrepreneurship literature has shown that the people who engage in entrepreneurial activity are not randomly determined. Certain individual-level characteristics are associated with the decision to engage in entrepreneurial activity. Figure 4.1 indicates the ways in which individual differences influence the entrepreneurial process. For example, psychological factors, including human motivation, core evaluation and cognition influence the discovery of opportunities; the willingness of people to exploit opportunities that they have discovered; their resource acquisition processes; and the strategies and organization designs of the entrepreneurs' new ventures. Although it is possible that demographic factors matter more than psychological factors (or vice versa) or influence different aspects of the decision to exploit opportunities, this book argues that differences in individual-level factors are important in explaining who exploits entrepreneurial opportunities.

This chapter and the next one summarize the research of entrepreneurship researchers who have identified specific human attributes associated with the decision to exploit entrepreneurial opportunities. In this chapter, I examine the arguments for and empirical support of the non-psychological individual-level attributes associated with the exploitation of entrepreneurial opportunity. In the

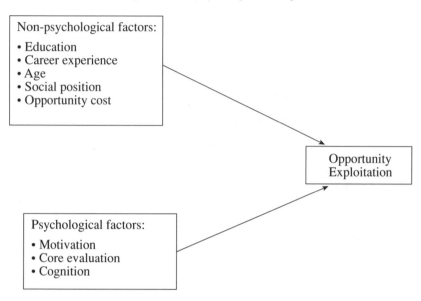

Figure 4.1   The effect of individual attributes on the decision to exploit

next chapter, I turn to the psychological factors. Because several different definitions of entrepreneurship have been employed in the literature, most notably firm formation and self employment, I consider all definitions in describing the empirical studies that have been conducted, and make reference to the definition used when describing each study.

THE DECISION TO EXPLOIT: A BASIC MODEL

To pursue uncertain opportunities, entrepreneurs must believe that they will gain more than they are giving up (Venkataraman, 1997). Consequently, when people make a decision to exploit an entrepreneurial opportunity, they do so because they believe that the expected value of exploitation (both monetary and psychic) exceeds the opportunity cost for alternative use of their time plus the premiums that they would like for bearing uncertainty and illiquidity.[1]

The entrepreneur is more likely to exploit an opportunity, the greater is the value that she expects to receive from exploitation. This expected value is influenced by three factors: the nature of the opportunity and the industry and institutional environment (which I will discuss in Chapters 6 and 7); psychological factors (which I will discuss in Chapter 5); and the non-psychological characteristics of the entrepreneur (which I discuss below).

The entrepreneur is less likely to exploit an opportunity, the greater is her opportunity cost and the premiums that she expects to earn for bearing uncertainty and illiquidity. The entrepreneur's opportunity cost and uncertainty and illiquidity premiums are affected by two factors: the entrepreneur's psychological composition (which I will discuss in Chapter 5) and the non-psychological characteristics of the entrepreneur (which I discuss below).

Opportunity Cost

Entrepreneurs always have an alternative use for their time. They can work for others or enjoy their leisure rather than exploit entrepreneurial opportunities. Because entrepreneurs always have an alternative use for their time, the exploitation of entrepreneurial opportunities has a positive opportunity cost (Hamilton and Harper, 1994).

In making a decision whether or not to exploit an opportunity, a potential entrepreneur implicitly compares the value of her utility from engaging in entrepreneurial activities with her opportunity cost of engaging in other activities (Johnson, 1986). As Kanbur (1980: 493) explains, 'it could be that the prospective entrepreneur has open to him a safe return in an alternative occupation. *Relative* to this return ... he could end up worse than if he had taken up a safe occupation.'

People are more likely to make decisions to exploit opportunities when the gap between expected utility of exploiting opportunities and the alternative uses of their time is larger. This gap is larger if a person has a lower opportunity cost to alternative uses to their time. As a result, for a given opportunity and equally capable individuals, those individuals with low opportunity costs should be more likely to exploit entrepreneurial opportunities (Amit *et al.*, 1993). In fact, some people might have such high opportunity cost that they will never exploit opportunities, whereas others have so little to lose that almost any opportunity is sufficient to lead them to act (Gifford, 1992). In the subsections below, I examine two factors that are associated with having a low opportunity cost of alternative activity: income and unemployment.

Income
The opportunity cost argument suggests that people who have higher incomes should be less likely to exploit opportunities, all other things being equal. Empirical research supports this argument. For example, Amit *et al.* (1995) examined data on 55 434 people from the 1988–1990 Labor Market Activity Survey in Canada, which gathered data on the non-military population between the ages of 16 and 69. These authors found that, before leaving, people who become self employed earned $2340 less, on average, than those who did not become self employed. Similarly, Evans and Leighton (1989) examined data on

2731 white men from the National Longitudinal Survey. They found that the probability of entering self employment went down as the respondents' wages went up. Johansson (2000) examined Finnish microdata on 103 482 people aged 18 to 65 for the period from 1987 to 1994, and found that higher wages reduced the likelihood that a respondent would become self employed. Dolton and Makepeace (1990) examined data on 4016 British people from the Survey of Graduates and Diplomates and found that the respondent's initial starting salary upon graduation reduced the likelihood of subsequent self employment.

The opportunity cost argument also suggests that the likelihood that a person will exploit an entrepreneurial opportunity increases with the gap between expected value of self employment earnings and the person's current wage employment earnings. Several studies provide empirical support for this version of the opportunity cost argument. For example, Rees and Shah (1986) examined data from the 1978 British General Household Survey, and found that the gap between expected self employment earnings and current wage earnings increased the likelihood of self employment. Taylor (1996) examined data from the 1991 British Household Panel Survey and found that the difference between predicted earnings from self employment and current earnings had a positive effect on the probability of self employment. Using Canadian data, Bernhardt (1994) found that the larger the wage differential between self and wage employment in a person's field, the greater the likelihood that a person would engage in self employment.

Unemployment

The opportunity cost argument also suggests that unemployed people should be more likely than employed people to exploit entrepreneurial opportunities. Once unemployed, a person's opportunity cost from their prior wage employment drops, increasing their likelihood of engaging in self employment. Several studies provide empirical support for this argument. For example, Mesch and Czamanski (1997) surveyed 275 immigrants to Israel from the former Soviet Union and found that people were more likely to intend to start a business if they were unemployed and unable to find a job.

Moreover, research shows that these intentions are translated into actual behavior. For example, using data from the British Household Survey, Taylor (2001) found that people who were unemployed in 1994 were significantly more likely to make the transition to self-employment between 1994 and 1996 than people who were employed in 1994. Similarly, Ritsila and Tervo (2002) examined data from a 0.2 per cent random sample of the Finnish population taken from the Finnish Longitudinal Employment Statistics and found that unemployment increased the probability that a person would found a business.

A related issue concerns the level of benefits that the individual receives during unemployment. The opportunity cost argument suggests that the greater the benefits that a person receives during unemployment, the greater the opportunity cost to self employment, and the lower the likelihood that an individual will engage in self employment.

Two studies provide empirical support for this argument. At a macro-level, Eisenhauer (1995) examined self employment in the United States from 1959 to 1991 and found that when the real level of unemployment benefits went up, the rate of self employment went down. At a more micro-level, Alba-Ramirez (1994) examined data on 5282 unemployed workers taken from the 1986 and 1988 US Displaced Worker Survey and found that people covered by unemployment insurance were less likely to become self employed than those not covered.

The opportunity cost argument also suggests that a person's likelihood of exploiting an entrepreneurial opportunity should increase with the duration of unemployment. As unemployment progresses, a person's unemployment benefits are used up. Consequently, a person's opportunity cost from exploiting an entrepreneurial opportunity goes down with the duration of unemployment, and their willingness to exploit entrepreneurial opportunities goes up.

Again, empirical research provides support for the argument. Using data from the National Longitudinal Survey, Evans and Leighton (1989) found that the probability of being self employed in 1981 increased with the duration of the respondent's unemployment. Similarly, using data from a government survey of Spanish Households undertaken in 1985 and data from the US Displaced Worker Survey, Alba-Ramirez (1994) found that the duration of unemployment increased the probability of entering self employment.

Given the opportunity cost argument, one would also expect a correlation between unemployment rates and entrepreneurial activity across geographic locations. In regions with more unemployed workers, the average level of opportunity cost and the threshold for opportunity exploitation, is lower. Several macro-level studies have reported such correlations. Both Johnson (1986) and Storey (1982) have demonstrated the existence of this correlation across regions in the United Kingdom. Guesnier (1994) examined the rate of firm formation per 100 existing firms and per 10 000 active workers from 1986 to 1991 across French regions and found a positive effect of the unemployment rate. Audretsch and Fritsch (1994) examined the rate of firm formation per 100 existing firms across regions of Germany from 1986 to 1989 and found a positive relationship between the unemployment rate and the rate of firm formation. Davidsson *et al.* (1994) examined the rate of new firm formation across regions in Sweden from 1985 to 1989 per member of the workforce-aged population and found a positive effect of the unemployment rate. Kangasharju (2000) examined regional variation in firm formation per 1000 workers in Finland from 1989 to 1993 and found that the unemployment rate had a significant positive effect on firm formation. Reynolds (1994a) looked at the rate of new firm birth across 382 labor market areas in the United States from 1986 to 1988 and found a positive effect of the percentage of the civilian workforce that was unemployed on the rate of firm formation. Storey and Jones (1987) examined the formation of new independent manufacturing plants in two northern counties in the United Kingdom between 1965 and 1978 and found that job losses through contractions and closings had a positive effect on formation of new firms. Given these results, it is not surprising that Bogenhold and Staber (1990) found a positive relationship between unemployment and self employment in ten OECD countries between the early 1950s and 1987.

Similar patterns exist when researchers have examined the relationship between rates of unemployment and new firm formation rates within the United States over time. For example, Audretsch and Acs (1994) examined new firm start-up activity as measured by the US Small Business Administration's database at six points in time between 1976 and 1986 for 117 industries, and found that firm formation was higher when unemployment was higher. Similarly, Grant (1996) examined the annual percentage change in new business incorporations in the 48 contiguous US states from 1970 to 1985 and found that the unemployment rate in the previous year had a positive effect on firm formation.

In short, the evidence for the relationship between low opportunity cost and a high probability of opportunity exploitation appears to be quite broad and robust. But what is the relationship between opportunity cost and performance at opportunity exploitation? If people with lower opportunity cost are more likely to exploit entrepreneurial opportunities than people with higher opportunity cost, then the population of entrepreneurs with low opportunity cost probably has less entrepreneurial talent and is engaged in the exploitation of worse opportunities, on average, than the population of entrepreneurs with high opportunity cost. To motivate them to engage in opportunity exploitation despite their high opportunity cost, the population of entrepreneurs with high opportunity cost must have greater entrepreneurial talent or better opportunities than those with lower opportunity cost

Several empirical studies provide support for this argument. One set of studies indicates that the greater an entrepreneur's opportunity cost, the lower is the likelihood that her new venture will fail. Using data from a survey of firm founders who were members of the National Federation of Independent Businesses, Cooper *et al.* (1988) showed that those ventures founded by people who quit their previous jobs because of their venture plans were more likely to survive three years than those who started businesses upon losing their jobs. Similarly, Reid (1999) examined a stratified random sample of 138 clients of the Enterprise Trusts in Scotland and studied their three-year survival. He found that people who started their businesses as an alternative to unemployment were more likely to fail than those who started their businesses when they were previously employed.

Another set of studies shows the relationship between levels of opportunity cost and the growth and profitability of new ventures. Cressy (1996b) examined a sample of 1189 new firms that established accounts with the National Westminster Bank in 1988, and showed that founders with higher pre-founding income had new ventures with higher annual rates of growth in cash flow than other new ventures. Similarly, using data from the National Longitudinal Survey of Youth, Evans and Leighton (1989) and Schiller and Crewson (1997) both found that the longer the unemployment of respondents, the lower their subsequent self employment earnings were.

Married/Working Spouse

Because exploiting an entrepreneurial opportunity involves acting on one's conjectures about the potential for profit inherent in particular information, it is uncertain. People demand compensation for bearing this uncertainty. However, some people demand greater premiums for bearing uncertainty than others. In general, those people for whom uncertainty has a greater negative effect demand a greater uncertainty premium than those people for whom uncertainty has a lesser negative effect. In the next chapter, I will discuss the effect of psychological attributes that lead people to demand a greater uncertainty premium – such as a lower risk-taking propensity or a lower tolerance for ambiguity. In the subsection below, I examine demographic characteristics that affect a person's uncertainty premium. Earlier research has shown that being married and having a working spouse increases likelihood of opportunity exploitation, presumably by reducing the person's expected uncertainty premium. Because the adverse effects of failure are cushioned by the income of a spouse, married people with working spouses should be more willing to exploit entrepreneurial opportunities than single people, all other things being equal.

Several studies have shown that being married increases the likelihood that a person will be self employed. For example, Butler and Herring (1991) examined data on 7542 respondents to the General Social Survey from 1983 to 1987 and found that being married increases the likelihood of self employment. Bates (1995b) explored data from the 1984 panel of the Survey of Income and Program Participation and found that married people were more likely than single people to become self employed. Schiller and Crewson (1997) and Evans and Leighton (1989) both examined data from the National Longitudinal Survey of Youth and found that being married increased the likelihood of self employment for women and men, respectively.

Studies using US census data find similar results. For example, Borjas (1986) examined a 1/100 sample of the 1970 US census and found that being married was positively related to self employment for white, Asian, Mexican, Cuban and other Hispanic individuals. Similarly, Robinson and Sexton (1994) examined data from the 1980 US census on people between the ages of 23 and 64, and found that being married increased the likelihood of self employment.

Similar results have also been found for studies conducted outside the United States. Johansson (2000) examined Finnish microdata on 103 482 people aged 18 to 65 for the period from 1987 to 1994 and found that married people were more likely to become self employed than single people. Taylor (1996) examined data on 2768 people who responded to the British Household Panel Survey in 1991 and found that being married had a positive effect on the probability of self employment. Lindh and Ohlsson (1996) examined data on 4402 people in the Swedish Level of Living Survey and found that married people were more likely than single people to engage in self employment.

Several studies provide more detailed information that directly addresses the mechanism through which being married makes a person better able to exploit an entrepreneurial opportunity. Blanchflower and Oswald's (1998) analysis suggests that the spouse's income is what allows a person to have a lower uncertainty premium, because these authors found that a *working* spouse was what increased the propensity to engage in self employment. Similarly, Bernhardt (1994) examined data from the Social Change in Canada Project and found that people were more likely to become self employed if their spouse worked. Examining data from the 1980 US census on people between the ages of 23 and 64 that were employed in 1979, Robinson and Sexton (1994) found that having other sources of family income, such as a spouse's salary, increased the likelihood of self employment. Macpherson (1988) examined the self employment of 1327 women from a 1/1000 sample of the US Census and found that the husband's income increased the respondent's probability of self employment.

Unlike opportunity cost, which has a negative effect on performance at entrepreneurial activity, having a lower uncertainty premium – at least as measured by being married and having a working spouse – appears to have a positive effect on performance at entrepreneurial activity. Using data from the National Longitudinal Survey of Youth, Schiller and Crewson (1997) found evidence of a positive relationship between being married and self employment income. Robinson and Sexton (1994) and Boyd (1991) found similar results from investigations of the 1980 US census, though Boyd only examined the self employment income of African-Americans.

INDIVIDUAL-LEVEL FACTORS THAT INFLUENCE THE VALUE OF ENTREPRENEURIAL OPPORTUNITIES

On the other side of the model of the decision to exploit an entrepreneurial opportunity is the expected value from opportunity exploitation. As I mentioned earlier, both psychological and non-psychological factors influence the expected value from opportunity exploitation. This expected value, in turn, influences the likelihood of opportunity exploitation. While I will discuss the effect of psychological factors in the next chapter, below I will discuss the effects of education, career experience, age and social position on the likelihood of opportunity exploitation.

For example, an entrepreneur with the right experience will do a better job at exploiting an opportunity than an entrepreneur without that experience. Even if the entrepreneur could hire others with the experience that they lacked, they must have sufficient knowledge to select the right employees. Moreover, the entrepreneur needs specific skills, including sales, negotiation, leadership, planning, problem solving, team building and communication skills (Shane *et al.*, forthcoming) to effectively develop and execute a plan for exploiting the opportunity, as the human capital literature in entrepreneurship (for example, Bates, 1990; Schoonhoven *et al.*, 1990) has shown. Those people with better skills will do a better job at opportunity exploitation and therefore be more likely to engage in the exploitation process.

Education

A person will be more likely to exploit an opportunity if they are better educated, because the information and skills that education provides will increase their expected returns to opportunity exploitation. As I indicated in Chapter 1, entrepreneurship involves the ability to assemble resources, develop a strategy, organize, and exploit opportunities. Certain information and skills facilitate these activities, including information about labor and product markets (Le, 1999), and the skills used to sell, bargain, lead, plan, make decisions, solve problems, organize and communicate. People who have the relevant information and skills should be more likely to exploit opportunities than people who lack these things.

Education increases a person's stock of information and skills, including those needed to pursue an entrepreneurial opportunity successfully. Moreover, education improves entrepreneurial judgment by providing people with analytic ability and an understanding of the entrepreneurial process (Casson, 1995). For example, Clouse (1990) found a significant change in his students' approach to the entrepreneurial process as a result of teaching them about new venture evaluation. In particular, the education about entrepreneurship increased the students' focus on cash flow and managerial fit.

To the extent that an individual has been educated in the relevant skills and information for opportunity exploitation, she faces less uncertainty about and has greater expectations of the value of opportunity exploitation (Hebert and

Link, 1988). These arguments suggest that education should increase the likelihood that a person will exploit an entrepreneurial opportunity.

A wide variety of studies have shown that people who have a higher education than the general population are more likely to exploit entrepreneurial opportunities (Storey, 1994b; Reynolds, 1997). First, several studies using US census data show that education increases the likelihood that people will engage in self employment. Borjas and Bronars (1989) examined the 1980 US census and found that, in comparison to the omitted category of people with between 13 and 15 years of education, having 16 or more years of education had a positive and significant effect on self employment propensity for white and African-American respondents. Boyd (1990) examined a 1980 public use microdata sample of the census to explore self employment of 21 290 African-Americans. He found that years of education had a positive and significant effect on self employment for African-Americans. Robinson and Sexton (1994) examined data from the 1980 US census found that education increased the likelihood of self employment. Macpherson (1988) examined the self employment income of 1327 women from a 1/1000 sample of the US census and found that years of schooling increased the probability of self employment.

The results are consistent when researchers examined the effect of education on the self employment of immigrant groups. Using a 1/100 sample of the 1970 US census, Borjas (1986) showed that the number of years of education had a positive and significant effect on self employment propensity for Asians, Mexicans, Cubans and other Hispanic immigrant groups. Fernandez and Kim (1998) examined a 5 per cent microdata sample of the US Census for Chinese, Korean, Indian and Vietnamese immigrants to the United States and found that education increased the likelihood of self employment for all groups. Sanders and Nee (1996) found that graduation from high school and college increased the likelihood of self employment for Chinese, Korean, Cuban, Mexican, Filipino and Puerto Rican immigrants in New York and Los Angeles.

Similar results have also been found using sources of data other than census data. Bates (1995b) explored the 1984 panel Survey of Income and Program Participation, which contacted approximately 24 428 people aged between 21 and 60 three times per year from 1983 to 1986, to predict transition to self employment during that period. He found that graduate education increased the likelihood of self employment among the subjects. Evans and Leighton (1989) examined the National Longitudinal Survey of Youth and found that the number of years of education had a positive and significant effect on self employment propensity for white males. Holmes and Schmitz (1993) examined 40 106 people in the Characteristics of Business Owners database and found that the probability of entering self employment increased with education.

The results are also consistent when data were gathered in other countries. Honig and Davidsson (2000) and Delmar and Davidsson (2000) compared a random sample of Swedes in the process of founding a business with a control group of workforce-aged Swedes not starting a business. Both studies found that the people who were in the process of founding a business were better educated than the control group. Mesch and Czamanski (1997) surveyed 275 immigrants to Israel from the former Soviet Union and found that those immigrants with secondary and college education were more likely to start a business than those with lesser education. Ritsila and Tervo (2002) used data from a random sample of the Finnish population from 1987 to 1997 to show that education increased the probability that a person would found a business.

Two studies found similar results in Great Britain. Rees and Shah (1986) examined 4762 people who were heads of household, aged between 16 and 65, and not in the military. They found that the number of years of education had a positive and significant effect on self employment propensity for a variety of ethnic groups. Dolton and Makepeace (1990) examined data on 4016 British people from the 1980 Survey of Graduates and Diplomates undertaken by the Department of Employment. They found that obtaining professional qualifications after graduation increased the likelihood of self employment.

More macro-level research has also confirmed the relationship between education and entrepreneurial activity. One set of studies shows this relationship across geographic locations. Bull and Winter (1991) examined *Inc* Magazine's measure of the new business birth rate for 129 communities and found that it was higher in locations where a greater percentage of people had more than 16 years of education than in places where a lower percentage of the population was highly educated. Schell and David (1981) examined the 1966 and 1976 county business patterns data for Alabama and found that the creation of new business units was positively correlated with median education in the county.

Other studies show support for the relationship between education and exploitation of entrepreneurial opportunities by comparing both across locations and across time. For example, Grant (1996) examined the annual percentage change in new business incorporations in the 48 contiguous US states from 1970 to 1985 and found that the percentage of people under 25 with a high school education or better in the previous year had a positive effect on firm formation. Black and Strahan (2000) examined the rate of new incorporations across US states from 1976 to 1994, as well as the number of business start-ups from 1986 to 1994. They found a positive effect of the share of the population with a college degree on both of these measures.

Similar results have been found for macro-level studies undertaken outside the United States. Guesnier (1994), for example, examined the rate of firm formation per 10 000 active workers from 1986 to 1991 across French regions and found a positive effect of percentage of adults with bachelor's degrees. Audretsch and Fritsch (1994) examined the rate of firm formation per 100 existing firms and per 10 000 workers in Germany from 1986 to 1999 and found a negative effect of the share of unskilled workers in the region. Garofoli (1994) examined the rate of firm formation across regions of Italy from 1987 to 1991 and found that the proportion of manual workers had a negative effect on the number of new firms per existing firm and per member of the population. Keeble and Walker (1994) examined the spatial variation in firm formation per capita in the United Kingdom from 1980 to 1990 and found a negative effect for the proportion of manual laborers.

Some studies have provided more direct evidence of the mechanism through which education operates on the exploitation of entrepreneurial opportunity. Dana (1987), for example, found that the provision of management training and the supply of educational material on start-ups made it easier for people to understand how to start a business in Australia, thereby enhancing the likelihood of opportunity exploitation. Similarly, Jackson and Rodney (1994) showed that education reduced perceptions of the difficulty of starting a business, thereby enhancing expectations of the value of exploiting entrepreneurial opportunities. Surveying a random sample of 1001 individuals in 1985, these authors showed that more educated people perceived that starting and growing a business was easier than did less-educated people.

One interesting study by Kent *et al.* (1982) showed that education provides people with specific types of knowledge that are useful to opportunity exploitation. Opportunity exploitation demands marketing, organization design and product development skills to a greater degree than finance and accounting skills. Therefore, people with these skills expect to capture greater value from opportunity exploitation and therefore be more likely to exploit opportunities than those without these skills. Consistent with this argument, Kent *et al.* (1982) compared 111 managers with 1259 entrepreneurs, defined as founders or purchasers of businesses drawn from the Action Council of the National Federation of Independent Businesses. They found that the managers were more likely than the entrepreneurs to have studied finance, statistics and accounting in college.

Given the evidence outlined above for the effect of education on the decision to exploit entrepreneurial opportunities, one might ask if education influences performance at entrepreneurial activity. I argue that it does. If education provides information and skills that encourage opportunity exploitation by increasing expectations of the value of opportunities, education should also have a positive effect on performance at entrepreneurial activity. The same information and skills that increase entrepreneurs' expectation of the value of exploitation should improve their skills at the process of exploitation.

Consistent with this argument, founder education appears to improve the performance of their new ventures. Several studies show that firms founded by better-educated entrepreneurs are less likely to fail. For example, Bates (1994, 1995b) examined survival from 1987 to 1991 of 19 463 firms founded between

1984 and 1987 using data taken from the Characteristics of Business Owners database. He found that founders with college and graduate education had ventures that were more likely to survive. Using the same dataset, Bates (1990) found that new ventures established between 1976 and 1982 with at least $5000 in sales and a capital investment of greater than zero were less likely to have failed by 1986 if their founders were more educated. Cooper *et al.* (1988) surveyed 2994 members of the National Federation of Independent Businesses who had founded new firms and compared three-year survivors with discontinued firms. They discovered that the founders of the surviving firms were better educated than the founders of the non-surviving firms. Bates and Servon (2000) used data from the US Bureau of the Census to examine the survival from 1992 to 1996 of 15 129 ventures founded between 1986 and 1992. They learned that founder education increased venture survival. Gimeno *et al.* (1997) examined 1547 firms that were members of the National Federation of Independent Business that had been in business for 18 months or less in 1985 and that responded to their follow-up surveys in 1986 and 1987. They discovered that the founder's formal education had a negative effect on the likelihood of venture failure.

Consistent results have also been found in studies outside the United States. Mata (1996) demonstrated that firms founded by more educated Portuguese had lower failure rates than firms founded by less educated Portuguese. Bruderl and Preisendorfer (1998) and Bruderl *et al.* (1992) showed that the founder's years of schooling increased survival rates for new ventures established in Upper Bavaria in 1985 and 1986. Westhead (1995) examined the factors that predicted the survival of 227 independent high technology firms in the United Kingdom that were in existence in 1986. He found that firms founded by someone who had a bachelor's degree or higher were more likely to survive than those founded by someone with less education.

Similar results have been found when failure has been measured as exit from self employment. For example, Fairlie (1999) examined 22 years of data on 6417 male heads of households from the Panel Study of Income Dynamics and found that graduating from college reduced the probability of exit from self employment.

Other studies indicate that founder education increases the growth rate of new ventures. For example, Reynolds and White (1997) examined 2624 new firms founded in three different states in 1985 and 1986, and found that firms with high growth rates had more highly educated founders. White and Reynolds (1996) followed 332 new firms sampled from the Wisconsin unemployment insurance files for two years and found that those firms with sales growth that was at least one half standard deviation above the median annual sales growth had start-up teams with a significantly greater percentage of people with college degrees. Roberts (1991a) examined 20 young technical firms and found that the educational level of the founding team was positively correlated with long-term sales growth.

Similar results have also been found when the studies were conducted outside the United States. Westhead's (1995) study of the factors that predicted the employment growth from 1986 to 1992 of 77 independent British high technology firms showed that businesses founded by someone with a bachelor's degree or better grew larger. Butt and Khan's (1996) study of 73 firm founders in book retailing and wholesaling, and light engineering manufacturing in Pakistan indicated that sales growth was positively related to prior management experience and the number of management courses attended. Burke *et al.*'s (2000) examination of data from the British National Child Development Study showed that the university educated self employed had larger firms than the non-university educated self employed. Van Praag and Cramer's (2001) survey of 258 self employed people from the Dutch province of Noord-Brabant showed that the employment size of their firms was positively related to the total amount of education that the subjects had received, but negatively related to an arts-oriented education.

Founder education also increases the profitability of new ventures. Denison and Alexander (1986) studied 927 entrepreneurs who participated in forums to bring entrepreneurs, investors and service providers together in 1983 and 1984. They learned that founder education was positively correlated with new venture income. Gimeno *et al.*'s (1997) examination of new firms whose founders were members of the National Federation of Independent Business showed that formal education increased the amount of income that the founders had taken out of the business. Kalleberg (1986) examined the earnings growth of 411 owner-operated small firms in Indiana in 1985 and found that founders' education increased one-year earnings growth.

Similar results for the relationship between founder education and profitability from entrepreneurial ventures have been found when entrepreneurial activity is measured as self employment. One set of studies supporting this argument comes from census data. For example, Borjas and Bronars (1989) used 1980 census data to show that education had a positive effect on self employment earnings for whites, blacks, and Hispanics. Robinson and Sexton (1994) examined data from the same census on people between 23 and 64 years of age, and found that education increased self employment earnings. Macpherson (1988) showed that years of schooling increased the self employment income earned by a random sample of self employed women.

Similar results have been found when sources of data other than the US census were examined. For example, Evans and Leighton (1989) and Schiller and Crewson (1997) examined data from the National Longitudinal Survey of Youth and found that education increased self employment income. Hamilton (2000) examined the 1984 panel of the Survey of Income and Program

Participation, which studied 8771 males, aged 18 to 65 in the non-farm sector, at four-month intervals from 1983 to 1986. He found that college graduates had higher self employment income and high school dropouts had lower self employment income than the rest of the population.

These results have also been confirmed by empirical research outside the United States. Burke *et al.* (2000) and Taylor (1996) examined data from the British National Child Development Study and found that the income of the self employed was higher if the person had passed O-level exams. Dolton and Makepeace (1990) examined data on 208 self employed British people taken from the Survey of Graduates and Diplomates and found that the higher the degree class of the graduate was, the greater their self employment income was. Rees and Shah (1986) examined data from the 1978 British General Household Survey and found that education increased self employment earnings. Wong (1986) looked at a 1/100 sample of the 1976 Hong Kong Census for people not employed in agriculture or fisheries, and found that education was positively correlated with self employment earnings for 1159 male entrepreneurs.

Career Experience

While education provides one useful route to gathering information and skills that are useful to the exploitation of entrepreneurial opportunities, career experience is another. Through career experience, people develop information and skills that facilitate the formulation of entrepreneurial strategy, the acquisition of resources, and the process of organizing. Thus, career experience reduces the uncertainty about the value to be gained from exploiting an entrepreneurial opportunity and increases the entrepreneur's expected profit (Shane and Khurana, 2001). As a result, people with more career experience will be more likely to exploit entrepreneurial opportunities than people with less career experience. To date the literature has suggested that five types of career experience encourage opportunity exploitation: general business experience, functional experience, industry experience, start-up experience and vicarious experience.

General business experience

General business experience increases the likelihood that a person will exploit an entrepreneurial opportunity that they have discovered. Through general experience, people learn information about many of the basic aspects of business that are relevant to opportunity exploitation, such as finance, sales, technology, logistics, marketing and organization (Romanelli and Schoonhoven, 2001; Klepper and Sleeper, 2001). Moreover, general business experience provides training in many of the skills needed for exploiting an opportunity, including selling, negotiating, leading, planning, decision-making, problem solving, organizing and communicating.

Earlier empirical research supports the argument that prior business experience increases the likelihood that a person will exploit an entrepreneurial opportunity. For example, Cobas (1986) examined a random sample of 220 Cubans living in San Juan drawn from the 1970 Census and found that those with a business background were more likely to be self employed. Using 1980 census data, Borjas (1986) demonstrated that self employment propensities increased with the number of years of work experience for all groups examined save African-Americans, except at very high levels of work experience. Robinson and Sexton (1994) also examined data from the 1980 US census and found that the respondent's amount of work experience increased the likelihood of self employment.

Other researchers found similar results from sources of data other than the US census. For example, Evans and Leighton (1989) and Schiller and Crewson (1997) examined data from the National Longitudinal Survey of Youth, and found that the probability of being self employed increased with labor market experience. Bates (1995b) explored the 1984 panel of the Survey of Income and Program Participation conducted by the US Bureau of the Census and found that work experience increased the likelihood of transition to self employment.

Studies undertaken outside the United States also show that general business experience increases the likelihood of opportunity exploitation. For example, Evans (1989) found that years of work experience had a positive and significant effect on self employment propensities for a sample of Australian migrants. Mesch and Czamanski (1997) found that immigrants to Israel from the former Soviet Union with prior business experience were more likely to start businesses than those without business experience, and Lerner and Hendeles (1993) found that Russian immigrants to Israel with prior managerial experience were more likely to become self employed than those without prior managerial experience. Honig and Davidsson (2000) and Delmar and Davidsson (2000) compared a random sample of 452 Swedes in the process of founding a business with a control group of 608 Swedes not in the process of founding a business and found that those founding a business had more years of managerial experience than the control group.

Researchers have also sought to understand the process by which previous business experience increases the likelihood that people will exploit entrepreneurial opportunities. Several studies suggest that business experience increases a person's intention to start a new business, thereby facilitating opportunity exploitation. For example, Vesalainen and Pihkala (1999) surveyed a random sample of 2899 people in 16 municipalities in Sweden and asked them about the probability that they would start a venture in the next year. They found that the amount of prior work experience was positively correlated with the intention to found a business. Similarly, in their survey of immigrants to Israel from the former Soviet Union, Mesch and Czamanski (1997) found that intentions to start a business were 7.8 times higher for those immigrants with prior business experience than for those without experience.

The studies outlined above indicate that general business experience increases the likelihood that a person will exploit an entrepreneurial opportunity. But will it improve performance at that activity? Given the argument that business experience encourages opportunity exploitation by providing information and skills that increase the expected value of opportunities, one would expect business experience to have a positive effect on performance at entrepreneurial activity. The same information and skills that increase entrepreneurs' expectation of the value of exploitation should improve their efforts at opportunity exploitation.

As expected, research has shown that the entrepreneur's business experience reduces the likelihood of new venture failure. Bruderl and Preisendorfer's (1998) investigation of new ventures founded in Upper Bavaria in 1985 and 1986 showed that founders' years of work experience increased their ventures' three-year survival rates. Similarly, Bruderl *et al.* (1992) used similar data to indicate that the failure rate of new German firms was reduced by general work experience. Bates (1994) used census data to show that entrepreneurs' management experience increased the survival of new firms founded by Asian immigrants. Duchesneau and Gartner (1990) compared 13 successful and 13 failed ventures in fresh orange juice distribution and found that the founders of the failed ventures had narrower managerial experience than the founders of the successful businesses. Taylor (1999) examined the duration of self employment of people responding to the British Household Panel Survey, and found that having prior paid employment reduced the rate of exit from self employment.

Some studies have actually demonstrated the mechanism by which prior business experience increases new venture performance. Consistent with the arguments made above, these studies have shown that prior business experience gives entrepreneurs the knowledge and skills needed to exploit opportunities successfully. For example, Lorrain and Dussault (1988) compared 38 firm founders whose businesses survived two years with 32 whose firms did not survive, and found that the survivors had greater business knowledge before starting than the non-survivors. Similarly, Schefczyk (2001) examined 103 transactions by 12 German venture capitalists and found that founder business management qualification reduced the risk of venture insolvency by providing founders with knowledge about how to exploit entrepreneurial opportunities.

Research also shows that entrepreneurs with more management experience tend to found ventures that have greater employment and sales growth than do founders with less management experience. Bruderl and Preisendorfer (1998) showed that the firm founder's years of work experience reduced three-year sales growth and three-year employment growth for a sample of new German firms. Butt and Khan's (1996) study of firm founders in Pakistan showed that sales growth was positively related to the amount of prior management experience that the founders had. Lee and Tsang (2001) examined the rate of growth of sales of 168 founder-run new ventures in China and discovered that the entrepreneur's prior managerial experience increased the rate of the new venture's sales growth.

One study provides direct evidence that founders' general business experience improves the performance of new ventures by providing them with the skills necessary for opportunity exploitation. Lerner *et al.* (1995) surveyed 220 women business owners in Israel. They found that an index of the founders' business skills, such as location selection, plant selection, product development, quality control, pricing, customer service, innovation, cost control, human resource management, marketing and financial management, and an index of their management skills, such as finance, forecasting, budgeting, human resources, marketing, innovation, operations, production, planning and strategy were positively correlated with the revenues of the founders' new ventures.

Entrepreneurs with greater management experience also have more profitable new ventures. Schefczyk's (2001) study of the investments of German venture capitalists showed that the level of the founder's business management qualifications enhanced the returns on investment in the new ventures. Moreover, Lerner *et al.* (1995) found that their index of founder business skills was positively correlated with the new venture's income. Examining data on firms founded by members of the National Federation of Independent Business, Gimeno *et al.* (1997) showed that the founder's management experience and supervisory experience both increased the amount of income that the founder took out of the business.

Similar results for the effect of management experience on income from the new venture have been found when entrepreneurship is measured as self employment. Using US Census data, Robinson and Sexton (1994) found that work experience increased self employment earnings. Using data from the National Longitudinal Survey of Youth, Schiller and Crewson (1997) and Evans and Leighton (1989) showed that the earnings of the self employed were higher if they had more labor market experience.

Functional experience
A person's functional area of expertise also influences the likelihood that they will exploit an entrepreneurial opportunity. Exploiting an entrepreneurial opportunity draws disproportionately on knowledge of marketing, management and product development rather than on knowledge of finance and accounting, because the former activities are undertaken earlier in the lives of new ventures and are harder to outsource (Roberts, 1991a). Therefore, people with functional experience in marketing, product development and management are more likely

to exploit opportunities than people with functional experience in accounting and finance.

Several studies support this proposition. Klepper and Sleeper (2001) examined 79 new laser firms that were founded by someone who had been previously employed by another laser firm and found that nearly all of the new firm founders had worked previously in technical fields, marketing or senior management. In 1993, Reynolds and White (1997) randomly sampled 1006 workforce-aged people and found that the 4 per cent of the respondents who were in the process of starting a business at the time of sampling were more likely to be administrators, managers, foremen/women or craftsmen/women than to have other types of jobs.

Researchers examining US census data have observed similar patterns. For example, Boyd (1990) found that people in managerial, technical and craft functions were more likely than those in other functions to be self employed, and that those in clerical functions were less likely to be self employed.

Industry experience

Because entrepreneurs face uncertainty about the value of the goods and services that they plan to produce, knowledge of the industry or market that they will enter has a strong influence on the decision to exploit an opportunity. Those people with prior experience in an industry as a customer or supplier often have a better understanding than others of how to meet demand conditions in that market place (Knight, 1921; Von Mises, 1949) because industry experience provides information that outsiders cannot gather (Johnson, 1986). Therefore, industry experience will increase the likelihood that a person will exploit an entrepreneurial opportunity.

Several different empirical studies provide support for this proposition. For example, using data from the National Longitudinal Survey of Youth, Praag and Pohem (1995) showed that public sector employees, who tend to lack industry experience, were less likely to become self employed than private sector employees, who tend to have relevant industry experience.

Other studies have shown that founders tend to start businesses in industries in which they were previously employed because their employment experience allows them to take advantage of information about the exploitation of opportunities garnered from their previous employment (Aldrich, 1999). Therefore, it is not surprising that Johnson and Cathcart (1979) found that employment in an industry had a positive effect on that industry's new firm formation rate in a study of the rate of new firm formation across industries in the Northern region of the United Kingdom in the early 1970s.

In a particularly creative test of the industry experience argument, Kaufmann (1999) examined whether prior industry experience influenced the decision to found an independent business rather than to purchase a franchise. If information gathered from prior industry experience enhances a person's likelihood of opportunity exploitation, one would expect that those individuals with more industry experience would be less likely to become self employed by purchasing franchises and more likely to start independent businesses. The reasoning is that these people already possess the industry knowledge necessary to exploit entrepreneurial opportunities and do not need the franchisor's information to act. Consistent with the industry experience argument, Kaufmann (1999) found that those people with previous experience in an industry who become self employed were less likely to purchase a franchise than to start an independent business.

As one might expect from the arguments made above, prior industry experience should increase performance at entrepreneurial activity. The information and skills garnered from industry experience increase entrepreneurs' expectation of the value of exploitation and should improve their efforts at exploitation.

Earlier research has shown that founder experience in the industry reduces the likelihood of new venture failure. In their studies of new German ventures, Bruderl and Preisendorfer (1998) and Bruderl *et al.* (1992) showed that the founders' industry experience increased their new ventures' survival rates. Wicker and King (1989) examined the two-year survival of 413 retail establishments created in California in 1985, and showed that the founders of surviving firms had more experience in the venture's industry than founders of failing firms. Cooper *et al.* (1988) examined the three-year survival of new ventures established by members of the National Federation of Independent Businesses. They found that the products, services, customers and suppliers of the surviving ventures were more closely related to the products, services, customers and suppliers of the entrepreneur's previous employer than were those of the failing ventures. Similarly, Gimeno *et al.* (1997) showed that firms founded by these members of the National Federation of Independent Business were more likely to survive if the entrepreneurs had experience in a similar business. Bates and Servon (2000) used data from the US Bureau of the Census to show that founder industry experience increased the survival of their new firms. Walsh *et al.* (1996) demonstrated that new firms in the semiconductor silicon industry survived longer if their founders had experience in the industry than if they did not. In a study of the survival of new firms in the laser industry, Sleeper (1998) found that those firms whose founders came from existing laser companies survived as long as diversifying firms from other industries, but firms whose founders did not have experience in the laser industry did not survive as long as diversifying entrants.

In fact, Klepper (2002) has shown that founders' prior industry experience allows new firms to perform as well as diversifying entrants from other industries. In a study of all of the entrants into the automobile industry from 1895 to 1966, Klepper (2002) showed that diversifying entrants were more likely to survive than *de novo* entrants. However, the disadvantage of *de novo* entrants was attributed entirely to those *de novo* entrants whose founders lacked experience in the same industries that the diversifying entrants came from. Those new automobile companies whose founders had previously led bicycle, wagon, engine, or carriage companies had equal or better chances of survival as diversifying entrants.

Research has also shown that entrepreneurs with greater industry experience have faster-growing firms. Reynolds (1993) examined representative samples of new firms in Pennsylvania and Minnesota and compared high performing firms (the 2 per cent of the sample that had sales growth greater than 100 per cent and annual sales greater than $5 000 000 per year) with the rest of the firms. He discovered that the founders of the high performing firms were more likely to have industry experience than the founders of the low performing firms.

Similar results for the effects of industry experience on new venture growth also have been found in studies conducted outside the United States. Dahlstrand (1997) compared 30 Swedish technology firms that were spin-offs from existing firms with 30 that were not spin-offs. She found that over ten years, the spin-offs grew faster, but were no more likely to produce new inventions than the non-spin-offs. Because the spin-off entrepreneurs were significantly more likely to have founded their firms because their previous employer would not exploit the opportunity that they discovered, she argues that employment within the parent firm enhanced the later growth of the spin-offs.

Two non-US studies provide more direct evidence of the relationship between founder industry experience and new venture growth. Bruderl and Preisendorfer (1998) showed that founder industry experience increased three-year sales growth for a sample of new firms in Germany. Similarly, Butt and Khan (1996) showed that sales growth was positively related to the venture team's experience for a sample of 73 new ventures in Pakistan.

The primary reason for the relationship between founder industry experience and venture growth is that ventures whose founders are without industry experience lack the necessary skills and information to exploit opportunities effectively. Baum *et al.* (2001) provide a fine-grained analysis that supports this interpretation of the relationship between industry experience and new venture performance. These authors surveyed 307 entrepreneurial woodworking companies run by active owner–managers who had founded or purchased their businesses between two and eight years earlier and who had more than one employee. The authors examined the founder's industry and technical competencies and found that they had a positive effect on annual sales growth over a two-year period.

Bayer (1991) also provides supportive evidence, though perhaps their evidence is more indirect than Baum *et al.* (2001). Bayer (1991) studied 315 German start-ups that went through a government assistance scheme. They found that those who used consultants had lower sales than those that did not. When they asked the founders why they used consultants, they found that the use of consultants was associated with a lack of professional experience among the founders.

Two studies show that entrepreneurs with more industry experience also have more profitable new ventures. Using data on ventures founded by members of the National Federation of Independent Business, Gimeno *et al.* (1997) showed that new ventures founded in a business similar to that of the entrepreneur's previous employer generated more income than new ventures founded in dissimilar businesses. Kalleberg (1986) examined the earnings growth of 411 owner-operated small firms in Indiana in 1985 and found that the number of years of experience the founder had in the industry had a positive effect on earnings growth.

Lastly, entrepreneurs with more industry experience also appear to found ventures that are more likely to experience an initial public offering. Shane and Stuart (2002) examined the life histories of 134 new companies founded to exploit intellectual property assigned to the Massachusetts Institute of Technology from 1980 to 1996. They found that the number of years of industry experience possessed by the founding team had a positive effect on the venture's hazard of initial public offering.

Start-up experience

Prior experience in starting new ventures also increases the likelihood that a person will exploit an entrepreneurial opportunity. While some of the information and skills necessary to exploit an opportunity can be learned through education or through management or industry experience, much of the necessary information about exploiting opportunities can only be learned by doing (Jovanovic, 1982; Hebert and Link, 1988). For example, the routines to form organizations may only be learned by creating organizations (Bruderl *et al.*, 1992), and gathering the right information and making effective decisions about opportunities may be something that can only be understood by undertaking those activities (Duchesneau and Gartner, 1990). Moreover, learning-by-doing may be more valuable than other ways of gathering the information and skills necessary to exploit an opportunity because it incorporates the entrepreneur in a network of suppliers and customers (Campbell, 1992). Furthermore, prior experience provides tacit knowledge that facilitates making decisions about entrepreneurial opportunities under uncertainty and time pressure. As a result, a person with more start-up experience should see a given opportunity as more desirable than other people see it, and therefore be more likely to exploit it.

Several studies of self employment provide support for this learning-by-doing argument for the effects of start-up experience on the likelihood of opportunity exploitation. Using data on 220 Cubans randomly sampled from the 1970 census, Cobas (1986) found that previous self employment increased the probability that the respondent would be self employed. Holmes and Schmitz (1993) examined data on 40 106 people from the Characteristics of Business Owners database and found that the probability of entering self employment was higher for those people with previous self employment experience than those without self employment experience.

Similar results were found when researchers used a more precise measure of the decision to exploit an opportunity, the transition to self employment (rather than the state of self employment). Using data from the National Longitudinal Survey of Youth, both Evans and Leighton (1989) and Praag and Pohem (1995) found that the likelihood of respondent's transition to self employment went up with their previous self employment experience. Similarly, Carroll and Mosakowski (1987) examined a nationally representative sample of 2172 West Germans and found that previous self employment experience increases the chance of a person's transition to self employment.

Studies of people in the process of organizing firms also support the results for the positive effect of previous start-up experience on the likelihood that a person will exploit an entrepreneurial opportunity. Reynolds (1997) surveyed a representative sample of 1016 people in the United States in 1993 and found that the 40 people in the process of starting a business at the time of the survey were more likely to have had self employment experience than the rest of the sample. Conducting the same type of study as Reynolds (1997), but on a larger scale, Delmar and Davidsson (2000) examined a random sample of 30 247 workforce-aged Swedes and compared the 405 people who were in the process of starting a business with a randomly selected control group not starting a business. They found that the people in the process of starting a business were more likely to have had prior self employment experience than the control group.

Perhaps the strongest evidence that previous entrepreneurial experience provides information that enhances the ability to exploit opportunities comes from efforts to compare people who purchase franchises from those who start independent businesses. Because franchisors provide support to their franchisees, people with start-up experience should be more likely to start independent businesses than franchises if previous start-up experience provides information and skills necessary to exploit entrepreneurial opportunities. Consistent with this argument, Williams (1999) examined the Characteristics of Business Owners database of the US Department of Census and found that people with previous self employment experience were less likely to purchase franchises than to found their own independent businesses. This result supports the notion that experience at entrepreneurship provides tacit knowledge that increases the probability that people will exploit entrepreneurial opportunities in the future.

Recent research has suggested several mechanisms through which previous start-up experience might operate to increase the likelihood that people will exploit entrepreneurial opportunities. The first mechanism is to provide a person with knowledge about how to develop and finance new organizations. Because new organizing efforts are disadvantaged *vis-à-vis* established ones, people are not inclined to exploit all of the opportunities that they discover. However, previous experience in starting ventures provides knowledge of how to overcome these liabilities of newness, thereby increasing the likelihood that people will exploit the entrepreneurial opportunities that they discover.

To test this argument, Shane (2001a) and Shane and Khurana (2001) examined the 1397 inventions patented by Massachusetts Institute of Technology between 1980 and 1996. In support of the argument, both studies found that patents belonging to inventors who had previously had more firm-founding patents were more likely to be exploited through firm formation than were patents belonging to other inventors. Shane and Khurana (2001) also found that firm formation was more common when the inventors of the technology had more patents licensed to externally financed start-up companies than when they had not.

Rueber and Fischer (1993) provide even more fine-grained evidence that previous start-up experience provides knowledge that helps an entrepreneur overcome the liabilities of newness that new ventures face. These authors surveyed 43 biotechnology and electronics firm founders about the value of previous experience to the opportunity exploitation process. They found that previous experience in a firm was useful for firm founders if that earlier experience was in a start-up or small business; if the experience was with a similar product or service; and if it involved supervising managers. This pattern indicates that previous start-up experience helps firm founders gather the knowledge that they need to overcome liabilities of newness in new ventures.

The second mechanism through which previous start-up experience makes people more likely to exploit entrepreneurial opportunities is by teaching entrepreneurs the right questions to ask and the right information to gather. Two studies provide empirical support for this argument. In survey of 220 founders of the 1983 cohort of Inc 500 firms, Shuman *et al.* (1985) found that entrepreneurs who had started previous businesses were more likely to analyse customer needs than those who had not started earlier businesses. Similarly, Cooper *et al.* (1995) studied the information search practices of 1176 entrepreneurs who were members of National Federation of Independent Business. These authors found that those entrepreneurs with no entrepreneurial experience sought more information, suggesting that experience was a substitute for information gathering.

A third mechanism through which previous start-up experience increases the likelihood of opportunity exploitation is to make attitudes toward firm formation more positive. Two studies support this argument. Begley *et al.* (1997) surveyed 861 MBAs from seven countries and found that owning one's own business increased a person's perception of the feasibility and desirability of starting a business. Similarly, Hills and Welsch (1986) surveyed 2000 students at two universities and found that students who had experience in owning a small business had greater intentions of starting a business in the future.

One might expect that people with previous start-up experience will found ventures that perform better than ventures founded by people without this experience. An entrepreneur's previous experience at founding firms will enhance the performance of her new venture because that experience provides the entrepreneur with valuable tacit knowledge about how to exploit an opportunity (Shepherd *et al.*, 2000). In particular, the entrepreneur might have learned from specific mistakes that she made in a previous entrepreneurial effort (Ripsas, 1998).

Several empirical studies provide support for this proposition. Shane and Delmar (2001) surveyed 225 new ventures initiated by a random sample of Swedish firm founders in the first nine months of 1998 and found that the likelihood of the venture disbanding over the first 24 months was reduced by the amount of start-up experience on the venture team. Similarly, Taylor (1999) examined duration in self employment of self employed people responding to the British Household Panel Survey. He found that previous self employment increased the duration of subsequent self employment.

Entrepreneurs with more start-up experience also have new ventures that grow faster. Reynolds (1993) examined representative samples of new firms in Pennsylvania and Minnesota and compared high performing firms to other firms in the sample. He found that high growth firms were more likely than the rest of the sample to have venture teams with previous start-up experience. Shuman *et al.* (1985) surveyed 220 founders of the 1983 cohort of Inc 500 firms, and found that founders who had started previous businesses had higher average annual sales growth than those who had not.

Similar results for the effect of previous start-up experience on new venture growth have been shown in studies undertaken outside the United States. Lerner *et al.*'s (1995) study of women business owners in Israel showed that founders' previous involvement in start-ups was positively correlated with the revenues of their new ventures. Butt and Khan's (1996) survey of firm founders in Pakistan showed that new venture sales growth was positively related to the founder's previous start-up experience.

Founder start-up experience also enhances the profitability of new ventures. Using the National Federation of Independent Business data, Gimeno *et al.* (1997) showed that new ventures whose founders had more previous start-up experience took more income out of their businesses. Using data from the National Longitudinal Survey of Youth, Evans and Leighton (1989) and Schiller and Crewson (1997) found that years of self employment had a positive effect on self employment income. Using data from the 1980 US Census, Boyd (1991) found that the self employment earnings of African-Americans in 52 metropolitan areas were higher if the entrepreneurs had more self employment experience.

Vicarious learning

An alternative (or complementary) explanation for the way that previous experience affects the likelihood that a person will exploit an entrepreneurial opportunity is the argument that much of the information and skills necessary for the exploitation of entrepreneurial opportunity can be learned through observation of others. As I explained above, the exploitation of entrepreneurial opportunities involves making decisions under uncertainty and with limited information about products, markets, ways of organizing, strategy and acquiring resources. The skills and information necessary to make these decisions are often unavailable in codified form, and cannot be easily gathered in real time. Consequently, the possession of tacit knowledge about how to make entrepreneurial decisions may be quite valuable in affecting the decision to exploit an opportunity (Busenitz and Lau, 1996).

Both Storey (1994b) and Reynolds (1997) explain that this tacit knowledge about how to exploit entrepreneurial opportunities can be developed from the close observation of entrepreneurs. For this reason, researchers have argued that the children of entrepreneurs should be more likely to exploit entrepreneurial opportunities than other people. Observation of their parents' efforts to exploit opportunities provides the necessary tacit knowledge to engage in the same activity (Minniti, 1999).

Several studies provide empirical evidence that the propensity to engage in self employment increases with parental self employment. For example, Dunn and Holtz-Eakin (1996) found that people whose parents were self employed were more likely to become self employed, controlling for the wealth of the parent. Roberts (1991a) compared 119 technical entrepreneurs with 296 scientists and engineers who were not entrepreneurs and found that the entrepreneurs were 20 per cent more likely to have had self employed fathers. Fairlie (1999) examined 22 years of data on 6417 male heads of households from the Panel Study on Income Dynamics. He found that having a self employed father increased the probability of self employment. Butler and Herring (1991) examined data on 7542 respondents from the General Social Survey from 1983 to 1987 and found that the self employment of the respondent's father increased the likelihood of the respondent's self employment.

Similar results for the effect of parental self employment on the exploitation of opportunities have been found outside the United States. For instance, De Wit and Van Winden (1989) found that Dutch men were more likely to be self employed in 1983 if their fathers were self employed in 1952, or if their fathers made the transition to self employment between 1952 and 1958. Using data on the British National Child Development Study, Burke *et al.* (2000) found that the probability of a subject's self employment in adulthood for a cohort of people born in 1958 was higher if the subject's father was self employed.

Studies undertaken outside the United States also show that parental self employment experience increases the likelihood of transition to self employment, a much more precise measure of opportunity exploitation than the state of self employment. Using a massive sample of 85 417 respondents from the Income Distribution Surveys conducted by Statistics Finland between 1990 and 1997, as well as a survey of 37 000 Finnish army recruits in 1982, Uusitalo (2001) found that parental self employment was a significant predictor of the respondent's transition to self employment. Similarly, Taylor (1996) and (2001) both examined data on respondents to the British Household Panel Survey. These studies showed that parental self employment increased signif-icantly the likelihood of the respondent's transition to self employment between 1994 and 1996. Carroll and Mosakowski 91987) examined a nationally repre-sentative sample of 2172 West Germans and found that parental self employment increased the subject's transition to self employment.

Other studies have demonstrated the effect of parental entrepreneurship on the likelihood that a person will exploit an entrepreneurial opportunity when opportunity exploitation is measured by firm formation. Using a representa-tive sample of the US population, Reynolds (1997) showed that the 40 people in the process of starting a business at the time of the survey were more likely than the other respondents to have self employed parents. Delmar and Davidsson (2000) conducted a parallel study to Reynolds' (1997) study on a larger sample in Sweden. Examining a random sample of 30 247 workforce-aged Swedes, they found 405 people who were in the process of starting a business at the time of the survey. They compared these 405 people with a randomly selected control group of respondents not in the process of starting a business at that time, and found that the respondents who were in the process of starting a business were significantly more likely than the others to have had parents who were self employed.

Some researchers have found patterns similar to the relationship between parental self employment and entrepreneurial exploitation described above for other close ties, such as friends and other relatives. The results of these studies are consistent with the underlying argument that the knowledge required to exploit entrepreneurial opportunities can be learned through the observation of others. For example, Honig and Davidsson (2000) compared a random sample of 452 Swedes who were in the process of starting a business with a control group of 608 Swedes who were not in the process of starting a business and found that those in the process of starting a business were more likely to have close friends and neighbors who were self employed. Similarly, Caputo and

Dolinsky (1998) examined a sample of 5159 women from the 1988 wave of the National Longitudinal Survey of Labor Market Experience. They found that the respondent was more likely to be self employed if her husband was self employed, and that the magnitude of the husband's annual self employment wage earnings predicted whether or not the respondent received wages from self employment.

Although the studies described above provide compelling evidence that people with self employed parents are more likely to exploit entrepreneurial opportunities, is the reason why really that the observation of self employed parents influences the child's knowledge and attitudes about entrepreneurship? Some researchers provide suggestive evidence that the answer to this question is yes – parental self employment transmits information that increases a person's intent to engage in entrepreneurial activity. For example, Hills and Welsch (1986) surveyed 2000 students at two American universities and found that students whose family members owned their own businesses had significantly greater intentions to start their own businesses. Mathews and Moser (1995) surveyed 267 graduating undergraduate business students from a Midwestern American university and found that those with an extended family member who owned his own business were significantly more likely to express a desire to own their own business. In a more precise test of this argument, Landry *et al.* (1992) surveyed 4850 high school seniors at 103 Canadian schools. They found that contact with entrepreneurs greatly increased students' intentions of becoming entrepreneurs, as well as their beliefs about entrepreneurship and needed competencies.

If entrepreneurs learn the necessary information and skills to exploit opportunities through observation of parental entrepreneurs or through participation in their businesses, those entrepreneurs whose parents were entrepreneurs should display greater entrepreneurial talent. In fact, the empirical evidence supports this proposition. Using data on 1547 new ventures founded by members of the National Federation of Independent Businesses, Gimeno *et al.* (1997) found that entrepreneurs whose parents had owned a business were less likely to fail. Similarly, Duchesneau and Gartner's (1990) comparison of successful and unsuccessful new ventures showed that the founders of the unsuccessful new ventures were less likely than the founders of the successful new ventures to have had self employed parents.

In an even more precise test of this proposition, Lentz and Laband (1990) used a structural model to determine if parental self employment influenced entrepreneurial talent. Using data on 514 entrepreneurs taken from the National Federation of Independent Business database on new firm owners, these authors found that second generation entrepreneurs started their businesses at a younger age and with less business experience than first generation entrepreneurs, but had higher income from their ventures. The authors argue that this result is only possible if the second generation entrepreneurs learned the information and skills necessary to exploit entrepreneurial opportunities from observing their parents or working in their parents' ventures.

Van Praag and Cramer (2001) also tested a structural model to show the effect of parental self employment on entrepreneurial talent and found similar results to those of Lentz and Laband (1990). These authors examined data on 1763 people from the Dutch province of Noord-Brabant who were surveyed for the first time as children in 1952 and again as adults in 1983 and 1993. Creating a structural model in which entrepreneurial talent was measured by the size of the firms created by those people who were self employed, the authors found that the subjects' level of entrepreneurial talent was positively related to the self employment of their fathers.

Age

Another important non-psychological individual difference that influences the tendency of people to exploit entrepreneurial opportunities is age. Unlike education and experience, which have a positive effect on the tendency of people to engage in self employment, age has a curvilinear relationship with the likelihood of opportunity exploitation because age incorporates the positive effect of experience, which increases with age, and the negative effects of opportunity cost and uncertainty premiums, both of which also increase with age. Initially, age increases the likelihood that people will exploit opportunities because people gather much of the information and skills necessary to exploit opportunities over their lives. Moreover, age provides credibility in transmitting that information to other people when people seek to obtain resources or design their organizations (Freeman, 1982). On the other hand, when people become much older, the effect of age on the tendency to exploit opportunities turns negative. As people age, their willingness to bear uncertainty declines because their time horizons shorten. In addition, as people age, their opportunity costs rise because their income tends to increase.

A significant amount of research supports the curvilinear relationship between age and the likelihood of opportunity exploitation. One set of studies provides evidence of this relationship by predicting self employment with US census data. Long (1982) used data from the 1970 US census to predict the self employment of males between the ages of 25 and 65. He found an inverted U-shaped relationship between age and self employment. Borjas and Bronars (1989) found a curvilinear relationship between age and the likelihood of self employment across ethnic groups in an examination of data from the 1980 US census. Boyd (1990) examined a public use microdata sample of the 1980 US Census to predict the self employment of 4200 Asian and 21 290 African-Americans. He found that age had a curvilinear relationship with self employment, first rising and then falling, for both African-Americans and Asians. Using a different public use microdata sample of the 1980 Census, Sanders and Nee (1996) found that age had a curvilinear effect on the likelihood of self employment for Chinese, Korean, Cuban, Mexican, Filipino and Puerto Rican immigrants in New York and Los Angeles.

Bates (1995b) found similar results for the curvilinear relationship between age and the likelihood of opportunity exploitation using data other than the US Census. He explored the 1984 panel of the Survey of Income and Program Participation and found that age had a curvilinear effect on the likelihood of self employment, first increasing and then decreasing.

Similar results for this curvilinear relationship between age and opportunity exploitation have also been found outside the United States. Alba-Ramirez (1994) examined data on 7657 individuals taken from a government survey of Spanish Households in 1985 and data on 5282 reemployed workers taken from the 1986 and 1988 US Displaced Worker Survey. In both the US and Spanish data, he found that age had an inverted U-shaped relationship with the probability of entering self employment. Rees and Shah (1986) examined data on 4762 people who were heads of households, between the ages of 16 and 65, and not in the military that were taken from the British General Household Survey in 1978. They found that age increased the probability of self employment and then reduced the probability at high levels. Taylor (1996) examined data on 2768 people who responded to the British Household Panel Survey in 1991. He found that age had an inverted U-shaped relationship with self employment.

Similar results have been found when the relationship between age and the likelihood of opportunity exploitation are analysed at a more macro-level of analysis. For example, Reynolds (1994a) examined rates of firm formation per existing establishment in the 382 US labor market areas between 1982 and 1984 and found that the percentage of the population in the area between the age of 25 and 44 increased firm formation rates.

While the research summarized above provides strong support for a curvilinear relationship between age and the decision to exploit entrepreneurial opportunities, it leaves open the question of whether people are making accurate decisions about opportunity exploitation. If age also has a curvilinear relationship with performance at opportunity exploitation, then researchers could conclude that people make rational decisions about this activity. Increases in age should initially enhance performance at entrepreneurial activity as people learn the information and skills necessary to be effective entrepreneurs over their life course. However, when they get very old, the effect of aging leads them to become uncertainty averse. As a result, they are no longer able to make the effective entrepreneurial decisions they once made and entrepreneurial performance turns negative.

In support of this argument, researchers have found that the entrepreneur's age has an inverted U-shaped relationship with the likelihood of venture failure. Using data from the Characteristics of Business Owners Database, Bates (1995b) found that age had an inverted U-shaped relationship with the four-year survival of a sample of 19 463 firms founded between 1984 and 1987. In an earlier study that examined the same database, but focused on only those businesses started by white males between 1976 and 1982, Bates (1990) also found similar results: entrepreneurs who were between the ages of 45 and 54 were less likely to have exited by 1986 than older and younger entrepreneurs. Bates and Servon (2000) used data from the US Bureau of the Census to examine 275 people who founded their firms between 1986 and 1992 because they could not find acceptable alternative work. This study also confirmed the predicted curvilinear relationship between founder age and new venture survival.

Similar results for the curvilinear relationship between age and performance at entrepreneurial activity have been found when entrepreneurship is measured as self employment. Holtz-Eakin *et al.* (1994b) used tax return data to examine the self employment duration of people who were beneficiaries of estates between 1982 and 1983. They found that age had a curvilinear relationship with the likelihood of continuing self employment, peaking at age 44.

Founder age also has an inverted U-shaped relationship with the growth of new ventures. For instance, Reynolds and White (1997) surveyed a representative sample of the founders of 2624 new firms and discovered that the firms with higher growth rates had significantly fewer 18 to 24-year-old founders and significantly more 25 to 34-year-old founders than other firms in their sample.

Similar results also have been found for the relationship between founder age and the profitability of entrepreneurial efforts. Taylor (1996) examined data on 466 self employed people who responded to the British Household Panel Survey and found that respondent age had an inverted U-shaped relationship with gross hourly earnings from self employment. Borjas and Bronars (1989) looked at 1980 US census data and found the same pattern.

Social Position

Another non-psychological individual difference that influences a person's tendency to exploit an entrepreneurial opportunity is her social position. Social position refers to a person's relationship to other members of the social community in which they live and work. Researchers have argued that two specific aspects of a person's social position influence her tendency to exploit entrepreneurial opportunities. The first is a person's social status, or how others perceive that they rank in the social ordering of people in their community. The second is a person's social ties, or their connection to other members of the community.

Social status

Social status increases a person's likelihood of exploiting an entrepreneurial opportunity. To exploit an entrepreneurial opportunity, a person must convince others that the opportunity that they have identified is valuable, despite the uncertainty and information asymmetry that such opportunities engender, because persuading others about the opportunity is necessary both to acquire resources and to organize. Under uncertainty and asymmetric information, researchers have shown that social status increases the likelihood that a person can persuade others that an opportunity is valuable because people are more likely to believe the claims of high status people than to believe the claims of low status people about uncertain events (Stuart *et al.*, 1999). Moreover, people are less likely to demand that high status individuals demonstrate the value of their private information because their status serves as a bond on their information.

Some empirical research supports this argument. Shane and Khurana (2001) examined the population of patents assigned to the Massachusetts Institute of Technology from 1980 to 1996 and found that the inventor's university rank increased the probability that a new firm would be formed to exploit the invention. Dolton and Makepeace (1990) examined data from the Survey of Graduates and Diplomates undertaken by the British Department of Employment and found that people of higher social classes were more likely to become self employed than people from lower social classes. Evans (1989) examined a 1 per cent public use sample of the 1981 Australian census and found that the probability of starting a business was higher, the greater the score of the respondent's occupation on a socioeconomic status scale.

Social ties

Social ties also increase the likelihood that people will exploit entrepreneurial opportunities. To exploit an opportunity, an entrepreneur must be able to gain access to resources and information that facilitate the exploitation process. These resources are often obtained through a person's direct and indirect social ties (Aldrich, 1999). For example, researchers have found that entrepreneurs use their social contacts to obtain information about such things as permits, management practices, appropriate investors, and trustworthy suppliers (Cromie and Birley, 1992). People who have direct and indirect ties to sources of information necessary to exploit opportunities, as well as to resource providers, are more likely to exploit the opportunities that they have discovered.

Several studies support this argument for the positive effect of social ties on the exploitation of entrepreneurial opportunities. Denison *et al.* (1994) found that the number of people in a person's social network positively predicted the likelihood that a person was trying to found a firm. Aldrich *et al.* (1987) examined 165 current and intended entrepreneurs over nine months using a sample drawn from the Research Triangle Council for Entrepreneurial

Development. They found that people who had more contact with the members of their core network were significantly more likely than others to found businesses. At a more macro-level of analysis, Cobas and DeOllos (1989) used a survey of 590 Cuban and Mexican immigrants to the United States to show that the likelihood of self employment increased with the number of relatives that the immigrant had in the same city.

One might expect that a person's social ties would also influence their performance at entrepreneurial activity because the performance of new ventures depends on obtaining resources and information from others, and obtaining these things depends on social interactions. As a result, entrepreneurs with broader and more diverse social networks should have better access to financial resources, develop stronger ties to customers and suppliers, obtain more accurate information, and hire people with better skills than other entrepreneurs (Bruderl and Preisendorfer, 1998; Hansen and Allen, 1992). Consequently, their ventures should perform better.

The empirical research supports this argument. Bruderl and Preisendorfer's (1998) examination of 1710 new ventures founded in Upper Bavaria in 1985 and 1986 showed that those ventures that received more support from strong ties (spouses, parents, friends and relatives) had higher three-year survival rates than those ventures that received less support from strong ties. Shane and Stuart (2002) examined the life histories of 134 new companies founded to exploit intellectual property assigned to the Massachusetts Institute of Technology from 1980 to 1996, and found that entrepreneurs who had indirect ties to investors before starting their firms had ventures with a lower likelihood of failure than did the ventures of other entrepreneurs. Singh *et al.* (1986b) examined the population of new voluntary social service organizations established in Toronto from 1970 to 1980 and found that the size of the board of directors at founding reduced the likelihood of failure, presumably because board size gave the new organizations broader social ties than those possessed by other new organizations.

The entrepreneur's social ties also appear to enhance other measures of new venture performance. Aldrich, Rosen and Woodward (1987) found a positive correlation between the interconnectivity of entrepreneurs' social networks and their ventures' profitability. Honig and Davidsson (2000) found that entrepreneurs who were members of a business network had ventures with a significantly higher probability of achieving first sales than did entrepreneurs who were not members of a business network.

Similar results have been shown for the relationship between entrepreneurs' social ties and the growth of their ventures. For example, Hansen (1991) and (1995) examined the social networks of 44 entrepreneurs who had created ventures within the previous five years and which were at least a year old and had at least one employee. Hansen (1991) found that the size of the pre-organization information network of the founder, its communication density, and its communication frequency were all positively associated with the subsequent employment size of the venture. Hansen (1995) found that the one-year growth in the venture's payroll in the year subsequent to hiring the first employee was positively correlated with the number of people in the entrepreneur's action set, and the degree of communication interaction between the members of that action set.

Reynolds and White (1997) also provide evidence that founder social ties influence new venture sales growth. These authors found that new venture sales growth was positively correlated with the entrepreneur's emphasis on industry contacts. Similarly, Bruderl and Preisendorfer (1998) found that the amount of support that founders reported receiving from their strong ties was positively correlated with the three-year sales growth of a sample of new firms in Germany. Lerner *et al.* (1995) surveyed 220 female business owners in Israel and found that the entrepreneurs' reported number of advisors was positively correlated with the new venture's revenue. Lee and Tsang (2001) examined the rate of growth of sales of 168 founder-run new ventures in China and found that frequency of external communication had a positive effect on the rate of venture sales growth.

SUMMARY

Unlike many explanations for entrepreneurship, which tend to ignore the role of human agency in entrepreneurial activity, the individual–opportunity nexus argues that the people who exploit entrepreneurial opportunities are not randomly determined, and identifying the individual characteristics associated with opportunity exploitation is an important and worthwhile endeavor.

At the most basic level, people become more likely to exploit opportunities as the gap between expected utility of exploiting opportunities and the alternative uses of their time increases. This gap is larger if a person has a lower opportunity cost to alternative uses to their time. As a result, people who have higher incomes are less likely to exploit opportunities and people who are unemployed are more likely to exploit them.

This gap is also larger if people have information and skills that will make them better able to exploit opportunities because these things will increase their returns to opportunity exploitation. Education increases a person's stock of information and skills useful for the pursuit of an entrepreneurial opportunity (for example, those needed to sell, bargain, lead, plan, make decisions, solve problems, organize a firm and communicate) and improves entrepreneurial judgment. Therefore, more-educated people are more likely to exploit opportunities than less-educated people.

Being married and having a working spouse increases the likelihood that a person will exploit an entrepreneurial opportunity because having a working spouse allows an individual to better bear the uncertainty of income from entrepreneurial activity. As a result, people with working spouses demand lower uncertainty premiums from entrepreneurial activity, and are more likely to exploit opportunities.

Career experience provides another source of information and skills useful to the pursuit of opportunity. General business experience, industry experience, functional experience in marketing, product development or management, and previous start-up experience all provide some of the information and skills that enhance entrepreneurial performance, thereby increasing the likelihood of opportunity exploitation. Similarly, parental entrepreneurial experience also increases the likelihood that a person will exploit an entrepreneurial opportunity because some of the information and skills useful for the exploitation of entrepreneurial opportunity can be learned through observation of others.

Age has a curvilinear relationship with the exploitation of opportunity. Initially, age will increase the likelihood that people will exploit opportunities because people gather much of the information necessary to exploit opportunities over the course of their lives and because age provides credibility in transmitting that information to others. However, as people become older, their willingness to bear uncertainty declines and their opportunity costs rise, swamping the information effect and making them less likely to exploit opportunities.

A person's social position also influences her tendency to exploit entrepreneurial opportunities. Social status makes it easier for a person to convince others that the opportunity that they have identified is valuable, despite the uncertainty and information asymmetry present with such opportunities. Social ties increase the likelihood that people will exploit entrepreneurial opportunities because social contacts provide information useful to the exploitation process.

Having explained the non-psychological characteristics that make people more likely to exploit opportunities, I now turn to a discussion of the psychological factors, the subject of the next chapter.

NOTE

1. As Venkataraman (1997) has explained, the decision to exploit an opportunity is made on the basis of payoffs from entrepreneurship relative to the entrepreneur's alternatives, not on the basis of payoffs to other entrepreneurs. As a result, the proper metric for evaluating whether or not someone engages in entrepreneurial activity differs from that used in strategic management, in which the metric for evaluating decisions is one's own performance relative to the performance of others.

5. Psychological factors and the decision to exploit

As I explained in the previous chapter, opportunity exploitation requires people to act on opportunities that they have discovered, indicating that individual characteristics are important to determining who exploits entrepreneurial opportunities. In addition to the non-psychological factors that were discussed in Chapter 4, several psychological factors also influence the tendency of people to exploit entrepreneurial opportunities.

Psychological characteristics influence the likelihood that people will exploit opportunities because these characteristics lead people to make different decisions about opportunities than other people with the same information and skills. It is important to note that psychological characteristics are not sufficient conditions and so do not cause people to exploit entrepreneurial opportunities. Rather, they influence the exploitation decision. Even if these characteristics are present, people might decide not to exploit opportunities. While researchers have analysed a wide range of psychological factors, they can be organized into three broad categories: aspects of personality and motives, core self-evaluation and cognitive characteristics (see Figure 5.1).

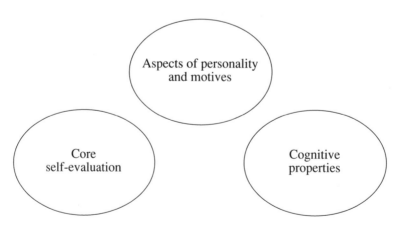

Figure 5.1   The psychological characteristics that influence the decision to exploit

The first two of these categories are composed of individual differences that researchers have argued are largely stable over time. People have certain aspects of personality and motives, and core self-evaluation, and these things tend to remain the same over long stretches of time. People can and do change their personalities, motivations and core self-evaluation, but these changes are rare in comparison to changes in cognitive characteristics and are relatively difficult to accomplish. In contrast, cognitive characteristics tend to vary significantly over time, and are largely situation dependent. For example, the representativeness bias tends to be influenced by the situation in which a person finds herself.

Whether they tend to be stable or not over long periods of time, psychological factors influence the exploitation of entrepreneurial opportunities. In the subsections below, I examine the effects of these three aspects of psychological characteristics, discussing the specific individual-level attributes that influence the exploitation of opportunity within each section. I begin with aspects of personality and motives.

ASPECTS OF PERSONALITY AND MOTIVES

Personality and motivations are fundamental characteristics of people that lead them to act in certain ways. People's personalities and motivations will influence the likelihood that they will exploit entrepreneurial opportunities because people with certain aspects of personality and motivations act differently from others in exactly the same situations. As a result, even if they face the same opportunities and have the same skills, information and opportunity cost, people with certain motivations will exploit opportunities that others will not exploit. Earlier researchers have identified five aspects of personality and motives that influence the exploitation of entrepreneurial opportunity: extraversion, agreeableness, need for achievement, risk-taking and independence.

Extraversion

Extraversion is an aspect of personality that incorporates the attributes of sociability, assertiveness, activeness, ambition, initiative, impetuousness, expressiveness, gregariousness, talkativeness, surgency and exhibitionism (Barrick and Mount, 1991). People possessing this aspect of personality are more likely than other people to exploit opportunities.

Because entrepreneurs identify opportunities that are not apparent to others, they often face the task of persuading others, particularly customers and employees, that the opportunity that they have identified is valuable. Under uncertainty, the ability to persuade others that one's judgment is valid depends heavily on sociability, assertiveness, initiative and gregariousness, all of which are aspects of extraversion. Thus, extraversion makes a person more likely to generate enthusiasm and support among others, and increases the likelihood that the individual will exploit an entrepreneurial opportunity (Baron, forthcoming).

For example, to make sales, entrepreneurs must satisfy customers' needs. This process requires them to be able to get beyond the customer's initial objections and overcome unarticulated fears to recognize unstated wants and requirements. Sociability and expressiveness enhance this ability because these characteristics help the entrepreneur to see the world through the eyes of others, to get others to provide information to her, and to recognize others' non-verbal cues (Bhide, 2000).

Some earlier research has indicated that entrepreneurs are more extroverted than other members of society. For instance, Wooten *et al.* (1999) compared 94 outplaced executives who did not start businesses during their outplacement counseling with 51 executives who started new businesses during the counseling period. Using Catell's personality inventory, these authors found that the entrepreneurs were more social than the non-entrepreneurs. Roberts (1991a) examined 72 members of the MIT Enterprise Forum and the 128 Venture Group, two groups of people interested in high technology entrepreneurship. He found that the 48 people in the sample who had started firms at some point in their lives were more extroverted than the rest. Sexton and Bowman (1984) administered a survey on several personality characteristics to 41 business students, 43 entrepreneurship students, and 51 non-business students. They found that the entrepreneurship students scored significantly higher than the other two groups on a scale of social adroitness. Babb and Babb (1992) surveyed 926 people in rural North Florida and compared firm founders to non-firm founders. They found that firm founders scored higher than non-founders on a scale of sociability. Burke *et al.* (2000) examined data from the National Child Development Study, which surveyed a cohort of people born in Great Britain in the first week of March 1958 five times over the first 33 years of their lives. They found that the probability of self employment was higher for people with higher anxiety acceptance scores, a measure of extraversion, gathered at age 11.

The evidence presented above supports the argument that people higher in extraversion are more likely to exploit opportunities than people lower in extraversion because they are better able to assemble resources and organize under conditions of information asymmetry and uncertainty. This argument also suggests that people who are higher in extraversion should perform better at entrepreneurial activity because the extraversion will improve their resource assembly and organizing efforts. In fact, prior research shows that firm founders who are more extroverted create better performing firms. For example, Burke *et al.*'s (2000) examination of data from the British National Child Development

Study showed that psychological tests conducted on respondents when they were children were related to the performance of the entrepreneurs' ventures as adults. In particular, if the psychological tests indicated that the subjects were introverted and unforthcoming as children, their ventures tended to be smaller than if the psychological tests indicated that they were extroverted and had higher anxiety acceptance scores as children.

Agreeableness

Agreeableness is an aspect of personality that incorporates the attributes of friendliness, social conformity, compliance, flexibility, tendency to trust, cooperativeness, tendency to forgive, tolerance, softheartedness and courteousness (Barrick and Mount, 1991). People possessing this aspect of personality are less likely than other people to exploit opportunities.

Entrepreneurs use information that others do not have or do not understand in order to identify and to act upon opportunities. As Baron (forthcoming) explains, the signal to noise ratio in entrepreneurial situations is very high. To separate more valuable information from less valuable information in the decision to exploit an opportunity, the entrepreneur must have a critical approach to information. Such an approach is enhanced by a suspicious and skeptical nature. Because a tendency to trust rather than to be skeptical is a dimension of agreeableness, people who are high in agreeableness are less likely to exploit opportunities than others.

Some empirical evidence supports this argument. Brodsky (1993) examined 47 self employed female entrepreneurs and compared them to 41 female managers and found that entrepreneurs were less trusting than managers, as measured by Catell's personality inventory. Wooten *et al.* (1999) examined 145 outplaced executives using Catell's personality inventory, and found that those who subsequently started businesses were less trusting, more suspicious, and more skeptical than those who did not. Fraboni and Saltstone (1990) compared 81 firm founders with 32 children of founders who were operating their family businesses and found that the founders scored higher than the non-founders on the suspiciousness scale of the 16-factor personality profile.

Need for Achievement

Need for achievement is a motivation that leads people to undertake activities and tasks that involve personal responsibility for outcomes, demand individual effort and skill, involve moderate risk and provide clear feedback (Shane *et al.*, forthcoming). People scoring more highly in need for achievement should be more likely to exploit entrepreneurial opportunities for several reasons. First, the exploitation of entrepreneurial opportunities requires solving novel and ill-specified problems. The willingness and ability to solve such problems demands an orientation toward meeting challenges, a characteristic of people who are high in need for achievement (Harper, 1996). Second, the exploitation of opportunities involves goal setting, planning and information gathering. Achievement-oriented people have a strong tendency to plan, to establish future goals, to gather information, and to learn (Miner, 2000). Third, need for achievement generates the drive to put forth effort to bring ideas into fruition. As a result, it increases the likelihood that a person will sustain goal-directed activity over a long period of time, persevering through the failures, setbacks and obstacles that are the inevitable result of decision making under uncertainty with incomplete information (Wu, 1989).

Much research supports the idea that people who exploit entrepreneurial opportunities are higher in need for achievement than other people. Some studies have shown this result by comparing entrepreneurs to the general population. For example, Begley and Boyd (1986), Hornaday and Bunker (1970) and Hornaday and Aboud (1973) all showed that firm founders were higher in need for achievement than the population in general, whereas DeCarlo and Lyons (1979) found that female entrepreneurs were higher in achievement motivation than women in general. Hines (1973) compared 80 entrepreneurs to 74 engineers, 68 accountants and 93 middle managers and found that the entrepreneurs had higher need for achievement than any of the other groups, while Caird (1991) compared 73 owner–managers of businesses to 189 teachers, nurses, clerical trainees, civil servants and lecturers and found that the entrepreneurs were higher than the other groups in need for achievement. Similarly, Ahmed (1985) compared 71 Bangladeshi entrepreneurs with 62 non-entrepreneurs and found that the entrepreneurs scored significantly higher than the others on a need for achievement scale.

Other studies have found that entrepreneurs are higher in need for achievement than managers. For example, Miner *et al.* (1989) compared 118 technical entrepreneurs to 41 managers who had applied for grants from the National Science Foundation. They found that the entrepreneurs scored significantly higher on self-achievement than the managers. Bellu (1988) administered the Miner Sentence Completion Scale to 70 firm founders and 77 managers, and found the firm founders to be higher in total task motivation and self-achievement than the managers. Furthermore, Lachman (1980) compared 29 entrepreneurs to 25 managers, and Cromie and O'Donaghue (1992) compared 73 entrepreneurs with 194 managers. In both studies, the authors found that the entrepreneurs scored higher on need for achievement than the managers.

Perhaps the strongest evidence in support of the argument that need for achievement increases the likelihood that people will exploit entrepreneurial opportunities comes from articles that summarize a large number of need for achievement studies. Johnson (1990) reviewed 23 studies on need for achievement and entrepreneurship and found that, despite different definitions of entrepreneurship, different sample selection criteria, and different measures, need for achievement differentiated firm founders from the rest of the population. Moreover, Collins *et al.* (2000) conducted a meta analysis of 63 need for achievement studies of entrepreneurship. They found that need for achievement significantly differentiated entrepreneurs from the rest of the population, and that the results were not affected by the measure of need for achievement used by the authors. The results held whether the authors administered the Thematic Apperception Test, questionnaires, or the Miner Sentence Completion Scale.

Some authors have sought to determine how need for achievement influences the tendency of people to exploit entrepreneurial opportunities. Perhaps most notable of these efforts is a series of studies that have shown that need for achievement increases people's interest in adopting the entrepreneurial role. For example, Hull *et al.* (1980) surveyed 307 alumni of the University of Oregon and found that the higher a person's need for achievement was, the greater the likelihood that the individual had plans to start a business in the next three years. In perhaps the most creative of all of these research projects, Kourilsky (1994) studied 685 children in 30 mini-societies (workshops that simulate economic activity). One of the key features of the mini-societies was that students were allowed to select the economic roles that they adopted. Kourilsky (1994) found that the students who adopted the entrepreneurial roles were higher in need for achievement and persistence than those who adopted other roles.

Type-A behavior is an aspect of personality related to need for achievement. Specifically, people who have type-A personalities are highly achievement oriented. Because type-A behavior is related to need for achievement, some researchers have argued that people with type-A personalities are more likely than other people to exploit entrepreneurial opportunities. Two studies provide support for this argument. Babb and Babb (1992) surveyed 926 people in rural North Florida through paper and pencil tests of psychological and demographic factors. They compared firm founders with other people and found that firm founders were more likely to engage in type-A behavior. Similarly, Begley and Boyd (1987) studied 471 executive members of the Smaller Business Association of New England and found that the members of the association who were firm founders scored significantly higher on tests of type-A behavior than the non-founders.

Although the studies reviewed above demonstrate that people higher in need for achievement are more likely to exploit entrepreneurial opportunities, they leave open the question of whether these people perform better at entrepreneurial activities. The explanations for the relationship between need for achievement and opportunity exploitation provided above suggest that need for achievement enhances performance at entrepreneurial activities. Need for achievement helps people to solve the novel and ill-specified problems that they face during the entrepreneurial process. Moreover, it encourages the goal setting, planning and information gathering activities that are central to opportunity exploitation. Furthermore, need for achievement leads people to persevere through the setbacks that are an inevitable part of entrepreneurial process.

The extant empirical research supports the argument that need for achievement enhances performance at entrepreneurial activity. Firm founders who are higher in need for achievement appear to have faster growing ventures than firm founders who are lower in need for achievement. For example, Johnson (1989) surveyed 79 small business owner–managers and found that the owner–manager's need for achievement was positively correlated with the business's sales growth. Lee and Tsang (2001) examined the rate of growth of sales of 168 founder-run new ventures in China and discovered that the firm founder's need for achievement increased the rate of venture sales growth. Moreover, in a meta analysis of 63 studies of need for achievement and entrepreneurship, Collins *et al.* (2000) found that entrepreneurs' need for achievement was correlated $r = 0.28$ with the sales performance of their firms.

Similar results have been found when researchers have focused on the specific case of high technology entrepreneurs. Wainer and Rubin (1969) looked at the relationship between founders' need for achievement and the annual sales growth of their ventures from the second to the most recent year for 51 technical entrepreneurs whose ventures were between four and ten years old and who had spun off from the Massachusetts Institute of Technology. These authors showed that the founder's need for achievement had a positive effect on the venture's growth. Roberts (1991a) studied 51 new technology companies and found that the sales growth of the companies whose founders received high scores on tests of need for achievement was more than double that of founders who received low or moderate scores on tests of need for achievement.

The results for the relationship between founder need for achievement and the performance of their firms are consistent across different measures of need for achievement. Miner *et al.* (1989) surveyed 118 technical entrepreneurs who had applied for grants from the National Science Foundation and found that the mean annual growth in sales for their ventures was positively correlated with the founder's self-achievement scores on the Miner Sentence Completion Test. Miner *et al.* (1994) followed up with 53 of these entrepreneurs approximately five-and-a-half years later. They found that the entrepreneur's self-achievement scores were positively correlated with sales growth measured as the growth in the dollar volume of sales five-and-a-half years later. Thuller (2001) examined the average annual rate of employment and sales growth for the ventures started by 58 Russian entrepreneurs who had participated in a training program four years earlier. He found that the entrepreneurs' self-achievement scores, as measured by the Miner Sentence Completion Test, were significantly positively correlated with both the employment and sales growth of their ventures.

Research has also shown that the founder's need for achievement increases the amount of income generated by the new firm. Lerner *et al.* (1995) found that achievement motives were positively correlated with income for a sample of female Israeli business owners. Miner *et al.* (1989) and (1994) found that the annual income of a sample of entrepreneurs who had applied for grants from the National Science Foundation was positively correlated with self-achievement.

Risk Taking

Risk-taking propensity is an aspect of personality that measures people's willingness to engage in risky activity. People higher in risk-taking propensity should be more likely to exploit entrepreneurial opportunities because risk-bearing is a fundamental part of entrepreneurship. Before a new product or service is introduced, a person cannot know with certainty that she can produce desired outputs, meet consumers' needs, generate a profit, or capture that profit in the face of competition because information about the future is unknowable (Wu, 1989). Because they often do not know the type and amount of resources that will be needed to introduce a product to market, what production processes will need to be created, how long it will take, or even if the product will work, entrepreneurs bear technical risk. Entrepreneurs also bear market risk because they often do not know how many customers will adopt the new product, the price at which they will adopt, or the pace of adoption. Entrepreneurs bear competitive risk because they do not know the pace at which their new products or services will be imitated and their profits eroded, or how their profits will be affected by the complex interdependence of actions by multiple competitors (Amit *et al.*, 1993). Therefore, when entrepreneurs exploit opportunities, they are bearing risks that cannot be insured or otherwise eliminated (Knight, 1921; Amit *et al.*, 1993).[1]

Earlier research shows that people who exploit entrepreneurial opportunities have a higher propensity to bear risk than those who do not exploit entrepreneurial opportunities. Some research has demonstrated this pattern by comparing entrepreneurs to the rest of the population. Caird (1991) compared 73 owner–managers of businesses to 189 teachers, nurses, clerical trainees, civil servants and lecturers, and found that the entrepreneurs were higher in risk-taking propensity than the other groups of people.

Other research supports the proposition that risk-taking propensity increases a person's tendency to exploit entrepreneurial opportunities by comparing entrepreneurs with managers. Begley (1995) studied 239 New England business people and discovered that risk-taking propensity differentiated firm founders from non-founders. Begley and Boyd (1987) compared 147 small business founders with 92 small business managers and showed that the founders had higher risk-taking propensity than the managers. Seth and Sen (1995) compared 20 firm founders with 20 managers and discovered that founders received higher scores on tests of risk-taking propensity than the managers. Stewart *et al.* (1999) compared 324 business owners with 342 managers and showed that the firm founders had higher risk-taking propensity than the managers. Cromie and O'Donaghue (1992) compared 73 entrepreneurs with 194 managers and found that the entrepreneurs received higher scores than the managers on a measure of risk-taking propensity.

Similar results have been found when entrepreneurs have been defined as owner–managers. Hull *et al.* (1980) surveyed 307 alumni of the University of Oregon and found that those respondents who owned their own businesses scored more highly on a risk propensity scale than did non-owners.[2] Ahmed (1985) compared 71 Bangladeshi owner–managers with 62 non-owner–managers and found that the owner–managers received higher scores than the others on a risk-taking propensity scale.

Still other research shows the positive effect of risk-taking propensity on opportunity exploitation by comparing people who were self-employed with people who were wage employed. Van Praag and Cramer (2001) examined data from a survey of 1763 people from the Dutch province of Noord-Brabant who were surveyed for the first time as elementary school children in 1952 and again in 1983 and 1993. Comparing the 258 that were ever self employed to the rest, the authors found that the decision to become self employed was related to attitude toward risk.

Even stronger results have been found for studies that predict the transition to self employment. Uusitalo (2001) examined data from the Income Distribution Surveys conducted by Statistics Finland between 1990 and 1997, as well as a survey of 37 000 Finnish army recruits in 1982 and found that the respondent's cautiousness score (related to risk aversion) was negatively correlated with the likelihood of the individual's transition to self employment. Similarly, Taylor (1996) examined data on 2768 people who responded to the British Household Panel Survey in 1991 and found that the importance of job security to the individual reduced the probability that they would become self employed.

Earlier research also shows people higher in risk-taking propensity have a greater preference for the entrepreneurial role. Sagie and Elizur (1999) compared 114 Dutch small business students to 171 general business students and found that the small business students had a greater preference for uncertain tasks and calculated risks. Douglas (1999) surveyed 3000 alumni of an undergraduate business program of an Australian university and found that responses to a risk-taking scale were positively correlated with the intention to found a firm. Sexton and Bowman (1984) administered a survey to 41 business students, 43 entrepreneurship students, and 51 non-business students and found the entrepreneurship students received significantly higher scores on a scale of risk-taking propensity and significantly lower scores on a scale of harm avoidance than the other two groups. Sexton and Bowman (1983) surveyed 401 students at Baylor University and found that entrepreneurial management majors received significantly lower scores on a scale to measure conformity and significantly higher scores on a scale to measure risk-taking propensity than non-business majors or non-entrepreneurship business majors. Koh (1996) surveyed 54 Hong Kong MBAs about their inclination to start a business and found that those who had a higher propensity to take risks were more likely to want to start their own businesses.

Stewart and Roth (2001) provided the strongest evidence for the relationship between risk-taking propensity and the tendency of a person to exploit entrepreneurial opportunities. They conducted a meta analysis of 12 previous studies of risk taking and opportunity exploitation. The authors found that people who exploit opportunities have a higher risk-taking propensity than managers, despite differences in the way opportunity exploitation was measured across the different studies.

A closely related measure to risk-taking propensity is tolerance of ambiguity, or a person's willingness to take action when outcomes are not known. Schere (1982) proposed that tolerance for ambiguity should increase a person's tendency to engage in opportunity exploitation because the exploitation of opportunity is, by nature, ambiguous. Research has shown that people higher in tolerance for ambiguity are more likely to exploit opportunities. Schere (1982) compared 52 firm founders with 65 managers and found that the managers had a lower tolerance for ambiguity than the firm founders. Begley and Boyd (1987) and Miller and Drodge (1986) compared samples of founders and non-founders and showed that the firm founders had a higher tolerance for ambiguity than the non-founders. Similarly, Koh (1996) surveyed 54 Hong Kong MBAs about their inclination to start a business and found that those who had a higher tolerance of ambiguity were more likely to want to start their own businesses.

While the studies described above show that people who have a higher risk-taking propensity are more likely than other people to engage in opportunity exploitation, do those people perform better at entrepreneurial activity? One might argue that people who have greater risk-taking propensity should perform better because they will be better able to make decisions about such uncertain things as the type and amount of resources that will be needed to introduce a product to market, how many customers will adopt the new product, or the pace at which their profits eroded. However, one might also argue that people who have a lower risk-taking propensity should perform better at entrepreneurial activity because they will take less risky approaches to resource acquisition, strategy, and organizing.

Although very little research has examined this question, the limited research that has been done suggests that the founder's risk-taking propensity appears to be *negatively* associated with the performance of their new ventures. For example, Miner *et al.* (1989) surveyed 118 technical entrepreneurs who had applied for grants from the National Science Foundation and found that mean annual growth in sales of the entrepreneurs' ventures was positively correlated with their tendency to avoid risks. Similarly, Forlani and Mullins (2000) conducted an experiment with 78 chief executive officers of fast-growing new firms culled from lists published in *Inc* Magazine, *Fortune* and *Business Week*. The authors asked the subjects to select between hypothetical ventures, of which one had low variable outcomes and the other had high variable outcomes. They found that the entrepreneurs preferred low variable outcome ventures to high variable outcome ventures. The authors also found that the entrepreneurs were more likely to choose ventures with a high upside and a high downside outcome than those with a low upside potential and a low downside potential.

Desire for Independence

Desire for independence is an aspect of personality in which people prefer to engage in independent action rather than action involving others. People with a strong desire for independence are more likely to exploit entrepreneurial opportunities because entrepreneurial activity entails following one's own judgment as opposed to following the judgment of others. Because entrepreneurs must make decisions contrary to the opinions of the majority to exploit opportunities, the tendency to do things in one's one way is an important motivation (Wu, 1989).[3]

Some empirical evidence supports this argument. Cromie (1987) reports that desire for autonomy was the most common reason given for starting their companies among the firm founders he surveyed. Boswell (1973) interviewed 31 firm founders and found that the desire to be one's own boss was the most common motivation to become an entrepreneur. Roberts and Wainer (1971) found similar results in a study of 69 former employees of the Massachusetts Institute of Technology who became entrepreneurs.

Some research has shown that entrepreneurs have a greater desire for independence than non-entrepreneurs by comparing entrepreneurs to the general population. For example, Hornaday and Aboud (1973) found that entrepreneurs scored more highly than the general population on independence, as measured by the Edwards personal preference scale. Similarly, Caird (1991) compared 73 owner–managers of businesses to 189 teachers, nurses, clerical trainees, civil servants and lecturers and found that the entrepreneurs were higher in need for autonomy than the other groups of respondents, while Cromie and O'Donaghue (1992) compared 73 entrepreneurs with 194 managers and found that the entrepreneurs scored more highly on need for autonomy than the managers.

Other research has shown that a preference for independence increases the likelihood of self employment. Using data from the British Household Panel Survey, Taylor (1996) found that a person's preference for the opportunity for job initiative had a positive effect on the probability that they would be self employed. Burke *et al.* (2000) examined data from the British National Child Development Study and found that the probability of self employment increased if the respondent believed that independence in one's job was important to them.

Still other research has shown that a desire for independence is correlated with the intention to found a business. For example, Hills and Welsch (1986) surveyed 2000 students at two universities and found that students receivng a high score on a composite scale of independence had stronger intentions to start new businesses than those scoring low on the scale. Sexton and Bowman (1983, 1984) administered surveys to business students, entrepreneurship students and non-business students and found the entrepreneurship students significantly lower on scales of interpersonal affect, conformity and succorance, and significantly higher on autonomy than the other students. Douglas (1999) surveyed 3000 alumni of an undergraduate business program of an Australian university and found a desire for independence scale was positively correlated with the intention to found a firm.

More precise research has sought to determine if the preference for independence actually influences the decision to exploit entrepreneurial opportunities. In general, this research has shown that it does. Wooten *et al.* (1999) administered Catell's personality inventory to a group of outplaced executives and then waited to see who started businesses. The authors found that the business starters were more self-reliant than the non-starters. Similarly, Vesalainen and Pihkala (1999) surveyed a random sample of 2899 people in 16 municipalities in Sweden and asked them about the probability that they were engaged in business start-up activities. They found that a desire for independence increased the likelihood that the respondent was engaged in start-up activity. Reynolds and White (1997) compared 81 people in the process of starting a business to a control group of 940 adults in Wisconsin who were not starting a business and found that those in the process of starting a business received higher scores on scales of autonomy and independence. Kaufmann (1999) surveyed 63 people who had attended a franchise exposition and evaluated who later became self employed. He found that those higher in independence were more likely to become self employed later on.

Although the research summarized above indicates that people who have a greater desire for independence are more likely to exploit entrepreneurial opportunities, people who have a greater desire for independence actually perform worse at entrepreneurial activities. One reason for this negative relationship is that the desire for independence means that entrepreneurs are less likely to build important social ties with customers, suppliers, employees or other stakeholders. Another reason is that the desire for independence keeps entrepreneurs from engaging in organizing or resource acquisition activities that are necessary to develop their new ventures.

Although relatively little empirical research has been conducted on this question, one study has shown that founders who establish their companies to obtain independence are less likely to have surviving ventures than those who found their companies for other reasons. Cooper *et al.* (1988) surveyed new firms founded by members of the National Federation of Independent Businesses and compared surviving firms with discontinued firms three years later. These authors found that the surviving ventures were less likely than the discontinued ventures to have been founded by someone whose primary goal in founding the firm was to avoid working for others.

Another study showed that entrepreneurs who found their firms to gain independence have slower growing ventures than those who found their firms for other reasons. Feeser and Dugan (1989) compared 39 computer firms listed on the Inc 500 list of the fastest growing private firms, with a matched sample of 39 low growth computer firms. They found that the low growth firms were significantly more likely than the high growth firms to be founded by people who started their firms because others would not let them do the work that they wanted to do.

CORE SELF EVALUATION

Core self evaluation is a psychological construct that includes the characteristics of self efficacy/self esteem and locus of control, dimensions that focus on people's sense of control over their external environment (Judge *et al.*, 2002). A person's core self evaluation will influence the likelihood that she will exploit an entrepreneurial opportunity for reasons that I will explain below.

Locus of Control

Locus of control is a person's belief that she can influence the environment in which she is found (Rotter, 1966). People with an internal locus of control have a stronger sense that they can control their own environment, and will be more likely than people with external locus of control to exploit an entrepreneurial opportunity. The beliefs that entrepreneurs form about the value of entrepreneurial opportunities depend, in part, on their evaluation of their own abilities to exploit those opportunities. This self evaluation, in turn, depends on the degree to which the entrepreneurs believe that they can influence the environment around them (Harper, 1996).

Earlier research provides support for this argument. Entrepreneurs have more internal locus of control than the rest of the population. Shapero (1975) and Caird (1991) all showed that firm founders have more internal locus of control than other groups of people, while Bowen and Hisrich (1986) showed this result for female firm founders, and Durand (1975) found it for African-American firm founders.

Moreover, firm founders have more internal locus of control than managers. Ward (1993) compared 44 small business managers who founded their businesses with 44 small business managers who did not found their own businesses and showed that the founders had significantly greater internal locus of control than the non-founders.

Similar results have been found in studies undertaken outside the United States. Cromie and O'Donoghue (1992) compared 73 entrepreneurs with 194 managers in the United Kingdom and found that the entrepreneurs had more internal locus of control than the managers. Similarly, Cromie and Johns (1983) and Cromie (1987) showed that Irish firm founders had more internal locus of control than Irish managers. Both Caird (1991) and Cromie and O'Donoghue (1992) found that British firm founders received significantly higher in internal locus of control scores on Durham's GET test than did British managers. Ahmed (1985) compared 71 Bangladeshi entrepreneurs with 62 non-entrepreneurs and found that the entrepreneurs received significantly more internal scores than the managers on the Rotter locus of control scale. Cachon (1988) compared 78 small firm owners in Ontario who founded their businesses with a control group that acquired their businesses and showed that the founders were significantly higher on Rotter's internal locus of control scale than the acquirers.

Internal locus of control also increases a person's propensity toward self employment. Evans and Leighton (1989) and Schiller and Crewson (1997) examined data from the National Longitudinal Survey of Youth and found that internal locus of control increased the subjects' likelihood of self employment.

Other research has shown that people with more internal locus of control are more likely to have entrepreneurial intentions. Bonnett and Furnham (1991) surveyed 190 students aged 16 to 19 to determine what psychological characteristics differentiated those students interested in the Young Enterprise scheme, a British entrepreneurship simulation, from the rest of the population. They found that those students who were interested in the scheme scored more internally on a scale of economic locus of control than did those who were not interested. Furthermore, Greenberger and Sexton (1987) surveyed 242 business students at two universities and found a significant positive correlation between internal locus of control and the intention to found a business.

The relationship between a person's sense of control over the environment and the tendency to engage in opportunity exploitation has been found when researchers examine measures of internal control other than locus of control. For example, Robinson *et al.* (1991) compared 57 business owners with 57 white-collar non-managers and found that the business owners received higher scores than the managers on a scale measuring personal control. Using Catell's personality profile, Brodsky (1993) compared 47 self employed female entre-preneurs with 41 female managers and found that the entrepreneurs had higher control needs than the managers. Lastly, Sagie and Elizur (1999) compared 114 Dutch small business students to 171 general business students and found that the small business students had a greater preference for tasks involving personal responsibility than the general business students.

The evidence presented above indicates that people who have more internal locus of control are more likely to exploit entrepreneurial opportunities. But do people with an internal locus of control perform better at entrepreneurial activities than people with an external locus of control? Theory suggests that the answer is yes. People who have more internal locus of control form stronger positive beliefs that they can exploit opportunities, obtain resources, organize firms and develop a strategy than people who have more external locus of control. Because success at any activity depends, in part, on a person's willingness to believe in their own ability to undertake that activity, those people with more internal locus of control perform better at entrepreneurial activity.

Several studies support this proposition. Internally motivated people are more likely to create new ventures that survive. Using data on the firms founded by members of the National Federation of Independent Businesses, Gimeno *et al.* (1997) showed that founders with more intrinsic motivation had firms that were less likely to fail than founders with more extrinsic motivation.

Internally oriented firm founders also create ventures that grow faster than externally oriented firm founders. Lee and Tsang (2001) examined the rate of growth of sales of 168 founder-run new ventures in China and discovered that the founders' internal locus of control was positively correlated with the new venture's rate of growth.

A founder's internal locus of control also appears to increase the amount of income that the founder earns from the new venture. Using data from the National Longitudinal Survey of Youth, Schiller and Crewson (1997) found that people with more internal locus of control had higher self employment income than people with more external locus of control.

A concept related to locus of control is that of the Protestant Ethic. A long tradition in sociology that started with the work of Max Weber (1947) has held that Protestants are more likely than Catholics to believe that they can influence their own environment. As a result, Weber (1947) and others have proposed that Protestants should be more likely to engage in opportunity exploitation than Catholics. Several studies have provided empirical support for this proposition. In their study of the characteristics that influenced British students to become interested in the Young Enterprise scheme, Bonnet and Furnham (1991) found that those interested in the scheme scored held beliefs more consistent with Protestantism than Catholicism. Similarly, Roberts (1991a) compared 50 technical entrepreneurs to 168 scientists and engineers and found that the group of entrepreneurs had 8 per cent more Jews and 10 per cent fewer Catholics than the group of non-entrepreneurs.

More macro-level studies also provide support for the positive effect of Protestantism on opportunity exploitation. Shane (1996) looked at the number of organizations per capita in the United States from 1899 to 1988 and found that the proportion of Protestants in the US population had a positive effect on this measure of entrepreneurial activity. Carroll and Mosakowski examined data on a representative sample of West Germans and found that being Catholic reduced the likelihood that the respondent would make the transition to self employment. Butler and Herring (1991) examined data on 7542 respondents to the General Social Survey from 1983 and found that being Catholic reduced the likelihood of self employment.

Self Efficacy

Self efficacy is the belief in one's own ability to perform a given task (Bandura, 1997). People who have higher self efficacy are more likely to exploit entrepreneurial opportunities than people who have lower self efficacy. When deciding whether or not to exploit entrepreneurial opportunities, Knight (1921: 269) argued that 'there must come into play the diversity among men in degree of confidence in their judgement and in disposition to act on their opinions, to "venture"'. Because entrepreneurs make subjective assessments about uncertain opportunities that differ from the subjective probabilities made by others (Casson, 1995), they must make judgmental decisions about resources that put their assessments at odds with those of other people (Wu, 1989). Consequently, they must have confidence in their own judgment and must not become too uncomfortable at the prospect of being wrong or at odds with a skeptical and disbelieving majority (Casson, 1995; Wu, 1989; Ripsas, 1998).

Several studies have shown that entrepreneurs have greater self efficacy than managers. Baron and Markman (1999a) surveyed 78 inventors and found that those who had started firms to exploit their inventions scored higher on a self efficacy scale than those who did not start firms. In their study, Robinson *et al.* (1991) found that business owners scored more highly on a self esteem scale than managers. Hull *et al.* (1980) found that alumni of the University of Oregon who were business owners scored more highly on an entrepreneurial task preference scale than non-owners.

Similar results for the positive effect of self efficacy on the decision to exploit an opportunity were found when researchers used more rigorous designs that focused on the decision to exploit opportunities. For example, Zietsma (1999) compared 52 technology firm founders with 22 senior technology managers who had considered exploiting entrepreneurial opportunities but decided against their pursuit. She found that non-founders were significantly less likely to be confident in themselves and their team than the firm founders were.

Researchers have also shown that self efficacy increases entrepreneurial intentions. Chen *et al.* (1998) surveyed 140 university students and found that entrepreneurial self efficacy was positively correlated with a scale score measuring the person's intention to set up their own business. De Noble *et al.* (1999) surveyed 87 MBA students and found that scales indicating the student's confidence in developing new product and market opportunities as well as those indicating their confidence in coping with unexpected challenges significantly distinguished entrepreneurship majors from non-entrepreneurship majors. In a survey of a random sample of Swedes, Vesalainen and Pihkala (1999) found that managerial self-efficacy predicted the intention to start a business as well as entrepreneurial education.

The studies described above demonstrate that self efficacy increases a person's tendency to exploit entrepreneurial opportunities. Given the importance of confidence in one's own judgment, persistence, and use of feedback to entrepreneurial activity, one might also expect that self efficacy would increase a person's performance at entrepreneurial activity.

Despite the apparent importance of this question, I could find only one empirical study that has examined it. Kalleberg and Leight (1991) studied the survival of 337 randomly selected owner-managed small businesses in Indiana from 1985 to 1987. They found that a two-item scale for the owner's confidence in their ability to run the business reduced the likelihood that the firms would go out of business over the observation period. Although this result supports the argument made above, it is probably too thin a base of evidence on which to draw any substantive conclusions.

COGNITIVE CHARACTERISTICS

Cognitive characteristics are factors that influence how people think and make decisions. As I mentioned at the opening of this chapter, cognitive characteristics tend to be much less stable over time than motives and core self evaluation, and tend to be more heavily influenced by a person's perception of a situation. Nevertheless, some evidence suggests that people who exploit entrepreneurial opportunities tend to display certain cognitive characteristics that other people do not display, indicating that these cognitive characteristics influence the decision to exploit entrepreneurial opportunities.

To exploit an entrepreneurial opportunity, a person must make a positive decision about something that is largely unknown, under uncertainty and with limited information, two conditions that allow cognitive biases and heuristics to influence decision-making (Baron, forthcoming). Moreover, making positive decisions about entrepreneurial opportunities requires the possession of cognitive characteristics that allow entrepreneurs to figure out how to exploit opportunities (Yu, 2001; Tyson *et al.*, 1994). Among the cognitive characteristics that are over-represented among people who exploit opportunities are: overconfidence, representativeness (Busenitz and Barney, 1997), and intuition (Baumol, 1993).

Overconfidence

Overconfidence, a facet of a more general optimism bias, is the belief in the accuracy of one's judgment that is too high given actual data. Overconfidence encourages people to exploit entrepreneurial opportunities (Busenitz, 1999) because it leads people to take action in situations in which they do not have enough information to assess the likelihood of their success, but where further investigation would reveal the poor odds, a short opportunity half-life, or the low value of the opportunity facing them (Busenitz and Barney, 1997; Johnson, 1986; Casson, 1995; De Meza and Southy, 1996; Wu, 1989). Moreover, over-confidence leads people to follow their own judgment instead of paying attention to the information or advice provided by others (Bernardo and Welsh, 2001), to disregard disconfirming information (Busenitz and Barney, 1997), and to misperceive the riskiness of actions (Venkatapathy, 1984; Busenitz, 1999; Corman *et al.*, 1988; Fry, 1993). For example, overconfident entrepreneurs often overstate their own skills and abilities (Aldrich, 1999) and exploit opportunities despite their lack of competitive advantage (Bhide, 2000).

Some research supports the proposition that overconfidence encourages people to exploit entrepreneurial opportunities. Gartner and Thomas (1989) surveyed 63 founders of computer software firms and found that they tended to be overconfident, with average sales forecasts that were 29 per cent above actual first year sales. Cooper *et al.* (1988) reported that one-third of the new firm founders that they surveyed were certain that they would succeed, and four-fifths were over two-thirds sure of their own success. Clearly, these estimates are too high given the new business failure rates that exist.

Several studies demonstrate that entrepreneurs tend to be more overconfident than managers. Busenitz and Barney (1997) compared 124 firm founders and 74 managers in large organizations and showed that firm founders were more over-confident than managers. Amit *et al.* (2001) interviewed 51 firm founders and

28 senior managers who investigated but did not found high technology companies in Canada. They found that the firm founders rated their chances of achieving 11 different goals significantly higher than the managers did.

Arabsheibani *et al.* (2000) provide perhaps the best evidence that entrepreneurs are overconfident. They examined data from the British Household Panel Study, which surveyed people from 1990 to 1996, and asked them at each survey wave if they believed that they would be better off in one year than they were at present. The authors found that 4.6 times as many self employed people forecast that they would see an improvement in their economic condition in one year when they actually experienced a deterioration in their economic condition, than forecast a deterioration in their economic condition when they actually experienced an improvement in their economic condition. Among the wage employed, this ratio was only 2.9.

Representativeness

Representativeness is the willingness to generalize from small samples that do not represent a population. A representativeness bias encourages a person to exploit entrepreneurial opportunities. Decisions to exploit opportunities have to be made in situations where there is little historical information to guide the decision. Moreover, these decisions have to be made under significant uncertainty, in settings in which greater effort to analyse information will not resolve that uncertainty (Busenitz and Barney, 1997). Furthermore, the breadth of the types of decisions that entrepreneurs must make demands that entrepreneurs make decisions about things for which often they are not experts. Finally, entrepreneurial opportunities often have a short half-life, requiring quick action to take advantage of them. These characteristics make the representativeness heuristic valuable to making decisions about opportunity exploitation (Busenitz and Lau, 1996).

Despite the logic of this argument, I could find evidence of only one study that has examined the effect of representativeness on opportunity exploitation. In that study, Busenitz and Barney (1997) compared 124 firm founders and 74 managers in large organizations. They found that firm founders scored more highly in representativeness than the managers. That is, the entrepreneurs were more likely than the managers to use rules of thumb rather than statistical analysis to make decisions. However, we don't know from this research whether the entrepreneurs engaged in the representativeness bias because they were different kinds of decision makers than the managers, or because the entrepreneurial situation leads people to engage in the bias. Nevertheless, Busenitz and Barney's (1997) work suggests that entrepreneurs and managers have different cognitive decision-making styles.

Intuition

Intuition is a belief or feeling that something is true without actually gathering evidence to demonstrate its veracity. Intuition will increase a person's tendency to exploit entrepreneurial opportunities (Allinson *et al.*, 2000). A decision to exploit an entrepreneurial opportunity is a decision that must be made under uncertainty, often under time pressure and with limited information (Busenitz and Barney, 1997). As a result, Schumpeter (1934) suggested that entrepreneurs must have an ability to make decisions about opportunities using intuition rather than by analysing information (Ripsas, 1998).

Some empirical research supports this argument. Allinson *et al.* (2000) compared 156 founders of high growth firms listed in the British publication *Local Heroes*, with 546 managers, and discovered that the firm founders were more intuitive in their decision-making than the managers were. Hills and Shrader (1998) surveyed 53 members of the Chicago area Entrepreneurship Hall of Fame and compared them to a sample of 187 business owners collected from a Dun and Bradstreet list of firms. They found that the members of the Hall of Fame were more likely than the typical entrepreneurs to consider their own gut feel as the most important part of judging the market potential of an opportunity. Similarly, Baron (2000a) compared 44 people who had founded businesses to 32 people who expressed no interest in starting a business and to 26 people who expressed strong interest in starting a business in the future. He found that people who had started businesses were less likely to engage in counterfactual thinking, or imagining what alternatives might have occurred, than people in the other two groups. Smith *et al.* (1988) conducted a field study in which 15 entrepreneurs and 13 managers from electronic manufacturing firms answered a series of questions about a decision-making scenario. They found that the entrepreneurs engaged in less formal analysis of data and were less likely to gather information from inside the organization than the managers.

Given the evidence just presented about the value of intuition to the decision to exploit entrepreneurial opportunities, one might suspect that people who rely on intuition perform better at entrepreneurial activity than those who rely on analytical decision-making. The use of intuition facilitates making decisions about resource acquisition, organizing and new venture strategy under uncertainty, intense time pressure and with limited information. By facilitating decision-making, the argument goes, the use of intuition enhances the performance at entrepreneurial activity.

Two studies provide empirical support for this argument. Carland (1982) compared growth-oriented firm founders to non-growth-oriented firm founders and discovered found that growth-oriented firm founders were more likely to be intuitive-thinking-perceptive types on the Myers–Briggs test while the other founders were more likely to be sensing-feeling-judging types. Similarly, Ginn and Sexton (1990) compared 143 founders whose firms were listed on the 1987 Inc 500 list with 150 founders of successful, slower growth firms. They discovered that the founders of the rapid growth firms were more likely than the founders of the slower growth firms to be intuitive and perceptive and were less likely to be judgmental and sensing on the Myers–Briggs personality inventory.

SUMMARY

This chapter reviewed three broad categories of psychological factors that influence the likelihood that a person will exploit entrepreneurial opportunities: aspects of personality and motives, core self-evaluation and cognitive characteristics. These psychological characteristics influence the likelihood that people will exploit entrepreneurial opportunities because people with psychological characteristics that other people do not have will make decisions to exploit the same opportunities that other people will not choose to exploit.

Research has shown that five aspects of personality and motives increase the likelihood that people will exploit entrepreneurial opportunities. Extraversion will increase the likelihood that a person will exploit an entrepreneurial opportunity because opportunity exploitation involves persuading others, particularly customers and employees, that the opportunity that she has identified is valuable, and extraversion is associated with persuasive ability. Agreeableness will reduce the likelihood that a person will exploit opportunities because opportunity exploitation requires a person to be critical and skeptical so as to separate more valuable information from less valuable information when making the decision to exploit. People who are higher in need for achievement will be more likely to exploit entrepreneurial opportunities because the exploitation of opportunity requires solving novel and ill-specified problems; involves goal setting, planning and information gathering; and requires sustaining goal-directed activity over a long period of time. People higher in risk-taking propensity will be more likely to exploit entrepreneurial opportunities because risk bearing is a fundamental part of entrepreneurship. People with a high level of independence will be more likely to exploit entrepreneurial opportunities because entrepreneurship entails following one's own judgment, as opposed to following the judgment of others.

Two aspects of core self evaluation – internal locus of control and self efficacy – increase the likelihood that a person will exploit an entrepreneurial opportunity. Internal locus of control has this effect because a person's willingness to exploit an opportunity depends on her beliefs about her ability to influence the environment around her. Self efficacy increases a person's willingness to exploit an entrepreneurial opportunity because exploitation requires confidence in one's subjective judgment under uncertainty.

Three cognitive characteristics influence the exploitation of opportunities: overconfidence, representativeness and intuition. People who are overconfident are more likely to exploit opportunities because overconfidence leads people to take action in situations in which they do not have enough information to assess the likelihood of their success, but where further investigation would reveal the poor odds, short opportunity half-life, or low opportunity value facing them. Moreover, overconfidence leads people to follow their own information instead of heeding that provided by others; to disregard disconfirming information; and to misperceive the riskiness of actions. Representativeness increases the likelihood of opportunity exploitation because representativeness makes people more likely to make decisions in situations where there is little historical information to guide decisions; where greater effort to analyse information will not resolve uncertainty; where people are not experts; and where quick action is needed. Intuitive decision-making will increase the likelihood of opportunity exploitation because the decision to exploit an opportunity must be made under time pressure, uncertainty and limited information, all of which hinder analytic decision-making.

Having discussed the individual-level psychological characteristics that make people more likely to exploit opportunities, I now turn to a discussion of the industry context of opportunity exploitation, the subject of the next chapter.

NOTES

1. Earlier research demonstrates that entrepreneurship is riskier than wage employment. Hamilton (2000) examined data from the 1984 panel of the Survey of Income and Program Participation, which surveyed 8771 males, aged 18 to 65 in the non-farm sector at four-month intervals from 1983 to 1986. He found that the distribution of self employment earnings was significantly more skewed and had greater dispersion than wage income.

2. They also found that those owners who had taken part in creating the business were higher on risk-taking propensity than those owners who had not taken part in creating the business, and that risk preferences were higher for those non-owners who indicated that they would start a business in the next three years than those who indicated that they would not.

3. Some research suggests that people choose self employment even when it pays less than wage employment because of the autonomy it provides (Hamilton, 2000), a point supported by the greater job satisfaction of the self employed relative to the wage employed (Blanchflower and Oswald, 1998). For example, Hamilton's (2000) examination of the 1984 panel of the Survey of Income and Program Participation showed that the distribution of self employment earnings was more skewed and had greater dispersion than the distribution of wage income. Ruling out the selection of low ability employees into self employment, he found that entrepreneurs start and continue their businesses despite the fact that initial earnings and earnings growth are lower than in paid employment, resulting in a 35 per cent discount for self employed earnings over ten years.

6. Industry differences in entrepreneurial activity

People do not make decisions to exploit entrepreneurial opportunities in a vacuum. Rather, they are influenced by the industry context in which they operate. As a result, two people with the same individual characteristics, both psychological and otherwise, will make very different decisions about founding a firm if the first one finds herself in an industry that favors opportunity exploitation through firm formation while the other finds herself in a industry context that hinders opportunity exploitation through firm formation. In this chapter, I review the effects of the industry context on the decision to exploit entrepreneurial opportunities through firm formation.

DO INDUSTRY DIFFERENCES IN FIRM FORMATION EXIST?

Are people more likely to exploit entrepreneurial opportunities by creating new firms in some industries than in others? The answer to this question appears to be yes. Many researchers have shown that the propensity for people to engage in opportunity exploitation through new firm formation differs significantly across industries. For example, Taylor (1996) used data from the British Household Panel Survey to show that people employed in agriculture, construction, distribution or finance were more likely to make the transition to self employment than people employed in other industries.

This tendency toward greater exploitation of entrepreneurial opportunities by creating new firms in some industries as compared to others means that the distribution of industries in a particular geographic area influences the tendency of people in that area to exploit entrepreneurial opportunities. Several authors have demonstrated this point. Using data from the 1980 US Census, Light and Sanchez (1987) found that the percentage of the labor force in retail industries was positively correlated with the self employment rate across 272 standard metropolitan statistical areas. Similarly, Georgellis and Wall (1999) examined 11 years of self employment data (1983–1993) for the ten standard regions of Britain and found a significant effect for industry composition across those regions.

Industry differences also appear to affect the performance of people at entrepreneurial activity. Several authors have found that the nature of the industry in which a new firm is founded influences its survival (Audretsch, 1991; Bates, 1994). Using data from the US Small Business Administration, Kirchhoff (1994) shows that new venture survival rates for firms founded in 1977 and 1978 differ across the one-digit standard industrial codes. Similarly, using data on exit rates from US manufacturing between 1963 and 1982, Dunne *et al.* (1988) found variation in survival rates across three-digit standard industrial codes.

Moreover, in studies undertaken across a wide variety of locations, at different times, and using different methodologies, several industries have been found to have higher new venture survival rates than others: the glass industry (Mata and Portugal, 1994), catering (Taylor, 2001; Cressy, 1996b), wholesaling (Gimeno *et al.*, 1997; Cressy, 1996b), manufacturing (Taylor, 2001; Gimeno *et al.*, 1997), distribution, hotels, banking, finance and insurance (Taylor, 2001; Gimeno *et al.*, 1997), construction, agriculture (Taylor, 1999; Gimeno *et al.*, 1997; Carter *et al.*, 1992), personal services and professional services (Littunen, 2000; Taylor, 1999; Gimeno *et al.*, 1997). Industries with particularly low survival rates include transportation and retail trade (Bruderl *et al.*, 1992; Reynolds, 1987; Cooper *et al.*, 1988; Carter *et al.*, 1992).

Some industries also appear more supportive of new venture growth than other industries (Cooper *et al.*, 1994). Across a wide variety of studies undertaken at different points in time, in different locations and using different methodologies, researchers have shown that distribution, construction (Reynolds, 1997), manufacturing (Reynolds and White, 1997; Reynolds, 1997; Reynolds, 1993; Dunkelberg *et al.*, 1987; Schutgens and Wever, 2000), financial services, business services (Reynolds and White, 1997; Schutgens and Wever, 2000; Reynolds, 1993), agriculture, and catering (Cressy, 1996b) are more supportive of the growth of new ventures than other industries. On the other hand, retail is particularly unsupportive of the growth of new ventures (Dunkelberg *et al.*, 1987).

Industry also influences the level of income earned from entrepreneurial activity (Kalleberg and Leight, 1991). Again, examining this issue across a variety of geographic locations, time periods and research methodologies, researchers have found that earnings from entrepreneurial activity were higher for engineering (Taylor, 1996; Taylor, 2001), manufacturing, (Gimeno *et al.*, 1997; Taylor, 1996; Taylor, 2001) construction (Taylor, 2001; Gimeno *et al.*, 1997) finance (Gimeno *et al.*, 1997; Taylor, 2001), transportation, wholesaling, agriculture, professional services and personal services (Gimeno *et al.*, 1997) than for other industries.

Industry differences also appear to influence the likelihood of initial public offering. For example, Hannan *et al.* (1996, 2002) examined new technology companies established in Silicon Valley between 1984 and 1994 and found that the likelihood of an initial public offering was positively related to being in medical technology and negatively related to being in research, manufacturing or computers.

While the evidence outlined above clearly demonstrates that people are more likely to engage in opportunity exploitation through new firm formation, or perform better at that exploitation process in some industries than in others, the identification of particular industries as supportive or unsupportive of new firm formation is unparsimonious. The imprecision of this answer has led some researchers to ask what it is about some industries that makes them more supportive of new firm formation than other industries. To explain the effect of industry differences on opportunity exploitation through firm formation in a more useful way, researchers have examined the effect of a smaller set of theoretically driven industry differences in the rate of new firm formation. In general, researchers have focused on five categories of industry differences. As Box 6.1 shows, these differences include knowledge conditions, demand conditions, industry life cycles, appropriability conditions and industrial structure. I discuss each of these perspectives below.

KNOWLEDGE CONDITIONS

Researchers have argued that the underlying knowledge conditions in an industry influence the level of opportunity exploitation by new firms in that industry (Winter, 1984). Knowledge conditions are the aspects of the industry that affect how people gather information about the production of goods and services in an industry. For example, is the industry technology simple or complex? Is it discrete or part of a larger system?

Researchers have shown that industries can vary on a wide variety of knowledge conditions, including the degree to which knowledge is tacit and held in the minds of people working in the industry, or codified and held in documentary form. Industries also vary on the locus of knowledge creation. For example, is most new knowledge created within or outside the value chain? If the knowledge is created within the value chain, do producers, their customers or their suppliers generate it? Industries also differ on the degree of uncertainty associated with knowledge creation, and the amount of knowledge output produced per unit of input. To date, researchers have provided empirical evidence for the relationship between four dimensions of the knowledge conditions in an industry and the level of opportunity exploitation through firm formation – the effect of R&D intensity, the locus of innovation, the size of innovating entities and the degree of uncertainty. In the subsections below, I review the results of these studies.

BOX 6.1 INDUSTRY DIFFERENCES THAT INFLUENCE OPPORTUNITY EXPLOITATION

- Knowledge conditions
  - R&D intensity
  - Locus of innovation
  - Size of the innovating entities
  - Uncertainty of the industry
- Demand conditions
  - Market size
  - Market growth
  - Market segmentation
- Industry life cycles
  - Industry age
  - Dominant design
  - Presence of a density of firms
- Appropriability conditions
  - Strength of patents
  - Importance of complementary assets
- Industry structure
  - Profitability of the industry
  - Cost of inputs
  - Capital intensity of the industry
  - Advertising intensity of the industry
  - Industry concentration
  - Average firm size

R&D Intensity

The research and development intensity of an industry should enhance opportunities for new firms to be used to exploit opportunities because the knowledge that makes entrepreneurial opportunities possible is often generated through research and development activities. By investing in research and development, firms and government entities produce new technologies that make possible new markets, new ways of organizing, new products, new processes and new raw materials. While some of that opportunity exploitation occurs through exploitation by established firms, some of it spills over and new firms are formed to exploit newly created technology. Because the level of knowledge creation and knowledge spillovers will increase with the level of R&D intensity in an industry, opportunity exploitation through firm formation should increase with the R&D intensity of an industry (Klepper and Sleeper, 2001).

Some research supports this proposition. For example, Dean *et al.* (1998) examined the number of small establishments entering each of 302 industries in three two-year periods: between 1976 and 1978, between 1982 and 1984, and between 1986 and 1988. They found that R&D intensity of the industry increased small firm entry. Using the US Establishment and Enterprise Longitudinal Microdataset, Dean and Brown (1995) examined the number of new independent firms formed in 306 industries between 1976 and 1980. These authors found that R&D intensity was positively correlated with new firm entry across industries. Similarly, Dean and Meyer (1992) examined the rate of creation of new independent establishments in 382 four-digit manufacturing industries from 1976 to 1980 and found that R&D intensity increased the rate of firm formation.

Locus of Innovation

Industries differ in the locus of innovation within them (Klevorick *et al.*, 1995). In some industries, firms within the value chain undertake most of the technology creation. In other industries, extra-industry entities, like universities and government research labs, are more important sources of technology creation. In industries in which government research labs and universities create most of the technology, opportunity exploitation through new firm formation is more prevalent.

The degree to which an industry relies on public sector institutions to innovate should enhance opportunity exploitation by new firms. Unlike the large, established firms that undertake research and development to create new technologies that they then identify commercial opportunities to exploit (Schumpeter, 1942), new firms cannot endogenize the innovation process. Instead, new firms must rely on new technologies that are created publicly or that spill over from the R&D efforts of private firms. Because technology created by the public sector makes entrepreneurial opportunities possible (Schumpeter, 1934) without limiting the property rights of those opportunities to large, established firms that might preclude their employees from exploiting them, public sector innovation encourages the exploitation of entrepreneurial opportunities by new firms.

Some empirical research supports this argument. Shane (2001b) examined the 1397 patents assigned to the Massachusetts Institute of Technology between 1980 and 1996 and found that in patent classes in which universities have a greater share of technology production, the likelihood that a newly founded firm will exploit the patent was higher than in industries in which universities have a smaller share of technology production. Similarly, Audretsch and Acs

(1994) examined new firm start-up activity in 117 industries at six points in time between 1976 and 1986 using a US Small Business Administration database. They found that industries with more university research have higher start-up rates.

Size of Innovating Entities

Another important knowledge condition that affects the rate of new firm formation in an industry is the nature of the innovation process. In some industries, innovation requires very large-scale operations, leading large firms to introduce most of the new products and services. In other industries, innovation requires flexible and nimble organizations, leading small firms to introduce most of the new products and services. Industries in which small firms tend to be better innovators have higher rates of firm formation than other industries because the knowledge conditions in these industries are closer to the knowledge conditions that facilitate new firm formation (Malerba and Orsenigo, 1996). In contrast, opportunities that require scale economies or large amounts of capital, and so favor large firm innovation, tend to be difficult to exploit on a scale that most new firms can achieve with the resources that they possess. Therefore, new firms tend to exploit those opportunities that result in innovations produced by small firms.

Despite the importance of this argument, only one empirical study has explored it. Acs and Audretsch (1989b) examined net entry by small firms into 247 manufacturing industries in the United States between 1978 and 1980 and found that the rate of entry was higher in those industries where the small firm innovation rate (the number of new product innovations per employee) in 1982 was higher.

Uncertainty of the Industry

Industries differ in the rate of change that occurs in them. Some industries, like pharmaceuticals, are more uncertain than others, and face a high rate of product, process and organizational innovation. Entrepreneurs are less likely to exploit opportunities in more uncertain industries. New firms have difficulty managing industry turbulence (Cooper and Bruno, 1978; Wyant, 1977) because techno-logical and market uncertainty reduce the likelihood that the new venture will be able to produce a new product or that there will be demand for it if it is produced (Audretsch, 2001). In contrast, large, established firms, which have economies of scale and scope, that allow them to diversify their operations across more activities, are less adversely affected by this uncertainty.

Two studies provide empirical support for this argument. Acs and Audretsch (1989a) examined the gross entry rate of new firms with fewer than 199 employees across 238 manufacturing industries from 1976 to 1982 and found a negative correlation between the number of innovations introduced in the industry in 1982 and gross entry of new, small firms. Similarly, Audretsch and Acs (1994) examined the US Small Business Administration's database on new firm formation at six points in time between 1976 and 1986 and found that, across 117 industries, those industries with more product changes had lower start-up rates.

While the above two studies indicate that opportunity exploitation through new firm formation is less common in more uncertain industries, it leaves open the question of the performance of new ventures in more uncertain industries. Do new firms founded in more uncertain industries perform worse than those founded in less uncertain industries, as one might expect if entrepreneurs' entry decisions were rational?

Two studies have examined this issue empirically and suggest that new ventures in more uncertain industries are, in fact, less likely to survive than new ventures in more certain industries. Audretsch (1991) examined the ten-year survival rates of 11 000 new firms established in the United States in 1976 and found that the innovation rate in the industry reduced the rate of new venture survival. Similarly, Audretsch and Mahmood (1995) examined the survival of 12 251 new establishments created in 1976 and found that the innovation rate in the industry increased the likelihood of new venture failure.

DEMAND CONDITIONS

Researchers have argued that the demand conditions in an industry influence the level of entrepreneurial opportunity present in that industry. Changes in demand that result from changes in culture, tastes, mood or attitudes can generate opportunities for the founding of new firms because producers need to respond to the preferences and purchasing habits of consumers (Schumpeter, 1934; Kirzner, 1997). First, if demand is high, the value of the opportunity may be enhanced by economies of scale. Given a fixed cost of exploiting an entre-preneurial opportunity, the expected value of the outcome will be larger if the market is bigger, all other things being equal. Second, if demand exceeds supply, that situation can create opportunities to increase capacity (Drucker, 1985). Third, demand growth might facilitate the formation of market niches (Chris-tiansen and Bower, 1996) because demand growth allows firms the opportunity to specialize (Geroski, 2001). In the subsections below, I review the research that discusses the effect of industry differences in demand conditions on the creation of opportunities for new organizing efforts.

Market Size

The size of a market should enhance opportunities for new firm creation because larger markets allow the fixed costs of organizing a firm to be amortized over more sales. As a result, participants in small markets might cede the exploitation of opportunity to established players, but attempt to exploit that opportunity themselves in larger markets.

Several empirical studies have supported this proposition. Pennings (1982b) examined firm formation rates in three industries – plastics, telecommunication equipment and electronic components – across 70 standard metropolitan statistical areas between 1967 and 1971 and between 1972 and 1975. The authors found a significant positive effect for industry size on firm formation rates. Schell and David (1981) examined the 1966 and 1976 County Business Patterns data for the state of Alabama and found that the creation of new business units was positively correlated with per capita retail sales in the county. Dean *et al.* (1998) examined the number of small establishments entering 302 industries during three time periods – between 1976 and 1978, between 1982 and 1984 and between 1986 and 1988 – and found that industry size increased entry. Ventresca *et al.* (1999) examined the rate of firm formation in the technology-based on-line database industry from 1972 to 1991, and found that the level of computer hardware sales in the United States had a positive effect on firm formation rates in this industry. Baum *et al.* (1995) examined the formation of facsimile transmission service organizations established in Manhattan from 1965 to 1992, and found that the sales level for digital facsimile machines had a positive relationship with the rate of firm formation. Mata (1994) examined the rate of entry of 2999 *de novo* firms into Portuguese manufacturing between 1982 and 1986 and found that larger industry markets had higher *de novo* entry rates.

The proposition that larger markets have more entrepreneurial activity than smaller markets has also been supported in studies that view entrepreneurship as self employment. Using US Census data, Borjas (1986) found that the percentage of a local market that is Hispanic had a significant positive effect on the likelihood that a Hispanic person would be self employed. Similarly, Evans (1989) found that the number of ethnic group members in a particular geographic area increased the likelihood that a person from that ethnic group would become self employed. In a study of the founding of day care centers in Toronto, Baum and Oliver (1992) found that formation rates increased with the level of demand for day care.

In contrast, excess capacity, which signifies insufficient demand, is negatively related to entrepreneurial activity. For example, Dean and Meyer (1992) examined the rate of creation of new independent establishments in 382 four-digit manufacturing industries from 1976 to 1980, and found that excess capacity was negatively correlated with the level of firm formation in the industry.

Given the evidence presented above for the argument that larger markets have more entrepreneurial activity than smaller markets, do new ventures perform better in larger markets than in smaller ones? One might argue that the answer to this question should be yes if entrepreneurs are rational. People are more likely to found firms in larger markets because larger market size allows them to amortize the cost of establishing a new firm over a larger potential customer base. For the same reason, larger market size should reduce new firm failure rates by providing a greater opportunity for scale economies. By exploiting scale economies, new ventures can reduce their average costs and therefore be more likely to survive.

Some empirical evidence supports this proposition. Eisenhardt and Schoonhoven (1995) examined 98 semiconductor firms founded in the US between 1978 and 1985, and found that the size of the semiconductor market had a negative effect on new firm failure rates. Carroll and Huo (1986) examined the formation of 2168 newspapers in the San Francisco Bay area from 1870 to 1980. Arguing that the relevant market for newspapers is the local population, these authors found that the area population had a negative effect on the failure rates of newspapers. Barnett (1990) examined the population of telephone companies operating in Pennsylvania up to 1934 and in Iowa from 1900 to 1930, and found that telephone market size reduced the failure rate of local telephone companies. Delacroix *et al.* (1989) examined the Californian wine industry from 1940 to 1985 and found that per capita levels of wine consumption had a significant negative effect on the failure of new wineries. Wade *et al.* (1998) examined the rate of failure of US breweries from 1845 to 1918, and found that state population and adjacent state population, two measures of local market size, had a negative effect on the failure of breweries.

Although I could identify no studies that examined the relationship between market size and the growth or profitability of new ventures, one study examined the relationship between market size and the likelihood that a new venture would achieve an initial public offering. Shane and Stuart's (2002) examination of the life histories of 134 new companies founded to exploit intellectual property assigned to the Massachusetts Institute of Technology from 1980 to 1996 showed that the size of the founding firm's industry increased its likelihood of initial public offering.

Market Growth

The growth of a market should enhance opportunities for new firm creation because new firms can enter growing markets to meet excess demand that established companies cannot meet (Dorfman, 1987). Moreover, if markets are growing, the new firm entrants do not need to compete directly with established firms for customers. Rather, they can seek customers from among potential new adopters.

Several empirical studies support the proposition that new firm creation is more likely in growing markets. Highfield and Smiley (1987) examined US Small Business Administration data on the rate of new firm formation in 40 industries across three time periods, 1976–77, 1978–79 and 1980–81, and found that high rates of industry growth were positively and significantly correlated with new firm formation rates in the industry. Dean *et al.* (1998) examined the number of small establishments entering 302 industries between 1976 and 1978, between 1982 and 1984, and between 1986 and 1988. These authors found that the growth rate of shipments in an industry increased small firm entry into that industry. Dean and Brown (1995) examined the number of new independent firms entering 306 industries between 1976 and 1980 and found that industry sales growth was positively correlated with new firm entry into the industry. Dean and Meyer (1992) examined the rate of creation of new independent establishments in 382 four-digit manufacturing industries from 1976 to 1980, and found that industry sales growth increased firm formation in the industry. Acs and Audretsch (1989b) examined net entry by small firms into 247 manufacturing industries in the United States between 1978 and 1980. They found that the rate of small firm entry into an industry was higher when the growth rate of shipments in that industry was higher. Acs and Audretsch (1989a) examined the gross entry rate of new firms with fewer than 199 employees into 238 manufacturing industries from 1976 to 1982, and found a positive correlation between gross entry and the growth of industry shipments.

If firm formation is more common in growing industries because high growth rates generate excess demand that established producers cannot satisfy, and because high growth rates make it possible for new entrants to avoid competing directly with established producers for customers, then it stands to reason that new venture performance should be better in high growth markets than in low growth markets. Several pieces of empirical evidence support this assertion.

Several authors have shown that high growth markets have lower new firm failure rates than low growth markets. Baum and Mezias (1992) examined the failure rates of Manhattan hotels from 1898 to 1990, and found that the hotel failure rate declined as the number of visitors to New York increased. Eisenhardt and Schoonhoven (1995) examined the performance of 98 semiconductor firms established in the United States between 1978 and 1985, and found that failure rates were lower when markets were at a growth stage. Mata and Portugal (1994) followed 3169 new Portuguese manufacturing firms established in 1983 from 1984 to 1988, and found that firm failure declined as market growth increased. Gimeno *et al.* (1997) examined the survival of 1547 new firms whose founders were members of the National Federation of Independent Business and had been in business for fewer than 18 months. They discovered that the growth of the gross state product in the location where the new venture was founded was negatively related to the new venture failure rate.

Market growth also appears to enhance the growth of new ventures. At least one study provides empirical support for this argument. Eisenhardt and Schoonhoven's (1995) study of new semiconductor firms showed that annual sales growth was higher for firms in growth stage markets than in markets at other stages of development.

Market growth also appears to enhance the profitability of new ventures. This proposition is supported by two pieces of empirical evidence. First, Dolton and Makepeace (1990) examined 208 self-employed British people using data from the Survey of Graduates and Diplomates undertaken by the Department of Employment. They found that respondents with a degree in a field in which real wages were growing 10 per cent per year or more had higher earnings from self employment than other respondents. Second, Gimeno *et al.* (1997), using the National Federation of Independent Business database on new firms, showed that the greater the gross state product in the state where the new venture was founded, the greater was the amount of income that the founders took out of the business.

Market Segmentation

Market segmentation should enhance opportunities for new firm creation because the exploitation of niches requires organizations that are quick and agile enough to take advantage of opportunities that are left unsatisfied by other players, and new firms tend to be quicker and more agile than large, established firms (Dean *et al.*, 1998; Dorfman, 1987). In addition, niche markets require organizations that can profit without significant scale economies (Cohen and Levin, 1989; Dorfman, 1987; Klepper and Sleeper, 2001). Because niche markets are often small, the level of demand in them is often insufficient for firms to achieve significant scale economies, and new firms, which can exploit opportunities on a smaller scale than large, established firms, are best able to serve them.

Empirical research supports the proposition that market segmentation increases the likelihood of new firm formation. Several authors have shown that the greater the level of market segmentation in an industry, the higher the rate at which employees will found firms to exploit opportunities that they have identified (Garvin, 1983; Christiansen, 1993; Anton and Yao, 1995). For example, Shane (2001b) examined the 1397 patents assigned to the Massachusetts Institute of Technology between 1980 and 1996. He compared the likelihood that a patent would be exploited by a newly founded firm with an industry-level measure of the tendency of the industry toward segmentation, and found a significant positive correlation. Similarly, Baum and Singh (1994b) examined the formation of 682 licensed day care centers in Metropolitan

Toronto from 1971 to 1989. These authors found that when the market was segmented into niches that represented different age groups of children, the firm formation rate was negatively related to the number of new firms already founded in the niche, but was positively related to the number of new firms already founded in other niches.

In many industries, researchers have shown that the presence of market niches also creates opportunities for new firm formation at the same time that opportunities exist for existing organizations to expand their operations. For example, the tendency of major airlines (for example, United, American, Delta, Northwest) to dominate large volume markets by establishing hubs actually created opportunities for entrepreneurs to found specialist carriers that fly point-to-point (Carroll and Hannan, 2000).

In a large sample statistical study, Mezias and Mezias (2000) found evidence of this proposition. These authors examined the production and distribution of all feature films in the United States between 1912 and 1929. They found that the concentration of production and distribution in the hands of a few players led to the formation of specialist producers and distributors.

INDUSTRY LIFE CYCLES

A third theoretical perspective on the relationship between industry character-istics and the rate of firm formation is that of the industry life cycle. Researchers have argued that industry life cycles influence the level of entrepreneurial opportunity present in that industry. When industries are young and pre-para-digmatic, they have few existing firms and new firm formation is relatively common. As industries age and develop, they tend to become composed of a larger number of firms, and new firm formation becomes relatively less common. In the subsections below, I review the research that discusses the effect of industry life cycles on opportunities for new organizing efforts. I focus on three areas for which empirical evidence has been amassed: industry age, dominant design and firm density.

Industry Age

Industry age should reduce opportunities for new firm creation for several reasons. First, the adoption of goods and services by customers tends to follow a normal distribution (Girfalco, 1991). As a result, the shift in adoption from the earliest adopters to the initial part of the customer mainstream will be marked by acceleration in demand growth, whereas the shift from the later part of the customer mainstream to the laggards will be marked by a deceleration in demand growth. Because demand growth shifts upward as adoption first increases and then shifts downward as adoption later decreases, new firm formation is more likely when industries are young than when they get older.

Second, when industries are mature, existing firms are available to meet increases in demand. However, when industries are young, no established firms exist to meet that demand. The lack of existing firms to meet demand means that most markets experience heavy waves of new firm formation when demand accelerates in the early days of the industry (Geroski, 1995).

Third, Malerba and Orsenigo (2000) explain that when an industry ages, the knowledge base underlying the industry becomes more stable. As a result, firms move up the learning curve and develop more efficient ways of developing new products and services and serving markets. Because much of this learning occurs by doing, new firms lack the opportunity to develop these learning curve advantages. Consequently, new firms become more disadvantaged as industries mature, and industry newness enhances the rate of new firm formation.

Some empirical support exists for the proposition that new firm formation declines as industries age. Both Garvin (1983) and Klepper and Sleeper (2001) found that the rate at which new firms spin off from established companies declines as the industry matures, suggesting that opportunity exploitation becomes more likely to remain in house at established firms as industries mature.

In a more direct test of the effect of industry age on the rate of new firm formation, Shane (2001b) examined the 1397 patents assigned to the Massachusetts Institute of Technology between 1980 and 1996. He found that that the older the patent class in which a technology was found, the less likely the patent was to be exploited by a newly founded firm. Furthermore, Barnett (1997) examined the founding rates of American breweries from 1633 until 1988, and Pennsylvania telephone companies from 1879 to 1934, and found that firm formation rates decreased as the average age of firms in the industry increased.

If entrepreneurs form their expectations about opportunities in a rational manner, the arguments presented above would suggest that new firms should perform better if they are founded in younger industries than if they are founded in older industries. Some empirical research lends support to this proposition.

Two studies show that the failure rate of new firms increases as industries age. Barnett's (1997) examination of American breweries and Pennsylvania telephone companies showed that the failure rate of new organizations increased with the average age of firms in the industry. Similarly, Wade *et al.* (1998) examined the rate of failure of American breweries from 1845 to 1918, and found that industry age had a positive effect on the likelihood of failure of new breweries.

Presence of a Dominant Design

New firm formation is more common before an industry converges on a dominant design. First, a dominant design limits the approaches that entrepreneurs can take to opportunity exploitation, thereby reducing the number of possible new means–ends frameworks that can be used in the industry. According to life cycle theory, industries operate within particular paradigms about how to produce products and services and how to serve customers (Dosi, 1988). These paradigms influence the nature of entrepreneurial opportunities by constraining the approaches that entrepreneurs take to opportunity exploitation. Consequently, when an industry is young, entrepreneurs propose a wide range of product offerings. Once a dominant design emerges, however, entrepreneurs only propose those designs that fit the dominant approach. The constraining effect of paradigm development means that the number of new firm alternatives that are offered decreases after a dominant design has been introduced.

Second, new organizing efforts tend to be more common before a dominant design emerges in an industry because success at firm founding is enhanced by the ability to influence the dominant design that emerges (Murmann and Tushman, 2001). As a result, entrepreneurs see the emergence of a dominant design as evidence that they can no longer influence the design in their industry in a way that will enhance their performance. This pattern, of course, makes them less likely to found firms.

Third, prior to the emergence of a dominant design, firms do not know their costs or quality, which makes large-scale investment problematic. However, when a dominant design emerges, the ability to make these investments increases. As a result, after the emergence of a dominant design, early entrants can move up the learning curve and create scale economies that disadvantage potential new organizing efforts (Geroski, 1995; Klepper and Graddy, 1990). This pattern means that new firms are more likely to be formed before a dominant design emerges than after it has been established.

Some research supports the proposition that the emergence of a dominant design reduces the likelihood of new firm formation. For example, Baum *et al.* (1995) examined the population of 170 facsimile transmission service organizations established in Manhattan from 1965 to 1992, and found that new firm formation was lower after a dominant design had been established in the industry. Similarly, Utterback (1994) provides evidence from several industries indicating that new firm entry declined after a dominant design had emerged in an industry. Tushman and Anderson (1986) confirmed this result for the jet aircraft and computer industries.

If new firm formation is more common before a dominant design emerges than after it has emerged, then it stands to reason that the development of a dominant design should influence new venture performance. Several researchers have shown that the development of a dominant design in an industry influences new venture failure rates. For example, Horvath *et al.* (2001) examined the American beer brewing industry between 1880 and 1890, and found that firms that entered the industry after the shakeout period had a higher hazard rate of failure than those that had entered before the shakeout. A more direct test of this argument by Baum *et al.* (1995) showed that the longer that facsimile service firms operated before a dominant design was established, the more likely they were to survive after the dominant design had emerged.

Density of Firms

When new firms are founded to exploit opportunities, this act of exploitation itself influences the likelihood of exploitation by other entrepreneurs through an endogenous dynamic process. Researchers have shown that new organizing efforts have a U-shaped relationship with the number of firms in the industry. Early in the life cycle, new firm formation spurs more new firm formation. However, ultimately this effect peaks and previous new firm formation reduces the likelihood of subsequent new firm formation.

Initially, the number of firms in the industry increases firm formation rates for four reasons. First, entrepreneurs use information about existing firms in making decisions about opportunities, and the presence of existing firms signals the existence of an opportunity worth pursuing (Johnson, 1986). Second, prior entry reduces technological and market uncertainty. The initial entrants provide information about both demand and templates for resource recombination, thereby facilitating entry (Horvath *et al.*, 2001; Aldrich, 1999). Third, stake-holders, including customers, suppliers, creditors and employees, need to form judgments about the accuracy of the entrepreneur's assessment of the opportunity. The more firms that are pursuing an opportunity, the more data points that are available to the stakeholders to evaluate the entrepreneur's opportunity (Aldrich, 1999), and the more comfortable stakeholders become with the actions of entrepreneurs to found firms (Carroll and Hannan, 2000). Fourth, increases in the density of firms lead to growth in the number of ties between them. Because these ties facilitate learning, more information about opportunities is transferred in environments that have a denser number of firms (Aldrich, 1999), leading to more firm formation.

However, at high levels, the density of firms decreases new organizing efforts by creating competition for resources. Capital, labor and entrepreneurial talent all face diminishing returns (Carroll and Delacroix, 1982; Delacroix and Carroll, 1983; Delacroix *et al.*, 1989) making it difficult to sustain increasing numbers of new firms as the stock of firms in an industry rises. As Carroll and Hannan (2000: 226) explain, 'the level of diffuse competition increases, more of the resources needed to build and sustain organizations have already been claimed by other organizations. Intense competition causes supplies of potential organizers, members, patrons and resources to become exhausted.'

The empirical literature shows strong evidence of a curvilinear relationship between number of firms and organizing efforts. Although the effects of density appear to be strongest at the local level (Carroll and Wade, 1991), perhaps because of the tendency of entrepreneurs to focus on local conditions and information in making their entrepreneurial decisions (Aldrich, 1999), the results are extremely robust to the geographical location, industry and time period in which the studies were undertaken.

Carroll and Wade (1991) examined the formation of US breweries from 1800 until 1988 and found an inverted U-shaped relationship between the density of firms in an industry and the rate of new firm formation. Similarly, Swaminathan (1995) examined the formation of new Californian wineries from 1941 to 1990 and found that there was an inverted U-shaped relationship between the rate of firm formation and density. Furthermore, Barnett (1997) examined the founding rates of American breweries from 1633 until 1988, and found an inverted U-shaped relationship between brewery density and brewery founding rates.

Similar results have been found in other industries. Ranger-Moore (1997) examined the founding of Manhattan banks from 1792 until 1980, and American life insurance companies from 1760 to 1937, and showed the predicted inverted U-shaped relationship between firm density and firm formation. Sorenson and Audia (2000) examined firm formation in the US footwear industry from 1940 to 1989, and found that the state level density of footwear firms had an inverted U-shaped relationship with the rate of firm formation. Mezias and Mezias (2000) examined the production and distribution of feature films in the United States between 1912 and 1929 and found that density had a U-shaped relationship with the formation of both specialist producers and specialist distributors. Baum *et al.*'s (1995) investigation of facsimile transmission service organizations in Manhattan showed that the likelihood of firm formation had an inverted U-shaped relationship with cohort density. Carroll and Hannan (1989a) examined the formation of newspapers in Argentina, Ireland and seven locations in the United States, and found that for seven of the nine locations, the density of firms had an inverted U-shaped relationship with firm formation. Ventresca *et al.* (1999) examined the rate of firm formation for technology-based on-line databases from 1972 to 1991 and found that density of firms in the industry had the predicted curvilinear relationship with firm formation. Dobbin and Dowd (1997) examined the founding of Massachusetts railroads between 1825 and 1922 and found that industry density had an inverted U-shaped relationship with the rate of firm formation. Hannan (1986) examined US labor unions from 1836 to 1985 and found evidence of an inverted U-shaped effect for the relationship between density of unions and the formation of new unions.

Despite the evidence presented above of the curvilinear relationship between industry density and the rate of venture formation, some researchers have argued that the logic of endogenous dynamic processes underlying the relationship between previous opportunity exploitation and subsequent opportunity exploitation really suggests an empirical test of the relationship between previous firm formation and subsequent firm formation rather than between industry density and subsequent firm formation. Several studies have examined the relationship between previous firm formation and subsequent firm formation and found evidence for a U-shaped relationship. The empirical evidence that supports this proposition has been found in a variety of populations, including cooperatives in Canada (Staber, 1989), American labor unions (Hannan and Freeman, 1989), American breweries (Carroll and Hannan, 1989a, 1989b), Californian wineries (Delacroix and Solt, 1988), Irish, San Francisco and Little Rock newspapers (Hannan and Carroll, 1992; Carroll and Huo, 1986), state life insurance companies (Ranger-Moore *et al.*, 1991), the Belgian automobile industry (Hannan *et al.*, 1995), film production and distribution (Mezias and Mezias, 2000), voluntary social service organizations (Tucker *et al.*, 1988), and facsimile transmission service organizations (Baum *et al.*, 1995).

Given the above arguments about the effect of firm density in the industry on the likelihood of new firm formation, one might expect that new venture performance would also have a curvilinear relationship with industry density. For instance, new venture survival should have a curvilinear relationship with the density or number of existing firms in an industry. Initially density should increase the likelihood of new venture survival by generating legitimacy for the new firms in the industry, but at high levels density should increase the likelihood of new venture failure by creating competition for resources (Hannan and Freeman, 1987, 1989; Hannan and Carroll, 1992).

Many researchers have found empirical support for the effect of industry density on the failure of new ventures. Barnett (1997) examined the failure rates of American breweries from 1633 until 1988, and found the predicted curvilinear relationship between failure rates and industry density. Hannan (1986) examined national labor unions from 1836 until 1985, and found that density of unions had a U-shaped relationship with the failure rate of unions, first declining and then increasing. Carroll *et al.* (1989) examined American and German breweries from 1900 to 1982 and found evidence of the same U-shaped relationship between industry density and venture failure. At a more local level of analysis, Wade *et al.* (1998) examined the rate of failure of American breweries from 1845 to 1918, and found that state brewery density had a U-shaped relationship with the rate of brewery failure.

In an attempt to obtain a more precise understanding of the relationship between industry density and new venture failure, several researchers have argued that density at founding will increase the likelihood of venture mortality. Arguing that the characteristics of an industry at the time of founding have long-term effects on the survival of new ventures even if industry conditions later change, researchers have proposed that new firms founded at the time of greater industry density have worse survival chances than new firms founded at the time of lesser industry density. New ventures founded at times of high density face greater competition for scarce resources, and cannot make as extensive investments in the development of their capabilities as ventures founded at times of low density (Carroll and Hannan, 2000; Singh and Lumsden, 1990).

Several researchers have provided empirical support for this proposition. Carroll and Wade (1991) examined the failure of American breweries and found a positive effect of industry density at the time that the venture was founded. Swaminathan (1996) examined American breweries and Argentinean newspapers and found that new firms founded in worse environments faced higher initial mortality rates than those founded in better environments. Carroll and Hannan (2000) used data on American labor unions, Argentinean newspapers, Irish newspapers, San Francisco newspapers, and American breweries to show that density at the time of venture formation had a positive effect on venture mortality. Tucker *et al.* (1988) examined voluntary social service organizations in metropolitan Toronto and found that the density of such organizations at the time of founding increased the rate of failure of those organizations. Wade *et al.* (1998) examined the rate of failure of US breweries founded between 1845 and 1918 and found that the density of breweries in the same state at the time of the venture's birth had a positive effect on the likelihood of venture failure.

In another set of attempts to obtain more precise evidence of the relationship between the density of the industry and the likelihood of new venture failure, researchers have examined the effect of industry failure rates on the likelihood of new venture failure. Wade *et al.*'s (1998) study of American breweries showed that the number of new breweries founded had a positive effect on the likelihood of brewery failure, and the number of brewery deaths in each state had a negative effect on failure, both of which are consistent with the density argument. Similarly, Delacroix *et al.* (1989) examined the Californian wine industry from 1940 to 1985 and found that the number of winery failures in the previous year had a significant negative effect on the likelihood of failure of new wineries.

APPROPRIABILITY CONDITIONS

Researchers have argued that appropriability conditions also influence the level of opportunity exploitation in an industry. Appropriability conditions are the characteristics of industry that allow entrepreneurs to capture the returns to their efforts to exploit an opportunity. Although entrepreneurs might see the potential for recombination of resources, they will only engage in that recombination if they believe that they can capture the returns from doing so (Levin *et al.*, 1987). The ability to profit from opportunity exploitation depends on the usefulness of patents, learning curves, lead time, complementary assets, first mover advantages and secrecy to capture the returns to exploitation of an opportunity (Cohen and Levin, 1989). Therefore, the willingness of people to exploit entrepreneurial opportunity through firm formation depends on the effectiveness of these means of appropriation in an industry. To date the empirical literature has examined the effect of only two of these means of appropriation on firm formation: patents and complementary assets. In the subsections below, I review the research that discusses the effect of industry differences in these two appropriability conditions on opportunities for new organizing efforts.

Strength of Patents

New organizing efforts are more common in industries in which patents are effective because patents are one of the few methods of appropriating entrepreneurial opportunities that do not require the possession of existing assets or capabilities. Because a patent can be obtained on the entrepreneur's underlying resource combination, it protects the combination against imitation by others very early in the life of the new venture. By contrast, other types of appropriability – learning curves, lead time, first mover advantages and complementary assets – depend heavily on the possession of other assets or capabilities that have not yet been created by the entrepreneur, and therefore cannot protect the recombination against imitation at as early a point in the exploitation process. The timing of the protection against imitation is important because entrepreneurs need to develop the value chain that they will use to exploit their opportunity before other firms imitate their efforts and appropriate the returns from exploiting the opportunity.

Moreover, patent protection encourages the formation of new firms because it facilitates knowledge disclosure (Arrow, 1962). In the absence of patents, people find it difficult to contract for resources to exploit their opportunities because they cannot risk disclosing their opportunities to others. Arrow (1962) pointed out that people are unwilling to contract for knowledge unless they know that the knowledge is valuable. However, efforts of the holder of knowledge to demonstrate its value reduce the motivation of others to pay for that knowledge because disclosure of knowledge makes the knowledge freely available. Patents mitigate this disclosure problem, thereby facilitating firm formation. By making it possible to ensure payment for any knowledge disclosed, patents make it easier for entrepreneurs to disclose information about their opportunities and therefore to contract for resources. Contracting for resources, in turn, encourages entrepreneurial activity because entrepreneurs typically need to obtain many missing parts of the value chain from others.

This means that in industries in which patent protection provides a strong mechanism for protecting an opportunity, such as biotechnology, firm formation should be more common than in other industries. For an industry to have strong patent protection two conditions must be met. First, patenting must be possible. That is, people must be able to demonstrate that they have created novel, non-obvious and valuable inventions – a situation that is more common in high technology industries than in low technology ones. Second, patents must be effective at protecting intellectual property. Patents are weak mechanisms of protection in an industry if they are unlikely to withstand a legal challenge, are unenforceable in courts, can be 'invented around', are unable to protect fast moving technologies, require too much disclosure, or require licensing or cross-licensing for legal reasons (Levin *et al.*, 1987). For example, patents are a weaker mechanism for protecting electronic devices than chemical formulas because electronic device patents are easier to invent around than chemical formula patents.

I could find evidence of only one empirical study that examined the relationship between the effectiveness of patents and the tendency of an industry to encourage new firm formation. Shane's (2001b) examination of patents assigned to the Massachusetts Institute of Technology showed that the effectiveness of patents in a line of business increased the likelihood that a newly founded firm would exploit the patent.

Importance of Complementary Assets

New organizing efforts tend to be less common in industries that are more marketing and manufacturing intensive. Although new firms often create innovative new products and services, they cannot develop the complementary assets in marketing, distribution and manufacturing that are necessary to provide these innovative products and services to customers, as readily as established firms can. Firms develop routines and exploit learning curves in manufacturing and marketing to serve markets in reliable and low cost ways (Katilla and Mang, forthcoming). As Teece and Pisano (1994) explain, when knowledge is tacit, a new firm cannot immediately replicate these assets overnight by entering the market and assembling marketing and manufacturing assets. Because it is easier for new firms to create innovative new products and services than the complementary assets to deliver these products and services to customers, new organizing efforts will be less common in industries in which complementary assets in marketing and manufacturing are relatively more important (Anton and Yao, 1995).

Again, I could find only one piece of empirical evidence to support the proposition that industries in which complementary assets in marketing and distribution are more important are less likely to facilitate new firm formation. Shane's (2001b) examination of patents assigned to the Massachusetts Institute of Technology between 1980 and 1996 showed that the more important complementary assets in marketing and distribution were to appropriating the returns to innovation in an industry, the less likely newly founded firms were to exploit the patents.

INDUSTRY STRUCTURE

Researchers have argued that industry structure influences the level of firm formation across industries. Industry structure is the set of characteristics that affect the long-term competitive dynamics, cost structure and profitability of an industry. Earlier research has examined six dimensions of industry structure that influence new firm formation: industry profitability, cost of inputs, capital intensity, advertising intensity, industry concentration and average firm size. In the subsections below, I review the research that discusses the effect of industry differences in industry structure on opportunities for new organizing efforts.

Profitability of the Industry

When industries are more profitable, new firm formation is more common. High profit margins increase the likelihood that a recombination will be profitable, making people more likely to undertake such efforts. Moreover, when industries are more profitable, an entrepreneur can enter with an uncertain opportunity and be more likely to remain above minimum average cost while the opportunity is being developed (Dorfman, 1987).

One empirical study provides support for the proposition that new firm formation is more common in more profitable industries than in less profitable industries. Acs and Audretsch (1989b) examined net entry by small firms into 247 manufacturing industries in the United States between 1978 and 1980 and found that the rate of entry was higher when the industry price–cost margin was higher.

Cost of Inputs

When an industry has lower cost inputs, it has more plentiful opportunities for firm formation. When input costs are low, many more situations exist in which a person can obtain the resources necessary to exploit an opportunity. Casual empiricism supports this claim. The numbers of people who exploit business ideas in industries in which firms have low cost structures are far greater than those in which businesses have high cost structures. Moreover, this relationship underlies the logic of incubators, which reduce the cost of development of new ventures through subsidies and cost sharing.

Some large sample empirical evidence supports the proposition that new firm formation is more common when input costs are lower. Baum and Oliver (1992) examined the founding of licensed day care centers in Toronto from 1971 until 1989 and found that the rate of firm formation went up as the number of early childhood education graduates increased, presumably because the increase in the number of graduates reduced labor costs. In a more direct test of this argument, Carroll and Huo (1986) examined the formation of 2168 newspapers in the San Francisco Bay area from 1870 to 1980. The authors found that the cost of newsprint had a negative effect on the rate of newspaper formation.

Similar results have been found at more macro levels of analysis. Arguing that countries with higher start-up costs should have fewer entrepreneurs, Fonseca *et al.* (2001) found that the number of weeks and the number of administrative procedures required to start a company were negatively correlated with the rate of transition of people from wage employment to self employment from 1990 to 1997 in 11 countries. Similarly, Bania *et al.* (1993) examined the number of start-ups formed from 1976 to 1978 for six two-digit manufacturing industries in 25 metropolitan areas and found that the start-up rate was inversely related to the labor costs in the area.

Although these studies indicate that lower costs encourage entrepreneurial activity, do those lower costs have any effect on performance at entrepreneurial activity? One might argue that in industries in which costs are relatively low, people will be more likely to identify opportunities in which revenues exceed costs, thereby facilitating entrepreneurial performance.

Some empirical research supports this assertion. Researchers have shown that new ventures are less likely to survive when costs are higher than when costs are lower. For example, Carroll and Huo (1986) found that the cost of newsprint was positively related to the failure of newspapers founded in San Francisco from 1870 to 1980. Similarly, Audretsch and Mahmood (1995) examined the survival of 12 251 new establishments created in 1976 and found that the likelihood of establishment failure was higher in industries in which average wages were higher. Furthermore, Reid (1999) examined the three-year survival of a stratified random sample of 138 clients of the Enterprise Trusts in Scotland and found that higher labor costs reduced the likelihood of new venture survival.

Capital Intensity of the Industry

New organizing efforts are inhibited by the capital intensity of an industry. The development and initial exploitation of an entrepreneurial opportunity results in negative cash flow for a certain period of time, as the venture incurs the cost of plant and equipment, and employees to develop an opportunity, but does not yet generate revenues (Dorfman, 1987). Because new firms do not have capital from existing operations to finance this negative cash flow, they must obtain capital from others. However, information asymmetry problems between entrepreneurs and investors make the financing of entrepreneurial activities problematic for investors (Holmstrom, 1989). These problems lead investors to demand a premium for financing new firms. As a result, the acquisition of external capital is more expensive than the acquisition of internal capital (Gompers and Lerner, 1999). Because this premium is more important to capital intensive ventures than to labor intensive ones, new organizing efforts are disproportionately less common in capital intensive industries.

Empirical research supports the proposition that capital intensity discourages new organizing efforts. Mata (1994) examined the rate of entry of 2999 *de novo* firms into Portuguese manufacturing industries between 1982 and 1986 and found that the more capital intensive the industry, the lower the *de novo* entry rate. Dean and Meyer (1992) examined the rate of creation of new independent establishments in 382 four-digit manufacturing industries from 1976 to 1980, and found that industry capital requirements reduced rates of firm formation.

Does the capital intensity of an industry make new firms founded in that industry more likely to fail? One might argue that capital intensity of an industry should reduce new venture performance. Following the argument presented above, firms founded in more capital intensive industries should find it harder to obtain the external capital that they need to survive and grow, thereby hindering their development.

Consistent with this argument, two empirical studies show that the greater is the capital intensity of an industry, the lower is the likelihood that new firms founded in it will survive. First, Audretsch (1991) examined the ten-year survival rates of 11 000 new firms established in the United States in 1976, and found that industry capital intensity reduced new firm survival rates. Second, Audretsch and Mahmood (1995) examined the survival of 12 251 new establishments created in 1976 and found that industry capital intensity increased the likelihood of new establishment failure.

Advertising Intensity of the Industry

New firm formation is less likely in advertising intensive industries for two reasons. First, brand reputations are developed over time through the cumulative effects of advertising. As a result, new entrants cannot build their brand names to the level of established firm brand names quickly. Second, size creates scale economies in advertising, making small firms less efficient at advertising than large firms (Dorfman, 1987). Because new ventures tend to begin small, their advertising efforts are less efficient than those of established organizations. These two patterns mean that people are less likely to form new firms in industries in which they need to rely heavily on advertising.

While provocative, this argument remains largely untested. I could find only empirical study that even indirectly supports it. In that study, Mata (1994) examined the rate of entry of the 2999 *de novo* firms into Portuguese manufacturing industries between 1982 and 1986. He found that consumer-oriented industries have a lower *de novo* entry rate, suggesting that the advertising intensity of an industry inhibits firm formation.

Industry Concentration

Concentrated industries have lower levels of new firm formation than more fragmented industries. When markets are concentrated, new ventures are more likely to directly challenge the customer base of powerful incumbents that have the resources to drive them out of business before they have gained a foothold in the market (Romanelli, 1989a). As a result, people often decide that it is not worthwhile to exploit opportunities in concentrated industries that they would exploit in more fragmented industries.

The empirical literature supports the proposition that industry concentration reduces the level of new firm formation. Dean *et al.* (1998) examined the number of small establishments entering each of 302 industries between 1976 and 1978, between 1982 and 1984, and between 1986 and 1988, and found a negative correlation between the four-firm concentration ratio and the level of small establishment entry into the industry. Acs and Audretsch (1989b) examined net entry by small firms into 247 manufacturing industries in the United States between 1978 and 1980, and found that the rate of entry was lower when the four-firm concentration ratio was higher. Acs and Audretsch (1989a) examined the gross entry rate of new firms with fewer than 199 employees across 238 manufacturing industries from 1976 to 1982, and found a negative correlation between net small firm entry and the concentration rate. Dean and Brown (1995) examined the number of new independent firms formed in 306 industries between 1976 and 1980, and found that industry concentration was negatively correlated with this measure of new firm entry. Dean and Meyer (1992) examined the rate of creation of new independent establishments in 382 four-digit manufacturing industries from 1976 to 1980 and found that industry concentration had a negative effect on the level of firm formation in the industry.

The argument presented above to explain why new firm formation is less likely in concentrated industries would also predict that new firms should perform better in less concentrated industries. In concentrated industries, new firms will have to tap the customer base of powerful incumbents who will seek to retaliate, driving the new ventures out of business.

Two studies provide empirical support for this argument. Eisenhardt and Schoonhoven's (1990) examination of new semiconductor firms founded between 1978 and 1985 showed that market concentration increased new firm failure rates. Similarly, Baldwin and Johnson (1996) reported that the likelihood of failure of new entrants in Belgian manufacturing was higher if there were more firms in the entry cohort, and if the industry had a higher concentration ratio.

Average Firm Size

New firm formation is less common in industries with larger average firm size. New organizing efforts are enhanced by low average firm size for several reasons. First, the capital constraints facing new organizing efforts increase with firm size because efforts to exploit opportunities through larger firms require more capital than efforts to exploit opportunities through smaller firms. Second, the incentive advantages that new organizing efforts have over established firms that result from their superior ability to distribute equity decrease with firm size. Third, the organizing constraints and risks facing entrepreneurs make it difficult to establish ventures on a large scale. As I will explain in greater detail in Chapter 9, entrepreneurs typically start ventures on a small scale because they are unsure of the value of their ideas. Only after the market informs them of whether demand for their product exists, and whether their offering is better than that of their competitors, do most ventures grow to a large scale. Because new organizing efforts have the smallest incentive advantages, and the largest capital and organizing constraints, in industries with the largest average firm size (Dorfman, 1987), these industries are the least supportive of new firm formation.

Some empirical evidence supports this argument about average firm size. Shane's (2001) examination of inventions patented by the Massachusetts Institute of Technology showed that patents were less likely to be exploited by firm formation when average firm size in an industry was larger. Similarly, Dean *et al.*'s (1998) investigation of the number of small establishments entering different industries showed that the average level of sunk costs per firm (asset size adjusted for depreciation and rental payments) in an industry reduced the rate of small firm entry.

Researchers have also shown that the proportion of small firms in a geographic location is associated with greater amounts of entrepreneurial activity. For example, Johnson and Cathcart (1979) examined the rate of new firm formation across industries in the Northern region of the United Kingdom in the early 1970s. These authors found that the percentage of people in the industry employed in plants of fewer than 100 people had a positive effect on the rate of firm formation in the region. Reynolds (1994a) looked at the rate of new firm birth across 382 labor market areas in the United States and found a negative effect of the size of existing establishments on the rate of firm formation in an area. Hart and Gudgin (1994) examined the rate of new manufacturing firm formation per 1000 manufacturing employees across 26 counties of Ireland from 1980 to 1990, and found a positive effect of the percentage of establishments employing 20 or fewer workers. Kangasharju (2000) examined regional variation in firm formation per 1000 workers in Finland from 1989 to 1993, and found that average establishment size had a significant negative effect on firm formation. Guesnier (1994) examined the rate of firm formation per 100 existing firms and per 1000 active workers from 1986 to 1991 across French regions and found a positive effect of the proportion of small firms.

The three arguments presented above for why new firm formation becomes less common as average firm size in an industry increases also suggest that new venture performance should be worse in industries with larger average firm size. In industries with larger size firms, new ventures face greater capital and organizing constraints, must bear greater risks, and have fewer incentive advantages, than in industries with smaller size firms. As a result, their performance is lower than in industries with smaller sized firms.

Two studies provide empirical support for this argument. Audretsch and Mahmood (1991) examined the survival of 7070 manufacturing establishments that were created in the United States in 1976 over the subsequent ten years. They found that the new establishments were more likely to fail when the minimum efficient scale in the industry was higher. Similarly, Audretsch's (1991) examination of the ten-year survival rates of new firms established in the United States in 1976 showed that the higher the level of economies of scale in an industry, the lower the survival rate of new firms in the industry.

SUMMARY

This chapter examined the effect of the industry context on the exploitation of entrepreneurial opportunities. It examined the empirical evidence for five theoretical perspectives on industry-level differences in the exploitation of entre-preneurial opportunities through the creation of new firms: knowledge conditions, demand conditions, industry life cycles, appropriability conditions and industry structure. Knowledge conditions influence the level of entrepre-neurial opportunity present in an industry, and include such factors as the research and development intensity of the industry, the reliance on innovation by small firms, the degree to which an industry relies on public sector institutions to innovate, and the level of uncertainty in the industry. The empirical evidence shows that firm formation is more common in industries that are more R&D intensive, in which extra-value chain sources of innovation are more important, that have a greater level of small firm innovation, and that are less uncertain.

Demand conditions influence the level of entrepreneurial activity in an industry, and include such factors as the size, growth rate and segmentation of the industry. The empirical evidence shows that firm formation is more common in industries that are larger, faster growing and more segmented.

Industry life cycles examine opportunity exploitation as a function of industry age, dominant design and the endogenous entry and exit of firms. The empirical evidence shows that firm formation is more common in industries that are younger and have not yet converged on a dominant design. In addition, new firm formation initially increases with the number of firms already in the industry and then declines when that number reaches a high level.

Appropriability conditions examine the ability of entrepreneurs to capture the returns to opportunity exploitation as a function of patents, complementary assets and other methods of appropriating the returns to innovation. The empirical evidence shows that firm formation is more common in industries in which patents are more important, and complementary assets in manufacturing, marketing and distribution are less important in appropriating the returns to innovation.

Industry structure considers opportunity exploitation as a function of industry profitability, input costs, capital intensity, advertising intensity, industry concentration and average firm size. The empirical evidence shows that firm formation is more common in industries that are more profitable, have lower cost inputs, are less capital and advertising intensive, are less concentrated and have lower average firm size.

Having explained the effect of the industry context on opportunity exploitation, I now turn to a discussion of the institutional environment, which is the subject of the next chapter.

7. The environmental context o entrepreneurship

As I explained in Chapter 6, people do not make decisions to exploit entrepreneurial opportunities in a vacuum, but instead are influenced by the context in which they operate. One important dimension of the context that influences opportunity exploitation is the institutional environment. The institutional environment consists of the economic, political and cultural context in which the entrepreneur finds herself. Thus, the institutional environment includes both the 'rules of the game' that economists believe generate incentives for certain types of action, and the social setting that sociologists believe determines legitimate and acceptable behavior. In this chapter, I explore the effect of the institutional context on the exploitation of entrepreneurial opportunity.

AN ENVIRONMENT FOR PRODUCTIVE ENTREPRENEURSHIP

Entrepreneurship researchers have long been interested in the institutional environment, both because the institutional context appears to influence entrepreneurial activity, and because it is amenable to the policy levers that government officials can use to influence the amount and form of entrepreneurial activity. Perhaps the most provocative thesis about the effect of institutional environment on entrepreneurial activity has been Baumol's (1990) argument that the number of enterprising individuals and valuable opportunities is constant over time and place, with only the distribution between productive and unproductive forms varying across these dimensions.

Baumol (1990) argued that society's rules and norms create incentives that influence the form that entrepreneurial activity takes. In some societies, at certain points in time, institutional factors provide incentives for rent-seeking entrepreneurial activities (for example, crime and corruption) as opposed to socially productive entrepreneurial activities (for example, founding new organizations).

However, when property rights and rule of law are strong (Baumol, 1990), and when productive entrepreneurial activity is legitimate (Aldrich and Fiol, 1994), entrepreneurial activity takes a socially productive form. Because illegal activities are costly to entrepreneurs, both financially and morally (Fadahunsi and Rosa, 2002), they opt to undertake productive entrepreneurship when that form of entrepreneurship is supported.

Lu (1994) provided a formal model that makes Baumol's (1990) argument more concrete. He showed that if firms are able to influence their tax rates through bribery or other means of influence, entrepreneurs are more likely to engage in unproductive entrepreneurial activity. As a result, Lu (1994) shows that productive and unproductive entrepreneurial activities are substitutes. Moreover, the choice between productive and unproductive entrepreneurship depends on the incentives provided by society's rules and norms, much as Baumol (1990) explained.

A few researchers have examined the distribution of entrepreneurial opportunities across productive and unproductive forms. For example, Fadahunsi and Rosa (2002) explored six case studies of Nigerian traders, and found that the lack of rule of law and property rights led entrepreneurs to engage in bribery to facilitate their entrepreneurial ventures. The importance of bribery to successful entrepreneurial activity also led the majority of people in Nigerian society to view illegal actions as legitimate aspects of business activity.

Moreover, these authors showed that government import–export policies, themselves, created opportunities for profit through smuggling. As Fadahunsi and Rosa, (2002: 397) explained, 'traders target any goods irrespective of their legal status if potential profit margins are high. Entrepreneurial advantage thus lies in the trade itself and making it work, not in its illegality.'

THE INSTITUTIONAL ENVIRONMENT

While many researchers (for example, Shane and Venkataraman, 2000; Venkataraman, 1997) would not accept Baumol's (1990) thesis in its entirety, they do believe that the institutional environment – the economic, political and social context in which an entrepreneur is found – influences people's willingness to engage in socially productive entrepreneurial activity. Box 7.1 summarizes the ways in which researchers have argued that the institutional environment influences opportunity exploitation.[1]

A variety of researchers have provided empirical evidence that sheds light on the basic concepts underlying this argument. In the subsections below, I discuss the empirical evidence for the effect of the institutional environment on the willingness of people to engage in productive entrepreneurial activity. I begin with the economic environment.

The Economic Environment

The nature of the economy in which an entrepreneur is found influences her tendency to engage in entrepreneurial activity. Earlier research has suggested

---

BOX 7.1   THE EFFECT OF THE INSTITUTIONAL
ENVIRONMENT ON OPPORTUNITY
EXPLOITATION

- Economic environment
  - Income, capital gains and property taxes reduce the level of opportunity exploitation
  - Economic growth and societal wealth increase the level of opportunity exploitation
  - Low rates of inflation and stable economic conditions increase the level of opportunity exploitation
- Political environment
  - Freedom increases the level of opportunity exploitation
  - Strong rule of law and property rights increase the level of opportunity exploitation
  - Decentralization of power increases the level of opportunity exploitation
- Socio-cultural environment
  - Social desirability of entrepreneurship increases the level of opportunity exploitation
  - Presence of entrepreneurial role models increases the level of opportunity exploitation
  - Specific cultural beliefs increase the level of opportunity exploitation

---

four areas in which the economic context influences the willingness of people to exploit entrepreneurial opportunities: societal wealth, economic stability, capital availability and taxation.

Wealth

Researchers have long argued that opportunity exploitation is enhanced by societal wealth. First, entrepreneurial activity is more viable when the economy is strong because demand for goods and services, and the ability to get credit tend to be higher during economic expansions than during economic contractions (Campbell, 1992). Second, greater wealth provides potential entrepreneurs with the capital that they need to self-finance their entrepreneurial activities. As I will discuss in the next chapter, most entrepreneurs are capital constrained, and these financial constraints affect their ability to self-finance their new ventures, an important solution to many problems engendered by the uncertainty and information asymmetry that are part of the entrepreneurial process. Third, wealth encourages positive attitudes toward entrepreneurship. In an interesting study of people's attitudes, Jackson and Rodney (1994) showed that income was positively correlated with positive attitudes towards entrepreneurship among a random sample of 1001 individuals. This finding suggests that wealth encourages entrepreneurial activity by making people more likely to consider exploiting entrepreneurial opportunities.

Several empirical studies support the argument that wealth is associated with opportunity exploitation. For example, Audretsch and Acs (1994) examined new firm start-up activity in 117 industries at six points in time between 1976 and 1986 and found that new firm formation was higher when the growth rate of the gross national product was higher. Grant (1996) examined the annual percentage change in new business incorporations in the 48 contiguous states from 1970 to 1985, and found that periods of economic recovery were positively correlated with firm formation, and periods of recession were negatively related to this variable.

Similar results have also been obtained when entrepreneurship was measured as a stock rather than as a flow. Shane (1996) looked at the number of organizations per capita in the United States, a measure of the stock of entrepreneurial activity, from 1899 to 1988. He found that economic growth had a positive effect on this variable. Blau (1987) examined the percentage of the male workforce that was self employed from 1948 to 1982, and found that total factor productivity had a positive effect on the rate of self employment.

Researchers have also obtained consistent results from studies undertaken in other geographic locations. For example, Ritsila and Tervo (2002) examined data on a random sample of Finnish people from 1987 to 1997, and found that a positive stage of the business cycle increased the probability that the subjects would found businesses.

Single industry studies have also produced consistent results for the effect of wealth on opportunity exploitation. Mezias and Mezias (2000) examined the production and distribution of feature films in the United States between 1912 and 1929 and found that growth of the gross national product had a positive effect on the formation of both specialist producers and specialist distributors. Ranger-Moore (1991) examined the formation of Manhattan banks from 1792 to 1980, and American life insurance companies from 1760 to 1937, and found a negative effect of the Great Depression on firm formation rates. Ventresca *et al.* (1999) examined the rate of firm formation in the technology-based on-line database industry from 1972 to 1991, and found that the level of the gross national product had a positive effect on firm formation.

Cross-sectional research that compares geographic locations with each other has shown consistent results for the proposition that economic wealth enhances entrepreneurial activity. Audretsch and Fritsch (1994) examined the cross-region rate of firm formation per 10 000 workers and per 100 firms in Germany from 1986 to 1991, and found a positive effect of per capita value added. Similarly, Keeble and Walker (1994) examined the spatial variation in firm formation per existing firm in the United Kingdom from 1980 to 1990, and found a positive effect for per capita economic growth.

Similar results have been obtained when studies have focused on comparing regions within the United States. Reynolds (1994a) looked at the rate of new firm births across 382 labor market areas in the United States from 1986 to 1988, and found a positive effect of inflation-adjusted per capita income growth. Black and Strahan (2000) examined the rate of new incorporations across US states from 1976 to 1994, and the number of new business start-ups from 1986 to 1994, and found a positive effect of personal income growth on both dependent variables.

The empirical research also supports the effect of wealth as a mechanism to facilitate resource acquisition. For example, Schell and David's (1981) study of county business pattern data in Alabama showed that the creation of new business units was positively related to median family income in the county. Similarly, Reynolds (1994a) examined the rates of new firm formation per existing establishment in 382 labor market areas between 1982 and 1984, and found that labor income and per capita household income in a labor market area increased the rate of firm formation in that area.

Given the argument that societal wealth facilitates opportunity exploitation presented above, one might expect that societal wealth would enhance the performance of new ventures. As I argued above, wealth increases demand, the availability of resources to exploit the opportunity, and positive attitudes toward entrepreneurship, all of which should enhance entrepreneurial performance.

Two empirical studies provide support for this argument. Baum and Mezias (1992) examined the failure rates of Manhattan hotels established between 1898 and 1990, and found that the higher the growth rate of the gross national product, the lower the likelihood that a new hotel would fail. Similarly, Freeman (2000) examined the hazard of failure of 4064 venture capital backed new businesses from 1987 to 1995, and found that the level of business failure in the economy in the month of observation increased the likelihood of new venture failure.

Economic stability

Researchers have argued that stable fiscal and monetary policies encourage opportunity exploitation because economic stability makes people more confident in their entrepreneurial decisions (Harper, 1997). When inflation is high or people do not expect economic or currency stability, they find it difficult to invest in entrepreneurial opportunities. Because entrepreneurs must obtain resources at one point in time and sell the output of the transformation of those resources at another, unstable economic conditions make it very difficult to make forward-looking decisions. Even the most valuable entrepreneurial opportunities are swamped by macro-economic forces, as occurs when an entrepreneur has obtained capital just as a deflationary cycle sets in. Similarly, McMillan and Woodruff (2002) explain that if buyers typically have 30 days to pay for goods, an economic shock, like a severe credit tightening, might lead them to renege on their commitment to pay. Fearing this possibility, entrepreneurs might demand immediate payment from their customers instead of offering credit, thereby inhibiting entrepreneurial activity.

Anecdotal evidence about societies that experience conditions of hyperinflation and economic instability support this argument. Most societies experiencing these economic conditions see a dramatic reduction in new firm formation and other entrepreneurial activity. For example, according to newspaper reports, during the periods of hyperinflation in Latin America in the 1970s and 1980s, the number of people founding new companies in Brazil and Argentina dropped dramatically from the level that they had experienced in more stable periods.

Two scientific studies support this anecdotal evidence about the relationship between inflation and entrepreneurial activity. In a comparison of transition economies, McMillan and Woodruff (2002) found that that entrepreneurial activity grew much faster in those countries that had lower rates of inflation than those that suffered from higher inflation. Similarly, Highfield and Smiley (1987) examined quarterly data on the growth rate of new incorporations in the United States from the third quarter of 1948 to the fourth quarter of 1977, and found that lower inflation led to greater new incorporation growth in subsequent periods.

Capital availability
Researchers have argued that a third dimension of the economic environment that influences opportunity exploitation is the availability of capital. Capital availability encourages opportunity exploitation by generating competition among investors to finance entrepreneurs, thereby reducing the threshold at which investors will provide resources (Amit *et al.*, 1998). Consequently, when capital is more readily available, more entrepreneurs can obtain financing for their opportunities, leading more of them to act to exploit entrepreneurial opportunities.

Empirical research supports the proposition that capital availability encourages opportunity exploitation. Pennings (1982a) found that availability of capital increased firm formation rates in the plastics and electronic equipment industries in a cross-sectional study of 70 metropolitan statistical areas from 1967 to 1975. Similarly, Dobbin and Dowd (1997) examined the founding of Massachusetts railroads between 1825 and 1922, and found that the condition of the British capital market, an important source for financing new railroad ventures in the United States at that time, had a positive effect on the rate of railroad formation. McMillan and Woodruff (2002), summarizing several studies of entrepreneurial activity in transition economies, found that credit availability was an important factor that influenced entrepreneurial activity in these economies.

A related argument to the capital availability argument is that concerning interest rates. Researchers have argued that firm formation should be more common when interest rates are lower. If people make decisions about exploiting opportunities that they have discovered by considering the expected value of the stream of payments from the exploitation of the opportunity, then the cost of the capital used to exploit the opportunity should influence their decisions. When capital costs are higher, the expected value of fewer opportunities will exceed the entrepreneur's opportunity cost, liquidity premium and uncertainty premium, making them less likely to exploit opportunities.

Two empirical studies shed light on this argument. First, Shane's (1996) examination of the number of organizations per capita in the United States over time showed that the average rate of interest in the economy had a negative effect on this measure. Second, Audretsch and Acs (1994) examined new firm start-up activity in 117 industries at six points in time between 1976 and 1986, and found that firm formation was lower when interest rates were higher.

The arguments and empirical evidence presented above indicate that fewer people exploit entrepreneurial opportunities when capital costs are higher because the expected value of fewer opportunities will exceed the entrepreneurs' opportunity costs, liquidity premiums and uncertainty premiums. This argument also suggests that entrepreneurs will perform better at entrepreneurial activity when interest rates are lower because the entrepreneurs' opportunities will generate greater profits under these conditions.

Three studies provide empirical support for this argument. First, Barron *et al.* (1994) examined state chartered credit unions in New York City from 1914 to 1990, and found that the credit unions were more likely to fail in the years of economic depression and in years when bond yields were high. Second, Audretsch and Mahmood (1995) examined the survival of 12 251 new establishments created in 1976, and found that interest rates had a positive relationship with the likelihood of new establishment failure. Third, Baum *et al.* (2000) examined the performance of 142 Canadian biotechnology firms founded between 1991 and 1996, and found that the amount of capital available in the biotechnology sector at founding and in the preceding year, had a positive effect on the new ventures' employment growth.

Because many people exploit entrepreneurial opportunities by using equity from their major asset – their home – house values should be positively associated with opportunity exploitation. House values provide equity that can be used to undertake efforts to exploit entrepreneurial opportunities. Moreover, the effect of house values should be relatively large because, as I will explain in greater detail in the next chapter, most entrepreneurs must self-finance the exploitation of their opportunities.

Several pieces of empirical research support the argument that house values are positively associated with opportunity exploitation. Three studies provide evidence at a macro-level by comparing across geographic locations. Keeble and Walker (1994) examined the spatial variation in firm formation per capita and per firm across regions of the United Kingdom from 1980 to 1990, and found a positive effect for house values. Similarly, Guesnier (1994) examined the rate of firm formation per 10 000 active workers across French regions from 1986 to 1991, and found a positive effect of percentage of owner-occupied dwellings. Reynolds (1994a) looked at the rate of new firm births across 382 labor market areas in the US from 1986 to 1988, and found positive effects for both the percentage of owner-occupied dwellings and the mean dwelling value. Barnett and Carroll (1993) provide support for the same argument about house values in a longitudinal study. These authors found that the formation of independent telephone companies from 1907 to 1942 increased with the value of farm buildings.

A fourth argument about capital availability and opportunity exploitation offered in the literature is that the availability of venture capital in an area will encourage the formation of new firms. To overcome information asymmetry and uncertainty problems in the financing of entrepreneurial opportunities, venture capitalists have emerged as specialists in financing entrepreneurial opportunities (Sahlman, 1990; Sorenson and Stuart, 2001; Gompers and Lerner, 1999; Gupta and Sapienza, 1992; Lerner, 1995). These financiers provide risk capital; connect entrepreneurs with suppliers, customers, lawyers and employees; and assist entrepreneurs with the development of their new ventures (Florida and Kenney, 1988; Gupta and Sapienza, 1992; Gorman and Sahlman, 1989; Gompers and Lerner, 1999; Sorenson and Stuart, 2001). The existence of these specialized sources of funds for financing entrepreneurial opportunities is important because some industries and some geographic locations receive greater amounts of venture capital funding than others (Amit *et al.*, 1998). In industries and geographic locations where venture capital is more readily available, new organizing efforts are more prevalent because more people are able to obtain the capital that they need to act on their entrepreneurial opportunities.

Several empirical studies support the argument that venture capital availability encourages opportunity exploitation. For example, Stuart and Sorenson (2002) examined biotechnology formation rates and found a positive effect of the number of venture capital firms in the same metropolitan statistical area as the start-ups. Similarly, Amit *et al.* (1998) demonstrated positive correlations between venture capital availability and rates of firm formation across industries in Canada.

Taxes

Taxes are a fourth dimension of the economic environment in which entrepreneurial activity takes place. Researchers have argued that higher marginal tax rates reduce opportunity exploitation for two reasons. First, higher marginal tax rates make people less willing to accept variable earnings, thus decreasing the likelihood of self employment (Hubbard, 1998). Second, high marginal tax rates reduce people's perceptions of the profitability of exploiting opportunities, thereby reducing the likelihood that they will act on the opportunities that they recognize (Harper, 1997).

In general, anecdotal evidence is quite supportive of the argument that taxes reduce the level of productive entrepreneurial activity. Many newspaper accounts have described how people choose not to exploit entrepreneurial opportunities that they have identified because the marginal tax rate that they would face was too high to make that effort worthwhile. Moreover, several policy-oriented studies that examine the problems that nations have in encouraging entrepreneurial activity indicate that high tax rates are a major culprit. For instance, Goldfarb and Henrekson (forthcoming) investigated why Sweden produces more new technology on a per capita basis than the United States, but has a much lower rate of new firm formation. The authors explain that Swedish tax policy makes entrepreneurial activity uneconomical.

Some scientifically generated empirical evidence also supports this argument. Gentry and Hubbard (2000) examined data from the Panel Study on Income Dynamics from 1979 to 1992, and found that the higher the marginal federal income tax rate was in the United States, the lower the rate of self employment. Blau (1987) examined the percentage of the male workforce that was self employed from 1948 to 1982, and found that the marginal tax rate on $7000 in 1967 dollars had a negative effect on the rate of self employment. Robson and Wren (1999) examined data on self employment for the OECD countries in the 1980s and found a negative relationship between marginal tax rates and self employment rates. Lastly, Dana (1987) examined the relationship between efforts to cut taxes and business formation. He found that business tax concessions encouraged firm formation in the Virgin Islands and Cayman Islands.

High capital gains tax rates also discourage productive entrepreneurial activity. Bygrave and Timmons (1985) examined the amount of venture capital flows from 1969 to 1982, and found that a reduction of the capital gains tax rate increased venture capital flows. Assuming that venture capital funds are used efficiently, the implication of the Bygrave and Timmons (1985) study is that the reduction in the capital gains tax rate encouraged opportunity exploitation by making more capital available to entrepreneurs.

Given the argument presented above, one might expect that taxes reduce performance at entrepreneurial activity. If higher taxes discourage people from exploiting opportunities or make them less willing to accept variable earnings, then they will distort entrepreneurial decision-making. These distortions could lead new ventures to generate less income, grow more slowly, or become more likely to fail.

Despite the importance of this question, very little empirical research has examined the effect of taxes on performance at entrepreneurial activity. However, newspaper accounts of entrepreneurship in many nations with high tax rates on entrepreneurial activity, such as Russia, indicate that entrepreneurs often refrain from growth to minimize the taxes that their new ventures have to pay.

One study that has examined the impact of taxes on the growth of new ventures scientifically is Carroll *et al.* (1989). In this study, the authors examined a random sample of 6817 sole proprietors aged 25 to 55 in 1985 who filed a schedule C (to report self employment income) on their federal tax returns between 1985 and 1988. They found that higher taxes reduced the growth of the entrepreneurs' ventures, an effect consistent with the problematic distortions to entrepreneurial activity that researchers have suggested result from taxation.

The Political Environment

Like the economic environment, the political environment is an important dimension of the context in which entrepreneurial activity takes place. The political environment influences the exploitation of entrepreneurial opportunity by influencing the perceived risks and returns of the entrepreneurial activity. Several dimensions of the political environment influence a person's willingness to exploit entrepreneurial opportunity, most notably, freedom, property rights and centralization of power (Harper, 1996).

Freedom

Political freedom is the freedom from being subjected to the will of others. It encourages opportunity exploitation for several reasons. First, opportunity exploitation involves the acquisition of information about entrepreneurial opportunities and political freedom encourages the free exchange of information (Hayek, 1945). Second, political freedom encourages the development of the internal locus of control that, as I described in Chapter 5, facilitates the exploitation of entrepreneurial opportunity (Harper, 1998). People who live in environments in which they are subject to the arbitrary exercise of the will of others tend to have less internal locus of control and therefore are less responsive to entrepreneurial opportunities (Harper, 1997).

Despite the importance of the theoretical argument that political freedom encourages opportunity exploitation, virtually no scientific studies have explored this question. However, some quasi-scientific evidence does exist. Several country-level measures of the degree of political freedom in different nations, such as those provided by the World Economic Forum, appear to be correlated positively with measures of the level of self employment, new firm formation and business people's perceptions of the ease of economic activity across nations. These correlations suggest that opportunity exploitation is facilitated by the provision of political freedom to the members of a society.

Property rights

Property rights are the rights to own and contract for assets according to an established set of rules and laws. Strong property rights enhance the exploitation of entrepreneurial opportunity for several reasons (Hebert and Link, 1988). First, the rule of law, a key component of strong property rights, increases freedom from coercion (Harper, 1997). As a result, under strong property rights, people believe that any entrepreneurial profit that they earn will not be taken away from them arbitrarily, facilitating opportunity exploitation. Second, rule of law makes the legal framework stable, allowing entrepreneurs to make plans to exploit perceived opportunities with a reasonable degree of confidence that the rules of the game will be the same in the future as in the past (Harper, 1997). Third, the rule of law facilitates the coordination of resources in transactions that occur at different points in time because it increases the confidence that those who provide them with access to resources have legitimate rights to them (Harper, 1997). Fourth, the rule of law allows for greater division of labor and specialization because it allows for the enforcement of contracts (Libecap, 1993). As a result, entrepreneurs can obtain financial and human resources from external parties, and do not have to internalize the entire value chain to exploit opportunities. These characteristics encourage opportunity exploitation at the margin by people whose opportunities are best exploited through contractual organizational arrangements, and who need to obtain capital and labor from external sources. Fifth, the rule of law encourages the investment in innovation because it facilitates the appropriation of the returns to innovation (Casson, 1995). As I described in the last chapter, people will not exploit entrepreneurial opportunities unless they believe that they can appropriate the returns from such exploitation. The use of trade secrets, patents and complementary assets – three of the major mechanisms for appropriating returns to innovation – depends, at least in part, on legal arrangements. Therefore, those environments in which property rights and the rule of law are stronger have greater levels of exploitation of entrepreneurial opportunities.

Again, this set of arguments would suggest a significant body of empirical evidence relating strong property rights to entrepreneurial activity. However, direct empirical evidence of this relationship is lacking. On the one hand, rigorous social science research demonstrates an empirical relationship between the rule of law and economic activity, but cannot directly attribute that improved economic activity to the tendency for people to exploit entrepreneurial opportunities. Rather, this research stream can merely assert that entrepreneurial activity is the mechanism through which this relationship operates. On the other hand, anecdotal evidence provides a more direct relationship between strong property rights and opportunity exploitation, but is subject to the criticism that this evidence is not scientific. For example, bivariate correlations between country-level measures of the perceived strength of property rights in different nations, such as those provided by the World Economic Forum, appear to be correlated positively with different measures of opportunity exploitation at the country level. Similarly, Johnson *et al.* (2002b) report that, during the transition from communism, a larger proportion of Russian entrepreneurs than Polish entrepreneurs explained that bribery was necessary to start a business, and that Russia had less entrepreneurial activity than Poland during this period. McMillan and Woodruff (2002) report that during transition, Russian entrepreneurs were less willing than Polish entrepreneurs to invest in their businesses and had to expend more time and money to start businesses, which is consistent with the argument that weak property rights discourage entrepreneurial activity. Researchers have also reported a relationship between an effective legal system and financial regulation, on the one hand, and the establishment of trade credit and the growth of trading partners by entrepreneurs on the other (Frye and Schleifer, 1997; Johnson *et al.*, 2002a).

Centralization of power
Centralization is the degree to which one political actor coordinates the economic, political and social activity in a society. The classic examples of centralized societies are communist and fascist nations, in which the government coordinates most human activity, ranging from where people can live, to where they can work, what they can read, and with whom they can associate. The exploitation of entrepreneurial activity is facilitated by decentralization. Hayek's (1945) famous critique of socialism was based on the problem of centralization. To Hayek, centralization is inferior to a market system because the central actor attempts to make all decisions, despite inferior information. Because the market system relies on the efficient exploitation of bits and pieces of information held by different actors, a decentralized market system can make most decisions better than a centralized one. As a result, in a decentralized market society, people can make decisions about the exploitation of entrepreneurial opportunities on the basis of idiosyncratic information gathered through their life course. Central actors simply lack the information to make the same decisions as efficiently, leading centralization to reduce the level of opportunity exploitation.

In addition, centralization influences people's attitudes toward opportunity exploitation. Specifically, centralization makes people's locus of control less internal because economic success in centralized societies depends less on one's own actions than on those of the state (Harper, 1997). Because internal locus of control facilitates the decision to exploit, centralization reduces the likelihood that people will exploit entrepreneurial opportunities (Earl, 1990; Gilad, 1982).

Furthermore, centralization reduces the dependence of rewards on one's own effort. In centralized societies, the relationship between entrepreneurial action and market-based rewards, in the form of entrepreneurial profit, is dampened or eliminated. Because the prospect of entrepreneurial profit provides an incentive for opportunity exploitation (Gilad, 1982), centralization reduces the incentive for entrepreneurship. As Libecap (1993) explained, when returns are constant or arbitrary, there is simply little incentive to search out or exploit entrepreneurial opportunities.

Researchers have gathered several types of evidence that supports the argument that opportunity exploitation is enhanced by decentralization. At a micro level, Shane (2000) shows that efforts by technology licensing officers to determine the entrepreneurial opportunities that emerge from university inventions are generally incorrect, and reduce the number of new ventures formed to exploit those inventions, as compared to letting market mechanisms decide how those entrepreneurial opportunities should be exploited.

At a more macro level, several observers have argued that the tremendous growth in new firm formation and self employment in the former communist nations of Eastern Europe that followed the transformation of those nations to free market systems, demonstrates the relationship between decentralization and the exploitation of entrepreneurial opportunities. By freeing people from the constraints of the central planner, potential entrepreneurs in all of these countries were able to use their idiosyncratic information to make decisions to exploit opportunities that the central planners had lacked the information to make. As a result, this transformation led to a dramatic growth in entrepreneurial activity.

The socio-cultural environment
The socio-cultural environment is a third dimension of the institutional environment that influences entrepreneurial activity. The socio-cultural infrastructure consists of the beliefs and attitudes of the members of society as to what are desirable and legitimate activities, as well as the social and cultural institutions that support a particular society's way of life. The socio-cultural environment influences the exploitation of entrepreneurial opportunity by influencing the desirability of entrepreneurial activity and the perceived risks and returns of such endeavors.

The social and cultural environment influences the amount of opportunity exploitation in a society in several ways. First, social and cultural norms influence the degree to which entrepreneurial activity is considered socially desirable among members of a community (Aldrich, 1990; Aldrich and Fiol, 1994). For example, positive attitudes toward profit-seeking behavior through the pursuit of opportunity enhance the status of an entrepreneurial career, thereby making people more willing to engage in such careers (Casson, 1995).

In contrast, negative attitudes towards entrepreneurship may discourage people from engaging in this activity (Gnyawali and Fogel, 1994) because people's behavior is influenced by what others think of them (Minniti, 1999). As a result, in societies in which people have negative attitudes toward entrepreneurial activity, people do not consider, or consider and reject, the exploitation of entrepreneurial opportunities when they are confronted with situations in which they could engage in that activity.

Second, social norms influence the number of people who have already engaged in entrepreneurial activity and thus the presence of experienced entrepreneurial role models. For reasons described in Chapter 4, much of the knowledge necessary for entrepreneurial activity is learned by doing, and is transmitted through social networks, apprenticeship or observation of others. The presence of experienced entrepreneurial role models influences the level of knowledge about entrepreneurship present in the social group, thereby facilitating access of people to that knowledge. As a result, societies with more experienced entrepreneurial role models have more novice entrepreneurs willing to exploit entrepreneurial opportunities.

Third, certain cultural beliefs encourage entrepreneurial activity. The exploitation of entrepreneurial opportunity involves certain types of decision-making, specific approaches to resource acquisition, distinct strategies and particular methods of organization design. Specific norms and cultural beliefs are associated with these types of actions. For example, social norms that encourage using one's own judgment to make decisions facilitate entrepreneurial activity because entrepreneurship involves making judgmental decisions. Similarly, cultural beliefs that support reciprocity and moral commitments encourage entrepreneurial activity by facilitating resource acquisition under conditions of uncertainty and information asymmetry (Harper, 1997). Because some societies hold the norms and beliefs that encourage entrepreneurial activity to a greater extent than others, the socio-cultural environment influences the tendency of people to exploit entrepreneurial opportunity.

Some empirical evidence supports these arguments. For example, entrepreneurial activity is more common among ethnic groups and in geographical locations where it is considered more socially desirable. For example, Butler and Herring (1991) examined 7542 respondents to the General Social Survey from 1983 to 1987 to determine which members of American society were self employed. They found strong evidence of cultural differences in self employment. In comparison to all other ethnic groups, Butler and Herring (1991) found that Irish, African, Hispanic and Polish people have a lower likelihood of self employment than other groups, and that Jews had a higher likelihood of self employment. These results support anecdotal arguments about the cultural characteristics of different ethnic groups that support or hinder entrepreneurial activity.

Blanchflower *et al.* (2001) found similar patterns by comparing nations rather than by comparing immigrant groups. These authors examined data from the International Social Survey, a random sample of people in 23 nations in 1997 and 1998. They found evidence of huge national differences in the preference for self employment, and that such preferences were positively correlated with actual self employment.

Some researchers have sought to determine whether cultural beliefs directly affect decisions to engage in opportunity exploitation. For instance, Swanson and Webster (1992) found that negative attitudes toward entrepreneurs discouraged people from starting companies in the Czech and Slovak republics. Similarly, Begley *et al.* (1997) surveyed 861 MBAs from seven countries and found that perceptions of high social status of entrepreneurs in a country increased the tendency of the MBAs to engage in entrepreneurial activity in that country.

The existing empirical evidence also supports the argument that the presence of role models who provide knowledge about the exploitation of entrepreneurial opportunities encourages opportunity exploitation. In a very interesting study of attitudes toward entrepreneurship, Walstad and Kourilsky (1998) used Gallop Organization survey data on a random sample of 1008 youths in 1995 to compare the attitudes of African-Americans and white youths. The authors found that African-American youths were significantly less likely than white youths to know someone who ran a small business or to have a parent who ran a small business. The survey also showed that African-American youths were also less likely than white youths to know that prices in a competitive market, like the United States, were determined by supply and demand, and were less likely to believe that prices should rise in response to a shortage of goods. The authors interpreted these responses to indicate a lack of positive cultural beliefs toward entrepreneurship among African-American youths, which they attributed to the lack of entrepreneurial role models in the African-American community.

The lack of entrepreneurial role models in the African-American community is corroborated by a series of studies. Borjas and Bronars (1989) examined the 1980 US census to show that able African-American people were less likely to choose self employment than able white people. Bates (1995b) used the 1984 panel of the Survey of Income and Program Participation to show that minorities were less likely than whites to become self employed. Schiller and Crewson (1997) examined data from the National Longitudinal Survey of Youth, to show that white respondents were more likely than African-American respondents to become self employed. Finally, Smith (1992) used data from the 1982 and 1987 General Social Surveys to demonstrate that white respondents were more likely than African-American respondents to own their own businesses.

Other evidence supports the argument that greater entrepreneurial experience within specific ethnic groups encourages self employment. For example, using

US census data, Cobas (1986) found that immigrant groups to the United States often had high levels of self employment in the United States because they had high levels of entrepreneurial activity in their home countries.

SUMMARY

This chapter examined the effect of the institutional environment in which entrepreneurs operate on the exploitation of entrepreneurial opportunities. The institutional environment is composed of both the set of incentives or 'rules of the game' to which economists believe that people respond, and the social legitimacy and acceptance which sociologists believe influence human behavior. The effect of the institutional infrastructure on productive entrepreneurial activity can be divided into three categories of factors: the economic environment, the political environment and the cultural environment. All three sets of factors influence the exploitation of entrepreneurial opportunities.

Four aspects of the economic environment influence the exploitation of entrepreneurial opportunities: wealth, economic stability, capital availability and taxation. Three aspects of the political environment influence the level of opportunity exploitation in a society: political freedom, the system of property rights and the centralization of power. The social and cultural environment influences the amount of opportunity exploitation that takes place in a society in three ways: by influencing the degree to which entrepreneurial activity is considered desirable among members of a community, by affecting the number of people who are entrepreneurial role models, and through specific cultural beliefs that encourage or discourage entrepreneurial activity.

Having explained the effect of the institutional environmental context on opportunity exploitation, I now turn to a discussion of the resource acquisition process.

.

NOTE

1. The institutional environment also probably influences the discovery of opportunity. However, I focus on the effect of the institutional environment on the exploitation of opportunity in this book because of the paucity of theoretical or empirical research discussing the relationship between the institutional environment and the discovery of opportunity.

8. Resource acquisition

This chapter explores the process by which people acquire financial resources to exploit entrepreneurial opportunities. Because the exploitation of an entrepreneurial opportunity requires the acquisition and recombination of resources before the sale of the output from that recombination, it must be financed. This financing process can and does include financing by the entrepreneur herself. In fact, in the vast majority of cases, founders finance the exploitation of entrepreneurial opportunity out of their own savings (Aldrich, 1999).

However, the financing of entrepreneurial opportunities can also involve the acquisition of capital from external sources. External financing can take a variety of forms, including equity investment, debt financing, asset-based financing, and grants from governments and not-for-profit agencies. The amounts of financial resources obtained through external financing can range from a few thousand dollars to hundreds of millions of dollars. The sources of external financing can include friends and family members, business angels, banks, venture capital firms, governments, and even, in very rare cases, public markets.

Regardless of the type of financing, source of financing, or the amount of financing, two basic characteristics of the exploitation of entrepreneurial opportunities influence the resource acquisition process – uncertainty and information asymmetry. As I explained in earlier chapters, entrepreneurship is a process in which people identify opportunities to recombine resources to bring future goods and services into existence (Venkataraman, 1997). To discover entrepreneurial opportunities, people must possess idiosyncratic information or beliefs (Kirzner, 1973). Resource owners would not make inputs available at a price that permitted entrepreneurial profit if they held the same beliefs and information as the entrepreneurs that seek their resources (Shane and Venkataraman, 2000). Moreover, entrepreneurial opportunities are uncertain because resources must be obtained and recombined before the profitability of the recombination is known (Arrow, 1974a).

The information dispersion and uncertainty that give rise to the existence and discovery of entrepreneurial opportunities make it difficult for entrepreneurs to acquire the resources that they need to pursue them (Venkataraman, 1997). In the next section of the chapter, I explain why resource acquisition is important to the pursuit of entrepreneurial opportunities. In the second section of the chapter, I explain why uncertainty and information asymmetry make such resource acquisition difficult. The remainder of the chapter then focuses on explaining the variety of solutions that entrepreneurs and investors use to cope with these problems, including self-financing, contractual provisions, pre-investment tools, post-investment tools, quality signaling, social ties and entrepreneurial behavior.

THE IMPORTANCE OF RESOURCE ACQUISITION

Obtaining adequate capital is important to the exploitation of entrepreneurial opportunities for several reasons. New ventures with more capital are more likely to survive, grow and become profitable because capital provides a buffer that entrepreneurs can use to respond to adverse circumstance (Carroll and Hannan, 2000; Ranger-Moore, 1997; Banaszak-Holl, 1991; Delacroix and Swaminathan, 1991; Baum and Mezias, 1992; Taylor, 2001). Moreover, having more capital overcomes liquidity constraints that limit the approaches that entrepreneurs can take to pursuing opportunities. Furthermore, capitalization influences external stakeholders' perceptions of the stability, legitimacy and dependability of new ventures (Baum, 1996).

The empirical evidence supports the proposition that adequate capitalization is important to the exploitation of entrepreneurial opportunities. For example, Bates (1990, 1994, 1995b) explored data from the Characteristics of Business Owners database on new ventures and found that new businesses with more start-up capital were more likely to survive over time. Similarly, Bruderl and Preisendorfer (1998) studied 1710 new ventures founded in Germany in the mid-1980s and found that their level of start-up capital increased their three-year survival rates. Cooper *et al.* (1988) and Gimeno *et al.* (1997) compared survivors and non-survivors among samples of new ventures founded by members of the National Federation of Independent Businesses, and found that the survivors had higher initial capitalization than non-survivors. Bates and Servon (2000) used data from the US Bureau of the Census to examine the survival of 15 129 firms founded between 1986 and 1992 over the 1992 to 1996 period. They found that the level of capital raised by the ventures increased their likelihood of survival.

Similar results have been found when entrepreneurship has been measured as self employment. For instance, Holtz-Eakin *et al.* (1994b) examined the performance of people who became self employed in 1982 and 1983, and found that the subjects' liquid assets were positively and significantly correlated with the continuation of self employment. Taylor (1999) used data from the British Household Panel Survey to show that the initial wealth of the self employed reduced the probability that they would exit self employment through bankruptcy.

Firms with greater access to capital at founding also appear to grow faster and larger, perhaps because firms with more capital can make greater investments and expand more rapidly (Taylor, 2001). Reynolds and White (1997) report that, in their study of 2624 new firms founded in the mid-1980s, growth rates were positively correlated with the level of initial financial support that the firms received. Bamford *et al.* (1997) examined the growth of 491 new banks founded between 1985 and 1988, and Bamford *et al.* (2000) examined the growth of 140 new banks established in 1988. Both studies found that the more capital a bank had at founding, the higher were its revenues in subsequent years.

Similar results for the value of access to capital have been found when the data on new firm growth have been collected outside the United States. Bruderl and Preisendorfer's (1998) study of new German ventures showed that the amount of start-up capital invested in the venture was positively correlated with three-year sales and employment growth. Lee *et al.* (2001) examined 137 Korean technology start-up companies who were enrolled in the Korean Small and Medium Business Administration, an organization that gives subsidies and tax breaks to new firms. These authors found that the firms that had greater invested capital and more venture capital investors had higher two-year sales growth than other firms in their sample. Westhead (1995) examined the factors that predicted the employment growth from 1986 to 1992 of 77 independent high technology firms in the United Kingdom. He found that firms that had obtained capital from external sources in an earlier period grew larger than those that had not obtained external capital.

Initial capitalization also appears to increase the profitability of new ventures. Gimeno *et al.* (1997) examined 1547 new firms whose founders were members of the National Federation of Independent Business, and found that the amount of initial capitalization increased the level of income that the founders subsequently took out of their businesses. Similarly, Holtz-Eakin *et al.* (1994a) examined the performance at self employment of people who received an inheritance in 1982 and 1983. They found that the receipt of an inheritance of $150 000, a sizeable capital inflow, raised self employment earnings by 20 per cent. Using data from the British National Child Development Study, Burke *et al.* (2000) also found that the receipt of a gift or inheritance increased the income of the self employed.

The positive effect of capitalization on new venture performance has been shown for the specific case of access to formal venture capital. Formal venture capital is a particularly important source of capital for the creation of high potential ventures. While venture capitalists finance less than 1 per cent of all new businesses, they finance approximately one-third of all companies that achieve initial public offerings. Moreover, because venture capitalists give strategic advice, find acquisition partners and identify suppliers and senior managers through their information networks, entrepreneurs often find them a very valuable source of external capital (Gorman and Sahlman, 1989).

The amount of venture capital received by new ventures increases their rate of employment and sales growth, reduces their likelihood of failure and increases their likelihood of achieving an initial public offering. Megginson and Weiss (1991) compared a matched sample of 320 venture capital and 320 non-venture capital backed firms that went public between 1983 and 1987 and found that the venture capital backed firms had higher initial returns and lower gross spreads at their initial public offerings. Shane and Stuart (2002) examined the life histories of 134 new companies founded to exploit intellectual property assigned to the Massachusetts Institute of Technology from 1980 to 1996. These authors found that the cumulative amount of venture capital raised by the firms reduced the likelihood of venture failure, and increased the likelihood of an initial public offering. Freeman (2000) examined the performance of 4064 venture capital backed new firms from 1987 to 1995 and also found that the cumulative amount of venture capital raised by the companies reduced the likelihood of failure and increased the likelihood of an initial public offering. Manigart (1999) looked at 187 venture capital backed firms in Belgium that received their investments between 1988 and 1995, and compared them with a matched sample of non-venture capital backed firms. They found that, over a five-year period, the venture capital backed firms had greater growth in assets, greater growth in profits and greater growth in personnel.

Another concept related to the amount of capital received by the venture is how efficiently that capital is used. New ventures often obtain debt in addition to the equity capital that they receive. The ratio of debt to equity varies across ventures and is measured by the amount of leverage that the venture has. Because ventures that have higher leverage actually obtain more capital to use for operating activities relative to the amount of their capitalization, one would expect that new ventures with higher financial leverage would perform better than new ventures with lower financial leverage.

In fact, two pieces of empirical research support this proposition. Using data from the Characteristics of Business Owners Database, Bates (1994) showed that the survival from 1987 to 1991 of 1615 firms founded by Asian immigrants from 1979 to 1987 was higher for firms with greater leverage. Similarly, Bates (1995b) used the same dataset to show that the survival from 1987 to 1991 of a larger sample of 19 463 firms founded between 1984 and 1987 was also enhanced by financial leverage.

THE DIFFICULTIES OF RESOURCE ACQUISITION UNDER UNCERTAINTY AND INFORMATION ASYMMETRY

While the discussion on the preceding pages shows that it is important for entrepreneurs to obtain adequate capital to exploit their entrepreneurial opportunities, obtaining capital is not easy. The information asymmetry and uncertainty that are necessary conditions of the discovery and exploitation of entrepreneurial opportunities create several obstacles to the acquisition of resources to pursue entrepreneurial opportunities. Box 8.1 summarizes these difficulties by dividing them into two categories – those created by information asymmetry and those created by uncertainty.

BOX 8.1   PROBLEMS IN RESOURCE ACQUISITION

Information asymmetry

Disclosure difficulties
Opportunism
Excessive risk taking
Adverse selection

Uncertainty

Inability to evaluate
Bargaining problems
Need for collateral

Information Asymmetry

Information asymmetry between entrepreneurs and potential capital providers creates four obstacles to capital acquisition. First, the entrepreneur's use of superior access to information, or better ability to recognize opportunities, means that the entrepreneur knows things about the opportunity and the method for exploiting that opportunity that potential capital providers do not know. Because this information advantage is what will enable the entrepreneur – if she is correct – to earn an entrepreneurial profit, the entrepreneur wants to keep this information secret, rather than disclose it to others. Disclosure of the information would spur others to seek the resources necessary to exploit the opportunity, bidding up their price and reducing the potential entrepreneurial profit (Casson, 1982). Moreover, because the resource providers have adequate financial resources to self-finance the exploitation of the entrepreneurial opportunity, they could exploit the opportunity without the entrepreneur if they learned all of what the entrepreneur knew about the opportunity and the method of exploitation. As a result, the entrepreneur cannot disclose all relevant information when seeking finance (Casson, 1995), and resource providers must make decisions about providing resources with less information about the opportunity and the method of exploitation than the entrepreneur possesses.

Second, the information asymmetry that the entrepreneur possesses makes it possible for her to act opportunistically toward capital providers. In addition to their greater knowledge about the opportunity and method of exploitation just described, entrepreneurs possess more information than resource providers about their own commitment, abilities and status of efforts to develop their ventures. Entrepreneurs could make use of this information advantage to take advantage of resource providers by extracting a better deal than is otherwise warranted, by obtaining more resources than their venture deserves (Shane and Cable, 2002), or by gaining greater concessions than a fully informed resource provider would supply. By engaging in such actions as threatening to depart from the venture (Shane and Stuart, 2002), failing to deliver the level of effort to develop the company that they promised to resource providers, or by taking action to generate private wealth at the expense of the resource providers (Shane and Cable, 2002), the entrepreneurs could use their superior information to take advantage of their investors. Consequently, the resource providers must protect themselves against the potential for opportunistic action by entrepreneurs.

Third, information asymmetry that exists between entrepreneurs and investors encourages entrepreneurs to undertake excessive risk with the investors' resources. The outcome of the venture is at least partially dependent on the actions of the entrepreneur. However, given information asymmetry, it is very difficult for the investor to monitor the entrepreneur's actions. As a result, the resource provider will need to compensate for the risk of default by offering fixed rate financing at a high interest rate. This financing arrangement would cause the entrepreneur to bear all of the risk of variation in potential outcomes, but to do so at a fixed cost. The potential for upside variation at a fixed cost will lead the entrepreneur to favor risky projects with high potential returns (Barzel, 1987).

Fourth, information asymmetry will allow for adverse selection. Most people do not identify and exploit valuable opportunities, in part because they lack the ability to do so. People lacking entrepreneurial ability who have discovered poor quality opportunities seek financing along with those people possessing entrepreneurial ability who have discovered high quality opportunities. If the investor cannot distinguish between these two groups of entrepreneurs, there is a potential for adverse selection. Because the resource providers face this potential for adverse selection – choosing the low ability entrepreneurs with the poor quality opportunities – they make financing offers to entrepreneurs at the average price across entrepreneurs and opportunities of all quality levels (Amit *et al.*, 1990b). Because this price is more attractive to low ability entrepreneurs with low quality opportunities than to high ability entrepreneurs with high quality opportunities, it drives high ability entrepreneurs and high quality opportunities from the market (Amit *et al.*, 1990b).

Uncertainty

Uncertainty creates three obstacles to capital acquisition. First, uncertainty about the entrepreneurial opportunity may make resource providers unable to evaluate the potential of new ventures. The ability of entrepreneurs to exploit specific opportunities, and the value of those opportunities themselves, are largely unknown prior to their exploitation. Much of the information that resource providers could use to evaluate a venture cannot be obtained until after resources have been provided to the venture and a functioning organization has been established, a new product or service created, and a track record started (Arrow, 1974a; Shane and Stuart, 2002). If the entrepreneur does not have an observable product or service or a historical track record, the resource provider must make her financing decision on little more than her own judgment about the value of a potential resource recombination (Bhide, 2000). Because this judgment is based on very little objective evidence, investors face high risks when selecting among entrepreneurs and opportunities (Low and Srivatsan, 1994).

Second, uncertainty means that the net present value of the new venture's profit stream cannot be objectively evaluated, leading the resource providers to develop perceptions about the profitability and attractiveness of the venture, which may differ from those of the entrepreneur (Wu, 1989). As a result, bargaining problems are likely to ensue, with the resource holder offering less than what the entrepreneur believes is the value of the opportunity.

Third, given the uncertainty of the process of opportunity exploitation, resource providers would like assurances that the entrepreneur will pay up if her judgment proves wrong. However, the entrepreneur cannot repay the resource provider from the proceeds of the venture if her judgment is incorrect because incorrect judgment will mean that the venture generates no profit (Casson, 1982). To overcome this problem, the resource provider wants the entrepreneur to provide collateral that has value that investors can tap into in the event that the venture fails (Blanchflower and Oswald, 1998). Unfortunately, this need for collateral means that only those entrepreneurs who have assets to pledge as collateral can obtain external capital.

THE SOLUTIONS TO THESE DIFFICULTIES

Given the problems engendered by the pursuit of uncertain opportunities by entrepreneurs with asymmetric information, the acquisition of resources involves several important characteristics: self-financing by the entrepreneur, contractual constraints on the exploitation process, pre-investment tools, post-investment tools, social ties, entrepreneurial behavior and quality signaling. In the subsections below, I explore each of these characteristics.

Self-Financing

Both uncertainty and information asymmetry between entrepreneurs and investors motivate the importance of self-financing to the entrepreneurial process. Knight (1921) argued that entrepreneurs need to use their own capital to exploit entrepreneurial opportunities because the information asymmetry between entrepreneurs and resource providers would create problems of moral hazard and adverse selection in the financing process. Specifically, the information asymmetry between entrepreneurs and investors makes resource providers reluctant to invest in the specialized assets that are used to develop the new venture for fear of being taken advantage of by unscrupulous entrepreneurs. This problem is mitigated if the entrepreneur makes large irreversible investments to the venture (Venkataraman, 1997). By investing, the entrepreneur makes the return on her investment at least partially contingent on her own effort. Because the value of the entrepreneur's investment in her own venture would fall if she does not put forth the required effort to exploit it, the investment serves as a bond to ensure that the entrepreneur is not acting against the interest of the investors (Barzel, 1987; Rumelt, 1987).

Moreover, self-financing overcomes the uncertainty inherent in the entrepreneurial process. By pledging her own assets, the entrepreneur can collateralize the venture for investors who cannot observe her opportunity, nor predict its outcome in advance. As a result, with self-financing, the investors are no longer required to bear all of the uncertainty of exploitation of the opportunity.

The empirical literature demonstrates the importance of self-financing as a solution to the uncertainty and information asymmetry problems present in new venture finance. According to the US Bureau of the Census data, approximately 70 per cent of people finance their new businesses with their own capital (Aldrich, 1999). In fact, apart from a small number of ethnic communities, even family members do not provide much capital to new businesses. The US Department of Census data indicates that, on average, family members (including spouses) provide less than 8 per cent of all capital borrowed by new ventures (Aldrich, 1999).

Several studies have documented the frequency with which entrepreneurs self-finance. Blanchflower and Oswald (1998) examined data on 243 self employed people from the National Survey of the Self-Employed, a random sample of 12 000 British adults. They found that more people used their own savings to finance their businesses than received money from banks and family and friends combined. In fact, the need for self-financing is so great that 20.1 per cent of the respondents cited in Blanchflower and Oswald (1998) explained that their biggest concern in becoming self employed was where to get capital. Moreover, the largest category of responses to a question about what help would have been most useful in the firm formation process, identified by 26.3 per cent of the sample, was help with money/finance.

This pattern does not appear to be very different across types of entrepreneurial opportunities, with high potential high technology ventures showing similar patterns to the average new venture. Roberts (1991a), for example, found that 74 per cent of the 154 technology start-ups he studied used personal savings as their initial source of capital, roughly the same percentage as the US Census data cited by Aldrich (1999).

The results described above suggest that people will fail to exploit entrepreneurial opportunities if they lack the capital to self-finance. Data presented by Blanchflower and Oswald (1998) provides support for this proposition. These authors report results from British Social Attitudes Survey, an annual sampling of 5947 members of the British population from 1983 to 1989, to explain why 451 people had given serious consideration to self employment, but did not become self employed. They found that lack of capital was the number one reason, in 51.3 per cent of cases.

Moreover, several studies indicate that people with greater income or assets are more likely to be self employed, presumably because they have the resources to self-finance the exploitation of their opportunities. For example, Butler and Herring (1991) examined data on 7542 respondents to the General Social Survey and found that income at age 16 increased the likelihood of self employment later in life. At a more macro-level of analysis, Eisenhauer (1995) examined self employment data in the United States from 1959 to 1991 and found that when the real level of assets per capita increased, the rate of self employment in the country went up.

More precise estimates of the effect of the ability to self-finance on entrepreneurship have been found in studies of the transition to self employment. For example, using data from the 1984 panel Survey of Income and Program Participation conducted by the US Bureau of the Census, Bates (1995b) showed that greater net worth increased the transition of people to self employment. Similarly, Fairlie (1999) examined a sample of 6417 male heads of households from the Panel Study on Income Dynamics from 1968 to 1989 and found that the amount of assets that they had increased their probability of self employment. Praag and Pohem (1995) and Evans and Leighton (1989) examined data from the National Longitudinal Survey and found that the probability of entering self employment increased with the amount of assets belonging to the subject.

Similar results have been shown in studies in other countries. Examining a random sample of workforce-aged Swedes, Delmar and Davidsson (2000) found that people who were in the process of starting a business had a higher net worth than a control group of people who were not in the process of starting a business. Johansson (2000) examined Finnish microdata on 103 482 people aged 18 to 65, for the period from 1987 to 1994, and showed that that wealthier people, and people who owned their own homes, were more likely to become self employed. Uusitalo (2001) examined a sample of 85 417 respondents from the Income Distribution Surveys conducted by Statistics Finland between 1990 and 1997, as well as a survey of 37 000 Finnish army recruits in 1982, and found that household wealth had a positive effect on the probability of self employment.

Similar results have been obtained when financial resource availability was measured as the value of one's home or investment income. For example, Bernhardt (1994) examined data from the Social Change in Canada Project survey and found that people with higher investment income, and who owned a home, were more likely than others to become self employed. Taylor (1996) examined data from the British Household Panel Study and found that the amount of equity that the respondent had in her home had a positive effect on their probability of self employment. Ritsila and Tervo (2002) examined data from a 0.2 per cent random sample of the Finnish workforce, collected from 1987 to 1997, and found that home ownership increased the probability that a person would found a business.

Unfortunately, all of the studies described above are subject to the criticism that assets, net worth and home equity value could all be correlated with unobserved factors that influence the discovery and exploitation of entrepreneurial opportunities. As Cressy (2000) has explained, greater wealth could make people more likely to take risks and therefore more likely to discover and exploit opportunities. Alternatively, people with greater wealth could have more entrepreneurial talent and therefore be more likely to discover and exploit opportunities.

To show that having capital increases the likelihood that people will exploit opportunities by allowing people to overcome constraints to self-financing, more sophisticated research designs are necessary. Three studies focus on the exogenous increase in capital generated by the receipt of an inheritance to examine this issue. Blanchflower and Oswald (1998) examined the National Child Development Study data, a longitudinal investigation of a cohort of 6885 people born in Britain in the first week of March, 1958 and resurveyed after 7, 11, 16, 23 and 33 years. These authors found that the receipt of an inheritance had a curvilinear relationship with self employment, first rising and then falling. As a result, a £5000 inheritance (in 1981 pounds) made people twice as likely to engage in self employment as those people who did not inherit. Burke *et al.* (2000) examined data on 1465 people from the same survey, and found that the probability of self employment increased if the individual received an inheritance or financial gift. For an inheritance of £75 000, the probability of self employment increased by 6 per cent. Holtz-Eakin *et al.* (1994a) examined the 1981 and 1985 US Federal income tax returns for people who received inheritances in 1982 and 1983. They found that the probability of having a schedule C (to report self employment income) on their tax forms in 1985, but not in 1981, increased upon the receipt of an inheritance, and that the effect was greater the fewer assets that the subject had in 1981. They estimated the magnitude of this effect to be a 3.3 per cent increase in the probability of shifting to self employment following the receipt of a $100 000 inheritance.

A third study examined an even better exogenous factor on transition to self employment – winning a lottery. Unlike receiving an inheritance, which could be correlated with the transfer of entrepreneurial talent or skills from parent to child, winning a lottery has nothing whatsoever to do with parental occupation, skills or abilities. Lindh and Ohlsson (1996) examined 4402 people in the Swedish Level of Living Survey who won the lottery. The authors found that the present value of the lottery winnings had an inverted U-shaped relationship with the probability of self employment. That is, people who won a moderate sized lottery became significantly more likely to become self employed, presumably because the lottery winnings provided an exogenous increase in their capital that facilitated the self-financing of the entrepreneurial opportunities that they discovered.

The limitations of self-financing
Although an entrepreneur could self-finance the purchase of the inputs needed to exploit an entrepreneurial opportunity, such an approach faces two limitations. First, many people lack the assets, income, inheritance, lottery winnings and even house values necessary to finance their entrepreneurial opportunities. Consequently, entrepreneurs are likely to face capital constraints, which limit their ability to actually exploit opportunities if they only rely on self-financing. Second, self-financing increases the risk of entrepreneurial activity because it requires the entrepreneur to bear all of the potential downside loss. For this reason, entrepreneurs often seek to obtain resources from others. Given the problems of uncertainty and information asymmetry inherent in the entrepreneurial process how do entrepreneurs obtain this external capital?

Contractual Solutions

One partial solution to the problems in resource acquisition generated by information asymmetry and uncertainty lies in the design of contracts between entrepreneurs and investors. While sometimes used by other investors, the use of contractual solutions to these problems are primarily adopted by venture capitalists, perhaps because of the significant transaction costs they impose and perhaps because other solutions (to be discussed below) are more effective for other types of investors than for venture capitalists (Landstrom *et al.*, 1998).

Researchers have identified four components of contractual solutions to the information problems that are present in new venture finance: the use of equity rather than debt as a source of financing, the use of convertible securities, the use of restrictive covenants on the behavior of entrepreneurs, and forfeiture and anti-dilution provisions.

Equity
As I explained above, one of the major problems engendered by the information asymmetry between entrepreneurs and investors is the potential for the

entrepreneur to engage in moral hazard. Specifically, entrepreneurs tend to engage in risky actions with investors' money when they obtain debt capital at a fixed interest rate. Ravid and Spiegel (1997) and Weinberg (1994) demonstrate formally that the exclusive use of equity is an optimal solution to this problem under conditions of uncertainty in which outsiders cannot observe the decisions of entrepreneurs. Using equity in place of debt to provide capital reduces the incentive for entrepreneurs to undertake activities with a negative net present value, thereby mitigating the moral hazard problem described above.

Convertible securities

Convertible securities are financial instruments that allow investors to own preferred stock, which has a liquidation preference, but which can also be converted to common stock at the investors' option. The use of convertible securities mitigates three of the problems in resource acquisition that result from the uncertainty and information asymmetry present in the entrepreneurial process. First, investors can use convertible preferred stock to identify high quality entrepreneurs and opportunities, mitigating adverse selection problems. Because entrepreneurs respond to contractual terms offered to them, the use of convertible preferred stock separates high and low quality entrepreneurs. Only high quality entrepreneurs with good opportunities are willing to accept convertible preferred stock because of the cost and risk it imposes upon them (Sahlman, 1990).

Second, convertible preferred stock minimizes the entrepreneur's tendency to take risks that the information asymmetry present in the entrepreneurial process makes possible. This change in behavior occurs because the convertible preferred stock makes the compensation of entrepreneurs more responsive to performance when investors, who are not involved in day-to-day operations of the venture, cannot judge actual performance (Kaplan and Stromberg, 2001).

Third, the liquidation preference that preferred stock provides gives investors preference over other parties in the event of a liquidation of the venture's assets. By increasing the likelihood that the investor will receive some value from their investment if the venture is liquidated, convertible preferred stock mitigates the need for collateral that results from uncertainty (Sahlman, 1994).

Gompers (1997) provides some empirical support for the value of convertible preferred stock in overcoming information problems in venture finance. Examining 50 venture capital contracts used by a variety of venture capital firms and the start-ups that they financed, he found a disproportionate (to random) use of convertible shares. Moreover, he found that investors tended to convert preferred stock to common stock after information was revealed about the venture, thereby demonstrating the value of convertible preferred stock as a tool to manage information problems.

Covenants

To protect themselves against moral hazard and hold-up by entrepreneurs, investors also forbid certain activities, which would allow the entrepreneur to take advantage of the investors by exploiting their greater information about the venture and its opportunity. The covenants used by investors include barring the sale or purchase of assets and the issuance or sale of shares by the founders without permission of the investors. They also include mandatory redemption rights that give investors back their investment at any time (Gompers, 1997).

Several empirical studies provide support for the use of covenants to protect investors from problems that result from information asymmetry and uncertainty in financing new ventures. For example, Gompers (1997) used his examination of 50 venture capital contracts to show that all venture capital contracts have at least some of the above mentioned restrictions on entrepreneurs' behavior. Similarly, Kaplan and Stromberg (2001) examined 213 investments by 14 venture capital firms in 119 new ventures and found that venture capitalists used these provisions plus vesting and non-compete provisions to make it more difficult for entrepreneurs to take problematic actions, particularly early in the venture when hold-up is more of a threat.

Forfeiture and anti-dilution provisions

Investors also use forfeiture and anti-dilution provisions to mitigate the problems in resource acquisition generated by information asymmetry and uncertainty. For example, Hoffman and Blakely (1987) explain that investors use provisions that cause entrepreneurs to lose ownership if their performance falls below target goals, and anti-dilution provisions that transfer ownership from entrepreneurs to investors if the venture fails to meet its performance targets. These provisions provide an excellent screen to weed out talented from untalented entrepreneurs. As Sahlman (1990: 510) noted, 'It would be foolish for the entrepreneur to accept these terms if they were not truly confident of their own abilities and deeply committed to the venture.'

They also provide an incentive for entrepreneurs not to engage in moral hazard. Anti-dilution provisions force entrepreneurs, not investors, to bear the cost of poor performance. With these provisions, the entrepreneurs' ownership declines if performance falters. Therefore, any efforts to divert resources to personal gain in place of efforts to build the venture will result in decreasing returns to the entrepreneur from venture ownership, thereby reducing their incentive to engage in such activity.

Limits to explicit contracting

While helping to overcome many of the problems in venture finance generated by information asymmetry and uncertainty, explicit contracting is necessarily an incomplete solution to these problems for several reasons. First, given the uncertainty present with new ventures, it is virtually impossible to write complete contracts to govern their financing. If contracts are incomplete, there is always the possibility of ex-post haggling by opportunistic entrepreneurs (Williamson, 1985). Second, contracts can never eliminate the ability or incentive for entrepreneurs to act against the interests of investors (Venkataraman, 1997; Arrow, 1974a) and so can never completely resolve moral hazard problems. Third, as I explained in Chapter 5, entrepreneurs are over-optimistic (Cooper, Woo, and Dunkelberg, 1988), which undermines the effectiveness of contract terms as screening mechanisms. While it might be wise for untalented entrepreneurs to self-select out of financing, entrepreneurial over-optimism hinders the effectiveness of self-selection. Fourth, investors cannot shift all of the risk of new venture finance to entrepreneurs while, at the same time, participating in financing the venture. The only way to shift risk to the entrepreneur completely would be to require the entrepreneur to self-finance. Any attempt to protect all of the resource provider's investment in the event of a negative outcome would be tantamount to asking the entrepreneur to self-finance completely.

Because contractual solutions to the problems of uncertainty and information asymmetry in venture finance are not completely effective, resource providers often use several pre- and post-investment tools to manage these problems. I discuss these tools below, describing the pre-investment tools first.

Pre-Investment Tools

Investors employ four pre-investment tools to overcome the problems of uncertainty and information asymmetry in venture finance. They are: due diligence, specialization, geographically localized investing and syndication.

Due diligence
One way that investors minimize information asymmetry in financing new ventures is to conduct due diligence. By collecting information about entrepreneurs and their opportunities prior to investing, investors can select out poor entrepreneurs and unprofitable projects (Sahlman, 1990). This effort helps to reduce the potential for adverse selection (Barry, 1994) because it reduces the level of asymmetric information that the entrepreneur possesses (Van Osnabrugge, 2000).

The empirical literature supports this argument. Kaplan and Stromberg (2001) report that venture capitalists spend a great deal of time engaging in due diligence before investing in new ventures. Similarly, Mason and Harrison (1996) conducted interviews with 31 business angels and 28 owner–managers in the United Kingdom and found that the typical investor talked at length to the entrepreneurs in whose ventures they were asked to invest, visited the venture's premises, and examined detailed information about the venture's financial structure, cash flow and profit forecasts.

Specialization

To select and monitor ventures better, investors also specialize in the industry in which the new venture would operate and the technology that it would use (Barry, 1994). Specialization generates contacts with suppliers, customers, operating firms and technical experts who can provide information that assists resource providers in learning about the entrepreneurs and opportunities in which they are considering investing. Moreover, the use of these contacts helps the investor to gauge the accuracy of information provided by those entrepreneurs by providing a source of verification of those data (Sorenson and Stuart, 2001). Furthermore, experience in an industry allows the investor to monitor new ventures more effectively by allowing the investor to learn about patterns across ventures that indicate trouble in a particular market or with a particular technology. Finally, greater industry experience provides industry-specific knowledge that facilitates the development of appropriate routines for selecting and monitoring investments (Sorenson and Stuart, 2001).

Some empirical evidence supports the idea that investors specialize to overcome moral hazard and adverse selection problems in new venture finance. The probability of venture capital investment in a start-up increases with a venture's similarity to the industries in which the investor has invested previously (Sorenson and Stuart, 2001). In a survey of 141 business angels, Van Osnabrugge (1998) found that investors were more likely to focus on industry sectors with which they were familiar than ones with which they were unfamiliar. Norton and Tenenbaum (1993) surveyed 98 venture capitalists and found that venture capitalists tend to focus on a single stage of venture development, a single technology, or a single product as a way to help them to evaluate the information about opportunities and methods of exploitation presented to them by entrepreneurs.

This argument also suggests that industry specialization should be more important in early stage investments than in later stage investments. Information asymmetry problems should decline as ventures become more advanced because, over time, ventures develop track records that can be used to evaluate them. Moreover, as ventures are developed, additional sources of information about them are created. Gupta and Sapienza (1988, 1992) found empirical support for this argument, showing that venture capitalists specializing in early stage ventures preferred to invest in a narrower range of industries than venture capitalists making later stage investments.

Geographically localized investment

To minimize information and uncertainty problems, investors also make highly localized investments in new ventures. By focusing on a geographic area, investors develop a network of trusted contacts that they can use to assess the accuracy of information about venture opportunities presented to them by entrepreneurs. Moreover, geographic concentration of effort increases the likelihood that the investor will receive redundant and overlapping information that can provide convergent validity about an entrepreneur or an opportunity (Sorenson and Stuart, 2001). Furthermore, geographic proximity facilitates monitoring by making frequent visits to the venture easier.

Some empirical evidence supports the argument that resource providers make localized investments to overcome problems in resource acquisition created by uncertainty and information asymmetry. Because monitoring is more difficult and more costly at a geographic distance, investors should be more likely to invest in and serve on the boards of directors of new ventures if those ventures are geographically proximate. Lerner (1995) examined 271 biotechnology firms that received venture capital between 1978 and 1989, and found that venture capitalists located within 5 miles of the start-up are twice as likely as those 500 miles away to be on a venture's board. Similarly, Sorenson and Stuart (2001) examined the investment decisions of venture capitalists and found that the investors are twice as likely to invest in new ventures within ten miles of their offices as those 100 miles away.

The need to monitor investments also means that when information asymmetry is highest, investors should make the most geographically proximate investments (Kelly, 2000). As I explained above, information asymmetry declines as firms become more developed, thereby reducing the need for geographically proximate investments. Gupta and Sapienza (1988, 1992) provided support for this argument when they examined the investment patterns of 169 venture capitalists. These authors found that venture capitalists specializing in early stage ventures were more likely to make geographically proximate investments than those specializing in later stage ventures.

Consistent with the idea that investors may learn information about opportunities from experience, older venture capitalists are able to make investments on opportunities for which they have less information. As a result, they can make less geographically proximate investments. In support of this argument, Sorenson and Stuart (2001) found that older and more experienced venture capitalists make less geographically constrained investments.

Syndication

Syndication of investments also helps resource providers to overcome information asymmetry and uncertainty problems in venture finance. Syndication helps to manage the irreducible uncertainty that is part of the entrepreneurial process by allowing investors to diversify their investments. By syndicating, resource providers can invest smaller amounts across a wider variety of investments than they could if they only made direct investments. Syndication also helps to reduce information asymmetry by facilitating the process of information acquisition. Information about entrepreneurs and opportunities moves within networks of investors who work in specific geographic and industry space. By syndicating, venture capitalists increase the number of parties from whom they can gather information about opportunities and entrepreneurs from outside those geographic and industry boundaries, thereby increasing the amount of information that they receive (Sorenson and Stuart, 2001). Furthermore, Lerner (1994) explains that syndication provides a way to check the validity of information, arguing that venture capitalists favor syndication as a way to compare their own evaluation with that of others.

Some empirical evidence supports the idea that syndication is a useful mechanism for controlling information asymmetry and uncertainty problems in new venture finance. Bygrave (1988) found that the top 21 venture capital firms investing in technology ventures were closely tied by joint investments. Van Osnabrugge (1998) surveyed 141 business angels and found that serial investors, who presumably had better knowledge of how to invest than one-time investors, were more likely to engage in co-investing. Lerner (1994) examined *Venture Economics* records on biotechnology firms financed by venture capital between 1978 and 1989, and found that experienced venture capitalists syndicate more with each other in early rounds, which is consistent with the idea that they syndicate to confirm their information about where to invest.

Post-Investment Tools

Investors also employ several post-investment tools to manage the problems in resource acquisition created by the information asymmetry and uncertainty present in the entrepreneurial process. The three key post-investment tools are: the allocation of control rights, real options approaches to investing, and involvement with new ventures.

Allocation of control rights
One post-investment tool to mitigate information and uncertainty problems in new ventures has been for entrepreneurs to allocate control rights to resource providers. Control rights are the rights to decide how to use the venture's assets. The investor can mitigate the entrepreneurial moral hazard in situations in which entrepreneurs have more information than resource providers, by preserving control rights over the firm's assets (Gompers and Lerner, 1999; Kaplan and Stromberg, 1999; Van Osnabrugge, 2000). By limiting the entrepreneur's use of venture assets, the allocation of control rights to investors makes it more difficult for entrepreneurs to take morally hazardous action.

Kirilenko (2001) provides a formal model to show that investors can control the behavior of entrepreneurs by retaining control rights in amounts that are disproportionate to their ownership stake and that increase as the information asymmetry between entrepreneurs and investors goes up. This argument suggests that venture capitalists will control the board of directors of new companies even if they do not have a majority share of ownership in the new venture.

In support of this argument, Gompers (1997) found disproportionate board seats to ownership stakes among venture capitalists. Similarly, Kaplan and Stromberg (2001) found that venture capitalists make cash flow, control and voting rights contingent on observable information about performance of the venture, and allocate voting, board and liquidation rights to preserve control of the venture if performance is poor. Moreover, Kaplan and Stromberg (2001) found that venture capitalists exerted greater control over the votes and board seats as the potential for entrepreneurial moral hazard increased, which is consistent with this argument.

Real options approaches to investing

Investors also mitigate the problems in resource acquisition created by uncertainty and information asymmetry by treating investments in new ventures as real options. Real options in venture finance provide the right, but not the obligation, to make future investments. Also known as staged financing, this process involves making a small initial investment in a venture. If the results of that investment prove to be negative, the investor can elect not to invest further (Sorenson and Stuart, 2001). However, if the results of the initial investment prove to be positive, then the investor can elect to make an additional investment.

Some empirical evidence supports the argument that investors treat investments in new ventures as real options to manage information asymmetry and uncertainty problems. For example, Bhide (2000) found that the average *Inc* 500 firm, the fastest growing private firms in the United States, was started with less than $30 000 in capital even though these ventures ultimately raised much greater amounts of capital from investors. Similarly, the US Census Department data indicate that 60 per cent of new businesses required less than $5000 of initial capital, only 3 per cent required more than $100 000 and less than 0.5 per cent required more than $1 000 000 of initial capital (Aldrich, 1999). However, the average amount of capital raised by new ventures over their entire lives is far greater than these amounts of initial capital.

One way in which real options help investors is to mitigate adverse selection problems. Staging of investments helps to separate high and low quality entrepreneurs and opportunities because only talented entrepreneurs with good opportunities would be willing to accept staged investments (Venkataraman, 1997). Entrepreneurs who have opportunities that they know to be poor or who know themselves to be incompetent would not accept staged investments because they would know that their low quality would be revealed before they received much capital.

Staging is also a useful device for precluding entrepreneurial moral hazard because it allows an investor to exit an investment with smaller loss than would be the case if a single up-front lump sum investment was made (Sahlman, 1990). An options approach allows the investor to gain information about the venture and not supply additional capital unless positive information is received (Giudici and Paleari, 2000). By having the ability to withdraw further funding, the investor can reduce the likelihood that an entrepreneur will invest in a negative net present value opportunity. Staging forces the entrepreneur to reveal information about the negative net present value investment before all of the funds necessary to pursue that opportunity have been received (Sahlman, 1994).

Some empirical evidence supports the argument that staging reduces the incidence of entrepreneurial moral hazard. Kaplan and Stromberg's (2001) examination of 213 venture capital investments showed that the greater the potential for entrepreneurial moral hazard that existed in a venture, the more that the investors limited financing until performance milestones were met.

Staging of investments also reduces the threat of entrepreneurial hold-up. Over time, the value of an opportunity and the entrepreneur's method of exploiting it become embedded in the venture itself. As a result, value of the venture's physical assets independent of the entrepreneur and her information about the opportunity tends to grow, increasing the venture's collateral value.

In the beginning, when the venture has little in the way of physical assets, the investor is subject to the potential for entrepreneurial hold-up. In the early days of the venture, the entrepreneur may attempt to renegotiate the terms of the contract by threatening to leave and fail to fully embed the opportunity into the venture's assets. By staging investments, the investor can protect the early rounds of investment from entrepreneurial hold-up because staged investments lower the financial gain to the entrepreneur of this opportunistic behavior. Later, when the gain from opportunistic renegotiation would be larger, the value of the venture's physical assets protects the investor against renegotiation (Neher, 2000).

One empirical study, that by Gompers (1995), provides empirical support for this argument. Gompers (1995) examined a random sample of 794 venture capital backed firms between 1961 and 1992 and found that as ventures age, investors stage investments with longer duration between rounds.

Researchers have also argued that hold-up is more common in industries with more firm-specific assets because asset specificity makes hold-up by the entrepreneur more feasible (Williamson, 1985). Gompers (1995) found empirical support for this proposition as well, demonstrating that investments in industries with more specific assets had more investment stages of shorter duration than industries with less specific assets.

Lastly, the use of real options approaches mitigates the problems that uncertainty creates in new venture finance. At the initial stage of discovery and shortly thereafter, opportunities are most difficult to evaluate. However, as the opportunity is developed, information about the value of the opportunity and the operations of the venture are revealed, and uncertainty is reduced (Sorenson and Stuart, 2001).

Given this pattern of uncertainty reduction, investors find it very difficult to make early investments, and find that staging those investments is valuable. Delaying a sunken investment until after some uncertainty is resolved by the achievement of particular milestones, such as the issuing of a patent or the launch of a product, has an option value. The achievement of these milestones reduces uncertainty by confirming that the venture has met necessary (but not sufficient) conditions for entrepreneurial profit to be earned (Neher, 2000).

The idea that investors delay investments until after uncertainty has been reduced suggests that self-financing of new ventures should transition into external financing after the venture has achieved observable milestones marking its development (Barzel, 1987). In fact, some empirical evidence supports this argument. Bates (1997) examined US Census data on the loan amounts received by 5882 non-minority borrowing firms from 1979 to 1987, and found that being an ongoing business had a positive effect on the amount of money these ventures received. Similarly, Basu and Parker (2001) examined the financing received by 82 British Asian entrepreneurs who obtained outside capital and found that the more hours the founders worked in their business, the more funding they received.

Earlier research also shows that the achievement of observable milestones is important to the acquisition of external capital. For example, the hiring of employees is an important milestone to investors because employees provide another source from which to gather information about the venture and the opportunity; because hiring employees indicates that the entrepreneur was able to persuade another individual of the value of the opportunity; and because the success of the opportunity depends on more than just the information and efforts of the entrepreneurial team. Making initial contact with customers is a valuable milestone to investors because ventures that have made contact with customers have information about customer needs, purchasing criteria and ways to market and promote the products to those customers. The creation of a product is a valuable milestone to investors because a venture cannot earn revenues unless it has a good or service that meets customers' needs. Lastly, the achievement of a first sale is a valuable milestone because it indicates that the venture has a product or service that meets the needs of at least one customer.

Some empirical evidence supports the argument that the achievement of venture development milestones facilitates the acquisition of external capital. For example, Roberts (1991a) studied 109 technology start-ups and found that those entrepreneurs who already had a product raised more capital than those who did not yet have a product. Similarly, Eckhardt *et al.* (2002) showed that 223 new Swedish ventures were more likely to receive external financing if they had already hired employees and had completed product development than if they had not yet achieved these milestones.

Involvement with new ventures

Investors also mitigate information problems in new venture finance through active involvement with new ventures (Kaplan and Stromberg, 2001). This involvement includes such actions as requiring entrepreneurs to provide them with regular updates of information about the venture (Kelly, 2000), and even includes participation in the day-to-day operations of the ventures. By participating in the day-to-day operations of the venture, investors can gather their own source of information about the venture, resolve problems if the information that they gather indicates that something is amiss (Sahlman, 1990), and maintain a credible threat to replace the venture's management if need be (Van Osnabrugge, 2000).

Presumably, if investors become involved in the operations of new ventures to mitigate information problems, this involvement should be higher when the problems of information asymmetry are greatest. Researchers have argued that information asymmetry decreases as ventures develop because venture development provides information that is available to the investor as well as the entrepreneur (Kelly, 2000). Moreover, innovativeness of the venture increases problems of information asymmetry because fewer sources of comparison information exist for more innovative ventures than for less innovative ventures.

The empirical evidence supports the proposition that venture involvement is higher in the early stages of venture development and for more innovative ventures. Sapienza (1989, 1992) examined 51 venture capitalist–entrepreneur dyads and found that investors were more involved with the ventures in early stage ventures and in ventures in which the founder had a small equity stake. Similarly, Sapienza and Gupta (1994) found more monitoring in venture capitalist–entrepreneur dyads when the ventures were in earlier stages of development or were more innovative.

Social Ties

Although investors certainly use the contractual mechanisms and pre- and post-investment tools described above to manage the problems of information asymmetry and uncertainty in the resource acquisition process, these explanations do not consider a whole range of behavioral (as opposed to economic) solutions to these problems. Sociologists, psychologists and organization theorists have long argued that, under conditions of uncertainty and information asymmetry, people make use of information about others' behavior and their social ties to make decisions (Granovetter, 1985; Venkataraman, 1997).

Therefore, one might expect that resource providers make use of these factors to determine which entrepreneurs and opportunities to finance.

Social ties are an important tool in overcoming information asymmetry and uncertainty problems in venture finance because they provide four benefits to investors. First, if the investor knows the entrepreneur, the relationship between the parties will reduce the likelihood that the entrepreneur will act opportunistically towards the investor. Social ties reduce the tendency for people to act in a self-interested manner by infusing the relationship with the logic of social obligation, generosity, fairness and equity (Marsden, 1981; Uzzi, 1996; Granovetter, 1985; Gulati, 1995). Working together generates familiarity, the ability to predict the counterpart's behavior, and the ability to understand the counterpart's character (Aldrich, 1999). These things, in turn, lead to trust (Low and Srivatsan, 1994) and feelings of friendship (Aldrich and Fiol, 1994). As Cable and Shane (1997) explain, information exchange is better when investors and entrepreneurs know each other, because social ties enhance trust.

Second, social ties preserve ongoing relationships. Not only do people in an ongoing relationship have an incentive to preserve that relationship for future interactions, but also social ties provide a way to enforce implicit contracts through the sanctioning mechanisms of social networks. This sanctioning occurs, for example, when investors communicate negative information about those who acted improperly (Macaulay, 1963; Granovetter, 1985; Bradach and Eccles, 1989; Coleman, 1990; Raub and Weesie, 1990; Stuart and Robinson, 2000).

Third, social ties provide an important mechanism for information transfer that overcomes problems of information asymmetry (Burt, 1992). Because information about new ventures and entrepreneurs is not publicly available, social networks provide a key mechanism for the rapid transmission of information about them (Aldrich and Zimmer, 1986; Gulati and Gargiulo, 1999; Uzzi, 1996). Moreover, social ties in an industry or location are useful for confirming the accuracy of information about an investment opportunity.

Fourth, social ties increase the level of positive attributions made about others under uncertainty. Investors often look to social status as a way to infer quality about new venture opportunities because the entrepreneur's competence and opportunity are uncertain (Podolny, 1994; Stuart *et al.*, 1999). Because people prefer to interact with others of similar social status, investors see this social interaction as 'evidence' of the quality of the entrepreneur and her judgment (Lounsbury and Glynn, 2001).

In sum, these arguments suggest that direct ties between entrepreneurs and investors should increase the likelihood of resource acquisition.

Direct ties
Direct ties are personal relationships between the entrepreneur and the investor (Larson, 1992). The empirical literature indicates that direct ties facilitate

resource acquisition under uncertainty and information asymmetry (Podolny, 1994). For example, Kelly (2000) found that private investors often use close friends and business contacts to locate investment opportunities. Aldrich and Waldinger (1990) showed that many ethnic groups raise resources through rotating credit associations of people known to each other. Through fieldwork and a survey of seed stage investors, Shane and Cable (2002) found that direct ties between entrepreneurs and investors increased the likelihood that new ventures would receive financing. Shane and Stuart (2002) used data on life histories of 134 new companies founded to exploit inventions assigned to the Massachusetts Institute of Technology from 1980 to 1996 to show that founders with direct ties to investors before start-up were more likely to raise venture capital than founders without such ties. Levie and Warhuus (1998) interviewed 48 entrepreneurs and their bankers in Denmark, Ireland, the United Kingdom and the United States, and found that familiarity of the banker with the entrepreneur increased the likelihood of a credit agreement. They also found that local banks were more likely to make a credit agreement than geographically more distant banks, a finding consistent with localized patterns of social interaction.

Indirect ties

Indirect ties are direct tie relationships between an entrepreneur and a third party who is also connected to an investor (Burt, 1987). Indirect ties overcome the information asymmetry and uncertainty problems in venture finance and enhance the likelihood of resource acquisition for several reasons. First, indirect ties transfer the sense of social obligation, behavioral expectations and debt of reciprocity that exists between the directly connected parties to the indirect relationship (Uzzi, 1996). By serving as an intermediary in trust (Coleman, 1990), the third party facilitates the level of trust in the indirect relationship by using his or her ties as a bond on the level of confidence in the relationship.

Second, investors are more favorably disposed to believe in the competence and trustworthiness of entrepreneurs who have been referred (Blau, 1964). Therefore, the go-between in indirect ties transfers attributions and behavioral expectations from the existing relationship to the new one, improving investors' perceptions of the venture (Uzzi, 1996).

Third, indirect ties provide information that would not have been possible to obtain without the tie, or that would be obtained too slowly without the tie, facilitating access to private information (Burt, 1987; Nohria, 1992). For example, indirect ties reduce the cost and speed of information acquisition because they allow information to be gathered through activities that do not demand additional allocation of time and attention (Coleman, 1990; Nahapiet and Ghoshal, 1998).

Fifth, indirect ties provide information about difficult to observe characteristics, such as competence or honesty, which are important in differentiating high and low quality entrepreneurs and opportunities (Fernandez and Weinberg, 1997; Burt, 1992; Kelly, 2000). As a result, these ties increase the level of information about the venture that is available to investors.

Some empirical evidence supports these arguments about usefulness of indirect ties to resource acquisition. For instance, Kelly (2000), Wilson (1985) and Tyebjee and Bruno (1982) have all observed that investors frequently make investments in ventures that were referred to them by their prior investees, lawyers and accountants. In fact, Fried and Hisrich (1995) found that venture capitalists rarely invest in deals that were not referred to them. Similarly, Tyebjee and Bruno (1981) and Roberts (1991a) found that venture capitalists were more likely to fund business plans referred to them by parties who had brought them previous deals, and that the likelihood of funding increased with the number of accepted opportunities presented previously by the referee. Haar *et al.* (1988) used a survey of 130 angel investors, and Hall and Hofer (1993) used 16 verbal protocols given to four venture capitalists, to show that investors were significantly more likely to invest in proposals that had been referred to them, particularly by close ties that they were more likely to trust.

Indirect ties other than referrals also appear to increase the likelihood of resource acquisition. In an in-depth case study, Steier and Greenwood (1995) showed that a new firm that had failed to get financing from numerous investors, received financing from several investors who had rejected it previously once one key investor had 'signed on'. Burton *et al.* (1998) showed that the founders of new technology start-ups in Northern California were more likely to raise money if they had stronger network ties in general. Using data from fieldwork and a survey of 202 seed stage investors, Shane and Cable (2002) found that indirect ties between entrepreneurs and investors increased the likelihood that the ventures would receive financing. Shane and Stuart (2002) examined the life histories of new companies founded to exploit inventions assigned to the Massachusetts Institute of Technology, and showed that those founders with pre-existing indirect ties to investors before start-up were more likely to raise venture capital. Finally, Verheul and Thurik (2001) studied 2000 Dutch firms founded in 1994 and discovered that networking had a positive effect on the amount of start-up capital raised by new ventures.

Behaviors and Actions

While investors certainly use social ties to overcome information asymmetry and uncertainty problems in the resource acquisition process, Bhide (2000) points out that many entrepreneurs do not possess either direct or indirect social ties to resource providers. In his *Inc* 500 sample, Bhide (2000) found that less than 30 per cent of the founders had any link to resource providers or customers from whom they received external financing. Moreover, in only a small number of ethnic groups do people receive much financing for new businesses from their closest direct social ties – their family members (Aldrich *et al.*, 1996; Bates, 1997; Renzulli, 1998; Zimmer and Aldrich, 1987). These observations raise the question: in the absence of direct and indirect social ties to resource providers, how do people raise resources to pursue entrepreneurial opportunities?

When entrepreneurs have no track record and resource providers have little reason to be confident that their new ventures will survive and flourish, entrepreneurs can obtain resources by engaging in behaviors and actions that generate an impression of legitimacy, trustworthiness and competence (Starr and MacMillan, 1990). In fact, given the uncertainty that is a necessary condition of the entrepreneurial process, resource providers do not have unequivocal evidence that one entrepreneur's plan for opportunity exploitation is actually better than another's. Successful entrepreneurs recognize that investors judge value from appearances, as well as actual content, and create the appearance that their opportunities are valuable and legitimate, and that they are competent and trustworthy (Dees and Starr, 1992). Specifically, researchers have identified three types of behavior that enhance the appearance of value and therefore enhance resource acquisition: communication strategies, equity ownership and business planning.

Communication strategies

One way that entrepreneurs enhance external perceptions of their competence and trustworthiness is to use persuasion and influence strategies (Dees and Starr, 1992). The ability to persuade others involves the successful implementation of impression management and influence strategies that overcome the resistance of others and achieve consent (Bird and Jelinek, 1988).

One important impression management and influence strategy is to share information by engaging in frank and open communication. Sharing information is a mechanism that signals trust (Low and Srivatsan, 1994). Therefore, as Cable and Shane (1997) explain, high-quality and frequent communication between entrepreneurs and their investors is important. In fact, Feeney *et al*'s (1999) interviews with 194 angel investors in Canada showed that an important reason why investors favored a potential entrepreneur was their perception of the entrepreneur's openness about the opportunity.

Another important impression management and influence strategy is to frame risk in a way that is more acceptable to investors. Roberts (1991b) found that venture capitalists were more likely to accept opportunities that were lower in perceived risk than ones that were higher in perceived risk. Moreover, Rea (1989) found that venture negotiations were often unsuccessful when investors perceived that there was a high risk that the venture would fail. Therefore, to obtain capital, the Inc 500 founders that Bhide (2000) interviewed framed their requests for capital from others in a way that minimized the investor's perceived risk. In particular, they compared themselves to even riskier competitors so as give the impression that their ventures were not very risky.

A third important impression management and influence strategy that entrepreneurs use to generate beliefs among resource providers in their competence and trustworthiness is to create a sense of urgency that leads resource providers not to seek disconfirming evidence (Bhide, 2000). One way entrepreneurs do this is to give resource providers immediate benefits that lead them to be myopic and disregard or fail to investigate long-term costs. Another way is for entrepreneurs to provide financial incentives to resource providers who are the first to finance them (Bhide, 2000).

A fourth important impression management and influence strategy that entrepreneurs use to generate beliefs in them and their opportunities lies in stressing the similarity between their new activities and activities with which stakeholders are familiar (Aldrich, 1999). One way that entrepreneurs do this is to imitate the behaviors of large established firms to give the impression of stability (Bhide, 2000). Another way is to cite tradition as justification of their actions (Aldrich, 1999). A third way is to frame the opportunity as less novel than it might actually be (Aldrich, 1999).

Equity ownership

Another important behavior that entrepreneurs engage in to acquire resources despite the information asymmetry and uncertainty of the entrepreneurial process is to own a significant portion of their own ventures (Carter and Van Auken, 1990). The fraction of equity owned by the entrepreneur is a valuable indicator of the entrepreneur's belief in the future earnings potential of the venture because the risk-averse entrepreneur will only invest heavily in a venture if her information suggests that its future looks promising (Amit *et al.*, 1998).

Some empirical evidence supports this proposition. Using US census data on the debt financing of approximately 6000 US firms from 1979 to 1987, Bates (1997) found that the dollar value of the founders' equity capital had a positive effect on the amount of loans the venture received. Similarly, Carter and Van Auken (1990) surveyed 132 entrepreneurs drawn from the Iowa business directory and found that the greater the portion of the venture's equity represented by the entrepreneur's personal funds, the fewer financing problems the venture had in its first year.

Business planning

In addition to the use of communication strategies and equity ownership, a third type of action that entrepreneurs engage in to overcome problems of information asymmetry and uncertainty in resource acquisition is business planning. Business plans are documents that present the entrepreneur's conjectures in written and visual form (diagrams and charts), which facilitate communication of those conjectures to resource holders. Specifically, the business plan and supporting financial statements lay out the entrepreneur's strategy for building the venture, the risks that the venture will face, the areas in which investment will be made, the venture's financial condition and structure, its assets and financial relationships with other entities, and the timing and amount of desired financing (MacMillan and Narasimha, 1987).

Business plans provide a signal of the quality of the entrepreneur and the opportunity. As I explained in Chapter 2, opportunities have varying attributes because founders perceive opportunities that vary on a variety of dimensions including value, risk, and capital requirements (Shane, 2000). Because entrepreneurs must pay for external finance (Bhide, 2000), they seek to make the investment only if they believe that the expected value of the venture justifies the cost. These differences mean that entrepreneurs will only want to seek external capital for certain opportunities. For those opportunities that they believe are valuable, it pays for entrepreneurs to invest in the development of a business plan that signals the value of the opportunity and the diligence of the entrepreneur.

In addition, business plans provide evidence of the legitimacy of a new venture. Business plans are the institutional form in which entrepreneurs tell their stories about their businesses (Zimmerman and Zeitz, 2002). When external validation of the entrepreneur's opportunity is difficult, such as when the venture relies on such unobservable assets as the founder's initiative or tacit knowledge (Aldrich, 1999), symbolic communication is important to gaining legitimacy. First, a good story can explain and rationalize an opportunity in a way that others will be willing to accept, despite uncertainty and information asymmetry (Lounsbury and Glynn, 2001). By framing the opportunity in terms that are familiar and understandable to the target audience and incorporating existing knowledge that they have, the entrepreneur can make the opportunity seem more acceptable and appropriate to resource providers (Lounsbury and Glynn, 2001). Second, a good story can demonstrate internal consistency, which generates confidence in the entrepreneur and makes the entrepreneur's expected outcome seem plausible (Fisher, 1985). This is the case, for example, when the business plan presents estimates for revenue generation that are consistent with its plans for hiring. Third, a good story is valuable because resource acquisition under uncertainty is often a self-fulfilling prophecy. If the entrepreneur convinces resource providers that the opportunity is a reality, they will be more likely to provide the resources necessary to make the entrepreneur's beliefs into a reality (Gartner *et al.*, 1992).

Some empirical evidence supports the argument that a business plan facilitates resource acquisition under uncertainty and information asymmetry. For example, Mason and Harrison (1996) conduced interviews with 31 business angels and 28 owner–managers in the United Kingdom and found that the attractiveness of a venture to investors is enhanced by the presence of a business plan. Similarly, Hustedde and Pulver (1992) surveyed 318 entrepreneurs in Minnesota and Wisconsin who sought equity capital of more than $100 000 and found that those with a written business plan and balance sheet were more likely to receive financing than those without these documents. Roberts (1991b) studied 109 technology start-ups and found that those entrepreneurs with business plans raised more capital than those without business plans. Finally, when Shane and Cable (2002) compared the most recent positive and negative seed stage investment decisions of 202 investors, they found that funding was more likely when investors perceived that the entrepreneurs had a good business plan than when investors did not.

Limits to business planning   Because business plans are documents created by entrepreneurs, however, they face significant limitations in overcoming information asymmetry and uncertainty problems in venture finance. As I explained in Chapter 4, entrepreneurs are often overoptimistic about the potential of themselves and their opportunities (De Meza and Southey, 1996; Busenitz and Barney, 1997), requiring resource providers to seek external sources of information rather than just information presented by entrepreneurs in their business plans to evaluate the potential of the entrepreneurs and the opportunities. For example, Feeney *et al.* (1999) interviewed 194 angel investors in Canada and found that one of the main reasons that investors did not invest in opportunities was that the entrepreneur's forecasts were overly optimistic or unsubstantiated. Similarly, Shane and Cable (2002) found that the size of the market claimed by the entrepreneurs in their business plans did not influence the investment decisions of seed stage investors because entrepreneurs' perceptions of their ventures and their markets were often unrealistically overoptimistic.

In fact, Roberts (1991b) compared venture opportunities evaluated by two venture capitalists and found that funded opportunities were *less* likely to have overly optimistic projections. Similarly, MacMillan and Subba Narasimha (1987) examined 82 business plans provided by a New York venture capital firm and found that plans that were not financed were *more* optimistic than plans that were financed. In particular, unfounded plans had higher sales to fixed asset ratios than funded plans.

Indicators of Quality

Given the limits to the use of business plans as evidence of the quality of the venture opportunity and the competence of the entrepreneur, investors often look to indicators not completely under the control of venture founders as evidence about the quality of the venture opportunity and the entrepreneur's method of exploitation.

Founder attributes

In general, resource providers seek to identify entrepreneurs with the individual level characteristics associated with opportunity exploitation that I described in Chapter 4. For example, investors appear to prefer ventures founded by larger teams of entrepreneurs because those entrepreneurs have a wider range of necessary competencies (Roberts, 1991a). In addition, they tend to prefer entrepreneurs who are higher in need for achievement and internal locus of control (Pandry and Tewary, 1979) because these psychological attributes are associated with opportunity exploitation and new venture success.

Perhaps the most important signal of entrepreneurial competence that investors look for is education, because more educated entrepreneurs tend to perform better than other entrepreneurs. Using US census data, Bates (1997) found support for this argument. He showed that education had a positive impact on the amount of money received for a sample of 5882 non-minority borrowing firms from 1979 to 1987. Similarly, Storey (1994a) surveyed firm founders in Cleveland, England in 1979 and 1990 and found that those with higher educational qualifications were more likely to receive bank loans or overdrafts. Hustedde and Pulver (1992) examined 318 entrepreneurs in Minnesota and Wisconsin who sought equity capital and found that those with a degree outside of business were less likely to receive financing than those with a business education. Lastly, Shepherd *et al.* (2000) conducted an experiment on 66 venture capitalists, using a fictive set of company attributes. These authors found that venture capitalists associated high levels of founder education with venture profitability.

The entrepreneur's industry, management and start-up experience also signal that the entrepreneur has the information to identify and exploit opportunities successfully without the investor actually knowing the entrepreneur's information about the opportunity (Casson, 1982; Amit *et al.*, 1993). As a result, several studies show that entrepreneurs with more management experience, industry experience and start-up experience are more likely to obtain financing than those without this experience. For example, Bates' (1997) examination of US Census data revealed that entrepreneurs' management experience had a positive impact on the size of the bank loans that they received. Similarly, Mason and Harrison's (1996) interviews with business angels and entrepreneurs in the United Kingdom indicated that investors preferred entrepreneurs with greater management experience. Feeney *et al.* (1999) used interviews with 194 angel investors in Canada to show that angels tended not to invest in new ventures when entrepreneurs lacked management knowledge.

Investors also prefer entrepreneurs with more industry experience. Shepherd *et al.*'s (2000) experiment with venture capitalists showed that investors associated founders' industry skills with venture profitability. Similarly, Kelly's (2000) data on British business angels revealed that investor confidence in entrepreneurs was higher when the founders had more industry experience.

The empirical evidence also supports the proposition that investors prefer entrepreneurs with more start-up experience. Feeney *et al.*'s (1999) interviews with Canadian business angels showed that investors view a track record of previous start-up success as the main desirable attribute in an entrepreneur. Similarly, Kelly's (2000) survey of British business angels indicated that investors' trust and confidence in entrepreneurs was higher when the founder had greater experience in starting companies.

Opportunity attributes

Resource providers also seek indicators of the value of the venture opportunity. These signals include evidence of a large market, acceptance of the product or service, appropriate firm strategy, competitive advantage, availability of the raw materials to produce the product, a viable production process, a product prototype, some evidence of external accreditation, endorsements, guarantees, bonds, licenses, or certification of the venture (Low and Abrahamson, 1997; Carter and Van Auken, 1990; Kaplan and Stromberg, 2001).

In general, investors seek to identify venture opportunities with the characteristics described in Chapter 2, as well as the characteristics associated with venture strategies that I will describe in the next chapter. For example, Rea (1989) compared 47 successful venture capital negotiations and 42 failed venture capital negotiations described by 18 venture capitalists. He found that these negotiations were more likely to fail when the entrepreneur's product had no clear competitive advantage in the market place. On the other hand, Roure and Keeley (1990) showed that 36 new venture investments of a single venture capital firm from 1974 to 1982 had higher internal rates of return if they had technically superior products.

As several empirical studies show, a particularly important signal of new venture quality is the possession of a proprietary competitive advantage that can be demonstrated objectively and externally (Bhide, 2000). Because competitive advantage is often difficult to observe, new venture finance is easier when the new venture has a patent or other form of intellectual property protection that the investor can evaluate.

For instance, Roberts (1991b) showed that venture capital funded firms were less likely than unfunded ventures to engage in price competition and more likely to compete on the basis of some kind of proprietary technology. Shane and Stuart (2002) showed that the effectiveness of patents in an industry increased the likelihood of obtaining venture capital for the population of start-ups that were founded to exploit intellectual property assigned to the Massachusetts Institute of Technology. Westhead and Storey (1997) examined 171 firms in science parks in the United Kingdom from 1992 to 1993, and found that firms that were significantly more reliant on intangible assets had greater problems than other firms in obtaining capital. Shane and Cable (2002) examined the seed stage investment decisions of 202 investors and found that funding was more likely when investors perceived that the entrepreneurs had technology that provided a strong and proprietary competitive advantage. Lastly, Shepherd *et al.*'s (2000) experiment with venture capitalists showed that investors associated low levels of competition, strong lead-time, and pioneering advantages with new venture profitability.

In addition to showing that their ventures are pursuing valuable opportunities with good strategies for exploitation, entrepreneurs need to demonstrate that their new ventures are legitimate entities – organizations as accountable and reliable as existing firms. Legitimacy is the degree to which people believe that the venture operates in ways consistent with existing rules, laws, standards, procedures, norms and beliefs (Aldrich and Fiol, 1994). Therefore, one way to achieve legitimacy is to act in a way consistent with these things (Scott and Meyer, 1983).

To appear as reliable and accountable as existing organizations, entrepreneurs make their new ventures adhere to the norms of legal authority by paying taxes and obtaining regulatory approvals, especially very early in the life of the new venture when there are few alternative bases for achieving legitimacy. By adhering to these norms publicly and voluntarily, the entrepreneur can also demonstrate commitment to them (Aldrich, 1999). In fact, researchers have argued that adherence to these norms enhances resource acquisition by facilitating interaction with resource providers who prefer to do business with legitimate actors.

SUMMARY

Because the exploitation of opportunity requires the acquisition and recombination of resources before the sale of the output from that recombination, opportunity exploitation must be financed. This chapter explored the process by which people acquire financial resources to exploit entrepreneurial opportunities.

Obtaining a sufficient amount of capital is important to the exploitation of entrepreneurial opportunities. New ventures with more capital are more likely to survive, grow, and become profitable because capital provides a buffer that entrepreneurs can use in response to adverse circumstance; because having adequate capital leads people to perceive the organization as more successful, legitimate and dependable; and because having more capital allows entrepreneurs to approach the organizing process in the most effective way possible.

The information dispersion and uncertainty that give rise to the existence and discovery of entrepreneurial opportunities make it difficult for entrepreneurs to acquire resources to pursue them. Information dispersion creates four problems in the resource acquisition process. First, to preserve the value of the opportunity against competition, the entrepreneur must keep the opportunity secret, forcing investors to make decisions with less information than the entrepreneur. Second, the entrepreneur's information advantage allows her to act opportunistically towards investors. Third, information asymmetry encourages entrepreneurs to undertake excessive risk with the investors' resources. Fourth, information asymmetry allows for adverse selection.

Uncertainty creates three problems in the resource acquisition process. First, the uncertainty may make resource providers incapable of evaluating new ventures. Second, uncertainty results in bargaining problems between the entrepreneur and the investor. Third, uncertainty leads investors to collateralize their investments in case the entrepreneur's judgment proves false.

Given the problems engendered by the pursuit of uncertain opportunities by entrepreneurs with asymmetric information, the acquisition of resources involves several important characteristics: self-financing by the entrepreneur, contractual constraints on the exploitation process, pre-investment tools, post-investment tools, social ties, entrepreneurial behavior and quality signaling.

Self-financing overcomes the information and uncertainty problems in venture finance in several ways. By investing in her own venture, the entrepreneur makes the return on her investment at least partially contingent on her own effort, mitigating moral hazard problems. Moreover, by pledging her own assets, the entrepreneur can collateralize the venture for investors who cannot observe the opportunity nor predict its outcome in advance. As a result, most entrepreneurs self-finance the exploitation of opportunities.

However, some people lack the capital to finance their entrepreneurial opportunities or seek to bear less risk by obtaining external finance, particularly when the size of the initial investment to exploit the opportunity is very large. As a result, investors often design contracts to mitigate the information asymmetry and uncertainty problems present in entrepreneurial finance. Typical contracts involve convertible securities with restrictive covenants, and forfeiture and anti-dilution provisions.

Complete contracts are difficult to write under uncertainty and cannot eliminate the ability or incentive for entrepreneurs to act against the interests of investors. Moreover, entrepreneurs are overoptimistic, which undermines the effectiveness of contract terms as screening mechanisms. Furthermore, investors cannot shift all of the risk of new venture finance to entrepreneurs, while, at the same time, participating in the venture. Therefore, investors use tools other than contracts to manage the information asymmetry and uncertainty problems in venture finance.

Among pre-investment tools, investors conduct due diligence to select out poor entrepreneurs and unprofitable projects, thereby reducing the potential for adverse selection. They specialize in the industry in which the new venture operates, which provides contacts, experience and routines that assist with selection and monitoring of investments. Investors also make geographically localized investments so that they can use a network of trusted contacts to assess the accuracy of information that entrepreneurs provide; to create redundant and overlapping information sources that can provide convergent validity about entrepreneurs and their opportunities; and to facilitate monitoring. Investors syndicate to diversify the irreducible uncertainty that is part of the entrepreneurial process, and to gather and verify information on which to make their investment decisions.

Investors also employ several post-investment tools to manage the problems in resource acquisition created by the information asymmetry and uncertainty present in the entrepreneurial process. They retain disproportionate control rights to decide how to use the venture's assets. Investors also treat investment in new ventures as real options in which they have the right, but not the obligation, to make future investments. Investors remain heavily involved with new ventures, requiring entrepreneurs to provide regular updates of information about the venture and even participate in the day-to-day operation of new ventures.

Investors also use social mechanisms to manage the problems of resource acquisition in the entrepreneurial process. Perhaps most important of these social mechanisms are social ties. These ties overcome information asymmetry and uncertainty problems in venture finance by reducing the likelihood that the entrepreneur will act opportunistically towards the investor; by providing a way to enforce implicit contracts; by transferring information; and by making attributions of the opportunity and entrepreneur more positive. As a result, direct and indirect ties between entrepreneurs and investors enhance resource acquisition.

While investors certainly use social ties to overcome information asymmetry and uncertainty problems in the resource acquisition process, many entrepreneurs do not possess social ties to resource providers. As a result, they must engage in behavior to encourage resource providers to give them needed capital. Effective behaviors include communication strategies; signaling commitment through equity ownership and involvement in the venture; and adhering to legitimate norms about business, such as business planning. Lastly, entrepreneurs appear to signal their quality by demonstrating individual and opportunity attributes associated with successful exploitation of entrepreneurial opportunities.

Having shown the problems in venture finance generated by information asymmetry and uncertainty in the entrepreneurial process, and having discussed the solutions offered by entrepreneurs and investors to these problems, I turn now to a discussion of the strategies used by entrepreneurs to exploit opportunities.

9.   Entrepreneurial strategy

In this chapter, I explore the strategies by which entrepreneurs exploit new venture opportunities. I define entrepreneurial strategy as those efforts to obtain and preserve private value from the exploitation of opportunities. Entrepreneurial strategy involves two major issues: first, how does the entrepreneur develop a competitive advantage that precludes the dissipation of the opportunity to competitors once she has begun to exploit it? Second, how does the entrepreneur manage the uncertainty and information asymmetry inherent in the exploitation of an opportunity when she seeks to generate value from the opportunity? This chapter will be divided into two sections, each of which explores one of these questions.

ENTREPRENEURSHIP, STRATEGY AND ENTREPRENEURIAL STRATEGY

Before turning to a discussion of these two issues, however, I would like to clarify the relationship between entrepreneurship and strategic management, thereby locating entrepreneurial strategy in intellectual space. I do this given the confusion that has emerged in the entrepreneurship field about the relationship between these two areas (see Zahra and Dess, 2001 and Shane and Venkataraman, 2001 for a discussion). As Figure 9.1 indicates, entrepreneurial strategy is the intersection between *all* strategic actions and *all* activity to exploit opportunities. Entrepreneurial strategy does not consider the non-strategic activities undertaken to discover and exploit opportunities, such as the organizing processes, the individual level characteristics that promote the decision to exploit opportunities, and the resource acquisition processes that are the subject of other chapters of this book. Similarly entrepreneurial strategy does not consider strategic action to engage in activities other than those to exploit entrepreneurial opportunities. For example, the strategic action of a nation state to obtain better trade concessions from other nations does not fall in the domain of entrepreneurial strategy (see Figure 9.1). Nor do those business strategies designed to improve the efficiency of existing operations rather than to exploit new opportunities, such as strategies to minimize transaction or agency costs. However, those aspects of business strategy that are concerned with firm efforts to exploit entrepreneurial opportunities, such as efforts to exploit dynamic capabilities, are aspects of entrepreneurial strategy.

Figure 9.1 The domain of entrepreneurial strategy

DEVELOPING A COMPETITIVE ADVANTAGE

As I mentioned above, one of the key questions for entrepreneurial strategy concerns how the entrepreneur appropriates the returns to the exploitation of an entrepreneurial opportunity, given that the act of exploitation provides information to potential competitors about how to imitate the entrepreneur's actions. To answer this question, I first explain why the returns to opportunity exploitation will dissipate to competitors unless the entrepreneur develops a competitive advantage.

The entrepreneur earns a profit for correctly identifying a valuable opportunity inherent in information that she observes in the economy. This entrepreneurial profit is transient for three reasons. First, the factors that made the opportunity possible are often replaced by changes that generate new opportunities in place of the old ones (Schumpeter, 1934). Second, the resource owners, whose inputs the entrepreneur recombines to exploit the opportunity, recognize that the entrepreneur has earned profits. Because they too would like to earn profits, they raise the price of their resources to take some of the entrepreneurial profit for themselves at the expense of the entrepreneur (Kirzner, 1997). Third, and most importantly for our purposes here, the opportunities are exhausted by competition.

When the entrepreneur identifies and initially exploits an opportunity, she has a monopoly position. As I explained in Chapter 3, the entrepreneur exploits private information or superior powers of recognition to identify a unique opportunity – one that others do not see. Unfortunately for the entrepreneur, the very act of exploiting this opportunity transmits to others information about how to identify and exploit the opportunity (Campbell, 1992). Therefore, potential imitators see the successful exploitation of an entrepreneurial opportunity as a signal to enter the market, using the initial entrepreneur's information to replicate the initial entrepreneur's effort to exploit the opportunity (Casson, 1982). For example, Baum and Haveman (1997) have shown that hotel entrepreneurs tend to found their hotels geographically close to established hotels and at similar prices to take advantage of information externalities that come from the success of previously established hotels.

By doing the same thing as the initial entrepreneur, the imitators capture some of the entrepreneurial profit for themselves (Schumpeter, 1934). As long as there is still entrepreneurial profit to be made from the exploitation of the opportunity, each imitator has an incentive to bid away from other imitators and the initial entrepreneur those resources necessary to exploit the opportunity (Casson, 1982). This effort to bid away resources causes their price to rise and ultimately exhausts the profitability of the opportunity (Schumpeter, 1934; Shane and Venkataraman, 2000).

The tendency of people to imitate the initial entrepreneur's method of opportunity exploitation leads the entrepreneur to preclude others from copying, thereby preserving the entrepreneurial profits for herself (Amit *et al.*, 1993; Casson, 1982). As Figure 9.2 shows, there are two different ways that the entrepreneur can preserve the profits from the exploitation of entrepreneurial

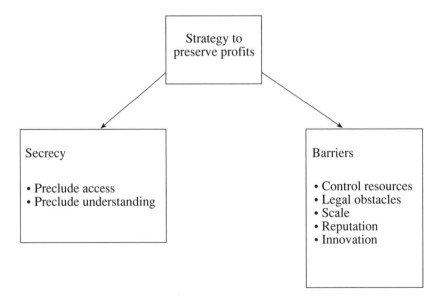

Figure 9.2   How entrepreneurs protect their opportunities against competition

opportunities. First, the entrepreneur can preclude others from gaining access to or understanding information about the opportunity (Rumelt, 1987). Second, the entrepreneur can preclude others from actually exploiting the opportunity, even if they have access to information about the opportunity and understand it (Casson, 1982).

Efforts to preclude others from gaining access to or understanding the opportunity generally involve secrecy. The entrepreneur could take efforts to keep secret the information that she used to discover the opportunity. For example, the entrepreneur might avoid telling others that she has made a technological discovery of a cure for cancer. As a result, others would not know that the technological discovery has occurred, and therefore they cannot exploit the opportunity to produce the cure for cancer.

To keep her opportunity secret, the entrepreneur cannot communicate to others the information that allowed her to discover the opportunity, and must prevent others from independently gaining access to it (Casson, 1982). Given the necessity of keeping information secret, these types of efforts work best when the exploitation of the opportunity requires knowledge of a new technical process to combine resources that the entrepreneur retains as a trade secret. A good example is development of a new chemical process to create a fertilizer.

The entrepreneur can also preclude others from imitation if she can keep them from understanding how to exploit the opportunity, even if they have gained access to information that allows them to discover the existence of the opportunity. This concept, called causal ambiguity by the resource-based view of the firm (Barney, 1991), preserves the profit from exploitation of the opportunity by ensuring that only the entrepreneur understands a method for exploiting it. For example, several people might learn that a cure for cancer can be made from the bark of a yew tree, but they would be unable to imitate the entrepreneur if they cannot figure out how to make a drug from the bark.

The ability to preclude others from understanding how to exploit the opportunity usually involves some type of tacit knowledge. If knowledge about how to exploit the opportunity is held by the entrepreneur in uncodified form, other people often have difficulty identifying the causal relationships that underlie the production, distribution and organizing processes necessary to exploit the opportunity in a profitable way (Nelson and Winter, 1982; Aldrich, 1999).

In particular, imitation is difficult if the explanation of how to exploit the opportunity lies in tacit knowledge about the use of specific human capital (skills and abilities) that make the entrepreneur good at the execution of the resource recombination (Amit *et al.*, 1993). With many entrepreneurial opportunities, the key to opportunity exploitation lies in just such tacit knowledge. For example, the entrepreneurial profit that is earned from a furniture store might be a result of the superior execution at sales by a particular entrepreneur. As a result, other potential entrepreneurs could locate next door to the first entrepreneur and fail to capture any of the entrepreneurial profit because they lack the first entrepreneur's sales skills.

Several empirical studies provide evidence that the performance of new ventures often depends on the entrepreneur's ability to implement her approach to exploiting the opportunity in ways that others cannot imitate. One set of studies indicates that exploitation of the entrepreneur's tacit knowledge about the exploitation process enhances the survival of new ventures. For example, Reynolds and White (1997) surveyed the founders of 627 new firms in Pennsylvania in 1986 and in Minnesota in 1987. They found that those ventures that emphasized marketing implementation were more likely than other ventures to survive at least one year. Similarly, Reynolds (1987) surveyed the founders of 551 new firms established in Minnesota between 1978 and 1984. He found that survival one year later was positively related to strategy implementation.

The exploitation of the entrepreneur's tacit knowledge about the exploitation process also enhances the growth of new ventures. For example, Reynolds' (1987) survey of new firms founded in Minnesota showed that strategic implementation was also correlated with the one-year increase in sales.

The use of causal ambiguity to deter imitation of the opportunity exploitation process is most effective when the process of exploitation requires the possession of knowledge, skills or experience that only a small number of people have (Amit *et al.*, 1990b). If large numbers of people have the knowledge, skills or experience to exploit the opportunity, it is unlikely that all of them will fail to figure out how to exploit it. However, the ability to preclude others from figuring out how to exploit an opportunity is much more plausible when only a small number of people have the knowledge, skills or experience to try.

Zucker *et al.* (1998) describe a situation in which entrepreneurs exploited opportunities that other people did not imitate quickly because of the limited distribution of necessary skills. Exploring the performance of new biotechnology firms, the authors found that certain biotechnology entrepreneurs earned entrepreneurial profits for many years because very few scientists were capable of employing the scientific techniques that they used to exploit technological discoveries in biology.

Most times, however, people can imitate the entrepreneur's approach to exploiting an opportunity once the entrepreneur has identified the opportunity. Under these circumstances, the entrepreneur can stop others from profiting from the opportunity only by creating impediments to their exploitation of it (Rumelt, 1987). Moreover, these impediments are useful even when the entrepreneur has sought to keep knowledge of the opportunity secret or when others cannot initially imitate the opportunity because of causal ambiguity. Secrecy can be breached even when people try to maintain it; and others can learn the skills necessary to exploit an opportunity even when that knowledge is tacit.

Therefore, entrepreneurs often seek to erect barriers to competition as a way to preserve the profits that they earn from exploiting an entrepreneurial opportunity (Casson, 1982).

The entrepreneur can erect five different kinds of barriers to competition: she can obtain control of resources needed to exploit opportunities; establish legal barriers to imitation; exploit opportunities at a scale that deters imitation; develop a reputation; and innovate to stay ahead of competition.

Control of Resources

The entrepreneur can create a barrier to competition by obtaining control of all the resources needed to exploit it, thereby precluding others from gaining access to the resources necessary to exploit the opportunity. For example, the entrepreneur can establish long-term contracts with all of the resource providers, making it impossible for a competitor to contract with any of them (Casson, 1982). Alternatively, the entrepreneur could identify a resource which is necessary for the exploitation of the opportunity, but which is limited in its supply, and purchase all sources of supply of that resource (Venkataraman, 1997). This would be the case if the entrepreneur bought up all deposits of a rare raw material (Casson, 1982); hired all of the labor with the skills to make a particular product or service; or leased all of the locations that would be appropriate for the distribution of a product or service.

Legal Barriers to Imitation

The entrepreneur can create a barrier to competition by obtaining a legal monopoly on the process of recombining or exploiting resources through a patent, government permit or exclusive contract, all of which create a legal barrier to duplication by others (Casson, 1982; Shane and Venkataraman, 2000). For example, an entrepreneur might obtain a patent to produce a drug that cures heart disease, precluding others from producing the same drug even if they see the value in the opportunity and know how to make the drug.

Some empirical evidence supports the argument that entrepreneurs seek legal barriers to imitation when they exploit their entrepreneurial opportunities. If entrepreneurs obtain patents to create barriers to imitation in the exploitation of the opportunities that they pursue, then the strength of patent protection should influence the likelihood of opportunity exploitation. When patents are stronger, they provide a greater ability to deter imitation of the entrepreneur's process for exploiting a technological opportunity than when patents are weaker. Therefore, people should be more likely to found firms to exploit entrepreneurial opportunities when patents are stronger. Consistent with the argument, Shane (2001a) examined the 1397 inventions patented by the Massachusetts

Institute of Technology between 1980 and 1996 and found that patent scope, a measure of the breadth of intellectual property protection offered by the patents, increased the likelihood that a new firm would exploit an invention.

If the above argument is correct, and entrepreneurs seek to deter imitation of their processes for exploiting opportunities, then those entrepreneurs who obtain legal barriers to the imitation of their opportunities should also perform better. Several studies indicate that those new ventures that establish legal barriers to imitation of their process for exploiting an opportunity are less likely to fail than other new ventures. Shane and Stuart (2002) examined the life histories of 134 new companies founded between 1980 and 1996 to exploit intellectual property assigned to the Massachusetts Institute of Technology. These authors showed that the number of patents obtained by the new firm at founding reduced the likelihood of its failure. Similarly, Barnett (1997) examined the failure rates of American breweries from 1633 until 1988. He found that a different type of legal barrier to imitation – a permit – influenced the likelihood of venture failure. Specifically, Barnett (1997) showed that the possession of a permit reduced the failure rate of the breweries in his sample.

Other studies have shown the effect of legal barriers to imitation on new venture growth. Lee *et al.* (2001) examined the performance of 137 Korean technology start-up companies who were enrolled in the Korean Small and Medium Business Administration. These authors found that those new firms with more patents submitted or issued, more utility models or designs registered, and who had more trademarks, had higher two-year sales growth than other ventures in their sample. Similarly, Baum *et al.* (2000) examined the performance of 142 Canadian biotechnology firms founded between 1991 and 1996. They found that the firms in the sample with more patents at the time of founding had faster revenue growth than other firms, but that firms whose rivals had more patents had lower employment and revenue growth.

Legal barriers to imitation also increase the likelihood of a new venture's initial public offering. Stuart *et al.* (1999) examined the rate of initial public offering for 301 venture capital backed biotechnology companies in human diagnostics and therapeutics funded by venture capitalists from 1978 to 1991. They found that the number of biotechnology patents belonging to the firm had a positive effect on the probability of initial public offering.

Scale

The entrepreneur can create a barrier to competition by exploiting the opportunity on such a scale that others cannot afford to imitate it. By committing to a scale that would saturate the market, the entrepreneur can make entry by others result in industry over-capacity. This over-capacity would lead all parties to lose money if imitative entry occurred. As a result, potential imitators would recognize that their added supply, coupled with inelastic demand, would drive down prices to below average costs and eliminate the profits that they were trying to share. Therefore, they would not enter (Casson, 1982).

In addition, by entering at a larger scale, a new venture can capture the benefits of scale economies. These scale economies allow the new venture to operate at a lower cost structure than potential imitators. The new venture preserves the profits from the exploitation of its opportunity by undercutting the prices of imitators. Because those imitators cannot exploit the opportunity at the same scale as the initial entrepreneur, they have a higher cost structure, and cannot match the initial entrepreneur's prices.

Some empirical evidence supports the argument that exploiting an entrepreneurial opportunity on a large scale deters imitation, thereby allowing the new venture to appropriate the profits from the exploitation of its opportunity, and survive.[1] A variety of researchers have provided support for the relationship between new venture size and new venture survival (Freeman *et al.*, 1983; Marple, 1982). For example, Evans (1987) examined all firms operating in a random sample of 100 manufacturing industries in 1976. He found a relationship between firm size and firm survival for 81 per cent of the industries.

Studies that have examined the effect of size at a lower level of analysis have found similar results. For instance, Mahmood (2000) examined the US Small Business Administration database, which is a census of US business establishments created between 1976 and 1986. He found that initial start-up size reduced the likelihood of new venture failure. Audretsch and Mahmood (1991) examined the 7070 manufacturing establishments that were created in the United States in 1976 over the subsequent ten years. They found that firms that were larger at start-up were more likely to survive. Audretsch and Mahmood (1995) examined the survival of 12 251 new establishments created in 1976 and found that the size of the establishment reduced the likelihood of failure. Freeman *et al.* (1983) examined the survival of American labor unions from 1860 until 1980; American newspapers in seven metropolitan areas from 1800 to 1875; and producers of semiconductor devices from 1950 to 1979. In all cases, he found that the failure rates were lower for larger organizations than for smaller ones.

The results have been similar when the studies have been conducted outside the United States. Wagner (1994) found that larger new entrants in German manufacturing had lower failure rates than smaller ones. Mata and Portugal (1994) followed 3169 new Portuguese manufacturing establishments over time and found that firm size at start-up increased the likelihood of venture survival. Fotopoulos and Louri (2000) examined 209 new firms established in Greece between 1982 and 1984. They found that larger firms had lower failure rates than smaller ones. Mata *et al.* (1995) examined data on new companies operating in Portugal between 1983 and 1990 and found that single plant firms that were larger at the time of formation were more likely to survive than those that were smaller at the time of formation. Bruderl *et al.* (1992) examined the five-year survival of 1849 businesses that had registered with the local chamber of commerce in Munich and Upper Bavaria. They found that venture size, whether measured as capital invested or employees, reduced the likelihood of venture failure.

Researchers have also documented the effect of size on venture survival when size has been measured in terms of assets. Ranger-Moore (1991, 1997) examined New York State life insurance companies from 1813 to 1935, and found that failure rates fell as the asset size of the companies increased. Banaszak-Holl (1992, 1993) examined the survival of Manhattan banks from 1840 to 1976, and showed that failure rates decreased as the companies' asset size increased. Barron *et al.* (1994) studied the survival of state-chartered credit unions in New York City from 1914 to 1990, and found that the size of assets had a negative effect on venture failure rates.

The effect of venture size on survival has also been shown when size has been measured as the venture's productive capacity. Delacroix *et al.* (1989) and Delacroix and Swaminathan (1991) examined Californian wineries from 1940 to 1985, and found that failure rates decreased as the storage capacity of wineries grew. Baum and Singh (1994a) and Baum and Oliver (1991, 1992) examined Toronto nursery schools from 1971 to 1987 and found that failure rates decreased as licensed capacity increased. Baum and Mezias (1992) examined Manhattan hotels from 1898 to 1990, and found that failure rates decreased as number of rooms in the hotels increased. Carroll *et al.* (1993) examined American breweries from 1878 to 1988, and found that failure rates decreased with initial level of production capacity. Barnett and Carroll (1987) examined Southeast Iowa telephone companies from 1900 to 1917 and found that size, measured as the log of the number of telephones in the system, reduced the likelihood of venture failure.

Several studies have shown the beneficial effect of capacity on survival in studies of chain organizations. For example, Ingram (1994) examined American hotel chains from 1896 to 1980, and found that failure rates decreased with the number of hotels in the chain. Similarly, Shane and Foo (1999) examined the survival of 1292 new franchise systems established in the United States between 1979 and 1996, and found that the number of outlets in the system reduced the likelihood of system failure.

Venture size also has a negative effect on venture failure when size has been measured as units sold. Wholey *et al.* (1992) examined group and independent health maintenance organizations from 1976 to 1991, and found that enrollment had a negative effect on failure of the organizations. Ingram (1993) examined US microcomputer manufacturers from 1975 to 1986 and found that failure rates declined with the number of units sold. Aldrich *et al.* (1994) examined

US trade associations from 1901 to 1990, and found that the liklihood of failure decreased as membership increased.

Previous studies have also shown that venture size increases the growth of new ventures. For example, Bamford *et al.* (2000) examined 140 new banks established in 1988 and found that the more branches the bank had at founding, the higher its sales were in every year from 1989 to 1994. Baum *et al.* (2000) examined the performance of 142 Canadian biotechnology firms founded between 1991 and 1996. These authors found that firms with manufacturing facilities at the time of founding had faster growth in the number of employees than did firms without manufacturing facilities at founding.

Reputation

The entrepreneur can create a barrier to competition by building up goodwill and making customers suspicious of any new entrants (Casson, 1982). If customers believe that the initial entrepreneur has a better product or superior service than any subsequent entrant, the entrepreneur can preclude subsequent entrants from serving those customers even if the entrants are able to exploit exactly the same opportunity as the initial entrepreneur.

One way to build this goodwill with customers is through advertising, in which the entrepreneur promotes the attributes of her new product or service to customers. As a result of this advertising, customers come to expect that any new product or service that is used to exploit the opportunity would have the characteristics of the entrepreneur's product or service. If imitators cannot copy all of the features of the entrepreneur's product or service, customers would be reluctant to adopt the products or services offered by the new entrants and the entrepreneur's profit from exploiting the opportunity would be protected against competition.

Another way for the entrepreneur to establish goodwill with customers would be through giving coupons. By offering a coupon that allowed the customer to obtain a discount on any subsequent purchases, the entrepreneur would force any imitator to meet the discounted price if she were to enter the market. The requirement that the competitor offer a discounted price to enter would reduce the profitability of entry (Casson, 1982). As a result, fewer imitators would be willing to enter, and the entrepreneur's profit from exploiting the opportunity would be preserved.

A strategy to build new venture reputation appears to enhance new venture growth. Reynolds (1993) examined representative samples of new firms in Pennsylvania in 1986 and Minnesota in 1987 and compared high performing firms with the rest of the sample. He found that the founders of high growth firms were more likely than the founders of other ventures to emphasize the quality of their goods and services.

Baum *et al.* (2001) studied 307 entrepreneurial woodworking companies run by active owner–managers who had founded or purchased their businesses between two and eight years before and who had more than one employee. They found that adopting a differentiation strategy, in which the new ventures sought to develop new products and services that were distinct from their competitors, had a positive effect on annual sales growth over a two-year period.

Reynolds and White (1997) surveyed 2624 new firms founded in several Midwestern states and found that those ventures with higher growth rates were more likely to have used marketing-oriented strategies to differentiate their products. Similarly, Reynolds (1987) surveyed 551 new firms founded in Minnesota between 1978 and 1984 and found that the one-year sales increase was positively correlated with an emphasis on marketing, sales and promotion in the previous year.

In contrast to the reputation-building strategy outlined above, adopting a price competition strategy increases the likelihood of new venture failure. For example, Stearns *et al.* (1995) examined the survival of 2653 new firms founded in Pennsylvania and Philadelphia between 1979 and 1985 and found that competing on price in 1985 lowered the rate of survival of the venture six years later.

Innovation

The entrepreneur can create a barrier to competition by continually advancing her method of exploiting the opportunity to keep it superior to that offered by others. This would occur, for example, if the entrepreneur changed the recombination used to exploit the opportunity through innovation. The innovation process allows the entrepreneur to remain a step ahead of imitators by exploiting a proprietary learning curve. As long as some of the knowledge of how to provide a product or service to customers is developed through the actual provision of that service, and can be kept secret from competitors, new ventures can keep imitators from copying their method of exploiting the opportunity. As a result, entrepreneurs can preserve the profit from exploiting the opportunity.

Two studies provide evidence in support of this proposition by demonstrating that new firms that introduce innovative new products more readily are more likely to survive. First, Eisenhardt and Schoonhoven (1995) examined the survival of 98 semiconductor firms founded in the United States between 1978 and 1985, and found that the more innovative the new product developed by the firm, the less likely it was to fail. Second, Littunen (2000) examined the three-year survival of 138 metal product manufacturers and 62 business service firms in Finland. He found that those firms that focused on developing new products were more likely to survive than were firms that did not focus on new products.

New ventures that innovate are also more likely to grow. Zahra and Bogner (2000) surveyed 116 US-based software companies that were less than eight years old, and found that firms that were more likely to introduce radical new products and to have product upgrades had higher market share growth than other ventures. Simon and Zahra (1994) examined 72 new biotechnology firms created by individual entrepreneurs and found that the percentage rate of sales growth was positively correlated with an innovation strategy.

A focus on innovation also enhances the profitability of new ventures and their likelihood of an initial public offering. Zahra and Bogner's (2000) study of software companies showed that new firms that had more product upgrades and introduced more radical new products had higher return on equity than other new firms. Hannan *et al.* (1996) examined 100 new technology companies established in Silicon Valley between 1984 and 1994 and found that the likelihood of initial public offering was positively related to a technology race strategy.

MANAGING UNCERTAINTY AND INFORMATION ASYMMETRY

The execution of entrepreneurial strategy involves the management of uncertainty and information asymmetry because these characteristics are fundamental to the existence, discovery and exploitation of entrepreneurial opportunities. First and foremost, entrepreneurial strategy involves undertaking strategic actions that help the entrepreneur to bear uncertainty. As I explained in Chapter 2, entrepreneurs make conjectures about resource combinations that are uncertain – that is, one cannot know *ex ante* whether these conjectures will be correct. In general, three types of uncertainty keep entrepreneurs from knowing ahead of time whether their conjectures will be correct. The first type of uncertainty is technical. The entrepreneur does not know if the product or service she is producing will work, and, if so, if it can be produced at a cost less than the price at which it will be sold (Amit *et al.*, 1990a, b).

The second type of uncertainty is market uncertainty. The entrepreneur does not know if demand will exist for the product or service, and, if so, if customers will adopt in large enough volumes, quickly enough, and at a high enough price, to make the effort profitable (Amit *et al.*, 1990a, b).

The third type of uncertainty is competitive uncertainty. The entrepreneur does not know if she will be able to appropriate the profits from the exploitation of the opportunity or if they will dissipate to competitors (Amit *et al.*, 1990a, b).

In addition, entrepreneurial strategy involves undertaking strategic actions that help the entrepreneur to manage information asymmetry. As I explained in Chapter 3, entrepreneurs discover and exploit opportunities that others do not recognize because of superior access to information or a superior ability to recognize opportunity inherent in that information. Moreover, to preserve that opportunity against imitation, the entrepreneur limits access to information about it. Both of these forces result in information asymmetry between entrepreneurs and others.

As I have shown in earlier chapters, uncertainty and information asymmetry influence many aspects of the entrepreneurial process, including the process of opportunity discovery, the decision to exploit, the identification of the individuals who pursue opportunities and the resource acquisition process. Therefore, it is not surprising that entrepreneurs tend to adopt specific strategies to manage uncertainty and information asymmetry. In the remainder of this chapter, I discuss how uncertainty and information asymmetry influence entrepreneurial strategies. As Box 9.1 shows, uncertainty and information asymmetry lead entrepreneurs to adopt six specific strategies: growth from small scale, entry via acquisition, focus, flexibility and adaptability, alliance formation, and legitimation.

BOX 9.1 STRATEGIES TO MANAGE UNCERTAINTY AND INFORMATION ASYMMETRY

- Growth from small scale
- Entry by acquisition
- Focus strategy
- Flexibility and adaptability
- Forming alliances
- Legitimation

Growth from Small Scale

The uncertainty and information asymmetry that are central conditions of the entrepreneurial process mean that it is difficult for entrepreneurs to establish new ventures on the same scale as large, established firms. First, as I explained in Chapter 8, the information asymmetry and uncertainty that pervade the entrepreneurial process require entrepreneurs to self-finance. Because most people have limited capital, this requirement means that most entrepreneurs cannot make large initial investments in their ventures to initiate high volume production, build a brand name, or serve broad market segments.

Second, as I explained in Chapter 2, the pursuit of opportunity requires the entrepreneur to bear risk. Because people are risk averse, most entrepreneurs want to minimize the risk borne in establishing their new ventures. As a result, entrepreneurs find it valuable to avoid large, irreversible investments. Therefore, entrepreneurs seek to initiate entrepreneurial activities on a small scale (Starr and MacMillan, 1990).

By entering on a small scale, entrepreneurs can make use of the logic of real options. The entrepreneur can minimize her potential downside loss if her conjecture about a market opportunity proves to be incorrect by entering a small market niche with particular needs at a small size (Bhide, 2000). On the other hand, if her capabilities prove adequate and demand is present, the entrepreneur can increase her investment (Caves, 1998). Therefore, as Caves (1998: 1959) explains, 'even if the industry's technology supports a large optimal scale, the less confident entrant might rationally start out small, incurring a unit-cost penalty but limiting its sunk commitment while it gathers evidence on its unknown capability'.

Several studies provide indirect evidence in support of the proposition that entrepreneurs adopt strategies to grow from a small scale. First, many of the venture capital studies described in the previous chapter indicate that sophisticated investors take a real options approach to the new ventures that they finance. Because venture capital backed firms perform better than average new firms (Gompers and Lerner, 1999), it appears that high potential ventures tend to start on a small scale and expand from there, if their initial forays prove successful.

Second, most new ventures begin life on a very small scale. According to Dun and Bradstreet data, two-thirds of new firms started with fewer than five employees, 85 per cent began with fewer than ten employees, 98 per cent began with fewer than 50 employees and over 99 per cent began with fewer than 100 employees (Aldrich, 1999). Moreover, the scale of production in an industry does not appear to deter entry. Geroski (1995) explained that new firms are typically founded at a size that is much smaller than the minimum efficient level of scale, and the size at entry appears to be independent of the industry's minimum efficient level of scale.

Third, Bhide (2000) examined the performance of a sample of companies listed in *Inc* magazine as the fastest growing private companies. He showed that most of these firms grew quite large, but had very few initial employees and very little initial capital. This pattern is consistent with growth from a small scale.

The evidence on age

If new ventures expand from a small scale because entrepreneurs enter markets with uncertain conjectures about the value of their venture ideas and expand if their conjectures prove to be correct, then the failure rate of new organizations should decline as they age. When entrepreneurs found new organizations, they are uncertain of whether they can find a market for their new product or service and do not know if they can produce that product or service in a cost-effective and competitive manner. Moreover, they lack the knowledge, skills, roles and routines to produce goods and services and to organize, as well as necessary social ties to stakeholders to coordinate activities under information asymmetry and uncertainty. Because knowledge, skills, roles and routines are learned by doing, new venture performance should be an increasing function of age (Jovanovic, 1982; Carroll and Hannan, 2000).

Empirical research supports this proposition. Several studies have shown that the likelihood of new venture failure declines with age. Kalleberg and Leight (1991) showed that firm age reduced the likelihood that 337 owner-managed small businesses in Indiana would go out of business. Reynolds (1987) found that the survival of 551 new firms established in Minnesota between 1978 and 1984 was positively related to firm age. Delmar and Shane (2001) examined 223 new ventures established by a random sample of Swedish firm founders and tracked over their first 30 months of life. They found that firm age reduced the likelihood of the ventures disbanding. Stearns et al. (1995) found that the survival probability of 2653 new firms founded in Pennsylvania between 1979 and 1985 increased with age. Gimeno et al. (1997) examined 1547 firms that were members of the National Federation of Independent Business, and found that months in business reduced exit. Shane and Foo (1999) examined the survival of 1292 new franchise systems established in the United States between 1979 and 1996 and found that firm age reduced the likelihood of new system failure.

Similar results have been found in single population studies. Researchers have shown that failure rates decline with venture age in populations of newspapers in Argentina, Ireland, Finland, San Francisco, Little Rock, Springfield, Shreveport, Elmira and Lafayette, as well as in populations of immigrant newspapers from around the United States (Hannan and Freeman, 1989; Carroll and Hannan, 1989a, 1989b; Carroll and Wade, 1991; Hannan and Carroll, 1992; Carroll and Delacroix, 1982; Carroll and Huo, 1986; Olzak and West, 1991; Amburgey et al., 1994; Freeman et al., 1983). New firm failure rates also decline as firms age in samples of labor unions, American breweries, semiconductor firms, nursery schools, Californian savings and loan associations, Californian wineries, New York state life insurance companies, and medical device companies (Hannan, 1988; Hannan and Freeman, 1989; Carroll and Hannan, 1989a, 1989b; Carroll and Wade, 1991; and Hannan and Carroll, 1992; Wade et al., 1998; Freeman et al., 1983; Haveman, 1992; Delacroix et al., 1989; Lehrman, 1994; Mitchell, 1994; Hannan et al., 1995; Barnett, 1997).

Industry-level studies have also shown that new venture failure decreases with firm age. Evans (1987) examined all firms operating in a random sample of 100 manufacturing industries in 1976. He found a negative relationship between firm age and survival for 83 per cent of the industries that he examined. Similarly, Carroll (1983) examined 52 datasets on new firms and found that older firms were less likely to die than younger firms in the majority of these data sets.

At a more micro level of analysis, two studies have shown evidence of a negative relationship between duration of self employment and the probability of exit from it. Using data on 2731 white men from the National Longitudinal Survey of Youth, Evans and Leighton (1989) found that the rate of exit from self employment dropped from 10.3 per cent after two years of self employment to 1.6 per cent after 12 years. Using Census data, Bates (1990) also found that the likelihood of exit from self employment declined with the duration of self employment.

Other studies have provided support for the proposition that new venture failure declines with venture age in studies undertaken outside the United States. Mata (1994) and Mata and Portugal (1994) examined the failure rate of new entrants to Portuguese manufacturing in 1983, and found that the failure rate declined with age. Reid (1999) examined the three-year survival of a stratified random sample of 138 clients of the Enterprise Trusts in Scotland, and found that the longer the firms had been in business, the more likely they were to survive. Westhead (1995) examined the factors that predicted the survival of 227 independent high technology firms in existence in the United Kingdom in 1986, and found that older businesses were more likely to survive than younger ones.

Research also supports the proposition that new venture growth increases with venture age. Eisenhardt and Schoonhoven (1990) found that annual sales growth was a positive function of firm age for a sample of 92 semiconductor firms founded between 1978 and 1995. Baum *et al.* (2000) examined the performance of 142 Canadian biotechnology firms founded between 1991 and 1996, and discovered that older firms had faster employment and revenue growth than younger firms.

Firm age also appears to increase the profitability of new businesses. Williams (1999) examined the Characteristics of Business Owners Database and found that firm profitability increased with age for both franchised and independent businesses. Gimeno *et al.* (1997) examined the National Federation of Independent Business Owners database and showed the amount of income that the founders had taken out of the business was an increasing function of firm age.

Similar results for the positive relationship between venture age and profitability have been found when entrepreneurship is measured as self employment. Burke *et al.* (2000) used data from the National Child Development Study to show that the income of the self employed increased with the length of time they had been self employed. Schiller and Crewson (1997) found the same result by examining data from the National Longitudinal Survey of Youth. Taylor (2001) examined the British Household Survey, a representative sample of 5500 British households, and found that the duration of self employment increased self employment income.

The evidence on growth

Given the above argument about growth from a small scale, it stands to reason that ventures that grow from a small scale should perform better than those that do not grow. Growth provides evidence that demand exists for the entrepreneur's product and that she has the capabilities to fulfill that demand. Moreover, growth allows new ventures to reach more efficient levels of production and distribution.

Because the achievement of a first sale is an important milestone in demonstrating that the firm founder's idea has market value despite the initial uncertainty concerning whether customers would demand it, the achievement of a first sale should reduce the likelihood of venture failure. Consistent with this argument, Shane and Delmar (2001) surveyed 225 new ventures initiated by a random sample of Swedish firm founders in the first nine months of 1998, and found that the likelihood of a venture disbanding over its first 24 months was reduced by the achievement of a first sale.

New venture sales growth also enhances new venture survival, as several studies have demonstrated. For example, Reid (1999) examined the three-year survival of a stratified random sample of 138 clients of the Enterprise Trusts in Scotland. He found that founder willingness to give up profits to gain growth was positively related to venture survival. Similarly, Littunen (2000) examined the three-year survival of 138 metal products manufacturers and 62 business service firms in Finland in 1990. He found that firms that concentrated on increasing market share and increasing production were more likely to survive than those that concentrated on other things. Fotopoulos and Louri (2000) examined 209 new firms established in Greece between 1982 and 1984. They found that firms with higher employment growth had lower failure rates. Romanelli (1989a) examined the five-year survival of all firms founded in the minicomputer industry between 1957 and 1981 and showed that increased sales had a positive effect on survival. Reynolds (1987) examined the one-year survival of 551 new firms founded in Minnesota between 1978, and found that survival was positively related to sales growth.

Entrepreneurs who adopt a growth strategy also have ventures that grow faster than those who do not adopt a growth strategy, as several studies have shown. White and Reynolds (1996) followed 332 new firms sampled from the Wisconsin unemployment insurance files for two years. They found that the firms whose founders expected higher sales and employment growth had actual sales and employment growth that was significantly higher than the median two years later. Cardozo *et al.* (1992) examined 551 firms established in Minnesota between 1979 and 1982, and found that firms with higher initial sales growth had higher subsequent sales growth. Schutgens and Wever (2000) examined the employment growth from 1994 to 1997 of 563 new firms registered with the Dutch Chamber of Commerce in the first quarter of 1994 and found that, the greater the venture's sales turnover was at founding, the higher its subsequent employment growth.

Sales growth also increases profitability and the likelihood of an initial public offering, as one would expect, given the expansion-from-a-small-scale argument. Using the Characteristics of Business Owners database of the US Department of Census, Williams (1999) found that sales growth was positively correlated with profit growth for both franchised and independent businesses. Hannan *et al.* (2002) examined the likelihood of initial public offering for 155 technology companies founded in Silicon Valley between 1984 and 1994, and found that a firms level of revenues increased its likelihood of initial public offering.

Entry Via Acquisition

A strategy of entry into entrepreneurship through the acquisition of an existing business helps entrepreneurs to manage the uncertainty inherent in the entrepreneurial process. If a business already exists, information is known about demand, procedures for producing and delivering a product or service, and the venture's ability to compete with other ventures (Bates, 1990). This information reduces uncertainty and therefore should enhance the performance of entrepreneurs at opportunity exploitation.

Some empirical evidence supports the proposition that entry into entrepreneurship through acquisition enhances the performance of new ventures. Using data from the 1982 Characteristics of Business Owner database to examine the longevity of new businesses started by white males between 1976 and 1982, Bates (1990) found that those ventures whose founders had purchased their businesses were less likely than the others to have exited by 1986. Similarly, Duchesneau and Gartner (1990) compared 13 successful and 13 failed ventures in fresh orange juice distribution, and showed that the founders of the failed ventures were less likely than the founders of the successful ventures to have purchased their firms.

Focus Strategy

New ventures tend to focus on a single product or service and a single market segment because that strategy best overcomes the uncertainty inherent in exploiting an entrepreneurial opportunity for two reasons. First, the resolution of uncertainty about the entrepreneur's conjecture involves the investment of resources in gathering information about the opportunity and the entrepreneur's plan for exploiting it. The process of gathering this information involves the expenditure of capital, which is very costly for new ventures (Anton and Yao, 1995). Because new ventures must raise funds from capital markets rather than use internally generated cash flows, they pay a premium for capital. By focusing and exploiting markets or products sequentially, the entrepreneur can use the cash flow generated from the exploitation of the first product/market to finance the exploitation of the second product/market. As a result, a focus strategy is less costly for entrepreneurs than a strategy of developing multiple products/markets simultaneously.

Second, a focus strategy is beneficial to new ventures because targeting a niche market that is not well served by established firms is much more effective than going head-to-head with an established player. Given the uncertainty of entrepreneurial conjectures, entrepreneurs often enter markets at less than minimum efficient scale. As a result, new ventures are initially less efficient than established players and do poorly in head-to-head competition with them. By focusing on an under-served niche, the entrepreneur can avoid being driven out of the market by an established competitor before she is able to prove and scale up her opportunity.

Some empirical evidence supports this argument. Bhide (2000) found that *Inc* 500 firms, which are better than average performing new ventures, have tended to focus on niche markets that large companies avoid, as well as on new markets where established players do not yet exist (Bhide, 2000). Similarly, Christiansen (1993) examined the rigid disk drive industry in the United States from 1976 to 1989, and found that the most successful start-ups in that industry focused on a single product. In contrast, unsuccessful start-ups attempted to diversify their operations from the start.

Several studies have shown that new ventures are more likely to survive if they adopt a focus strategy. For example, Romanelli (1989a) examined the five-year survival of all firms founded in the minicomputer industry between 1957 and 1981 and found that the breadth of the market pursued (number of segments) had a negative effect on survival. Gimeno *et al.* (1997) examined 1547 new firms whose founders were members of the National Federation of Independent Business, and discovered that a broader geographic radius of initial sales increased new venture failure. Bruderl *et al.* (1992) examined the five-year survival of 1849 businesses registered with the local chamber of commerce in Munich and Upper Bavaria and found that specialist businesses, which focused on a single market or product, were less likely to fail than generalist businesses.

New ventures also are more likely to grow if they have adopted a focus strategy. Reynolds (1987) surveyed 551 new firms founded in Minnesota between 1978 and 1984 and discovered that one-year sales growth was positively correlated with the adoption of strategic focus. Simon and Zahra (1994) examined 72 new biotechnology firms created by individual entrepreneurs and found that the percentage rate of sales growth was positively correlated with the adoption of a focus strategy. Bamford *et al.* (2000) examined 140 new banks established in 1988. These authors found that the more concentrated a firm's product mix was, the higher its sales were every year from 1989 to 1994.

Flexibility and Adaptability

Given the technical, market and competitive uncertainty that pervades the pursuit of opportunities, entrepreneurs need to be flexible and adaptive. The fundamental uncertainty of the entrepreneurial process means that entrepreneurs cannot predict the future. Events transpire that have the potential to derail entrepreneurs' plans for opportunity exploitation. Consequently, new ventures must often adapt to develop new solutions to unanticipated problems (Bhide, 2000).

Some empirical evidence supports this argument. For example, Starr and MacMillan (1990) found that entrepreneurs typically minimize commitment to a particular course of action by investing only in assets that can be re-deployed easily. This emphasis on flexibility means that many technology ventures begin as consulting or contract organizations to avoid making investments in the fixed assets that reduce strategic flexibility (Roberts, 1991a). Over time, as uncertainty is reduced, these ventures evolve into manufacturing firms.

Christiansen (1993) provides perhaps the best example of the use of a flexible, adaptive strategy by new ventures to overcome uncertainty in the entrepreneurial process. Examining the rigid disk drive industry in the United States from 1976 to 1989, he found that start-up companies had to identify new market applications for their disk drives. The new architectures inherent in their products precluded them from selling their disk drives to large computer makers. As a result, they had to evolve over time by iterating from segment to segment until they found a market segment interested in buying their product (Christiansen and Bower, 1996).

Forming Alliances

The exploitation of entrepreneurial opportunity generates several problems that make forming alliances with established firms an important part of entrepreneurial strategy. First, opportunities are often short-lived and the effort to create all of the assets that are needed to pursue the opportunity may take too long (Katilla and Mang, forthcoming). The establishment of alliances provides a way to speed up the entrepreneurial process by allowing the entrepreneur to tap a source of already existing assets.

Second, opportunity exploitation is enhanced by strategies that allow the entrepreneur to obtain control over resources without purchasing them. Because entrepreneurship involves the recombination of resources held by others, it requires entrepreneurs to obtain control over those resources. Although an entrepreneur could conceivably purchase all of the resources needed to exploit an opportunity, such an approach is inhibited by the entrepreneur's capital constraints. By allying with others, the entrepreneur can gain access to necessary assets without incurring the large capital costs of purchasing those assets (Larson, 1992).

Moreover, contracting reduces the risk borne by the entrepreneur because it reduces the magnitude of the potential downside loss. If resources must be transformed into a specialized form to exploit an opportunity, the owner of the transformed resources must bear the risk that the specialized form proves to be without value. By allying with others, the entrepreneur can shift this risk to others (Venkataraman, 1997).

Third, the entrepreneur faces a fundamental problem in convincing others that the product or service that she has developed to exploit an opportunity is valuable. The fact that potential customers have not identified the opportunity makes them disinclined to believe that it is valuable. The entrepreneur can mitigate this problem by selling the new product or service under the brand name of an established firm through an alliance, licensing agreement or marketing arrangement (Eisenhardt and Schoonhoven, 1996). Because the established firm would lose its valuable reputation if it associated with a new venture whose product or service proved not to be valuable (Shepherd *et al.*, 2000; Baum *et al.*, 2000), the use of alliances mitigates the problem of demonstrating the value of new products and services to potential customers. Even though they are still faced with significant uncertainty and information asymmetry, people seeking to evaluate the worth of the new venture's product or service can look to the reputation of the alliance partner as evidence that the product or service is valuable (Stuart *et al.*, 1999).

Several empirical studies support the argument that forming alliances is an effective strategy for new ventures. For example, Larson (1991) examined seven new firms and found that new firms were better able to exploit opportunities if they formed alliances with other firms. These alliances allowed the new ventures to be more flexible and responsive without raising costs or slowing operations, and allowed them to use their partners' reputations to convince others of the value of their products and services.

Bruderl *et al.* (1992) showed that forming alliances with other firms reduced the likelihood that new ventures would fail. Using data on the five-year survival of 1849 new business ventures registered with the local chamber of commerce in Munich and Upper Bavaria in the mid-1980s, these authors found that those new ventures that were affiliated with an existing business were less likely to fail than those without an affiliation.

Moreover, forming alliances appears to enhance the growth of new ventures. Baum *et al.* (2000) examined the performance of 142 Canadian biotechnology firms established between 1991 and 1996. They found that firms with a more efficient (non-redundant) network of marketing or research and development alliance partners at the time of founding had faster revenue growth than firms with a less efficient network of partners. Stearns (1996) studied 82 new firms drawn from Wisconsin state unemployment insurance files and found that high growth ventures (those with greater than 50 per cent sales growth over five years) had more marketing and international strategic alliances than other firms in his sample. Zahra and Bogner (2000) surveyed 116 US-based software companies that were less than eight years old, and found that those firms that had more alliances and licensing relationships had higher market share growth.

The profitability of new ventures and the likelihood of their achieving an initial public offering also increase with the use of alliance strategies. Zahra and Bogner's (2000) study of young software companies showed that firms that had more alliances and licensing agreements had higher return on equity. Similarly, Stuart *et al.* (1999) examined the rate of initial public offering from 1978 to 1991 of 301 venture capital backed dedicated biotechnology companies in human diagnostics and therapeutics, and found that the number of alliance partners exerted a positive effect on the probability of initial public offering.

The value of forming alliances is even greater when the alliances are formed with high status actors. People are more likely to believe the claims of high status actors than the claims of low status actors because status gives people credibility. Consequently, it is easier for new ventures to overcome problems of information asymmetry and uncertainty in ascertaining the value of their products and services when their alliance partners are of higher status (Stuart *et al.*, 1999).

Several studies have shown that the quality of a new venture's alliance network also increases its likelihood of achieving an initial public offering. Baum *et al.* (2000) report that biotechnology and semiconductor start-ups allied to prominent established firms have faster initial public offerings and higher valuations than other start-ups in these industries. Stuart *et al.* (1999) found that technical and commercial prominence of alliance partners had a positive effect on probability of initial public offering in their sample of biotechnology companies. Freeman (2000) examined the likelihood of initial public offering, acquisition and failure for 4064 venture capital backed new firms from 1987 to 1995, and found that the centrality in the investment community of the firms' venture capitalist backers, a sociological measure of status, had a positive effect on the new firm's likelihood of an initial public offering.

Legitimation

As I explained in Chapter 3, potential stakeholders are uncertain about the entre-preneur's conjecture about how to exploit an entrepreneurial opportunity because that conjecture is based on information that they do not possess or do not understand (Aldrich and Baker, 2001). Moreover, other stakeholders lack much of the information that the entrepreneur possesses, and this information asymmetry makes it difficult for others to take for granted the entrepreneur's opportunity and method for exploiting it. As a result, the entrepreneur needs to take strategic actions that indicate that the opportunity and her approach to exploiting it are socially acceptable (Aldrich and Baker, 2001).

Entrepreneurs can undertake a variety of actions to demonstrate the legitimacy of their opportunities and their approaches to exploiting them. Sometimes the process of legitimating involves imitating existing firms' routines and competencies, which people already take for granted (Aldrich, 1999). By imitating others, the entrepreneur can minimize the uncertainty and information asymmetry inherent in the opportunity by reducing the external perception that the opportunity is different from what people already know.

Other times the process of legitimating involves achieving collective agreement on standards and designs, which reduces stakeholders' confusion about the acceptability of the approaches taken by new ventures. Moreover, convergence on standards and designs means that observers need to use less cognitive effort to learn that the opportunity is reliable and valid than is the case if multiple competing variants exist. These efforts to minimize stakeholders' confusion and reduce the cognitive demands placed on them increase stakeholders' perceptions of the entrepreneurs' reliability (Aldrich, 1999).

Still other times, legitimating involves engaging in actions that allow the venture to be certified by reputable authorities (Rao, 1994). For example, a new venture might obtain an endorsement by a scientific authority, or obtain a Good Housekeeping seal of approval. By obtaining certification from reputable authorities, the entrepreneur can demonstrate that her opportunity and method of exploiting it is legitimate and acceptable, and therefore is worthy of the support of others.

Some empirical evidence supports the proposition that certification and other legitimating actions enhance new venture performance. For example, Rao (1994) studied new American automobile companies at the turn of the 20th century and found that carmakers were more likely to survive if they won certification contests put on by reputable publications. Singh *et al.* (1986b) examined the population of new voluntary social service organizations founded in Toronto from 1970 to 1980. They found that the acquisition of a community directory listing and a charitable registration number, two actions that provided the venture with external credibility and legitimacy, reduced the likelihood of failure. In a study that spanned several hundred years, Miner *et al.* (1990) found that Finnish newspapers had lower failure rates if they were affiliated with political parties. Baum and Oliver (1991) found that Toronto day care centers and nursery schools that had ties to schools, community centers or other agencies had significantly lower failure rates than those centers without such ties. Loree (1993) found that integrated circuit manufacturers had lower failure rates if the US military approved them for manufacture. Lastly, Shane and Foo's

(1999) study of new franchise systems showed that the franchisor's ranking by *Entrepreneur* magazine (a trade publication that was a source of franchisor certification) had a negative effect on the likelihood of system failure.

Externally legitimated new firms also grow faster than other firms. Lerner (1999) examined 1435 new firms over a ten-year period and found that the sales growth and employment growth of Small Business Innovation Research grant awardees was greater than those of a matched set of firms. He also found that this effect was much stronger in high technology industries and was confined to firms in geographic areas with high early-stage venture capital disbursements. Because the Small Business Innovation Research grant recipients were no more likely to get venture capital than the matched sample before the award but significantly more likely to receive it afterwards, Lerner (1999) attributed the recipients' superior ability to garner outside capital and to grow, to the certification that the receipt of the grant provided.

SUMMARY

This chapter explored the strategies by which entrepreneurs exploit new venture opportunities. In general, entrepreneurial strategy involves two major issues: first, how does the entrepreneur develop a competitive advantage that precludes the dissipation of the opportunity to competitors once she has begun to exploit it? Second, how does the entrepreneur manage the uncertainty and information asymmetry inherent in the exploitation of an opportunity when she seeks to generate value from it?

The entrepreneur would like to preserve the profits she earns from exploiting entrepreneurial opportunities. She can do this in two ways. First, the entrepreneur can preclude others from gaining access to or understanding the information about the opportunity. This effort includes keeping secret the information that led to the discovery, as well as exploiting causal ambiguity to preclude people from understanding how to use that information, even if they have access to it. Second, the entrepreneur can preclude others from actually exploiting the opportunity even if they have access to information about the opportunity and understand it. The entrepreneur precludes others from exploiting the opportunity by erecting five different kinds of barriers to competition: controlling the resources needed to exploit opportunities, establishing legal barriers to imitation, exploiting opportunities at a scale that deters imitation, establishing a reputation, and innovating to stay ahead of competition.

Entrepreneurial strategy also involves managing the uncertainty and information asymmetry present in the process of exploiting opportunities. To do this, the entrepreneur engages in several actions. The entrepreneur starts on a small scale and grows the venture if the opportunity proves valuable. She also frequently enters via acquisition to reduce demand and production uncertainty. The entrepreneur adopts a focus strategy to resolve uncertainty about her conjecture and to keep the new venture from competing head-to-head with established firms. To overcome uncertainty, the entrepreneur also makes her venture flexible and adaptive. She forms alliances with established firms to obtain the assets needed to pursue the opportunity quickly; to obtain control over resources without purchasing them; and to use the established firm's reputation. The entrepreneur also takes strategic actions that indicate that the opportunity and the approach to exploitation are legitimate by imitating existing firms' routines and competencies; by achieving collective agreement on standards and designs; and by obtaining certification from reputable authorities.

I now turn to the next chapter, which explores the process by which the entrepreneur organizes the entity that exploits the entrepreneurial opportunity.

NOTE

1. The mechanism by which size reduces new venture failure has not been tested. Thus, the empirical evidence could support any argument in favor of a correlation between new venture size and survival.

10.   The organizing process

To exploit an opportunity for which she has gathered resources, an entrepreneur must engage in organizing. Organizing involves creating the routines and structures that support the goal-directed, boundary-maintaining system of collective activities that recombine resources according to the entrepreneur's conjectures (Aldrich, 1979).

In contrast to much of the static description of organization in the academic literature, organizing is a process, not a state. It takes place over time, as founders engage in a set of activities, such as obtaining equipment, establishing production processes, attracting employees and setting up legal entities (Katz and Gartner, 1988). Although the range of time that this organizing process can take is quite large, and varies with the nature of the opportunity being pursued, Reynolds and White (1997) provide evidence to suggest that the average organizing process – the time until a new venture organizing effort is an operating firm – takes about one year.

Researchers have observed that organizing efforts are fairly common in modern society. In fact, Reynolds and White (1997) report that between 4 and 6 per cent of the working age population in the United States is engaged in organizing a new firm at any point in time. Because many entrepreneurs exploit opportunities through market mechanisms, this estimate likely understates the true amount of organizing activity that is occurring at any point in time. Moreover, this high level of organizing activity means that more than 40 per cent of the population engages in organizing activity at some time during their careers (Aldrich, 1999).

In this chapter, I explore the activities that entrepreneurs undertake to organize the exploitation of entrepreneurial opportunities. In doing so, I first discuss the dynamic nature of organizing, emphasizing that it is a process, not a state. Second, I discuss the role of planning in organizing efforts. Third, I discuss the entrepreneur's choice of the mode of opportunity exploitation, focusing on the decision to spin off from an employer, and the choice between market mechanisms and hierarchical arrangements. Fourth, I examine several core dimensions of the organizing process, including the selection of the legal entity, the determination of the size of the new entity, the selection of employees, the allocation of employment between permanent and temporary workforce, and the structure of the new organization and its production process.

THE ORGANIZATION DESIGN PROCESS

To profit from the discovery of an opportunity, an entrepreneur needs to establish the organization or market mechanism that she will use to exploit it. This process – called organizing – involves creating routines and structures that will be used to recombine resources into the product or service sold to customers, and to create the entity that will undertake the recombinatory activity (Venkataraman, 1997).

The organizing process is uncertain because the future of efforts to exploit opportunities is unknown before the entrepreneur takes action. The routines and structures that will be used to recombine resources and to create the entity that will undertake that activity have to be created before much of the information about technology, ways to coordinate, strategy, stakeholder networks and customer demand is known with certainty. Therefore, as I explained in Chapter 3, at the time that the entrepreneur organizes, she must base her decisions on conjectures (Arrow, 1974a). Because the entrepreneur cannot identify all possible actions and all expected outcomes of those actions, the organizing process is fundamentally uncertain (Harper, 1996).

Moreover, the information asymmetry that gives rise to the discovery of entrepreneurial opportunities also influences the organizing process. Because organizing requires people to use their information to make decisions, the knowledge people possess influences their organization designs (Azoulay and Shane, 2001). In general, entrepreneurs design their organization by basing routines and structures on knowledge gained from education, working in an industry, or from imitation of established firms (Aldrich and Von Glinow, 1992; Katz *et al.*, 2000; Klepper, 2001).

Several authors provide empirical support for this explanation of the origin of organization designs in new ventures. For example, Hannan *et al.* (1996) found that new company human resource practices typically have their origin in founders' employment models. Thus, Baron *et al.*'s (1999) investigation of 100 technology companies founded in Silicon Valley between 1984 and 1994 showed that the founders' employment model predicted the degree of administrative intensity of their new organizations. And Cooper *et al.*'s (1990) examination of new ventures whose founders were members of the National Federation of Independent Businesses showed that founders who had more management experience were more likely than other founders to pursue administrative goals in their new ventures.

The fact that prior information influences the designs of new ventures suggests that entrepreneurs adopt a wide variety of approaches to organizing their new ventures. Some of these approaches will be better than others (Aldrich, 1999). In general, entrepreneurs that have worse knowledge of organization design will design their new organizations on the basis of 'erroneously imagined decision frameworks' (Kirzner, 1997: 355), and will establish routines and structures that prove to be ineffective.

Some empirical evidence supports this argument. For example, Azoulay and Shane (2001) examined quantitative data on 170 new franchise systems and interview data on 16 new franchise systems established between 1992 and 1995. They found that franchise systems that used exclusive territories were more likely to survive over time because the use of exclusive territories mitigated hold-up problems. While the adoption of exclusive territories was survival enhancing, many entrepreneurs did not adopt this organization design because they simply did not know or understand how exclusive territories solved hold-up problems.

When initial designs for organizations prove to be ineffective, entrepreneurs often adapt them through a process of improvisation (Aldrich, 1999). For example, Baker *et al.* (forthcoming) examined 68 technology start-up ventures and observed that entrepreneurs engaged in significant improvisation of their approaches to human resources when they found that their initial designs were ineffective at attracting employees.

However, many entrepreneurs are unable to design the right routines or structures in their new organizations, or to adapt those routines or structures into an effective form through improvisation. Consequently, many organizing efforts fail, with estimates ranging as high as half of the total (Aldrich, 1999).

THE ROLE OF PLANNING

Although many entrepreneurs engage in improvisation when their initial organizing efforts are not successful and develop a flexible and adaptive strategy (see Chapter 9), entrepreneurship also involves planning. Specifically, the entrepreneur formulates a plan, in mental or written form, for the organizing process that she will use to recombine resources to exploit an opportunity. This planning then leads to organizing activities (Reynolds, 1994b; Reynolds and White, 1997).

Planning is a valuable part of the organizing process because it overcomes several problems that result from the uncertainty and information asymmetry present in the exploitation of entrepreneurial opportunities. First, planning tests the accuracy of the entrepreneur's conjectures about opportunities. Efforts to exploit new opportunities generally begin as unsubstantiated claims based on the entrepreneur's interpretation of the information that she possesses. Planning tests the accuracy of the entrepreneur's conjectures about demand, production and governance by forcing the entrepreneur to articulate assumptions and formulate hypotheses that can be tested for internal consistency, plausibility and accuracy, given potentially disconfirming information (Harper, 1996).

Second, planning can indicate the human, physical and financial resources that the venture will need, and can show how the parts of the organizing effort will link together before the expense of trial and error effort is incurred. Because human beings have limited cognitive capacity, they need planning tools to help them analyse complex tasks and to avoid making errors in decision-making. Planning facilitates this analysis by allowing people to incorporate more information in more complex ways and make more accurate decisions than they otherwise would (Tolchinsky and King, 1980).

Third, planning increases people's ability to learn new information by focusing their attention (Langer and Applebee, 1987; Locke and Latham, 1990). By planning, the entrepreneur learns where she should search for information that the venture is lacking (Duchesneau and Gartner, 1990), and becomes better able to absorb this additional information once it is found (Castrogiovanni, 1996).

Fourth, planning clarifies goals and sets specific objectives, which facilitate the achievement of those goals (Locke and Latham, 1990; Rousseau, 1997). In support of this argument, researchers have shown that having a vision for the future enhances the development of an organization only if the entrepreneur has set concrete objectives (Baum, 1994).

Fifth, planning helps to communicate information to others, thereby facilitating organizing (Castrogiovanni, 1996). Planning leads the entrepreneur to understand the logic of her own conjectures, thereby facilitating her ability to communicate them to others. In addition, referencing a plan helps the founder to transfer information to others about their role in the exploitation of an opportunity. In particular, assembling facts and presenting conjectures in oral, written, visual and physical form enhances communication with others (Harper, 1996). Thus, Van de Ven *et al.* (1984) examined 14 software start-ups and found that those founders who engaged in business planning more clearly articulated to stakeholders their vision of the business and its specific goals.

The empirical literature supports the value of planning to the organizing process (Aldrich and Baker, 2001). Several studies have shown that inadequate pre-start-up and post-start-up planning by entrepreneurs hinders the acquisition of necessary information (Trow, 1961; Woodruff and Alexander, 1958) and that planning enhances the development and performance of start-ups after founding (Van de Ven *et al.*, 1984) For example, Delmar and Shane (2001) examined 223 new ventures established by a random sample of Swedish firm founders in the first nine months of 1998 and followed over the subsequent 30 months. They found that completing a business plan increased the lilelihood that the founders would gather inputs, talk to customers, complete product development and initiate marketing and promotion. Shuman *et al.* (1985) surveyed 220 founders of *Inc* 500 firms and found that those who engaged in business planning were more likely to develop mechanisms to allocate resources and to institute procedures for control and coordination in their ventures. Similarly, Duchesneau and Gartner (1990) found that entrepreneurs who spent less time planning also conducted less market research and had a narrower strategic vision.

Planning also increases the growth of new ventures. Reynolds and White (1997) surveyed 2624 new firms in three different states and found that those that engaged in formal business planning had higher high growth rates than those that did not. Dunkelberg *et al.* (1987) surveyed members of the National Federation of Independent Business who founded new ventures in the mid-1980s. These authors found that business planning was correlated with the growth of the new ventures. Schutgens and Wever (2000) examined employment growth from 1994 to 1997 of 563 new firms registered with the Dutch Chamber of Commerce in the first quarter of 1994 and found that those that had better planning and preparation had higher employment growth.

Similar results have been found from studies that have examined the founder's tendency to plan rather than the creation of business plans. Miner *et al.* (1989) surveyed 118 technical entrepreneurs who had applied for grants from the National Science Foundation and found that mean annual growth in sales of their ventures was positively correlated with the entrepreneur's tendency to plan for the future. Miner *et al.* (1994) followed up with 53 of these entrepreneurs and reexamined the relationship between planning and growth five-and-a-half years later. The authors again found that the entrepreneur's tendency to plan for the future was positively correlated with the venture's sales growth. Tullar (2001) examined the average annual rate of employment and sales growth for ventures founded by 58 Russian entrepreneurs who had participated in a training program four years earlier, and found that the entrepreneur's tendency to plan for the future significantly increased the employment growth of their ventures.

Planning also appears to increase the income earned by the entrepreneur from the new venture. Miner *et al.*'s (1989) survey of technical entrepreneurs and Miner *et al.*'s (1994) follow-up both showed that their ventures' annual income was positively correlated with their tendency to plan for the future.

As I explained above, one reason that planning is valuable is that it allows the entrepreneur to articulate a clear vision, which, in turn, encourages the growth of the new venture. A clear vision allows the venture's employees, customers and investors to share the entrepreneur's approach to exploiting the opportunity and make commitments to it (Bird and Jelinek, 1988). A clear vision also facilitates the entrepreneur's efforts to communicate her idea to others. Furthermore, it allows the entrepreneur to motivate others without the use of tangible resources (Baron, forthcoming).

Several empirical studies provide support for the value of a clear vision for the venture on new venture performance. For example, Baum *et al.* (1998) examined the two-year sales growth of 183 new ventures in architectural woodworking. They found that other organization members' perception that the founder had a vision, the written or oral communication of that vision, and the growth content of that vision had significant positive effects on venture growth. Similarly, Ensley *et al.* (2000) surveyed 116 lead entrepreneurs of *Inc* 500 firms in 1994, and found that sales growth of the firms was positively correlated with the vision scores of the lead entrepreneurs.

THE MODES OF EXPLOITATION

Another important aspect of the organizing process concerns the mode of opportunity exploitation. The choice of the mode of exploitation depends on the answer to two questions: first, does the individual who identified the opportunity want to exploit it on behalf of someone else or do they want to exploit it on their own? Second, does the individual want to use a market mechanism, such as licensing or franchising, to exploit the opportunity or does he want to use a hierarchical mechanism, such as a firm?

Figure 10.1 shows how four common types of entrepreneurial activity – independent start-up, corporate venturing, licensing/acquisition and spin-off – can be categorized by just considering whether the person discovering the opportunity was within or outside the exploiting organization at the time of discovery and whether the entrepreneur exploits the opportunity through a market mechanism or a firm.

		Discovery	
		Independent individual	Organization member
Exploitation	Independent individual	Independent start-up	Spin-off
	Organization member	Acquisition/ licensing	Corporate venturing

Figure 10.1   The modes of exploitation

The Decision to Spin-off

Audretsch (2001) observed that human agency is necessary for the discovery of entrepreneurial opportunities. Individuals, whether they are working in an existing organization, or are retired or unemployed at the time of their discovery, are the entities that discover opportunities. The organizations that employ people are inanimate and cannot engage in discovery. Therefore, any explanation for the mode of opportunity exploitation must be based on choices made by individuals about how they would like to exploit the opportunities that they have discovered.

In the less common case in which the discoverer of the opportunity is not employed at the time of discovery, the situation is easy to explain. Markets for the sale of entrepreneurial opportunities generally fail because of problems of information disclosure (Casson, 1982). As a result, individuals can sell their opportunities to existing organizations only under a small number of circumstances. (The conditions under which opportunities can be sold are described below.) Most of the time, if a person is not employed by an existing organization at the time of discovery, the opportunity will be exploited through the creation of a new firm.

Because most of the people who discover entrepreneurial opportunities are employed at the time they discover their opportunities, a more interesting question concerns how an employee makes the decision about how to exploit the opportunity that she has discovered (Audretsch, 2001). Specifically, does she spin off and start a new company or does she exploit the opportunity on behalf of her employer?

Risk-adjusted expected value

One explanation for how people make this decision is cost–benefit analysis. The discoverer of the opportunity calculates her expected compensation from the exploitation of the opportunity on behalf of her employer and compares that compensation to the discounted expected value of profits from founding a firm. While the entrepreneur might weight this decision by the non-economic factors such as desire for independence described in Chapter 5 and might include the liquidity and uncertainty premiums discussed in Chapter 4, the basic decision-making model is simple. When the expected value from founding a firm is larger than the expected value from exploiting the opportunity on behalf of the employer, the individual spins off instead of engaging in corporate venturing (Audretsch, 2001).

The uncertainty of the opportunity

While comparison of expected values provides a basic explanation of the decision to spin off, several characteristics of the opportunity, including its uncertainty and its radicalness influence the decision to spin off. First and foremost, the uncertainty of the opportunity increases the likelihood of a spin-off. Knight (1921) explained that decision-making under uncertainty requires formulating opinions based on partial knowledge. People formulate different opinions because they have different individual attributes and different information. Differences between the attributes and information of the discoverer and her employer are likely to lead the two parties to form different expected values for the opportunity. These differences in expected values will be larger when uncertainty is higher because the opinions of the two parties will be based less on common objective information and more on private information and opinion (Audretsch, 2001). If the expected value of the opportunity formulated by the discoverer is greater than that formulated by the employer, the discoverer is likely to see any compensation offered by the employer as insufficient to justify undertaking the opportunity on behalf of the employer. As a result, Klepper and Sleeper (2001) point out, the discoverer of the opportunity often becomes frustrated with the employer, who the discoverer believes is failing to capitalize properly on the opportunity, and quits to found a new firm to exploit the opportunity.

Some empirical research supports this argument. Several observers have noted that uncertain technologies often lead people to spin off from existing companies after their employers have rejected their efforts to pursue the opportunity on behalf of the employer (Cooper, 1971; Amit and Muller, 1994; Bhide, 2000). Christiansen (1993) examined the rigid disk drive industry in the United States from 1976 to 1989 and found such a pattern underlying spin-offs. He discovered that the founders of new disk drive companies were often members of an engineering team at a previous disk drive company who had developed a new disk drive architecture that their employer was unwilling to pursue. Similarly, Lowe (2001) examined 489 inventions disclosed to the University of California between 1986 and 1995 and found that when knowledge was more uncertain, the inventors were more likely to start new firms to exploit their inventions in large part because they could not persuade others to license them.

The radicalness of the opportunity

The radicalness of the opportunity will also increase the likelihood that the entrepreneur will exploit it by spin off for several reasons. First, when an opportunity is based on radical technology that undermines the competence advantages of existing firms, the employer is not likely to want to exploit the opportunity (Tushman and Anderson, 1986). Established firms avoid investing in opportunities that cannibalize their existing operations (Arrow, 1962). Moreover, existing routines lead the employer to discount or ignore opportunities based on technology that they do not have (Henderson, 1993).

Second, established firms do not provide strong incentives for employees to pursue opportunities that are based on radical innovation. Not only do such uncertain opportunities require the high powered incentives that can be created only through significant equity holdings, but established firms give employees incentives to focus their attention on what they have always been doing instead of on innovation (Foster, 1986; Holmstrom, 1989).

Third, Henderson and Clark (1990) explain that radical innovations are difficult for existing firms to pursue, given their structures and communication channels. The routines and organization structures that established firms find useful for searching and refining local, familiar information, often perform poorly in identifying and developing new information, leading established organizations to reject radical opportunities (Henderson, 1993; Henderson and Clark, 1990; Nelson and Winter, 1982).

Fourth, established firms seek to serve their existing customers, who prefer suppliers that focus on making incremental improvements to existing products and services rather than making radical changes to those products and services (Christiansen and Bower, 1996). Because radically new products or services are often inferior to existing alternatives on the dimensions that customers care about when they are first introduced, customers do not have an incentive to adopt radically new products or services. In fact, Christiansen (1993) explains that spin-offs will exploit radical opportunities because an established firm's existing customers will not be interested in purchasing products or services based on radical technology.

Some empirical evidence supports this proposition. For example, Shane (2001a) examined the 1397 inventions patented by the Massachusetts Institute of Technology between 1980 and 1996 and found that more radical patents were more likely to lead to firm formation than more incremental patents. Similarly, Tushman and Anderson (1986) examined the cement industry from 1872 to 1980, the minicomputer industry from 1956 to 1980, and the airline industry from 1924 to 1980, and found that new firms were disproportionately likely to introduce competence-destroying technologies. In contrast, Baum *et al.* (1995) report that the shift from analog to digital technology in the facsimile transmission business enhanced the competence of established producers, and reduced the formation rate of new firms.

Other aspects of the opportunity

Several other aspects of the opportunity also influence the likelihood that an entrepreneurial opportunity will be exploited via a spin-off. First, the discreteness of the entrepreneur's opportunity increases the likelihood that the entrepreneur will spin off. New firm formation is easier when an entrepreneur can enter with a discrete piece of knowledge than when the knowledge necessary to exploit the opportunity is embedded in a system belonging to established firms (Winter, 1984). When the opportunity is embedded in a system controlled by someone else, the entrepreneur will find it difficult to exploit the opportunity without replicating the entire system, a proposition that is seldom cost effective.

Second, the individual is more likely to spin off if the basis of the opportunity lies in human, rather than physical, capital (Klepper and Sleeper, 2001). While human beings can move relatively easily from an existing organization to pursue an entrepreneurial opportunity, physical assets are much less mobile. Therefore, the discoverer will be more likely to spin off if the key to the opportunity lies in her head than if it lies in something that resides physically on the premises of the employer.

Firm characteristics

Several attributes of the discoverer's employer also influence her tendency to spin off. First, a bureaucratic organizational structure will increase the likelihood of a spin-off because the exploitation of uncertain entrepreneurial opportunities requires organizational flexibility. Many organizations minimize flexibility in order to monitor employees closely. By monitoring employees, the organization can hold them accountable for failure to perform at the expected level, and therefore improve efficiency. However, this approach will restrict the employee's freedom of action and thus undermines her ability to engage in opportunity exploitation (Holmstrom, 1989). Moreover, a bureaucratic organization design will create structures and institutional pressures that make the organization slow to respond to change (Hannan and Freeman, 1977, 1984). This inertia will inhibit its ability to take actions quickly enough to exploit entrepreneurial opportunities.

In a test of this argument, Klepper and Sleeper (2001) examined 79 laser firms that were founded by someone who had been previously employed by a laser firm. They found that large, bureaucratic, diversified firms generated more spin-offs than small, flexible organizations.

Second, an organization that generates more new products will also generate more spin-offs (Klepper, 2001). Organizations that introduce more new products provide their employees with more information than other firms about how to pursue opportunities in their industry (Hannan and Freeman, 1987). Moreover, the tendency of a firm to create new products leads its employees to develop confidence that they have the necessary skills to pursue opportunities (Aldrich, 1999). In support of this argument, Brittain and Freeman (1986) found that semiconductor firms with more products had more spin-offs; and Klepper and Sleeper (2001) found that laser firms with more products had more spin-offs.

Third, organizations that offer better incentives to their employees to exploit their opportunities on behalf of the employer will have fewer spin-offs (Romanelli, 1989b). For example, if the organization does not allow employees to receive equity in the exploitation of an opportunity, the individual would not be able to share in the potential returns to exploitation as an employee (Audretsch, 1997). As a result, the individual would be more likely to engage in a spin-off.

Fourth, the discoverer will be more likely to spin off from a firm with a stronger brand name reputation. Established firms are often reluctant to pursue entrepreneurial opportunities for fear that they will make incorrect decisions that will harm their reputations (Holmstrom, 1989). The greater the magnitude of their reputations, the greater the potential damage from incorrect decisions, and the lower the likelihood that the existing organization will exploit an opportunity that an employee has discovered.

Hierarchies Versus Markets

To exploit an opportunity, the entrepreneur must develop the production process that she will use to transform those resources into new products or services (Bhave, 1994). One important decision that the entrepreneur has to make about developing this production process concerns whether to vertically integrate the process within a new firm hierarchy or to use a more market-based mode of exploitation, as would be the case if the entrepreneur engaged in licensing or franchising. Most of the time, the production process will be vertically integrated within a new firm. However, four different factors influence the decision of which mode of organizing to use: cost, speed, capabilities and information (Venkataraman, 1997).

Cost

Market mechanisms are often used in place of vertically integrated new firms to exploit opportunities because they are less costly. Because entrepreneurs lack cash flow from existing operations, they must raise capital externally to pursue opportunities. External capital is more costly than internal capital due to information asymmetry problems that require entrepreneurs to pay a premium to investors. Moreover, capital is often rationed, precluding new firms from obtaining the full amount that they need to pursue their opportunities effectively (Evans and Leighton, 1989). As a result, entrepreneurs sometimes use mechanisms, such as franchising and licensing, which permit the use of others' capital to exploit their opportunities (Shane, 1998). In addition, they sometimes take approaches that require the ownership of fewer assets, such as leasing, to reduce capital needs (Martin, 1988). In fact, several empirical studies have shown that when new ventures lack capital or fail to obtain financing through capital markets, they are more likely to engage in licensing and franchising (Martin, 1988; Shane, 1998).

Speed

Market mechanisms are also used to exploit entrepreneurial opportunities to accelerate the process of opportunity exploitation. The rapid development of the value chain used to exploit the opportunity is often necessary when the opportunity is time-dependent or short-lived (Venkataraman, 1997). In particular, market mechanisms are often used to exploit one-time trading opportunities or when a new firm faces a race to become a first mover in a new technology market. For example, market mechanisms were the major vehicle to exploit opportunities to capitalize on price discrepancies for fruits and vegetables between East and West Germany immediately following the fall of the Berlin Wall. Similarly, entrepreneurs often use market mechanisms to exploit new biotechnologies when they need to develop and commercialize new drugs before potential competitors.

Capabilities

Differential capabilities also motivate the use of markets to exploit opportunities. Because different people have different information, and that information motivates the discovery of opportunities, the discoverer of an opportunity is not always the entity with a comparative advantage in the exploitation of the opportunity. Other parties might be better suited to exploit the opportunity because they have better access to capital, better knowledge of markets, more complementary assets in marketing, distribution and manufacturing, or, simply, because they have more experience at organizing. This differential capability means that the discoverer can gain from selling the opportunity to those more capable of exploiting it (Teece, 1980). The surplus profit from the sale of the opportunity to the more capable party would leave the discoverer with a greater gain than would be the case if she exploited the opportunity on her own.

One important example of the capabilities explanation for the use of markets to exploit opportunities lies in university technology licensing. Many university inventors do not found firms to exploit their technological inventions, but instead license them to other parties who have more relevant business and market experience. Not only does this use of a market to exploit the opportunity extend to licensing to established firms with existing cash flow and complementary assets in marketing, distribution and manufacturing, it also leads university inventors to license their technology to experienced entrepreneurs who shop for promising university technologies at technology licensing offices (Shane, 2002).

Information

Because information is difficult to sell through markets, entrepreneurs generally create new firms to exploit their opportunities directly. However, market mechanisms are also used to pursue opportunities when mechanisms, like patents, can be used to protect information against appropriation. They are also used to exploit opportunities when information about opportunities can be codified more easily. Finally, market mechanisms are more likely to be used to exploit opportunities when the information problems that come from the use of market-based mechanisms are low relative to the information problems that come from the use of hierarchical mechanisms.

Patent strength   Entrepreneurs tend to use market mechanisms to exploit opportunities when patents are effective at protecting intellectual property, as is the case with biotechnology. Patent protection provides three specific benefits that facilitate the exploitation of opportunities through markets. First, it reduces the disclosure problem that plagues the sale of knowledge. Arrow (1962) pointed out the paradox of selling knowledge, such as the knowledge of entrepreneurial opportunities and how to exploit them. A buyer of such knowledge would be unwilling to purchase the knowledge unless its value could be demonstrated. However, demonstration of the knowledge would allow imitation and would undermine the buyer's incentive to pay for the knowledge. Patents mitigate this problem by requiring the buyer to pay to use knowledge after it has been disclosed.

Second, patent protection reduces the likelihood of the moral hazard that occurs when the buyer or seller shirks in her commitment to a deal. Patents mitigate this problem by making it easier for third parties to verify adherence to an agreement (Anand and Khanna, 2000). When others cannot verify whether or not parties are adhering to their agreements about the amount or quality of knowledge transfer, the buyer may refuse to pay, knowing she cannot unlearn transferred knowledge (Arora, 1996). Similarly, the seller can economize on the cost of knowledge transfer by providing less knowledge or lower quality knowledge than the agreement specified (Arora, 1995). By making it possible for others to verify at least some of the knowledge transfer, patents minimize the incentive for both parties to engage in morally hazardous behavior (Anand and Khanna, 2000), as well as providing a bargaining tool to enforce agreements about uncodified knowledge (Arora, 1996).

Third, patents facilitate the writing of contracts, which minimize the potential for hold-up (Teece, 1981). Because entrepreneurial opportunities are uncertain, it is hard to write complete contracts about these opportunities (Pisano, 1991). In the absence of complete contracts, the parties to an agreement have an opportunity to take advantage of specific investments made by their counterparty by opportunistically renegotiating the terms of the agreement (Pisano, 1989). Patents mitigate this problem by codifying information. By making information less ambiguous, patents make contracts governing agreements more precise, mitigating the potential for *ex post* renegotiation (Teece, 1981).

Several studies provide empirical support for the argument that market mechanisms are more common modes of opportunity exploitation when patent protection is strong. For example, Lowe's (2001) examination of University of California inventions showed that when knowledge was more tacit, inventor-founded start-ups were more common. Similarly, Shane (2002) examined inventor and non-inventor efforts to exploit inventions at the Massachusetts Institute of Technology from 1980 to 1996 and found that inventor start-ups were less common when patents provided a strong method of protecting intellectual property. Hsu and Bernstein (1997) conducted case studies of 14 inventions at the Massachusetts Institute of Technology and Harvard University, and found that inventors believed that licensing to others was more effective in fields in which patents worked better. Barnes *et al.* (1997) found that patent effectiveness influenced the likelihood that University of California patents would be licensed to others. Finally, Gans, Hsu and Stern (2000) examined the strategies of 100 new technology firms. Arguing that profitability would be much greater if the start-ups cooperated with established firms through licensing or acquisition (cooperation would preclude the creation of duplicative assets), they found that the firms were more likely to use market-based mechanisms to obtain access to complementary assets if they had at least one patent than if they had no patents.

Codification   Entrepreneurs are more likely to use market-based mechanisms to exploit opportunities when opportunities can be codified in written contracts that govern their sale because codification mitigates the information problems inherent in market-based mechanisms while holding the information problems from hierarchies constant (Casson, 1996). When opportunities cannot be codified, market transactions often break down because the parties cannot agree on the value of the opportunity, causing them to value the opportunity differently (Audretsch, 1997). By codifying the opportunity, the parties can reduce the variance in different people's perception of its value. For example, Michael (1996) demonstrates that franchising, a market-based mechanism to exploit opportunities, is more common in industries in which opportunities can be codified, than in industries in which they cannot.

Information problems from markets and hierarchies   Entrepreneurs are also more likely to use market-based mechanisms to exploit opportunities when the information problems from hierarchical organizational arrangements exceed those from market-based arrangements. For example, franchising is a very popular mode of exploitation for many retail opportunities, where the need for owner–operators to prevent the shirking of employees is so great that it overwhelms any threat that independent entrepreneurs will free-ride off of the advertising efforts of others (Shane, 1998). In contrast, hierarchical mechanisms are used when hold-up problems become very severe because small numbers of potential participants, uncertainty and asset specificity create bargaining problems (Williamson, 1975). With retail opportunities, this problem often leads entrepreneurs to own retail outlets when franchisees would be afraid that franchisors would hold them up through encroachment on their territories

(Azoulay and Shane, 2001). Specifically, the balance between markets and hierarchies depends on the relative importance of two types of information problems: adverse selection and moral hazard.

Adverse selection

Entrepreneurs will be more likely to use market-based mechanisms to exploit opportunities if they face the potential for adverse selection in hiring employees. In the absence of some mechanism to separate high and low quality individuals, employees often misrepresent their abilities to obtain employment for which they are not qualified. This tendency requires entrepreneurs to engage in expensive efforts to screen potential employees. By using market-based mechanisms that turn potential employees into residual claimants, entrepreneurs can reduce the cost of screening potential employees. Because residual claimancy on the proceeds of one's effort will prove rewarding only for qualified individuals, the use of residual claimancy provides an effective mechanism to separate high and low quality candidates.

Some empirical evidence supports this argument. Shane (1996) examined 138 firms that first began franchising in the United States in 1983. He found that an emphasis on franchising enhanced the survival and growth of the firms because franchising minimized the problems of selecting competent employees. Because franchisees become residual claimants on the proceeds of their efforts, Shane (1996) argued that they would only undertake work that they knew they were capable of performing, and therefore would not misrepresent their abilities like employees.

Similarly, Shane and Foo (1999) examined the survival of 1292 new franchise systems established in the United States between 1979 and 1997. These authors found that system growth increased the likelihood of failure if the firm had a large reliance on company-owned outlets, presumably because of human resource constraints on selecting and monitoring managers. Because franchisees are less likely than employees to engage in adverse selection, firms that relied on company-owned outlets for growth faced greater problems selecting competent new outlet operators than those structured to use franchisees more heavily.

Finally, Shane (1998) argued that franchisees would make a large cash investment to purchase a franchise only if they had the right skills and abilities to manage that outlet because franchises become residual claimants on the proceeds of their own efforts. In contrast, the cash required to open an outlet would have no effect on the decision of employees to manage the same outlet because employees face no cost to opportunistic misrepresentation of their abilities. Consistent with this argument, Shane (1998) showed that the survival of new franchisors established in the United States between 1981 and 1983 was higher for those systems that required franchisees to make larger cash investments to purchase an outlet than those that required a lower level of investment.

Moral hazard

Entrepreneurs will be more likely to use market-based mechanisms to exploit entrepreneurial opportunities if the threat of employee shirking is high. Shirking is a problem that occurs when a person does not put forth the amount of effort that she is capable of providing. One of the major solutions to shirking is to give people ownership incentives. By turning employees into owners, their incentives to shirk in the provision of effort are reduced because, as residual claimants, they bear the cost of their own shirking. Therefore, when the threat of shirking by employees is high, entrepreneurs are more likely to use market mechanisms to exploit their opportunities.

Because market mechanisms are effective solutions to shirking problems, entrepreneurs who use market mechanisms to exploit opportunities when the threat of shirking by employees is high should perform better than those who use hierarchical arrangements to exploit these opportunities. Several pieces of empirical evidence support this argument. First, Shane (1996) examined 138 firms that first began franchising in the United States in 1983 and found that an emphasis on franchising enhanced survival and growth because franchising minimized the shirking problems of hiring employees. Shane (1998) found that the survival of 157 new franchisors established in the United States was enhanced by geographic concentration and organizational simplicity of the chain because those attributes allowed the firm to use market-based mechanisms without incurring large monitoring costs. Similarly, Shane (1998) found that survival was inhibited by passive ownership because passive ownership undermined the incentives provided by residual claimancy. Similarly, Ingram (1998) examined the population of US hotel chains from 1896 to 1980 and found that the use of franchising increased growth of the system because it turned employees into owners.

THE DIMENSIONS OF NEW ORGANIZATIONS

Despite the importance of explaining the mode that entrepreneurs use to exploit opportunities, the fact remains that most entrepreneurs exploit opportunities by organizing new firms. Consequently, a complete framework for entrepreneurship must also explain the organization of new firms. In particular, this explanation must account for how the aspects of entrepreneurial process discussed in previous chapters, particularly the conditions of uncertainty and information asymmetry that pervade the organizing process, influence the organization of new firms. In the remainder of the chapter, I examine this issue by exploring several dimensions on which the organization of new firms can be examined: the type of legal entity established, the size of the new entity, the selection of the employees that undertake the exploitation of the opportunity, the allocation of employment between permanent and temporary workforce, and the structure of the new organization and its production process.

Legal Entity

When an entrepreneur begins to exploit an opportunity through the creation of a new firm, she must establish the legal form for the new organization. The establishment of a legal entity enhances the creation of a new firm by facilitating organizing activities. The establishment of the legal entity makes the new venture appear more legitimate and establishes property rights.

One empirical study shows that the establishment of a legal entity increases the likelihood of venture organizing activities in new firms. Delmar and Shane (2001) examined 223 new ventures established by a random sample of Swedish firm founders in the first nine months of 1998 and followed them over the subsequent 30 months. These authors found that establishing a legal entity increased the likelihood that the new ventures would gather inputs, talk to customers, complete product development, and initiate marketing and promotion.

When an entrepreneur creates a legal entity, she must choose between three basic types of legal organization: a sole proprietorship, a partnership or a corporation. A sole proprietorship is the default legal form. With a sole proprietorship, the individual engages in entrepreneurial activity and records that activity as a source of income for tax purposes. A partnership is an agreement for two or more people to work together to exploit an opportunity as joint owners of the residual claim on that activity. A corporation is a legal entity that exploits the opportunity, but which has limited liability.

The use of a corporation as the legal form of the organization provides an advantage to the exploitation of opportunity because uncertainty is a fundamental part of the entrepreneurial process. Uncertainty means that the entrepreneur's conjecture about the resource combination that the new venture will exploit may be incorrect. As a result, she may lose the value of her investment in the opportunity. By limiting her liability to the amount that she has invested, the use of a corporation minimizes the entrepreneur's downside risk, thereby encouraging entrepreneurial action. Therefore, one would expect the use of the corporate legal form to be associated with better performance of new ventures.

Several empirical studies have shown that the corporate legal form of the new venture enhances new venture performance. In particular, newly established corporations are more likely to survive than partnerships or sole proprietorships.

For example, Wicker and King (1989) studied 413 retail establishments created in California in 1985, and found that corporations were more likely than sole proprietorships and partnerships to survive two years. Similarly, Kalleberg and Leight (1991) studied 337 owner-managed small businesses in Indiana selected randomly from the yellow pages, and found that incorporation reduced the likelihood that the firms would go out of business. Cressy (1996b) examined a sample of 1189 new firms that established accounts with National Westminster Bank in 1988 and found that incorporated start-ups were more likely to survive until 1992 than sole proprietorships or partnerships. Finally, Bruderl *et al.* (1992) examined the survival of 40 018 firms registered with the local chamber of commerce in Munich and Upper Bavaria during the 1980s and found that incorporated firms had lower failure rates than other firms.

Incorporated new ventures also appear to have faster growth than those ventures that are not incorporated. For example, Reynolds and White (1997) analysed the growth of 2624 new firms founded in three different US states in the mid-1980s and found that corporations had higher growth rates than partnerships and sole proprietorships. Similarly, White and Reynolds (1996) followed 332 new firms sampled from the Wisconsin unemployment insurance files over a two-year period. They found that firms that were initially a corporation had employment growth that was, on average, one half standard deviation above the median for the ventures in the sample.

Incorporated firms also appear to be more profitable than unincorporated firms. For example, Kalleberg (1986) examined the one-year earnings growth of 411 owner-operated small firms in Indiana in 1985, and found that incorporated firms had higher earnings growth than partnerships and sole proprietorships. Similarly, Kalleberg and Leight (1991) studied 337 owner-managed small businesses in Indiana selected randomly from the yellow pages over the 1985 to 1987 period and found that incorporation increased the venture's level of gross earnings.

Venture Size

Entrepreneurs must establish the size at which their organizing effort occurs. The choice of size is important because new ventures founded by larger teams and with more employees are better able to overcome the information asymmetry and uncertainty problems that pervade the entrepreneurial process. First, much of the information necessary to exploit the entrepreneurial opportunity successfully cannot be known completely at the time that the opportunity is initiated, but must be gathered in real time during the development of the new venture. Because different people possess different information, the larger the number of people involved in the organizing effort, the greater the likelihood that someone involved in the entrepreneurial effort has the necessary information to develop the venture. Second, much of the knowledge necessary for the exploitation of opportunities is complementary with other knowledge. For example, the value of knowledge about the market is greater if the venture also possesses knowledge of a technology to create a new product. Given the specialization of labor in society, ventures with more founders and more employees are more likely to ensure that complementary knowledge about the entrepreneurial process lies within the new organization. Third, vetting a venture idea with more people leads to the selection of better venture opportunities. Because many entrepreneurial conjectures prove to be incorrect, effort by multiple people to exploit an opportunity provides a better test of the plausibility of the entrepreneurial conjecture than effort by one person.

In the subsections below, I examine two dimensions of the size of the organizing effort: the size of the team of founders and the size of the group of people that these founders employ.

Team size
New ventures can be exploited by a single entrepreneur or by a team of entrepreneurs. In many instances, after discovering an opportunity, the initial entrepreneur builds a team of other people to join her as equity owners and active participants in the new venture. Therefore, one of the most important decisions that entrepreneurs must make in the organizing process is to determine how large the founding team should be.

Venture teams provide several advantages to new ventures. First, given the cognitive limits that human beings have, solo entrepreneurs find it difficult to gather and process all the information necessary to create a new venture (Hansen and Allen, 1992). Second, teams draw upon complementary knowledge of the founders, giving them more complete knowledge of relevant areas of new venture activity than single founder ventures (Klepper, 2001; Roberts, 1991a; Roure and Maidique, 1986). Third, assembling a team of people who all have different beliefs and information verifies the validity of the venture idea (Cooper and Daily, 1998). Fourth, teams allow entrepreneurs to combine people who have worked together previously and can communicate with and trust each other (Cooper and Daily, 1998).

Some empirical evidence supports the argument that ventures founded by teams perform better than ventures founded by individuals. Eisenhardt and Schoonhoven (1995) examined 98 semiconductor firms established in the United States between 1978 and 1985 and found that team size reduced new venture failure rates. Cooper *et al.* (1988) compared three-year survivors with discontinued firms among a sample of firms established by members of the National Federation of Independent Businesses. They found that the surviving ventures had more full time partners than the discontinued firms. Duchesneau and Gartner (1990) compared 13 successful and 13 failed ventures in fresh orange juice distribution and found that the failed ventures were less likely to have had partners than the successful ventures. Westhead (1995) examined the factors that predicted the survival of 227 independent high technology firms in the United Kingdom. He found that firms with more than one shareholder were more likely to survive than firms with only one shareholder.

Klepper (2001) found that team size made up for the disadvantages that new firms face in comparison to diversifying entrants. In a study of firm survival in several high technology industries, Klepper (2001) found that spin-off firms with more than one founder were as likely to survive over time as diversifying firms from other industries, and that both of these groups had higher chances of survival than new firms established by a single founder.

New ventures founded by teams also grow larger and faster than those founded by individuals. Reynolds and White (1997) analysed the growth of 2624 new firms founded in three different US states in 1985 and found that venture team size was positively correlated with venture growth rates. Eisenhardt and Schoonhoven's (1990) study of new semiconductor firms showed that annual sales growth was higher for those ventures with larger founding teams. Reynolds (1993) examined representative samples of new firms in Pennsylvania in 1986 and Minnesota in 1987 and found that teams were much more common among high performing firms than among the rest of the sample. Tyebjee and Bruno (1982) studied 197 technology start-ups founded between 1978 and 1980 in 17 high technology industries, and found that the number of people founding the venture had a positive and significant relationship with the venture's sales level.

Furthermore, Cooper *et al.* (1994) compared 1053 entrepreneurs who were members of the National Federation of Independent Businesses in 1985, who had become business owners over the previous 17 months and who could be re-contacted two years later. Using a multinomial logit model in which firms were defined as failures, non-growing survivors (which had less than a 50 per cent increase in employment or had added fewer than 2 employees), or growing survivors (which had more than a 50 per cent increase in employment or had added more than 2 employees), the authors found that larger venture teams were more likely than smaller venture teams to have high growth firms.

Similar results have been found for studies conducted outside the United States. Schutgens and Wever (2000) examined the employment growth from 1994 to 1997 of 563 new firms registered with the Dutch Chamber of Commerce in the first quarter of 1994 and found that those firms founded by more than one person were more likely to grow than those founded by a single individual. Lee and Tsang (2001) examined the rate of growth of sales of 168 founder-run new ventures in China and found that the number of partners in the venture increased the rate of venture growth.

One reason offered above for the effect of team size on firm growth is that a larger team provides access to more varied information about how to exploit the entrepreneurial opportunity. Some empirical evidence supports this argument directly. For example, Eisenhardt and Schoonhoven's (1990) study of new semiconductor firms showed that annual sales growth was higher for teams with more heterogeneous industry experience. Similarly, Roure and Maidique (1986) examined 36 ventures that a venture capital firm invested in between 1974 and 1982. These authors found that a more complete founding team, in terms of breadth of knowledge, led to a higher internal rate of return for the new venture.

Number of employees
In addition to their own labor, founders often need other human resources in the new venture. These resources include employees and external service providers, such as lawyers and accountants. One of the most important decisions that entrepreneurs need to make during the organizing process is to determine the number of employees and service providers to hire.

Larger numbers of employees provide several advantages to new ventures. First, employees provide a source of knowledge that the entrepreneur can use to exploit her opportunity. Second, the more employees the venture has, the faster the organization can acquire information that no one in the organization yet knows, but that is necessary to understand to pursue the opportunity. The reason is that the organization can only acquire information to the extent that each organization member obtains it.

The empirical evidence supports the proposition that new ventures with more employees perform better than other new ventures. One set of studies shows that new ventures that are started with more employees are more likely to survive (Baum, 1996; Fichman and Levinthal, 1991). For example, Loree (1993) found that failure rates decreased with the number of employees for a sample of integrated circuit manufacturers founded between 1971 to 1981. Gimeno *et al.* (1997) found that failure rates declined with the number of employees for a sample of 1547 firms whose founders were members of the National Federation of Independent Business. Halliday *et al.* (1987) found that the number of workers reduced the likelihood of failure of state bar associations from 1870 to 1930. Bates (1994, 1995b) found that the number of employees increased the likelihood of survival for a sample of new ventures founded between 1984 and 1987.

The number of employees also increases the rate of new venture growth. Schutgens and Wever (2000) found that employment growth rates for 563 new Dutch firms were higher for those firms that had more employees at founding. Using data on 332 new firms sampled from the Wisconsin unemployment insurance files, White and Reynolds (1996) showed that firms with employment growth one half standard deviation above the median after two years had higher numbers of employees at founding. Ensley *et al*. (2002) found that cumulative five-year sales growth was positively correlated with the number of employees in 70 *Inc* 500 companies. Using a sample of 77 independent high technology firms in the United Kingdom, Westhead (1995) found that ventures with more employees in 1986 grew larger by 1992.

The employment size of a new venture also appears to increase its profitability. Kalleberg and Leight's (1991) study of 337 owner-managed small businesses in Indiana showed that the number of employees had a positive effect on the venture's gross earnings. Gimeno *et al.*'s (1997) study of members of the National Federation of Independent Business showed that the amount of income that the founders removed from their businesses increased with the employment size of their new ventures.

The number of employees in a venture also increases its likelihood of initial public offering. Hannan *et al*. (1996) examined 100 new technology companies established in Silicon Valley between 1984 and 1994 and found that the likelihood of initial public offering was positively related to the number of employees in the firm.

Given the arguments presented above, one might expect that full-time employment by the founder should increase survival of new ventures by providing the same type of information acquisition as that generated by higher numbers of employees. Several studies support this argument. For example, Wicker and King (1989) used a sample of 413 retail establishments created in California in 1985 to show that those ventures whose founders worked full time were more likely to survive two years. Using data taken from the characteristics of business owners database of the US Census Bureau, Bates (1994, 1995b) showed that owner labor input increased the four-year survival of 19 463 firms founded between 1984 and 1997. Bates and Servon (2000) used data from the US Bureau of the Census to examine the duration of new ventures from 1992 to 1996 for 275 people who founded their firms between 1986 and 1992, and who claimed that they could not find acceptable alternative work. These authors found that owner labor input increased new venture survival.

Similar results have been observed for venture growth. Reynolds and White (1997) analysed the growth of 2624 new firms founded in three different US states and found that those ventures with greater involvement of the principals had higher growth rates than other ventures. Similarly, Boyd (1991) looked at the public use micro-samples for 1980 census and found that the 1979 self employment earnings of African-Americans in 52 metropolitan areas were higher if they worked more hours.

Selection of Employees

In addition to deciding the number of employees to hire at founding, the organizing process also involves selecting which potential employees to hire.

This process is far from simple because the asymmetric information between the entrepreneur and the potential employee generates the potential for adverse selection, moral hazard, and hold-up in the hiring process. Moreover, the uncertainty inherent in the entrepreneurial process makes it difficult for the entrepreneur to obtain labor with useful and relevant competencies (Aldrich, 1999).

Although there might be many ways that entrepreneurs can overcome these problems in the attraction and selection of employees, very little research has explored this question. To date, the literature has only explored one way that entrepreneurs mitigate the uncertainty and information asymmetry problems in the selection of employees for new ventures – through the exploitation of social ties.

Direct ties
Entrepreneurs frequently hire people with whom they have direct ties, such as their friends or close social contacts, in early recruiting efforts (Aldrich, 1999; Francis and Sandberg, 2000). This approach to initial hiring offers several advantages to new ventures. First, hiring people with whom the entrepreneur has a direct social tie provides the entrepreneur and the employee with greater knowledge of the other party, minimizing the difficulties of determining competencies that uncertainty creates (Nohria, 1992), and reducing the recruiting and retention costs that the entrepreneur otherwise would face to overcome this uncertainty (Jovanovic, 1984).

Second, given the uncertainty and information asymmetry inherent in exploiting a venture opportunity, it is difficult for the entrepreneur to prove the value of her opportunity to others. By hiring people with whom she has direct ties and making use of the trust inherent in friendships, the entrepreneur can select employees who will believe her without proving every aspect of the venture opportunity.

Third, a social tie between the parties mitigates the tendency for either party to engage in opportunistic behavior (Williamson, 1985), allowing the founder to transfer information about the venture idea with less fear of loss. As a result, the entrepreneur can hire people with whom she can exchange more information, allowing for the more effective development of the organization.

Fourth, much of the early organizing process involves coordinating people into a collective entity without the benefit of firmly established rules. Coordination of strangers is difficult to accomplish without explicit rules because strangers do not necessarily agree on the same implicit rules and norms. The use of implicit norms and rules is facilitated if entrepreneurs initially hire people who know each other (Aldrich, 1999).

The empirical evidence supports this argument about the selection of direct ties as early employees in new ventures. Several studies show that entrepreneurs typically hire their spouses and other family members as early employees in new ventures (Zimmer and Aldrich, 1987). Moreover, Baker and Aldrich (1994) conducted a study of the hiring practices of new ventures in two industries in the Research Triangle in North Carolina. In both industries, they found that the first hires were typically people with whom the entrepreneur had a direct tie, such as a friend or prior colleague.

Indirect tie

Founders also use their social networks and informal contacts to hire people who are known to people that they trust (Aldrich and Von Glinow, 1992) for many of the same reasons that direct ties help the entrepreneur to hire initial employees. In addition, entrepreneurs use indirect ties as part of a legitimating process that facilitates recruiting. Entrepreneurs often have difficulty recruiting because job seekers lack information about new ventures; see new ventures as less legitimate than established organizations; and do not include new ventures in their consideration set (Williamson *et al.*, 2002). Because new ventures cannot rely on their own reputations to overcome these problems, they exploit indirect ties and key employment brokers, like recruiting offices of universities, to find early employees.

The empirical evidence collected to date appears to support entrepreneurs' use of indirect ties to hire early employees. For example, Aldrich (1999) found that entrepreneurs often select their early hires on the basis of the recommendations of their suppliers and customers. Similarly, Baker and Aldrich (1994) examined the early hiring by technology companies in the Research Triangle in North Carolina and found that the recommendations and social contacts of early recruits were used to hire subsequent employees.

Permanent vs. Temporary Workforce

Another important aspect of organizing is the allocation of employees between permanent and temporary workers (Aldrich, 1999). On the one hand, new ventures often start with temporary workers because this design reduces fixed costs, a desired approach given the uncertainty of new ventures. If the entrepreneur's initial conjectures prove wrong, the flexibility of a temporary workforce facilitates changing direction during the early life of the new venture.

On the other hand, the desire to minimize fixed costs must be balanced against the development and codification of information, which is facilitated by permanent staff (Aldrich, 1999). As Van de Ven *et al.* (1984) explained, hiring permanent employees ensures continuity, increases learning and retention of organizational knowledge, enhances commitment and reduces selection and hiring costs. In contrast, Rao and Argote (1992) explained, reliance on temporary employees inhibits the retention of knowledge by new ventures.

Some empirical evidence supports these arguments. For example, Matusik (1997) conducted detailed interviews with 15 software start-ups in Washington and found that they used contingent workers to have flexibility and speed in acquiring knowledge. In contrast, Aldrich and Langdon (1998) surveyed 229 new firms in Vancouver and found that only 14 per cent of the new firms had part-time workers because such workers do not allow organizational learning and retention of knowledge.

Creation of the Organization Structure and Production Process

Entrepreneurs also need to establish production processes that will transform resources into new products and services, market the output from those production processes, and establish the organization structures in which those production processes will reside (Schumpeter, 1934; Nelson and Winter, 1982). Because new ventures often involve people who are working with new production processes or will involve new teams of people working together, entrepreneurs need to define organizational policies, establish communication mechanisms, define organizational roles and develop routines for monitoring employees in new ventures.

Organizational policies and procedures

During the organizing process, the entrepreneur must define the policies and procedures that the organization will use to recombine resources into new products and services. Although some of the organization's routines are brought to the new organization through the experience of the founders, many of them relate to the new opportunity that the entrepreneur is exploiting and must be created by organization members during the process of opportunity exploitation (Schutz, 1967).

These new policies and procedures can be formal or informal. Ultimately, the new venture needs formal policies and procedures. Because people suffer from limits in their span of control (Arrow, 1974b), they cannot process unlimited amounts of information, and face diminishing returns to decision-making quality as information increases. To mitigate this problem, entrepreneurs formalize policies and procedures to allow them to manage more information (Gifford, 1992). By specifying decision rules, the entrepreneur can delegate tasks to others (Casson, 1996).

However, because of the uncertainty inherent in the exploitation of entrepreneurial opportunities, new ventures tend to begin with more informal policies and procedures. This informality allows the entrepreneur to change the policies and procedures in response to changes in the venture opportunity and the entrepreneur's method of exploitation. Over time, as the organizing effort becomes less uncertain, and begins to involve the coordination of more people, policies and procedures become more formalized.

Some empirical evidence supports this argument. For example, De Kok and Uhlaner (2001) examined 16 small Dutch firms and found that small firms tend not to have formalized human resource management practices. However, over time, as the ventures develop, this informality in policies and procedures tends to decrease. Hanks and Chandler (1995) studied 121 high technology firms in Utah that were under 15 years old and found that firms became more formalized in terms of documentation, structure, reporting, planning and control as they advanced through development stages. Similarly, Cooper *et al.* (1988) surveyed 2994 founders of new firms who were members of the National Federation of Independent Businesses in 1985 and found that venture size was correlated with a reduction in the allocation of founder time to selling or making things, and an increase in the allocation of time to administrative activities.

Communication mechanisms

During the organizing process, the entrepreneur must also establish internal and external communication mechanisms for the new venture. The entrepreneur needs to create a collective understanding of the entrepreneurial opportunity so that employees can take common action. Because of the uncertainty and information asymmetry that pervade opportunity exploitation, each employee typically has a different and incomplete perspective on the new venture and its opportunity. Therefore, the entrepreneur sets up mechanisms to communicate to others her strategy for and design of the venture (Bouwen and Steyaert, 1990; Thakur, 1999). Moreover, as employees begin to recombine resources to produce new products and services, they need to communicate with each other to coordinate activity, leading to the development of internal communication mechanisms.

The entrepreneur also needs to create external communication mechanisms because the exploitation of the opportunity requires the acquisition of information from customers, suppliers and investors (Shepherd *et al.*, 2000). Moreover, communication enhances the development of the social ties that are an important lubricant to economic action (Granovetter, 1985; Arrow, 1974b). As a result, entrepreneurs seek to establish external communication mechanisms to strengthen their social ties with external stakeholders (Aldrich and Zimmer, 1986).

The empirical research supports this argument. External communication frequency and quality are associated with the organization of new ventures. For example, Aldrich, Rosen and Woodward (1987) found that the creation of new ventures was positively associated with the entrepreneur's frequency of communication with network members. Similarly, in an in-depth qualitative study, Martin *et al.* (1985) showed that high levels of internal communication frequency and quality were associated with the development of a common understanding among members of the new organization about how to exploit a venture opportunity.

The creation of communication mechanisms also enhances the performance of new ventures. For example, Littunen (2000) examined the three-year survival of 138 metal products firms and 62 business service firms and found that businesses with a network style of management were more likely than other firms to survive.

Specialization of labor

The organizing process also involves the determination of who will undertake what activities to exploit the opportunity. In general, new ventures begin with little specialization of labor in undertaking these activities but, over time, evolve toward specialization.

Initially, new ventures do not engage in much specialization of labor for two reasons. First, the uncertainty associated with new firm opportunities suggests the value of generalist skills and activities (Casson, 1982). As new ventures develop, their members must engage in improvisation (Aldrich, 1999) and respond to crises (Katz *et al.*, 2000). Generalists are better than specialists at improvisation and crisis management because they have a wider range of skills. Second, the benefits of specialization are limited until organization members develop the necessary routines and competencies that the venture will employ (Katz *et al.*, 2000).

Some empirical evidence supports the argument that new ventures have little initial specialization of labor. Aldrich (1999) found that entrepreneurs initially undertake almost all tasks in new ventures and delegate very little. They do not formalize specific roles or job titles and typically hire generalists with significant industry knowledge and give them broad responsibilities. Neiswander *et al.* (1987) surveyed 52 entrepreneurs in the Cleveland area and found that early employees at their new ventures were mostly generalists. Similarly, O'Reilly and Anderson (1982) examined 127 firms and found selection and training in organizations with fewer than 300 employees generally was done by a few regular employees rather than by human resource specialists.

However, over time, the roles and responsibilities of people in new ventures become more specialized. The entrepreneurs themselves focus on the identification and exploitation of opportunities and hire others to take on more managerial roles (Holmes and Schmitz, 1990). In addition, the entrepreneurs create a division of labor with specific structures and roles for members of the new organization (Aldrich, 1999).

Some empirical evidence supports this argument of a transition toward specialization of labor in new ventures over time. McCarthy *et al.* (1989) examined data on 125 firms whose founders were members of the National Federation of

Independent Business. These authors showed that, as their ventures grew, founders reallocated their time toward specific tasks of managing employees, financing and planning, and away from more general activities. Van de Ven *et al.* (1984) compared six early stage software companies to six later stage software companies and found that there was a greater tendency towards the use of specialized professional help in later stage companies. Hanks and Chandler (1995) studied 121 high technology firms in Utah that were under 15 years old, and found that labor in these firms became more specialized as the companies advanced through development stages.

Monitoring

The entrepreneur must also develop routines for monitoring the effort of employees. Initially the organization has a very rudimentary monitoring system because the entrepreneur herself does much of the work to exploit the opportunity (Aldrich, 1999). Moreover, in the early days of the new venture, even when the entrepreneur does not do the work herself, she typically engages in direct monitoring of employees.

However, as the entrepreneur hires more people, she needs to develop routines for monitoring employees. At a certain point, the entrepreneur reaches her span of control in supervising others. As she can no longer directly monitor more employees, she delegates monitoring to others.

Everyone hired by the entrepreneur (including managers who monitor the work of employees producing and selling the new venture's product or service) has an incentive to shirk (Norton, 1988). Therefore, once the entrepreneur hires managers to monitor and delegates to them the task of supervising employees, the entrepreneur needs to develop a structure and set of monitoring routines (Jones and Butler, 1992; Gifford, 1992).

Some empirical evidence supports the argument that the entrepreneur needs to establish mechanisms to monitor and control employees. Reynolds and White (1997) report the results of a survey of 627 new firms interviewed during their first year in Pennsylvania and Minnesota. They found that firms that emphasized financial controls to monitor the behavior of employees were more likely to survive until they were re-interviewed at least one year later. Similarly, Reynolds (1987) surveyed 551 new firms founded in Minnesota between 1978 and 1984. He found that one-year survival of the venture was positively related to the founder's emphasis on financial controls.

New venture growth is also enhanced by the use of monitoring and behavioral controls. For example, Ingram (1998) examined the population of American hotel chains from 1896 to 1980, and found that the use of internal controls increased growth of the systems. Similarly, Reynolds and White's (1997) study of new firms found that the use of financial controls was positively correlated with venture growth. Dunkelberg *et al.*'s (1987) study of new firms founded by members of the National Federation of Independent Businesses showed that the time that founders spent monitoring and managing employees was positively correlated with venture growth. Reynolds' (1987, 1993) studies of new ventures showed that the founder's emphasis on financial management and controls was positively correlated with venture growth.

An alternative approach to monitoring as a way to control the behavior of employees is to create a culture of commitment and lack of self-interest in the organization. This commitment culture leads employees to perform the work that is necessary for organization development without shirking or free riding off the efforts of others. Hannan *et al.* (2002) examined 155 technology companies founded in Silicon Valley between 1984 and 1994 and found that new firms established with a commitment employment model were less likely to fail than those with an engineering employment blueprint. Similarly, Welbourne and Andrews (1996) examined 136 non-financial firms that went public in 1988, and found that those firms that focused on human resources and mechanisms to generate commitment among employees were more likely than other ventures to survive.

A culture of commitment and lack of self-interest also enhances new venture growth and likelihood of achieving an initial public offering. Ensley *et al.* (2002) studied 70 *Inc* 500 companies and found that cumulative five-year sales growth was positively correlated with the top management team's sense of belonging and negatively related to affective conflict among team members. Similarly, Hannan *et al.*'s (2002) examination of Silicon Valley start-ups showed that the commitment employment model increased the likelihood of initial public offering.

SUMMARY

To exploit an opportunity for which she has gathered resources, an entrepreneur must engage in organizing. Organizing is the process of creating the routines and structures that will support the goal-directed, boundary-maintaining system of collective activities that recombine resources according to the entrepreneur's conjectures. This chapter explored the activities that entrepreneurs undertake in organizing to exploit an opportunity.

Entrepreneurs create new organizations through a dynamic process that involves such activities as obtaining equipment, establishing production processes, attracting employees and setting up legal entities. To design the entity that will exploit the opportunity, the entrepreneur draws upon information from her previous education and experience, or engages in the imitation of established firms. The use of prior information to make organizing decisions leads to variation in routines and structures, some of which are better than others. Entrepreneurs adapt unfit designs through a process of improvisation or their ventures fail.

Although entrepreneurs engage in improvisation and develop flexible and adaptive strategies, the process of organizing also involves planning. Specifically, the entrepreneur formulates a plan, in mental or written form, for the organizing process that she will use to recombine resources to exploit an opportunity. Planning overcomes several problems that result from the uncertainty and information asymmetry present in the exploitation of opportunities. It tests the accuracy of the entrepreneur's conjectures about opportunities; indicates the necessary resources and how those resources will be linked together without the expense of trial and error; increases people's ability to learn new information; clarifies goals and objectives; and helps to communicate information to others.

Another important aspect of the organizing process concerns the choice of the mode of exploitation of the opportunity. This choice seeks to answer two questions: First, does the individual who identified the opportunity want to exploit it on behalf of someone else or do they want to exploit it on their own? Second, does the individual want to use market mechanisms, such as licensing or franchising, to exploit the opportunity or does she want to use a hierarchical mechanism, like a firm?

Individuals are the entities that discover opportunities. Therefore, any explanation for the mode of opportunity exploitation must be based on choices made by individuals about how they would like to exploit the opportunity that they have discovered. At the most basic level, people spin off new companies to exploit opportunities if the expected compensation from exploitation as an employee is less than the expected value of the profits from founding a firm. However, several other factors affect this calculus. The greater the uncertainty or the radicalness of the opportunity discovered, the greater the likelihood of a spin-off. The discreteness of the entrepreneur's opportunity increases the likelihood that the entrepreneur will spin off, as does the human capital intensity of the opportunity. Several attributes of the discoverer's employer also increase likelihood of a spin-off, including a bureaucratic organizational structure, the generation of more new products, the provision of fewer equity incentives for employees, and a stronger brand name reputation.

Another important decision that the entrepreneur has to make about exploiting the opportunity concerns whether to integrate that process vertically within a new firm hierarchy or to use a market-based mode of exploitation. Most of the time, the production process will be vertically integrated within a new firm. However, four different factors influence the decision of which mode of organizing to use: cost, speed, capabilities and information. Market mechanisms are used in place of firms to exploit opportunities because they are less costly; because they accelerate the process of opportunity exploitation; because the entrepreneur sometimes lacks the capabilities to exploit the opportunity in house; and because information problems from market-based approaches are sometimes small relative to information problems from hierarchical mechanisms.

This chapter also explored the process by which the entrepreneur creates the entity that exploits the opportunity. One part of this process involves choosing the legal form of organization – sole proprietorship, partnership or corporation. The use of a corporation as the legal form of the organization provides an advantage to the entrepreneur because limited liability helps the entrepreneur to manage the uncertainty of the entrepreneurial process.

Another part of the organizing process involves establishing the size at which the organizing effort occurs. Research has shown that new ventures with larger teams and more employees are better able to overcome the information asymmetry and uncertainty problems that pervade the entrepreneurial process.

In addition to deciding on the number of employees to hire, the organizing process involves selecting which potential employees to hire. To date little research has explored this question. However, the research that has explored it tends to show that the selection of initial employees involves the exploitation of direct and indirect social ties.

Another important aspect of organizing is the allocation of the employees between permanent and temporary workers. Research has shown that entrepreneurs balance the flexibility provided by temporary workers with the continuity, increased learning, enhanced commitment and reduced selection and hiring costs that come from permanent employees.

Entrepreneurs also establish the processes that transform resources into new products and services, as well as the organization in which these production processes reside. To create an organization structure, the entrepreneur establishes internal and external communication mechanisms, and develops policies and procedures, organizational roles and monitoring mechanisms. In general, the entrepreneur begins with informal organizational policies and procedures to manage the uncertainty of the opportunity exploitation process, and moves toward more formal policies and procedures as the organization develops. Similarly, the organizing effort begins with little specialized labor and evolves toward specialization, and begins with simple monitoring mechanisms and develops more complex monitoring systems over time.

11. Conclusions

As I explained in Chapter 1, entrepreneurship is one of the most popular, but least understood aspects of business. Given the level of interest devoted to the topic, one might think that the academic field of entrepreneurship would have a deep understanding of the phenomenon, and a well-established intellectual framework to explain it. In reality, however, no coherent conceptual framework has yet emerged to integrate the field.

The purpose of this book was to outline the individual–opportunity nexus (Eckhardt and Shane, 2003; Shane and Venkataraman, 2000; Venkataraman, 1997) as a conceptual framework for the field of entrepreneurship, and to provide empirical support for the various propositions that emerge from this framework. Moreover, this book sought to develop a comprehensive explanation for entrepreneurship. Rather than focusing on only one part of the entrepreneurial process – such as the characteristics of the entrepreneurs themselves; the opportunities to which they respond; their strategies, their acquisition of resources; or their organizing processes – without consideration for whether the explanations that offered have any explanatory power for, or even relationship to, other parts of the entrepreneurial process, the perspective outlined here provides a framework for the field.

Specifically, the book examined the characteristics of opportunities; the individuals who discover and exploit them; the processes of resource acquisition and organizing; and the strategies used to exploit and protect the profits from those efforts. It also outlined the relationships between the different parts of the entrepreneurial process discussed in each chapter, and provided evidence for the arguments presented. To ensure that all parts of the framework could be linked together easily, the same fundamental assumptions were invoked for all parts of the nexus framework presented here. The end result of this effort was the individual–opportunity nexus of entrepreneurship summarized in Figure 11.1.

Because the economy operates in a continual state of disequilibrium, technological, political/regulatory and social/demographic changes occur, and generate situations in which people can transform resources into a form (new goods and services, new production processes, new ways of organizing, new materials and new markets) that have greater value than their cost to create (Venkataraman, 1997). The entrepreneurial process begins when alert individuals discover these opportunities, and formulate conjectures about how

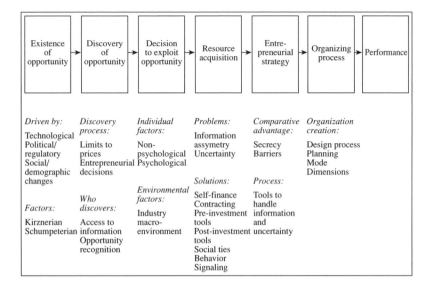

Figure 11.1 The entrepreneurial process

to pursue them, including the development of the product or service that will be provided to customers. These individuals then obtain resources, design organizations or other modes of opportunity exploitation, and develop strategies to exploit these opportunities.

A REVIEW OF THE CHAPTERS

Each of the chapters of this book provided the explanation behind, and empirical evidence in support of, different dimensions of the entrepreneurial process. Chapter 2 examined the role of entrepreneurial opportunities in the individual–opportunity nexus. The chapter summarized two major perspectives on entrepreneurial opportunities: the Kirznerian perspective, which holds that the existence of opportunities requires only differential views toward existing information, and the Schumpeterian perspective, which posits that new information is important to explaining the existence of entrepreneurial opportunities.

The second chapter also examined three major sources of entrepreneurial opportunities, and the forms that these opportunities take. Three major types of change create entrepreneurial opportunities: technological change, political/regulatory change, and social/demographic change. Technological change is an important source of opportunity because the introduction of new solutions to problems makes it possible for people to allocate resources in different and potentially more productive ways. Political and regulatory changes are important sources of opportunity because they alter the relative rewards gained from or costs incurred to undertake particular activities. Social and demographic changes are important sources of opportunity because they facilitate the creation of, and transmission of information about, ways to satisfy wants and needs. As I explained in Chapter 2, entrepreneurial opportunities take five different forms: new products or services, new ways of organizing, new raw materials, new markets and new production processes.

Chapter 3 examined the process of entrepreneurial discovery and identified the individual differences that explain why some people, and not others, make entrepreneurial discoveries. Entrepreneurial discovery occurs because the price system does not always allocate resources effectively. When people use the price system to make decisions, they optimize within known means–ends frameworks using mathematical rules. However, when the price system fails to allocate resources effectively, people must make decisions by means other than optimizing within existing means–ends frameworks – that is, they must make entrepreneurial decisions. Entrepreneurial decisions are non-optimizing decisions that require the formulation of new means–ends frameworks for buying, selling or transforming resources. The creation of a new means–ends framework involves judgmental decision-making, or holding different beliefs from others. To hold these different beliefs, an entrepreneur must either possess different information than others, or interpret the same information that others hold differently from them.

Exercising judgment is much more difficult than making decisions by optimizing within existing means–ends frameworks because judgmental decision-making requires forming a causal argument about a future market. When people exercise judgment, decision-making involves creativity. Moreover, because judgmental decisions can be wrong, these decisions are actually conjectures (or hypotheses). If the entrepreneur's conjectures about such things as production, market opportunities, new ways of producing existing products, or new products that satisfy customer wants or needs, are proved right, the entrepreneur earns a profit; otherwise she incurs a loss.

Because the discovery of entrepreneurial opportunities requires the formulation of a conjecture based on specific information or beliefs, not everyone will recognize all entrepreneurial opportunities. In general, people discover opportunities that others do not see for two reasons: first, they have better access to information about the existence of the opportunity through prior life experience, their social network structure, or through information search. Second, they are better able to recognize opportunities in a given amount of information about the opportunity because they have better absorptive capacity or cognitive processes. Research suggests that the most important aspects of absorptive capacity are prior knowledge about markets and prior knowledge about how to serve markets; while the most important cognitive processes are intelligence, perceptive ability, creativity, and seeing opportunity where others see risk.

Chapter 4 discussed the individual-level differences that explain the exploitation of opportunity. Unlike many sociological explanations for entrepreneurship, which tend to ignore the role of human agency, the individual–opportunity nexus underlying this book argues that the people who exploit entrepreneurial opportunities are not randomly distributed, and identifying the individual characteristics associated with opportunity exploitation is an important and worthwhile endeavor.

People make decisions to exploit opportunities because the gap between the expected utility of exploiting opportunities is higher than the expected utility gained from alternative uses of their time. This gap is larger if a person has a lower opportunity cost. As a result people who have higher incomes are less likely to exploit entrepreneurial opportunities, and people who are unemployed are more likely to exploit these opportunities.

The gap between the expected utility of exploiting opportunities and the expected utility from alternative uses of one's time is also larger if a person has information that will make her better able to exploit opportunities. That information will increase their returns to opportunity exploitation, all other things being equal. Education increases a person's stock of information and skills useful for the pursuit of an entrepreneurial opportunity (for example, those needed to sell, bargain, lead, plan, make decisions, solve problems, organize a firm, and communicate) and improves entrepreneurial judgment. Therefore, more educated people are more likely to exploit opportunities than less educated people.

Career experience provides another source of information useful to the pursuit of opportunity. General business experience; industry experience; functional experience in marketing and management; and prior start-up experience all provide knowledge and skills that enhance entrepreneurial performance, and therefore enhance opportunity exploitation. Similarly, parental entrepreneurial experience will increase the likelihood that a person will exploit an entrepreneurial opportunity because some of the knowledge and skills useful for the exploitation of entrepreneurial opportunities can be learned through the observation of others.

Being married and having a working spouse also increases the likelihood that a person will exploit an entrepreneurial opportunity because having a working spouse allows an individual to bear more easily the uncertainty of income from entrepreneurial activity.

Age has a curvilinear relationship with the exploitation of opportunity. Initially, age will increase the likelihood that a person will exploit an entrepreneurial opportunity because people gather much of the knowledge necessary to exploit opportunities over the course of their lives, and because age provides credibility in transmitting that information to others. However, as people become older, their willingness to bear risks declines, their opportunity costs rise, and they become less receptive to new information. As a result, people become reluctant to exploit entrepreneurial opportunities when they reach an advanced age.

A person's social position also influences her tendency to exploit entrepreneurial opportunities. Social status makes it easier for a person to convince others that the entrepreneurial opportunity that they have identified is valuable, despite the uncertainty and information asymmetry present in the identification of entrepreneurial opportunities. Social ties increase the likelihood that people will exploit entrepreneurial opportunities because social contacts help people to obtain information and resources useful to the exploitation process.

Chapter 5 reviewed three broad categories of psychological factors that influence the likelihood that a person will exploit entrepreneurial opportunities: aspects of personality and motives, core evaluation, and cognitive characteristics. Aspects of personality and motives influence the likelihood that people will exploit opportunities because people with certain aspects of personality and motives will make decisions to exploit the same opportunities that other people will not choose to exploit.

Extraversion will increase the likelihood that a person will exploit an entrepreneurial opportunity because extraversion facilitates the process of persuading others about the value of an opportunity. Agreeableness will reduce the likelihood that a person will exploit an entrepreneurial opportunity because critical and skeptical thinking makes people better able to separate more valuable information from less valuable information in the entrepreneurial decision-making process. People higher in need for achievement will be more likely than others to exploit entrepreneurial opportunities because the exploitation of opportunity requires solving novel and ill-specified problems; setting goals, planning, and gathering information; sustaining goal-directed activity over a long period of time; and persevering through failures, setbacks and obstacles. People higher in risk-taking propensity will be more likely to exploit entrepreneurial opportunities because risk bearing is a fundamental part of the entrepreneurial process. People with a high level of independence will be more likely to exploit entrepreneurial opportunities because entrepreneurship entails following one's own judgment, as opposed to the judgment of others.

Two aspects of core evaluation – internal locus of control and self-efficacy – will increase the likelihood that a person will exploit an entrepreneurial opportunity. Internal locus of control has this effect because it increases a person's belief in her ability to influence the environment around her. Self-efficacy has this effect because it increases a person's confidence in her subjective judgment about uncertain events.

Three cognitive characteristics influence the exploitation of opportunities: overconfidence, representativeness and intuition. Overconfidence makes a person more likely to exploit an entrepreneurial opportunity because it leads a person to take action in situations in which she does not have enough information to assess the likelihood of success, but where further investigation would reveal the poor odds, short opportunity half-life, or low opportunity value facing her. Moreover, overconfidence leads a person to follow her own information instead of heeding that of others; to disregard disconfirming information; and to misperceive the riskiness of actions. Representativeness increases the likelihood of opportunity exploitation because it makes a person more likely to make positive decisions in situations where there is little historical information to guide the decision; where greater effort to analyse information will not resolve that uncertainty; where a person is not an expert; and where quick action is needed. Intuitive decision-making will increase the likelihood of opportunity exploitation because the decision to exploit an opportunity must be made under time pressure, uncertainty and limited information, all of which hinder analytic decision-making.

Chapter 6 examined the impact of the industry context on opportunity exploitation. This chapter examined the effect of five categories of industry-level differences on the exploitation of entrepreneurial opportunities through the creation of new firms: knowledge conditions, demand conditions, industry life cycles, appropriability conditions and industry structure. Knowledge conditions influence the exploitation of opportunity in an industry by affecting the amount, locus and uncertainty of knowledge that make opportunities possible. The empirical evidence shows that firm formation is more common in industries that are more R&D intensive, in which extra-value chain sources of innovation are more important, that have a greater level of small firm innovation, and are less uncertain.

Demand conditions influence the exploitation of opportunity in an industry by increasing the size, growth rate and segmentation of the market. The empirical evidence shows that firm formation is more common in industries that are larger, faster growing and more segmented.

Industry life cycles examine opportunity exploitation as a function of industry age, dominant design and endogenous entry and exit dynamics. The empirical evidence shows that firm formation is more common in industries that are younger and have not yet converged on a dominant design. In addition, new firm formation initially increases with the number of firms already in the industry and then declines when that number reaches a high level.

Appropriability conditions examine the ability of entrepreneurs to capture the returns to opportunity exploitation as a function of patents, complementary assets and other methods of appropriating the returns to innovation. The empirical evidence shows that firm formation is more common in industries in which patents are more important, and complementary assets in manufacturing, marketing and distribution are less important.

Industry structure considers the exploitation of opportunity as a function of industry profitability, input costs, capital intensity, advertising intensity, industry concentration and average firm size. The empirical evidence shows that firm formation is more common in industries that are more profitable, have lower cost inputs, are less capital and advertising intensive, are less concentrated and have lower average firm size.

Chapter 7 discussed the institutional environment – the economic, political and cultural context – in which entrepreneurial activity takes place. This chapter explained that several aspects of the institutional environment affect the exploitation of entrepreneurial opportunities. Four aspects of the economic environment influence the level of opportunity exploitation: societal wealth, economic stability, capital availability and taxes. The empirical evidence indicates that opportunity exploitation increases with societal wealth, economic stability and capital availability, and decreases with rates of taxation. Three aspects of the political infrastructure influence the exploitation of opportunity: freedom, property rights and decentralization. The empirical evidence indicates that opportunity exploitation increases with political freedom, property rights, and economic and political decentralization. Three aspects of the social and cultural infrastructure influence the exploitation of opportunity: the degree to which entrepreneurial activity is considered desirable, the effect of social norms on the number entrepreneurial role models, and through cultural beliefs that encourage entrepreneurial actions and behaviors. The empirical evidence indicates that opportunity exploitation increases with the social desirability of entrepreneurship, the number of entrepreneurial role models, and the presence of cultural beliefs that encourage particular aspects of the entrepreneurial process.

Chapter 8 explored the process by which people acquire financial resources to exploit entrepreneurial opportunities. Because the exploitation of opportunity requires the acquisition and recombination of resources before the sale of output from that recombination, opportunity exploitation must be financed. In fact, obtaining a sufficient amount of capital is important to the exploitation of entrepreneurial opportunities because capital provides a buffer against adverse circumstance; allows more effective organization; and enhances legitimacy.

The information dispersion and uncertainty that give rise to the existence and discovery of entrepreneurial opportunities make it difficult for entrepreneurs to acquire resources to pursue them. Information asymmetry creates four problems in the resource acquisition process. First, the entrepreneur's need for secrecy forces investors to make decisions with less information than the entrepreneur. Second, the entrepreneur's information advantage allows her to act opportunistically towards investors. Third, information asymmetry encourages entrepreneurs to undertake excessive risk with the investors' resources. Fourth, information asymmetry allows for adverse selection.

Uncertainty creates three problems in the resource acquisition process. First, it makes resource providers unable to evaluate the potential of new ventures. Second, it creates bargaining problems between the investor and the entrepreneur. Third, it creates a need to collateralize investments in case the entrepreneur's judgment proves false.

To overcome these problems, venture finance takes on several attributes: self-financing by the entrepreneur, contractual constraints, pre-investment tools, post-investment tools, social ties, entrepreneurial behavior and quality signaling. Self-financing makes the entrepreneur's return on investment at least partially contingent on her own effort, mitigating moral hazard problems. Moreover, by pledging her own assets, the entrepreneur can collateralize the venture for investors who cannot observe her opportunity, nor predict its outcome in advance. Investors also design contracts to mitigate the information asymmetry and uncertainty problems present in entrepreneurial finance, and use convertible securities with restrictive covenants and forfeiture and anti-dilution provisions when they provide financing to entrepreneurs. Among pre-investment tools that investors use to manage information asymmetry and uncertainty in venture finance are: due diligence; specialization by industry and stage of development; geographically localized investing; and syndication.

Investors also employ several post-investment tools to overcome information asymmetry and uncertainty problems. They maintain disproportionate control rights over the disposition of the venture's assets; they treat investment in new ventures as real options in which they have the right, but not the obligation, to make future investments; and they remain heavily involved with new ventures.

Investors also use social mechanisms to manage the information asymmetry and uncertainty problems in the resource acquisition process. Perhaps most important of these social mechanisms is the use of direct and indirect social ties, which reduce the likelihood that the entrepreneur will act opportunistically towards the investor; provide a way to enforce implicit contracts; increase the transfer of information; and make attributions about the new venture more positive.

Entrepreneurs also engage in behaviors that encourage resource providers to give them needed capital. These behaviors include communication strategies, signaling commitment through equity ownership and involvement in the venture, and adhering to legitimate norms about business, such as engaging in business planning. Lastly, entrepreneurs appear to signal their quality by demonstrating the individual and opportunity-level attributes associated with successful exploitation of entrepreneurial opportunities.

Chapter 9 explored the strategies by which entrepreneurs exploit new venture opportunities. Entrepreneurial strategy involves two major issues: first, how does the entrepreneur develop a competitive advantage that precludes the dissipation of the opportunity to competitors once she has begun to exploit it? Second, how does the entrepreneur manage the uncertainty and information asymmetry inherent in the exploitation of an opportunity when she seeks to generate value from that opportunity?

The entrepreneur earns a profit for using her information to correctly identify and exploit a valuable opportunity. Unfortunately for the entrepreneur, the act of exploitation leads other entrepreneurs to learn about the opportunity and compete to exploit it. Because opportunities are exhausted by competition, the entrepreneur would like to minimize competition, which she does in two ways. First, the entrepreneur precludes others from gaining access to or understanding information about an entrepreneurial opportunity. This effort includes keeping secret the information that led to the discovery of the opportunity, as well as by exploiting causal ambiguity about how to take advantage of it. Second, the entrepreneur precludes others from exploiting the opportunity even if they have gained access to and understand information about the opportunity. This is done by erecting five different kinds of barriers to competition: obtaining control of resources needed to exploit opportunities, establishing legal barriers to imitation, exploiting opportunities at a scale that deters imitation, establishing a reputation and innovating to stay ahead of the competition.

Entrepreneurial strategy also involves managing the uncertainty and information asymmetry present in the process of opportunity exploitation. To do this, the entrepreneur engages in several actions. She starts on a small scale and expands the venture if the opportunity proves valuable. She also frequently enters via acquisition to reduce demand and production uncertainty. The entrepreneur adopts a focus strategy to facilitate the resolution of uncertainty about the entrepreneurial conjecture, and to keep the new venture from competing head-to-head with an established player. The entrepreneur also makes her venture flexible and adaptive so it can respond as information is revealed about the opportunity. She forms alliances with established firms to obtain needed assets quickly; to obtain control over resources without purchasing them; and to use the established firm's reputation to gain the support of stakeholders. The entrepreneur also takes strategic actions to show that the opportunity is legitimate, such as imitating existing firms' routines and competencies; achieving collective agreement on standards and designs; and obtaining certification from reputable authorities.

Chapter 10 explained that, to exploit an opportunity for which an entrepreneur has gathered resources, she must engage in organizing. Organizing involves creating the routines and structures that will support the system of collective activities that recombine resources.

Entrepreneurs create new organizations through a dynamic process that takes place over time, as founders engage in such activities as obtaining equipment, establishing production processes, attracting employees and setting up legal entities. The process of organizing involves selection and adaptation because entrepreneurs must make organizing decisions on the basis of unproven conjectures that arise from their prior education and experience or that are developed from imitation of established firms. The use of prior information to make organizing decisions leads to variation in routines and structures, some of which prove to be better than others. If designs prove to be ineffective, entrepreneurs adapt them through a process of improvisation, or their ventures fail.

Although entrepreneurs engage in improvisation and develop flexible and adaptive strategies, the process of entrepreneurship also involves planning. Specifically, the entrepreneur formulates a plan, in mental or written form, for the organizing process that he or she will use to recombine resources to exploit an opportunity. Planning overcomes several problems that result from the uncertainty and information asymmetry present in the exploitation of opportunities. Planning tests the accuracy of the entrepreneur's conjectures; indicates the validity of assumptions before expenses are incurred; increases the ability to learn new information; facilitates the achievement of goals; and helps to communicate information to others.

Another important aspect of the organizing process concerns the choice of the mode of exploitation. The choice of mode involves answering two major questions: first, does the individual who identified the opportunity intend to exploit it on behalf of an existing firm or through the creation of a new firm? Second, does the individual intend to use market mechanisms, such as licensing or franchising, to exploit the opportunity or does she plan to use a hierarchical mode, like a firm?

Several factors influence people to spin off new companies to exploit opportunities rather than to exploit them on behalf of their employers. In general, the discoverer of an opportunity compares her expected compensation from the exploitation opportunity as an employee with the liquidity and uncertainty-adjusted expected value of the profits from founding a firm, and spins off when the latter value is larger than the former. Research has shown that spin-offs are more likely when the opportunity discovered is more uncertain, more radical, more discrete and more human capital intensive. Several attributes of the discoverer's employer also influence whether she will spin off, including a bureaucratic organizational structure; the generation of more new products; weaker ownership incentives for employees; and a stronger brand name reputation.

Another important decision that the entrepreneur has to make about exploiting an entrepreneurial opportunity concerns whether to vertically integrate the exploitation process within a firm or to use a market mechanism. Most of the time, the exploitation process will be vertically integrated within a new firm. However, market mechanisms are often used in place of firms to exploit opportunities because they are less costly; because they accelerate the pace of exploitation; because the entrepreneur lacks the capabilities to exploit the opportunity in house; and because the information problems from the use of market mechanisms are small relative to information problems from the use of hierarchical mechanisms.

Chapter 10 also explored how the entrepreneur creates the entity that exploits the opportunity. One part of this process involves choosing the legal form of organization – a sole proprietorship, partnership or corporation. Research has shown that the use of a corporation as the legal form of the organization provides an advantage to the entrepreneur because limited liability helps the entrepreneur to manage the uncertainty of the entrepreneurial process.

Another part of the organizing process involves establishing the size of the organizing effort. This decision is important because research has shown that new ventures with larger teams and more employees are better able to overcome the information asymmetry and uncertainty problems that pervade the entrepreneurial process.

In addition to deciding the number of employees to have at founding, the organizing process involves selecting potential employees. To date, research has shown that the selection of initial employees in new ventures often involves the exploitation of direct and indirect social ties.

Another important aspect of the organizing process is the allocation between permanent and temporary workers. Research has shown that entrepreneurs balance the flexibility provided by temporary workers with the continuity, increased learning, knowledge retention, commitment, and lower selection and hiring costs that come from permanent employees.

The organizing process also establishes the processes that transform resources into new products and services, as well as the organization in which these production processes reside. To create these processes and this structure, the entrepreneur establishes internal and external communication mechanisms, develops policies and procedures, establishes organizational roles and creates monitoring mechanisms. In general, the entrepreneur begins with informal organizational policies and procedures, which help her to manage the uncertainty of the process and move toward more formal policies and procedures as the organization develops. Similarly, the organizing effort generally begins with very little specialized labor, and with simple monitoring systems, and evolves toward specialization of labor and more complex systems over time.

ISSUES FOR THE FUTURE

Because this book is an invitation to other scholars to investigate the phenomenon of entrepreneurship and to further advance the individual–opportunity nexus, I would like do more than just summarize the previous chapters in this conclusion. Therefore, I would like to use the remaining pages to be provocative and highlight topics that I believe require more investigation and discussion.

A Need For Interdisciplinary Investigation

My selection of the topics discussed in this book was driven by three somewhat conflicting goals. First, I sought to discuss what was central to the phenomenon of entrepreneurship. Second, I tried to discuss what was theoretically important. Third, I paid attention to topics for which some empirical evidence provided guidance one way or another. I say that these goals are somewhat conflicting because what is central to the phenomenon of entrepreneurship is not always what is theoretically interesting, and what is theoretically interesting is not always what has been the subject of empirical investigation.

My effort to balance these three goals has had a particular effect on the perspective expressed in this book. It is inherently interdisciplinary. The book drew from economic, psychological and sociological perspectives on entrepreneurship with equal abandon. As a result, this book should be accessible to readers from a variety of perspectives. As long as they are willing to make a few basic assumptions, readers from any social science discipline can find something in this book that is relevant to their field's approach to entrepreneurship.

At the same time, readers should have noticed that this book is very different from books on the same topic written by people from social science disciplines. This difference exists for a reason. Entrepreneurship is not sociology, psychology or economics. Scholars in the field of entrepreneurship are not searching for inviolate truths that hold regardless of the phenomenon under investigation. Rather, they are seeking to explain a very specific phenomenon and are willing to use any tools or frameworks that get them closer to that goal. As a result, this book may have seemed incomplete or contradictory to people looking for a particular discipline's perspective on entrepreneurship.

On the other hand, for readers truly interested in the phenomenon of entrepreneurship, the approach taken here has eliminated many of the artificial barriers present in entrepreneurship research. Take, for example, the unwillingness of sociologists to consider the possibility that individual differences in personality, motivations, core evaluation and cognition influence the decision to exploit entrepreneurial opportunities (Aldrich, 1999). To people immersed in understanding the entrepreneurial phenomenon, it is difficult to believe that variation across people has no effect whatsoever on the various decisions necessary to exploit entrepreneurial opportunities. In fact, as Chapters 3 and 5 indicated, the wealth of empirical evidence gathered to date confirms that differences between people in their psychological composition influence the discovery and exploitation of entrepreneurial opportunities.

Do not get me wrong. I do not believe that sociology is to blame for this problem. Psychologists, too, have proved quite resistant to consideration of the perspectives on entrepreneurship provided by other social science disciplines. Most psychologists have not considered the idea that variation in entrepreneurial opportunities is a central part of the entrepreneurial process. Very few comparisons of individual differences in opportunity exploitation or the performance of new ventures consider the effect of differences in the value of the opportunities that entrepreneurs pursue or the industries in which they operate. In psychological research on entrepreneurship, studies are often conducted as if the entrepreneurs under investigation have all been given exactly the same opportunity to pursue. However, that is clearly not the case. As Chapters 6 and 7 indicated, huge variations in opportunity exploitation exist across industries and institutional environments.

To the interdisciplinary entrepreneurship researcher, the effort spent by disciplinary scholars to support the theoretical foundations of their disciplinary field, rather than to examine the most important aspects of the entrepreneurial phenomenon, seems misplaced. This book provides a framework for scholars truly interested in entrepreneurship to develop explanations – and empirical tests of those explanations – that consider the entrepreneurship in a way that incorporates the relevant elements and theories from multiple disciplinary perspectives, as long as those perspectives further our understanding of the phenomenon.

Specific Areas in Greatest Need of Investigation

In the chapters that proceeded, I argued for paying greater attention to a wide variety of dimensions of entrepreneurship. However, some areas discussed in the earlier chapters are truly in greater need of scholarly inquiry than others. In the spirit of intellectual triage, I would like to stress several areas that seem to demand the greatest immediate scholarly attention.

First, and foremost, the field of entrepreneurship needs much more information about entrepreneurial opportunities than we currently have. As one can see from the discussion in Chapter 2, much of what we know about opportunities is observed at a very high level of abstraction. This raises some very fundamental questions that are, to date, unanswered. For example, what do specific entrepreneurial opportunities look like? What forms do they take?

To date, we do not even know basic demographics about entrepreneurial opportunities. At the most fundamental level, how often are entrepreneurial opportunities Schumpeterian opportunities and how often are they Kirznerian opportunities? We know that most opportunities are not very novel, and only a few are truly innovative. But what is the relative distribution between not very novel and truly innovative opportunities? Moreover, are these different types of opportunity equally likely to generate entrepreneurial profit, and if so, is the profit that they generate of the same magnitude?

We need more research that examines the relationship between sources of opportunity and the opportunities themselves. This book talks about three main sources of opportunity: technological change, political/regulatory change and social/demographic change. But are there others? More importantly, how do the different sources of opportunity actually create opportunities? We have no micro-level explanation of the processes by which technological, political/regulatory and social/demographic change make opportunities for profit possible. All we know is that these changes are associated with the creation of opportunities, with the mechanisms left unspecified.

One of the most important unanswered questions about these differences is which of these sources generates the most opportunities? Alternatively, does one of these sources of opportunity generate fewer opportunities, but opportunities that are of greater commercial value?

We also need more information about the relationship between sources of opportunity and forms of opportunity. We need to know the specific types of opportunities that emerge from different sources of change. Moreover, we need to know if these three sources of opportunity generate opportunities that are equally likely to take the form of new products and services, new markets, new ways of organizing, new raw materials and new processes. Furthermore, we do not know if the processes of discovery and exploitation of opportunities, the processes of resource acquisition and organizing, and the strategies for capturing the returns to the exploitation of opportunity differ across the five different forms of opportunity.

Chapter 3 explains that entrepreneurship involves a different decision-making process than that used by participants to buy and sell standard resources in the market place. This theoretical explanation is valuable, but is largely unsupported by empirical investigation. Moreover, while we have theoretical descriptions of the judgmental decision-making processes that entrepreneurs use (Casson, 1982; Sarasvathy, 2001), we have little empirical evidence for how they work. For example, what do new means–ends frameworks look like? How are they formed? What is the role of creativity versus discovery in their formulation?

Moreover, research has described entrepreneurial decision-making as involving the formulation of Popperian conjectures (Harper, 1996). But that observation raises a whole set of questions about the dynamic processes that underlie opportunity discovery and evaluation that are, to date, unanswered. For instance, how are those conjectures tested? What is the role of feedback in the process of opportunity development?

Another important set of questions concerns the opportunity identification process itself. We know relatively little about how this process works. For instance, do people search for opportunities or are they discovered without a search? What is the relative importance of information access and recognition processes to opportunity identification?

Chapter 3 also provides valuable information about the cognitive process of opportunity discovery. However, research in this area is really in its infancy. We have little empirical evidence to show that any cognitive characteristic enhances the likelihood of opportunity discovery. Future research would do well to identify the effects of different cognitive characteristics on opportunity discovery.

While we know more about the individual characteristics that influence opportunity exploitation than we do about cognitive processes underlying opportunity discovery, even here we have very limited information. We need to know much more about the effect of experience on opportunity exploitation. To date, we have very crude measures of experience. We know, for example, that people with more industry, management and start-up experience are more likely to exploit opportunities. But what types of industry experience matter most? When is start-up experience most valuable and when is it least valuable? For these types of subtle questions we have little in the way of answers.

The evidence on social factors and opportunity exploitation is also rather limited. We have a small amount of evidence that social ties and social status facilitate entrepreneurial exploitation. But we do not know if other social factors also matter. Moreover, we do not know what types of social ties – direct vs. indirect, strong vs. weak, and so on – matter the most for opportunity exploitation and under what conditions they tend to matter.

Furthermore, we could use more research that examines the actual decision to exploit opportunities rather than the static state of being an entrepreneur. Most of the research to date compares entrepreneurs to managers, raising many methodological and conceptual questions about the findings. Research on the actual decision to exploit opportunities among people at risk of such exploitation would overcome many of the limitations inherent in much of our existing research on this topic, as well as provide more precise explanations for how individual differences influence the entrepreneurial process.

Chapter 4 explained the importance of opportunity cost to the decision to exploit an opportunity. While this research informs us greatly about the role of opportunity cost in the exploitation decision, researchers could do much more with it. Opportunity cost matters, not in the absolute sense, but relative to the expected value of profit from exploiting an opportunity. Therefore, researchers should measure the gap between the expected profit from the opportunity and the opportunity cost of exploitation. Moreover, a true consideration of the relationship between expected value of the opportunity and opportunity cost of alternative activity should estimate the liquidity and uncertainty premiums that people demand to engage in entrepreneurial activity.

Additional research could be done to develop further our understanding of the topics discussed in Chapter 5. Despite over 30 years of research on the personalities and motives of entrepreneurs, more still could be done. Researchers have explored a very small range of personality characteristics and motives, even though a wider range of them would be theoretically relevant. Moreover, much more research is necessary to truly understand the effect of cognitive characteristics on opportunity exploitation. A careful reading of the evidence presented in Chapter 5 shows how thin the empirical support for cognitive factors appears to be.

Researchers interested in explaining the effect of individual differences on the exploitation of entrepreneurial opportunities should also consider the potentially conflicting effects of specific individual differences on different aspects of the entrepreneurial process, and on performance at entrepreneurial activity. For example, a desire for independence appears to increase the likelihood of opportunity exploitation, but appears to reduce the performance of new ventures. To date our arguments and evidence for entrepreneurship almost always assume that the factors that lead to entrepreneurial activity also enhance performance at that activity, but this need not be the case, and researchers should consider this possibility.

The information described in Chapters 6 and 7 about industry and institutional differences in opportunities is also informative, but leaves many questions unanswered. For example, do industries differ in the total amount of opportunity that is present in them or just in the form that the exploitation of opportunity takes? Similarly, does the institutional environment change the overall amount of opportunity that exists or just the distribution between productive and unproductive entrepreneurship as Baumol (1990) suggests?

Chapter 8 provides much useful information about resource acquisition in new ventures, but much more could be known about this topic. For instance, are there other contract provisions that investors use to overcome problems engendered by information asymmetry and uncertainty in the entrepreneurial process than those described in this book? What are the relationships between contract provisions and specific problems that they solve? In particular, we need more information about the use of contract provisions by investors other than venture capitalists because venture capitalists are a very small part of the total population of investors and are not representative of the entire group.

Moreover, we know very little about the similarities and differences in mechanisms that different types of investors use to overcome problems in resource acquisition. For example, business angels and venture capitalists appear to invest in many of the same ventures. So why do we have both types of resource providers? Do they solve uncertainty and information asymmetry problems in venture finance in the same way? Similarly, do people solve uncertainty and information asymmetry problems in venture finance the same way for $5000 investments as for $5 000 000 investments? Anecdotal evidence suggests that the answer is no, but we lack theoretical explanations for why such differences should exist, as well as rigorous scientific evidence to support those explanations.

Chapter 8 also describes a wide range of mechanisms used by investors, including such things as contracts, social ties, and pre- and post-investment tools. To what extent are these mechanisms substitutes for each other and to what extent are they complements? For example, should we expect investors to use social ties in place of contracts or do they employ both?

On the subject of social ties, we really should know several things that we do not yet know. As Chapter 8 explains, direct and indirect ties between entrepreneurs and investors facilitate resource acquisition in entrepreneurship, but what about other aspects of ties? For example, are investors positioned in a structural hole better able to finance entrepreneurial ventures than those not well connected to others? Are strong ties more valuable than weak ties in the venture finance process? More importantly, how do entrepreneurs obtain social ties? When seeking external capital, can the entrepreneurs actually use networking techniques or social skills to build ties with investors, or are they constrained by the social ties that they developed in school or through prior experience?

Lastly, Chapter 8 explains that entrepreneurs engage in certain behaviors and actions that facilitate resource acquisition. However, many of the explanations for particular actions and behaviors provided in this chapter have not yet received any widespread empirical support. Therefore, more research outlining effective actions and behaviors is clearly needed. Moreover, certain behaviors may be particularly important if entrepreneurs lack social ties or contractual arrangements that overcome information asymmetry and uncertainty problems in venture finance. However, we know very little about potential complementarities between these behaviors and other aspects of the venture finance process.

Chapter 9 explains the role of strategy in the entrepreneurial process. Unfortunately, a careful read of this chapter shows the lack of evidence for the use of many strategies that the theoretical literature says that entrepreneurs should use. In fact, we do not even have evidence of the basic frequencies with which entrepreneurs use different strategies. For example, how often is the control of resources strategy actually used by entrepreneurs?

Moreover, we have virtually no evidence of contingent relationships between the choice of strategy and the entrepreneurial opportunity being exploited. This raises the question: is there really no relationship between the strategies that entrepreneurs use and types of opportunities that they exploit? Alternatively, are certain strategies more common with Kirznerian opportunities, and others with Schumpeterian opportunities? Similarly, is there any relationship between the form that opportunities take and the strategies that entrepreneurs employ to exploit them?

Chapter 9 also examines several of the ways in which entrepreneurs overcome uncertainty and information asymmetry problems. However, researchers seem only to have scratched the surface of this topic. Many contingencies appear largely unexplored. For instance, are certain techniques for managing uncertainty and information asymmetry more effective than others with certain forms or types of opportunities or at certain stages in the development of new ventures?

The discussion presented in Chapter 10 points out the need for more information about the organizing process. While the chapter explains that organizing is a process that takes place over time, the research conducted to date does not yet tell us whether that process occurs through selection or adaptation. Moreover, we still need to know more about the process by which entrepreneurs create organizations, and establish the roles, routines, structures, procedures and monitoring systems that they use. Do they design optimal roles, routines and structures to meet the conditions that they face? Do they blindly offer variation that is selected by the environment? Or do they improvise and adapt from their initial approaches? Furthermore, do these aspects of organization evolve and change as the organization emerges? If so, how and when?

We could also use more investigation of the organizational forms through which opportunities are exploited. Most entrepreneurship research appears to assume (perhaps implicitly) that opportunities are exploited through the formation of new firms, and does not consider when opportunities are exploited through market mechanisms or by established firms. As a careful reading of Chapter 10 shows, I was able to identify only a few empirical studies that have examined when an entrepreneur would exploit an opportunity by franchising or licensing as opposed to developing the entire value chain of a new firm, or when an entrepreneur would choose to spin off from their employer and found a new firm.

The lack of explanation and evidence about organizing is particularly glaring with respect to the attraction and organization of human resources. We have a paucity of theory and evidence to account for how entrepreneurs find initial employees and put them to work producing new products and services. Much more research on this topic is clearly necessary.

A Call for New Methods

Entrepreneurship researchers also need to make changes to their research methodologies. First and foremost, researchers need to develop hypotheses and test explanations rather than just assemble facts. It is hard to know what researchers should do with the large assembly of facts gathered so far in descriptive studies. How do we make use of the knowledge that '70 per cent of entrepreneurs self-finance'; 'most new ventures fail' and 'entrepreneurs tend to hire their friends' unless we provide and test some theory to explain why and how these facts should be organized?

The entrepreneurship field also needs to use research methods that are appropriate to the study of the phenomenon. Entrepreneurship is a dynamic process and therefore demands investigative techniques that take this dynamism into consideration. However, most research about entrepreneurship – whether it is psychological or economic in nature – tends to be static, seeking to explain outcomes as if they are found in equilibrium or are in some sort of permanent state.

Failure to treat entrepreneurship as a dynamic process obscures the fact that most entrepreneurial activity is episodic, staged, short-lived and involves much selection (Shane *et al.*, forthcoming). By using a dynamic approach to investigation, researchers could capture these essential features. For example, certain individual characteristics might have very different effects on opportunity evaluation than on resource acquisition, as would be the case if overconfident people were more likely to evaluate opportunities positively, but were less likely to impress investors. Failure to consider the dynamic nature of the entrepreneurial process has led the field to develop an ignorance about these differences, which hinders the development of a true understanding of entrepreneurship.

Another advantage of taking dynamic approaches to entrepreneurship would be that such approaches would permit the incorporation of information about the tremendous selection that occurs throughout the entrepreneurial process. Rather than unrealistically assuming that a snapshot of data represents the population from which the researcher wishes to draw inference, researchers could generate more accurate empirical results by incorporating information about who remains in a population over time.

Entrepreneurship research methods need to consider the interaction of opportunities and individuals and find ways to measure both in fair comparisons. The joint investigation of both factors is critical to the investigation of the individual–opportunity nexus described in this book. However, very little research has ever incorporated both parts of the puzzle in a fair way. For example, to measure the effect of individuals on the entrepreneurial process properly, researchers must properly control for opportunities. Entrepreneurs might make different decisions about whether to exploit a given opportunity because they have different motivations, but they might also make different decisions if they are examining opportunities of different magnitude. If researchers fail to control for the effect of opportunities when measuring the effects of individual differences on the likelihood of opportunity exploitation, then the variance attributed to motivation might actually be an artifact of unobserved correlation between the motivation and the expected value of the opportunity (Shane, 2000).

One way for researchers to measure the value of the opportunity would be to have people examine the same simulated opportunities whose value is held constant. Another way would be for researchers to have third parties code the value of the opportunities under investigation. The specific way does not matter that much. However, controlling for differences in opportunities when measuring the effects of individuals, and vice versa, is crucial to obtaining accurate empirical evidence about entrepreneurship.

Another methodological issue concerns the need for researchers to study people who are at risk of exploiting opportunities. Much of the empirical research in entrepreneurship examines subjects who may not be at risk of opportunity exploitation. For example, many researchers have compared entrepreneurs, who have discovered opportunities, with managers who have not. The problem with such an approach is that one cannot tell whether the differences in opportunity exploitation that these researchers seek to explain is a result of the differences in the individual attributes about which the researchers hypothesize, or the fact that the experimental group has discovered opportunities while the control group has not.

Researchers could design studies to overcome this problem. For example, they could compare people who are all in the processes of investigating entrepreneurial opportunities to see who exploits the opportunities and who does not. While some researchers have adopted such designs, comparing people who have all investigated a particular technology, or who have all considered buying a franchise, these types of designs are relatively rare in the entrepreneurship literature.

Researchers could also make greater use of meta-analysis to combine the results of multiple studies about entrepreneurial phenomena. Many entrepreneurship researchers have rejected hypotheses about the effect of certain factors – for example, the effect of risk-taking propensity on the decision to exploit opportunities – because they attributed the lack of significant results in a single study to lack of validity rather than to measurement error. By using meta-analysis, this problem can be mitigated because patterns that were not present in individual studies often emerge when sampling error is reduced.

A FINAL COMMENT

This book outlined the individual–opportunity nexus framework to explain the phenomenon of entrepreneurship. It extends a discussion of this topic presented in much more abbreviated form in Eckhardt and Shane (2003), Shane and

Venkataraman (2000), and Venkataraman (1997). The book provided expla-nations for why, when and how, entrepreneurial opportunities exist; the sources of those opportunities and the forms that they take; the processes of opportunity discovery, opportunity evaluation, resource acquisition and opportunity exploitation; why, when and how some individuals and not others discover, evaluate, gather resources for, and exploit opportunities; the strategies used to pursue opportunities; and the organizing efforts to exploit them. For all of these topics, the book presented the logical arguments offered by the individual–opportunity nexus and the empirical evidence gathered to date in support of the dimensions of this approach. Given the early stage of the development of the field, much of this evidence is limited. Therefore, I have suggested many areas for future research. I hope that this book stimulates other researchers to join the effort to refine the individual–opportunity nexus framework and gather robust empirical evidence in support of it.

References

Acs, Z. and D. Audretsch (1989a), 'Births and firm size', *Southern Economic Journal*, **56**(2), 467–76.

Acs, Z. and D. Audretsch (1989b), 'Small firm entry in US manufacturing', *Economica*, **56**(222), 255–66.

Acs, Z. and D. Audretsch (1990), *Innovation and Small Firms*, Cambridge, MA, US: MIT Press.

Acs, Z. and D. Audretsch (1992), 'The social and economic impact of entrepreneurship', in D. Sexton and J. Kasarda (eds), *The State of the Art of Entrepreneurship*, Boston, MA, US: PWS-Kent, pp. 45–67.

Ahmed, S. (1985), 'nAch, risk taking propensity, locus of control and entrepreneurship', *Personality and Individual Differences*, **6**(6), 781–2.

Alba-Ramirez, A. (1994), 'Self-employment in the midst of unemployment: The case of Spain and the United States', *Applied Economics*, **26**, 189–204.

Aldrich, H. (1979), *Organizations and Environments*, Englewood Cliffs, NJ, US: Prentice-Hall.

Aldrich, H. (1990), 'Using an ecological perspective to study organization founding rates', *Entrepreneurship Theory and Practice*, **4**(3), 7–24.

Aldrich, H. (1999), *Organizations Evolving*, London: Sage.

Aldrich, H. and T. Baker (2001), 'Learning and legitimacy', in K. Schoonhoven and E. Romanelli (eds), *The Entrepreneurial Dynamic*, Stanford, US: Stanford University Press, pp. 40–67.

Aldrich, H., A. Elam and P. Reese (1996), 'Strong ties, weak ties, and strangers: Do women business owners differ from men in their use of networking to obtain assistance?', in S. Birley and I. MacMillan (eds), *Entrepreneurship in a Global Context*, London: Routledge, pp. 1–25.

Aldrich, H. and M. Fiol (1994), 'Fools rush in? The institutional context of industry creation', *Academy of Management Review*, **19**(4), 645–70.

Aldrich, H. and N. Langdon (1998), 'Human resource management and organizational life cycles', in P. Reynolds, W. Bygrave, N. Carter, S. Manigart, C. Mason, G.D. Meyer and K. Shaver (eds), *Frontiers of Entrepreneurship Research*, Babson Park, US: Babson College, pp. 349–58.

Aldrich, H., B. Rosen and W. Woodward (1987), 'The impact of social networks on business foundings and profit: A longitudinal study', in N. Churchill, J.

Hornaday, B. Kirchhoff, O. Krasner and K. Vesper (eds), *Frontiers of Entrepreneurship Research*, Babson Park, US: Babson College, pp. 154–68.

Aldrich, H. and M. Von Glinow (1992), 'Business start-ups: The HRM imperative', in S. Birley and I. MacMillan (eds), *International Perspectives on Entrepreneurship Research*, New York, US: Elsevier, pp. 233–53.

Aldrich, H. and R. Waldinger (1990), 'Ethnicity and entrepreneurship', *Annual Review of Sociology*, **16**, 111–35.

Aldrich, H. and G. Wiedenmayer (1993), 'From traits to rates: An ecological perspective on organizational foundings', *Advances in Entrepreneurship, Firm Emergence and Growth*, **1**, 145–95.

Aldrich, H. and C. Zimmer (1986), 'Entrepreneurship through social networks', in D. Sexton and R. Smilor (eds), *The Art and Science of Entrepreneurship*, Cambridge, MA, US: Ballinger Publishing Company, pp. 3–23.

Aldrich, H., C. Zimmer, U. Staber and J. Beggs (1990), 'Trade association foundings in the 20th century', paper presented at the annual meeting of the American Sociological Association, Washington, DC, US.

Aldrich, H., C. Zimmer, U. Staber and J. Beggs (1994), 'Minimalism, mutualism, and maturity: The evolution of the American trade association population in the 20th century', in J. Baum and J. Singh (eds), *Evolutionary Dynamics of Organizations*, New York, US: Oxford University Press, pp. 223–39.

Allinson, C., E. Chell and J. Hayes (2000), 'Intuition and entrepreneurial behaviour', *European Journal of Work and Organizational Psychology*, **9**(1), 33–43.

Amburgey, T., T. Dacin and D. Kelly (1994), 'Disruptive selection and population segmentation: Interpopulation competition as a segregating process', in J. Baum and J. Singh (eds), *Evolutionary Dynamics of Organizations*, New York, US: Oxford University Press, pp. 240–54.

Amit, R., J. Brander and C. Zott (1998), 'Why do venture capital firms exist? Theory and Canadian evidence', *Journal of Business Venturing*, **13**(6), 441–66.

Amit, R., L. Glosten and E. Muller (1990a), 'Does venture capital foster the most promising entrepreneurial firms?', *California Management Review*, **32**(3), 102–11.

Amit, R., L. Glosten and E. Muller (1990b), 'Entrepreneurial ability, venture investments, and risk sharing', *Management Science*, **38**(10), 1232–45.

Amit, R., L. Glosten and E. Muller (1993), 'Challenges to theory development in entrepreneurship research', *Journal of Management Studies*, **30**, 815–34.

Amit, R., K. MacCrimmon, C. Zietsma and J. Oesch (2001), 'Does money matter? Wealth attainment as a motive for initiating growth-oriented technology ventures', *Journal of Business Venturing*, **16**(2), 119–44.

Amit, R. and E. Muller (1994), '"Push" and "Pull" entrepreneurship', in W. Bygrave, S. Birley, N. Churchill, E. Gatewood, F. Hoy, R. Keeley, W. Wetzel (eds), *Frontiers of Entrepreneurship Research*, Babson Park, US: Babson College, pp. 27–42.

Amit, R., E. Muller and I. Cockburn (1995), 'Opportunity costs and entrepreneurial activity', *Journal of Business Venturing*, **10**(2), 95–106.

Anand, B. and T. Khanna (2000), 'The structure of licensing contracts', *Journal of Industrial Economics*, **48**(1), 103–35.

Anton, J. and D. Yao (1995), 'Startups, spinoffs, and internal projects', *Journal of Law, Economics, and Organization*, **11**, 362–78.

Arabsheibani, G., D. De Meza, J. Maloney and B. Pearson (2000), 'And a vision appeared unto them of a great profit: Evidence of self-deception among the self-employed', *Economics Letters*, **67**, 35–41.

Arora, A. (1995), 'Licensing tacit knowledge: Intellectual property rights and the market for knowhow', *Economics of Innovation and New Technology*, **4**, 41–59.

Arora, A. (1996), 'Contracting for tacit knowledge: The provision of technical services in technology licensing contracts', *Journal of Developmental Economics*, **50**, 223–56.

Arrow, K. (1962), 'Economic welfare and the allocation of resources for inventions', in R. Nelson (ed.), *The Rate and Direction of Inventive Activity*, Princeton, NJ, US: Princeton University Press, pp. 609–25.

Arrow, K. (1974a), 'Limited knowledge and economic analysis', *American Economic Review*, **64**(1), 1–10.

Arrow, K. (1974b), *The Limits of Organization*, New York, US: Norton.

Audretsch, D. (1991), 'New firm survival and the technological regime', *Review of Economics and Statistics*, **73**(3), 441–50.

Audretsch, D. (1997), 'Technological regimes, industrial demography and the evolution of industrial structures', *Industrial and Corporate Change*, pp. 49–82.

Audretsch, D. (2001), 'Research issues relating to structure, competition, and performance of small technology-based firms', *Small Business Economics*, **16**, 37–51.

Audretsch, D. and Z. Acs (1994), 'New firm startups, technology, and macroeconomic fluctuations', *Small Business Economics*, **6**, 439–49.

Audretsch, D. and M. Fritsch (1994), 'The geography of firm births in Germany', *Regional Studies*, **28**(4), 359–65.

Audretsch, D. and T. Mahmood (1991), 'The hazard rate of new establishments', *Economic Letters*, **36**, 409–12.

Audretsch, D. and T. Mahmood (1995), 'New firm survival: New results using a hazard function', *Review of Economics and Statistics*, **77**(1), 97–103.

Autio, E., R. Keeley, M. Klofsten and T. Ulfstedt (1997), 'Entrepreneurial intent among students: Testing an intent model in Asia, Scandanavia, and USA', in P. Reynolds, W. Bygrave, N. Carter, P. Davidsson, W. Gartner, C. Mason and P. McDougall (eds), *Frontiers of Entrepreneurship Research*, Babson Park, US: Babson College, pp. 133–55.

Azoulay, P. and S. Shane (2001), 'Entrepreneurs, contracts and the failure of young firms', *Management Science*, **47**(3), 337–58.

Babb, E. and S. Babb (1992), 'Psychological traits of rural entrepreneurs', *The Journal of Socio-Economics*, **21**, 353–62.

Baker, T. and H. Aldrich (1994), 'Human resource management and new ventures', paper presented at the Babson Conference on Entrepreneurship, Babson Park, MA, US.

Baker, T., A. Miner and D. Eesley (forthcoming), 'Improvising firms: Bricolage, account giving and improvisational competencies in the founding process', *Research Policy*.

Baldwin, J. and J. Johnson (1996), 'Survival of new Canadian manufacturing firms: The importance of financial structure', working paper, Micro-economic Studies and Analysis Division, Statistics Canada, US.

Bamford, C., T. Dean and P. McDougall (1997), 'Performance strategies for high-growth entrepreneurial firms', in P. Reynolds, W. Bygrave, N. Carter, P. Davidsson, W. Gartner, C. Mason and P. McDougall (eds), *Frontiers of Entrepreneurship Research*, Babson Park, US: Babson College, pp. 375–89.

Bamford, C., T. Dean and P. McDougall (2000), 'An examination of the impact of initial founding conditions and decisions upon the performance of new bank start-ups', *Journal of Business Venturing*, **15**(3), 253–77.

Banaszak-Holl, J. (1991), 'Incorporating organizational growth into models of organizational dynamics: Manhattan banks', 1791–1980, Ph.D. Dissertation, Cornell University, US.

Banaszak-Holl, J. (1992), 'Historical trends in rates of Manhattan bank mergers, acquisitions, and failures', working paper, Brown University, US.

Banaszak-Holl, J. (1993), 'Avoiding failure when times get tough: Changes in organizations' responses to competitive pressures', working paper, Brown University, US.

Bandura, A. (1997), *Self-efficacy: The Exercise of Self-control*, New York: W.H. Freedman.

Bania, N., R. Eberts and M. Fogarty (1993), 'Universities and the startup of new companies: Can we generalize from route 128 and Silicon Valley', *The Review of Economics and Statistics*, **75**(4), 761–6.

Barnes, M., D. Mowery and A. Ziedonis (1997), 'The geographic reach of market and non-market channels of technology transfer: Comparing citations and licenses of university patents', paper presented at the Academy of Management Meetings, Boston, MA, US.

Barnett, W. (1990), 'The organizational ecology of a technological system', *Administrative Science Quarterly*, **35**, 31–60.

Barnett, W. (1997), 'The dynamics of competitive intensity', *Administrative Science Quarterly*, **42**, 128–60.

Barnett, W. and G. Carroll (1987), 'Competition and mutualism among early telephone companies', *Administrative Science Quarterly*, **32**(3), 400–21.

Barnett, W. and G. Carroll (1993), 'How institutional constraints affected the organization of early American telephony', *Journal of Law, Economics, and Organization*, **9**, 98–128.

Barney, J. (1991), 'Firm resources and sustained competitive advantage', *Journal of Management*, **17**(1), 99–120.

Baron, J., M. Hannan and M. Burton (1999), 'Building the iron cage: Determinants of managerial intensity in the early years of organizations', *American Sociological Review*, **64**, 527–47.

Baron, J., M. Hannan and M. Burton (forthcoming), 'Labor pains: Change in organizational models and employee turnover in young, high-tech firms', *American Journal of Sociology*, **106**(4), 960–1012.

Baron, R. (2000a), 'Counterfactual thinking and venture formation: The potential effects of thinking about what might have been', *Journal of Business Venturing*, **15**(1), 79–92.

Baron, R. (2000b), 'Psychological perspectives on entrepreneurship: Cognitive and social factors in entrepreneurs' success', *Current Directions in Psychological Science*, **9**(1), 15–18.

Baron, R. (forthcoming), 'OB and Entrepreneurship: Why both may benefit from closer links', in B. Staw and R. Kramer (eds), *Research in Organizational Behavior*.

Baron, R. and G. Markman (1999a), 'The role of entrepreneurs' behavior in their financial success: Evidence for the benefits of effective social skills', paper presented at the Babson Conference on Entrepreneurship, Babson Park, MA, US.

Baron, R. and G. Markman (1999b), 'Cognitive mechanisms: potential differences between entrepreneurs and non-entrepreneurs', in P. Reynolds, W. Bygrave, S. Manigart, C. Mason, C. Mason, G. Meyer, H. Sapienza and K. Shaver (eds), *Frontiers of Entrepreneurship Research*, Babson Park, US: Babson College, pp. 123–37.

Barrick, M. and Mount, M. (1991), 'The big five personality dimensions and job performance: A meta analysis', *Personnel Psychology*, **44**, 1–26.

Barron, D., E. West and M. Hannan (1994), 'A time to grow and a time to die: Growth and mortality of credit unions in New York City, 1914–1990', *American Journal of Sociology*, **100**, 381–421.

Barry, C. (1994), 'New directions in research on venture capital finance', *Financial Management*, **23**(3), 3–15.

Barzel, Y. (1987), 'The entrepreneurs reward for self-policing', *Economic Inquiry*, **25**, 103–16.

Basu, A. and S. Parker (2001), 'Family finance and new business start-ups', *Oxford Bulletin of Economics and Statistics*, **63**(3), 333–58.

Bates, T. (1990), 'Entrepreneur human capital inputs and small business longevity', *The Review of Economics and Statistics*, **72**(4), 551–9.

Bates, T. (1994), 'A comparison of franchise and independent small business survival rates', *Small Business Economics*, **7**, 1–12.

Bates, T. (1995a), 'Analysis of survival rates among franchise and independent small business startups', *Journal of Small Business Management*, **33**(2), 26–36.

Bates, T. (1995b), 'Self-employment entry across industry groups', *Journal of Business Venturing*, **10**(2), 143–56.

Bates, T. (1997), 'Financing small business creation: The case of Chinese and Korean immigrant entrepreneurs', *Journal of Business Venturing*, **12**(2), 109–24.

Bates, T. and L. Servon (2000), 'Viewing self employment as a response to lack of suitable opportunities for wage work', *National Journal of Sociology*, **12**(2), 23–53.

Baum, J. (1996), 'Organizational ecology', in S. Clegg, C. Hardy and W. Nord (eds), *Handbook of Organization Studies*, London: Sage, pp. 77–114.

Baum, J., T. Calabrese and B. Silverman (2000), 'Don't go it alone: Alliance network composition and startups' performance in Canadian biotechnology', *Strategic Management Journal*, **21**, 267–94.

Baum, J. and H. Haveman (1997), 'Love thy neighbor? Differentiation and agglomeration in the Manhattan hotel industry, 1898–1990', *Administrative Science Quarterly*, **42**(2), 304–38.

Baum, J., H. Korn and S. Kotha (1995), 'Dominant designs and population dynamics in telecommunications services: Founding and failure of facsimile transmission service organizations, 1965–1992', *Social Science Research*, **24**, 97–135.

Baum, J. and S. Mezias (1992), 'Localized competition and organizational failure in the Manhattan hotel industry, 1898–1990', *Administrative Science Quarterly*, **37**, 580–604.

Baum, J. and C. Oliver (1991), 'Institutional linkages and organizational mortality', *Administrative Science Quarterly*, **36**, 187–218.

Baum, J. and C. Oliver (1992), 'Institutional embeddedness and the dynamics of organizational populations', *American Sociological Review*, **57**, 540–59.

Baum, J. and J. Singh (1994a), 'Organizational hierarchies and evolutionary processes: Some reflections on a theory of organizational evolution', in J. Baum and J. Singh (eds), *Evolutionary Dynamics of Organizations*, New York, US: Oxford University Press, pp. 3–22.

Baum, J. and J. Singh (1994b), 'Organizational niches and the dynamics of organizational founding', *Organization Science*, **594**, 483–501.

Baum, J. and J. Singh (1994c), 'Organizational niches and the dynamics of organizational mortality', *American Journal of Sociology*, **100**(3), 346–80.

Baum, J.R. (1994), 'The relation of traits, competencies, vision, motivation, and strategy to venture growth', unpublished Doctoral Dissertation, University of Maryland, US.

Baum, J.R., E.A. Locke and S. Kirkpatrick (1998), 'A longitudinal study of the relation of vision and vision communication to venture growth in entrepreneurial firms', *Journal of Applied Psychology*, **83**(1), 43–54.

Baum, J.R., E.A. Locke and K.G. Smith (2001), 'A multi-dimensional model of venture growth', *Academy of Management Journal*, **44** (2), 292–303.

Baumol, W. (1990), 'Entrepreneurship: Productive, unproductive, and destructive', *Journal of Political Economy*, **98**(5), 893–921.

Baumol, W. (1993), 'Formal entrepreneurship theory in economics: Existence and bounds', *Journal of Business Venturing*, **8**(3), 197–210.

Bayer, K. (1991), 'The impact of using consultants during venture formation on venture performance', in N. Churchill, W. Bygrave, J. Covin, D. Sexton, D. Slevin, K. Vesper and W. Wetzel (eds), *Frontiers of Entrepreneurship Research,* Babson Park, US: Babson College, 291–305.

Begley, T. (1995), 'Using founder status, age of firm, and company growth rate as the basis of distinguishing entrepreneurs from managers of smaller businesses', *Journal of Business Venturing*, **10**(3), 249–63.

Begley, T. and D. Boyd (1986), 'Psychological characteristics associated with entrepreneurial performance', in R. Ronstadt, J. Hornaday, R. Peterson and K. Vesper (eds), *Frontiers of Entrepreneurship Research*, Babson Park, MA, US: Babson College, pp. 146–65.

Begley, T. and D. Boyd (1987), 'A comparison of entrepreneurs and managers of small business firms', *The Journal of Management*, **13**, 99–108.

Begley, T., T. Wee-Liang, A. Larasati, A. Rab, E. Zamora and G. Nanayakkura (1997), 'The relationship between socio-cultural dimensions and interest in starting a business: A multi-country study', in P. Reynolds, W. Bygrave, N. Carter, P. Davidsson, W. Gartner, C. Mason and P. McDougall (eds), *Frontiers of Entrepreneurship Research*, Babson Park, US: Babson College, pp. 156–82.

Bellu, R. (1988), 'Entrepreneurs and managers: Are they different?', in B. Kirchhoff, W. Long, W. McMullan, K. Vesper and W. Wetzel (eds), *Frontiers of Entrepreneurship Research*, Babson Park, US: Babson College, pp. 16–30.

Bernardo, A. and I. Welch (2001), 'On the evolution of overconfidence and entrepreneurs', *Journal of Economics and Management Strategy*, **10**(3), 301–30.

Bernhardt, I. (1994), 'Comparative advantage in self-employment and paid work', *Canadian Journal of Economics*, **27**, 273–89.

Bhave, M. (1994), 'A process model of entrepreneurial creation', *Journal of Business Venturing*, **9**(3), 223–42.

Bhide, A. (2000), *The Origin and Evolution of New Businesses*, New York, US: Oxford University Press.

Bird, B. (1992), 'The operation of intentions in time: The emergence of the new venture', *Entrepreneurship Theory and Practice*, **17**(1), 11–20.

Bird, B. and M. Jelinek (1988), 'The operation of entrepreneurial intentions', *Entrepreneurship Theory and Practice*, **13**(2), 21–9.

Black, S. and P. Strahan (2000), 'Entrepreneurship and bank credit availability', working paper, Federal Reserve Bank of New York, US.

Blanchflower, D. and A. Oswald (1998), 'What makes an entrepreneur?', *Journal of Labor Economics*, **16**(1), 26–60.

Blanchflower, D., A. Oswald and A. Stutzer (2001), 'Latent entrepreneurship across nations', *European Economic Review*, **45**, 680–91.

Blau, D. (1987), 'A time-series analysis of self-employment in the United States', *Journal of Political Economy*, **95**, 445–67.

Blau, P. (1964), *Exchange and Power in Social Life*, New York, US: Wiley.

Boeker, W. (1988), 'Organizational origins: Environmental imprinting at the time of founding', in G. Carroll (ed.), *Ecological Models of Organization*, Cambridge: Ballinger, pp. 33–51.

Bogenhold, D. and U. Staber (1990), 'Selbständigkeit als ein reflux auf arbeitslosigkeit? Makrosoziologische befunde einer international vergleichenden studie', *Kolner Zeitschrift für Soziologie und Sozialpsychologie*, **42**, 265–79.

Bonnett, C. and A. Furnham (1991), 'Who wants to be an entrepreneur? A study of adolescents interested in a Young Enterprise scheme', *Journal of Economic Psychology*, **12**, 465–78.

Borjas, G. (1986), 'The self-employment experience of immigrants', *The Journal of Human Resources*, **11**, 485–506.

Borjas, G. and Bronars, (1989), 'Consumer discrimination and self-employment', *Journal of Political Economy*, **97**, 581–605.

Boswell, J. (1973), *The Rise and Decline of Small Firms*, London: Allen and Unwin.

Bouwen, R. and C. Steyaert (1990), 'Construing organizational texture in young entrepreneurial firms', *Journal of Management Studies*, **27**(6), 637–49.

Bowen, D.D. and R.D. Hisrich (1986), 'The female entrepreneur: A career development perspective', *Academy of Management Review*, **11**, 393–407.

Boyd, R. (1990), 'Black and Asian self-employment in large metropolitan areas: A comparative analysis', *Social Problems*, **37**(2), 258–74.

Boyd, R. (1991), 'Black entrepreneurship in 52 metropolitan areas', *Social Science Research*, **75**(3), 158–63.

Bradach, J. and R. Eccles (1989), 'Markets versus hierarchies: From ideal types to plural forms', *Annual Review of Sociology*, **15**, 97–118.

Brittain, J. and J. Freeman (1986) 'Entrepreneurship in the semiconductor industry', paper presented at the Academy of Management Meeting, Chicago, IL.

Brock, W. and D. Evans (1986), *The Economics of Small Businesses: Their Role and Regulation in the US Economy*, New York, US: Holmes and Meier.

Brodsky, M. (1993), 'Successful female corporate managers and entrepreneurs', *Group and Organization Management*, **18**(3), 366–79.

Brophy, D. (1992), 'Financing the new venture: A report on recent research', in D. Sexton and J. Kasarda (eds), *The State of the Art of Entrepreneurship*, Boston, US: PWS-Kent, pp. 387–401.

Bruderl, J. and P. Preisendorfer (1998), 'Network support and the success of newly founded businesses', *Small Business Economics*, **10**, 213–25.

Bruderl, J., P. Preisendorfer and R. Ziegler (1992), 'Survival chances of newly founded business organizations', *American Sociological Review*, **57**, 227–302.

Bull, I. and F. Winter (1991), 'Community differences in business births and business growths', *Journal of Business Venturing*, **6**(1), 29–43.

Burke, A., F. Fitzroy and M. Nolan (2000), 'When less is more: Distinguishing between entrepreneurial choice and performance', *Oxford Bulletin of Economics and Statistics*, **62**(5), 565–87.

Burt, R. (1987), 'Social contagion and innovation: Cohesion versus structural equivalence', *American Journal of Sociology*, **92**, 1287–335.

Burt, R. (1992), *Structural Holes: The Social Structure of Competition*, Boston, US: Harvard University Press.

Burton, D.M., J. Sorenson and C. Beckman (1998), 'Coming from good stock: Career histories and new venture formation', paper presented at the Academy of Management Meetings, San Diego, US.

Busenitz, L. (1996), 'Research in entrepreneurial alertness', *Journal of Small Business Management*, **36**(5), 35–44.

Busenitz, L. (1999), 'Entrepreneurial risk and strategic decision making', *Journal of Applied Behavioral Science*, **35**(3), 325–40.

Busenitz, L. and J. Barney (1997), 'Differences between entrepreneurs and managers in large organizations: Biases and heuristics in strategic decision making', *Journal of Business Venturing*, **12**(1), 9–30.

Busenitz, L. and C. Lau (1996), 'A cross-cultural cognitive model of new venture creation', *Entrepreneurship Theory and Practice*, **20**(4), 25–39.

Butler, J. and C. Herring (1991), 'Ethnicity and entrepreneurship in America: Toward an explanation of racial and ethnic group variations in self-employment', *Sociological Perspectives*, **34**(1), 79–95.

Butt, A. and W. Khan (1996), 'Effects of transferability of learning from pre-start-up experiences', in P. Reynolds, S. Birley, J. Butler, W. Bygrave, P. Davidsson, W. Gartner and P. McDougall (eds), *Frontiers of Entrepreneurship Research*, Babson Park, US: Babson College, pp. 108–16.

Bygrave, W. (1988), 'The structure of the investment networks of venture capital firms', *Journal of Business Venturing*, **3**(2), 137–57.

Bygrave, W. and M. Minniti (2000), 'The social dynamics of entrepeneurship', *Entrepreneurship Theory and Practice*, **24**(3), 25–36.

Bygrave, W. and J. Timmons (1985), 'An empirical model for the flows of venture capital', in J. Hornaday, E. Shils, J. Timmons and K. Vesper (eds), *Frontiers of Entrepreneurship Research*, Babson Park, US: Babson College, pp. 105–25.

Bygrave, W. and J. Timmons (1992), *Venture Capital at the Crossroads*, Boston, US: Harvard Business School Press.

Cable, D. and S. Shane (1997), 'A prisoner's dilemma approach to entrepreneur–venture capitalist relationships', *Academy of Management Review*, **22**(1), 142–76.

Cachon, J. (1988), 'Venture creators and firm buyers: A comparison of attitudes toward government help and locus of control', in B. Kirchhoff, W. Long, W. McMullan, K. Vesper and W. Wetzel (eds), *Frontiers of Entrepreneurship Research*, Babson Park, US: Babson College, pp. 568–79.

Caird, S. (1991), 'The enterprising tendency of occupational groups', *International Small Business Journal*, **9**, 75–81.

Calvo, G. and S. Wellisz (1980), 'Technology, entrepreneurs and firm size', *Quarterly Journal of Economics*, **95**, 663–77.

Campbell, C. (1992), 'A decision theory model for entrepreneurial acts', *Entrepreneurship Theory and Practice*, **17**(1), 21–7.

Caputo, R. and A. Dolinsky (1998), 'Women's choice to pursue self-employment: The role of financial and human capital of household members', *Journal of Small Business Management*, **36**(3), 8–17.

Cardozo, R., A. Ardishvilli, P. Reynolds and B. Miller (1992), 'New firm growth and the role of founding circumstances', in N. Churchill, S. Birley, W. Bygrave, D. Muzyka, C. Wahlbin and W. Wetzel (eds), *Frontiers of Entrepreneurship Research*, Babson Park, US: Babson College, pp. 275–87.

Carland, J. (1982), 'Entrepreneurship in a small business setting: An exploratory study', Ph.D. Dissertation, University of Georgia.

Carroll, G. (1983), 'A stochastic model of organizational mortality: Review and reanalysis', *Social Science Research*, **12**, 303–29.

Carroll, G. and J. Delacroix (1982), 'Organizational mortality in the newspaper industries in Argentina and Ireland: An ecological approach', *Administrative Science Quarterly*, **27**, 169–98.

Carroll, G. and M. Hannan (1989a), 'Density delay in the evolution of organizational populations: A model and five empirical tests', *Administrative Science Quarterly*, **34**, 411–30.

Carroll, G. and M. Hannan (1989b), 'Density dependence in the evolution of newspaper organizations', *American Sociological Review*, **54**, 524–41.

Carroll, G. and M. Hannan (2000), *The Demography of Corporations and Industries*, Princeton, NJ, US: Princeton University Press.

Carroll, G. and P. Huo (1986), 'Organizational task and institutional environments in ecological perspective: Findings from the local newspaper industry', *American Journal of Sociology*, **91**, 838–73.

Carroll, G. and E. Mosakowski (1987), 'The career dynamics of self-employment', *Administrative Science Quarterly*, **32**, 570–89.

Carroll, G., P. Preisendorfer, A. Swaminathan and G. Wiedenmayer (1993), 'Brewery and Brauerei: The organizational ecology of brewing', *Organization Studies*, **14**, 155–88.

Carroll, G. and A. Swaminathan (1991), 'Density dependent organizational evolution in the American brewing industry from 1633 to 1988', *Acta Sociologica*, **34**, 155–76.

Carroll, G. and J. Wade (1991), 'Density dependence in organizational evolution of the American brewing industry across different levels of analysis', *Social Science Research*, **20**(3), 271–302.

Carroll, R., D. Holtz-Eakin, M. Rider and H. Rosen (1989), 'Personal income taxes and the growth of small firms', in G. Libecap (1993), *Advances in the Study of Entrepreneurship, Innovation and Economic Growth*, pp. 121–47.

Carter, N., T. Stearns, P. Reynolds and M. Williams (1992), 'The effects of industry and founding strategy on new firm survival', in N. Churchill, S. Birley, W. Bygrave, D. Muzyka, C. Wahlbin and W. Wetzel (eds), *Frontiers of Entrepreneurship Research*, Babson Park, US: Babson College, pp. 161–72.

Carter, R. and H. Van Auken (1990), 'Personal equity investment and small business financial difficulties', *Entrepreneurship Theory and Practice*, **15**(2), 51–60.

Casson, M. (1982), *The Entrepreneur*, Totowa, NJ, US: Barnes and Noble Books.

Casson, M. (1995), *Entrepreneurship and Business Culture*, Aldershot, UK and Brookfield, US: Edward Elgar.

Casson, M. (1996), 'The nature of the firm reconsidered: Information synthesis and entrepreneurial organization', *Management International Review*, **36**, 55–94.

Castrogiovanni, G. (1996), 'Pre-startup planning and the survival of new small businesses: theoretical linkages', *Journal of Management*, **22**(6), 801–22.

Caves, R. (1998), 'Industrial organization and new findings on the turnover and mobility of firms', *Journal of Economic Literature*, **36**, 1947–82.

Chen, C., P. Greene and A. Crick (1998), 'Does entrepreneurial self-efficacy distinguish entrepreneurs from managers?', *Journal of Business Venturing*, **13**(4), 295–316.

Christiansen, C. (1993), 'The rigid disk drive industry: A history of commercial and technological turbulence', *Business History Review*, **67**, 531–88.

Christiansen, C. (1997), *The Innovators Dilemma*, Cambridge, MA: Harvard Business School Press.

Christiansen, C. and J. Bower (1996), 'Customer power, strategic investment, and the failure of leading firms', *Strategic Management Journal*, **17**, 197–218.

Clouse, V. (1990), 'A controlled experiment relating entrepreneurial education to students' start-up decisions', *Journal of Small Business Management*, **28**(2), 45–53.

Cobas, J. (1986), 'Paths to self-employment among immigrants: An analysis of four interpretations', *Sociological Perspectives*, **29**(1), 101–20.

Cobas, J. and J. DeOllos (1989), 'Family ties, co-ethnic bonds, and ethnic entrepreneurship', *Sociological Perspectives*, **32**(3), 403–12.

Cohen, W. and R. Levin (1989), 'Firm size and R&D intensity: A re-examination', *The Journal of Industrial Economics*, **35**(4), 543–66.

Cohen, W. and D. Levinthal (1990), 'Absorptive capacity: A new perspective on learning and innovation', *Administrative Science Quarterly*, **35**(1), 128–53.

Coleman, J. (1990), *Foundations of Social Theory*, Cambridge, MA: Belknap Press.

Collins, C., E. Locke and P. Hanges (2000), 'The relationship of need for achievement to entrepreneurial behavior: A meta-analysis', working paper, University of Maryland, US.

Cooper, A. (1971), *The Founding of Technology-Based Firms*, Milwaukee, US: The Center for Venture Management.

Cooper, A. (1984), 'Contrasts in the role of incubator organizations in the founding of growth-oriented companies', in J. Hornaday, F. Tarpley, J. Timmons and K. Vesper (eds), *Frontiers of Entrepreneurship Research*, Babson Park, US: Babson College, pp. 159–74.

Cooper, A. (1985), 'The role of incubator organizations in the founding of growth-oriented firms', *Journal of Business Venturing*, **1**(1), 75–86.

Cooper, A. and A. Bruno (1978), 'Success among high technology firms', *Business Horizons*, April, pp. 16–23.

Cooper, A. and C. Daily (1998), 'Entrepreneurial teams', working paper, Purdue University, US.

Cooper, A. and W. Dunkelberg (1987), 'Entrepreneurship research: Old questions, new answers, and methodological issues', *American Journal of Small Business*, **11**(3), 11–23.

Cooper, A., W. Dunkelberg and C. Woo (1988), 'Survival and failure: A longitudinal study', in B. Kirchhoff, W. Long, W. McMullan, K. Vesper and W. Wetzel (eds), *Frontiers of Entrepreneurship Research*, Babson Park, US: Babson College, pp. 225–37.

Cooper, A., W. Dunkelberg and C. Woo (1990), *New Business in America*, Washington, US: NFIB Foundation.

Cooper, A., T. Folta and C. Woo (1995), 'Entrepreneurial information search', *Journal of Business Venturing*, **10**(2), 107–20.

Cooper, A., J. Gimeno-Gascon and C. Woo (1994), 'Initial human and financial capital as predictors of new venture performance', *Journal of Business Venturing*, **9**(5), 371–95.

Cooper, A., C. Woo and W. Dunkelberg (1988), 'Entrepreneurs' perceived chances for success', *Journal of Business Venturing*, **3**(2), 97–108.

Corman, J., B. Perles and P. Vancini (1988), 'Motivational factors influencing high-technology entrepreneurship', *Journal of Small Business Management*, **26**, 36–42.

Cressy, R. (1996a), 'Are business startups debt-rationed?', *Economic Journal*, **106**, 1253–70.

Cressy, R. (1996b), 'Pre-entrepreneurial income, cash-flow, growth and survival of startup businesses: Model and tests on UK data', *Small Business Economics*, **8**, 49–58.

Cressy, R. (2000), 'Credit rationing or entrepreneurial risk aversion? An alternative explanation for the Evans and Jovanovic finding', *Economics Letters*, **66**, 235–40.

Cromie, S. (1987), 'Motivations of aspiring male and female entrepreneurs', *Journal of Organizational Behaviour*, **8**, 251–61.

Cromie, S. and S. Birley (1992), 'Networking by female business owners in Northern Ireland', *Journal of Business Venturing*, **7**(3), 237–51.

Cromie, S. and S. Johns (1983), 'Irish entrepreneurs: Some personal characteristics', *Journal of Organizational Behavior*, **4**, 317–24.

Cromie, S. and J. O'Donoghue (1992), 'Assessing entrepreneurial inclinations', *International Small Business Journal*, **10**, 66–73.

Dahlstrand, A. (1997), 'Growth and inventiveness in technology-based spin-off firms', *Research Policy*, **26**, 331–44.

Dana, L. (1987), 'Entrepreneurship and venture creation – An international comparison of five commonwealth nations', in N. Churchill, J. Hornaday, B. Kirchhoff, O. Krasner and K. Vesper (eds), *Frontiers of Entrepreneurship Research*, Babson Park, US: Babson College, pp. 573–83.

Dana, L. (1990), 'Saint Martin/Sint Maarten: A case study of the effects of culture on economic development', *Journal of Small Business Management*, **28**(4), 91–8.

Davidsson, P., L. Lindmark and C. Olofsson (1994), 'New firm formation and regional development in Sweden', *Regional Studies*, **28**(4), 395–410.

Dean, D. and R. Brown (1995), 'Pollution regulation as a barrier to new firm entry: Initial evidence and implications for future research', *Academy of Management Journal*, **38**(1), 288–303.

Dean, T., R. Brown and C. Bamford (1998), 'Differences in large and small firm responses to environmental context: Strategic implications from a comparative analysis of business formations', *Strategic Management Journal*, **19**, 709–28.

Dean, T. and G. Meyer (1992), 'New venture formation in manufacturing industries: A conceptual and empirical analysis', in N. Churchill, S. Birley, W. Bygrave, D. Muzyka, C. Wahlbin and W. Wetzel (eds), *Frontiers of Entrepreneurship Research*, Babson Park, US: Babson College, pp. 173–87.

DeCarlo, J.F. and P.R. Lyons (1979), 'A comparison of selected personal characteristics of minority and non-minority female entrepreneurs', *Journal of Small Business Management*, **12**, 22–9.

Dees, G. and J. Starr (1992), 'Entrepreneurship thought through an ethical lens: Dilemmas and issues for research and practice', in D. Sexton and J. Kasarda (eds), *The State of the Art of Entrepreneurship*, Boston, US; PWS-Kent, pp. 89–116.

De Kok, J. and L. Uhlaner (2001), 'Organization context and human resource management in the small firm', *Small Business Economics*, **17**, 273–91.

Delacroix, J. and G. Carroll (1983), 'Organizational foundings: An ecological study of the newspaper industries of Argentina and Ireland', *Administrative Science Quarterly*, **28**, 274–91.

Delacroix, J. and A. Swaminathan (1991), 'Cosmetic, speculative, and adaptive organizational change in the wine industry', *Administrative Science Quarterly*, **26**, 631–61.

Delacroix, J., A. Swaminathan and M. Solt (1989), 'Density dependence versus population dynamics: An ecological study of failures in the California wine industry', *American Sociological Review*, **54**, 245–62.

Delacroix, J. and M. Solt (1988), 'Niche formation and foundings in the California wine industry, 1941–1984', in G. Carroll (ed.), *Ecological Models of Organization*, Oxford: Oxford University Press, pp. 53–68.

Delmar, F. and P. Davidsson (2000), 'Where do they come from? Prevalence and characteristics of nascent entrepreneurs', *Entrepreneurship and Regional Development*, **12**, 1–23.

Delmar, F. and S. Shane (2001), 'Legitimating first: Organizing activities and the survival of new ventures', working paper, University of Maryland, US.

De Meza, D. and C. Southey (1996), 'The borrower's curse: Optimism, finance and entrepreneurship', *The Economic Journal*, **106**, 375–86.

Denison, D. and J. Alexander (1986), 'Patterns and profiles of entrepreneurs: Data from entrepreneurship forums', in R. Ronstadt, J. Hornaday, R. Peterson and K. Vesper (eds), *Frontiers of Entrepreneurship Research*, Babson Park, US: Babson College, pp. 578–93.

Denison, D., A. Swaminathan and N. Rothbard (1994), 'Networks, founding conditions, and imprinting processes: Examining the process of organizational creation', paper presented at the Academy of Management Meetings, Dallas, Texas, US.

Dennis, W. (1986), 'Explained and unexplained differences in comparative state business starts and start rates', in R. Ronstadt, J. Hornaday, R. Peterson and K. Vesper (eds), *Frontiers of Entrepreneurship Research*, Babson Park, US: Babson College, pp. 313–27.

De Noble, A., D. Jung and S. Ehrlich (1999), 'Entrepreneurial self-efficacy: The development of a measure and its relationship to entrepreneurial action', in P. Reynolds, W. Bygrave, S. Manigart, C. Mason, C. Mason, G. Meyer, Sapienza, H. and K. Shaver (eds), *Frontiers of Entrepreneurship Research*, Babson Park, US: Babson College, pp. 73–87.

De Wit, G. (1993), 'Models of self-employment in a competitive market', *Journal of Economic Surveys*, **7**, 367–97.

De Wit, G. and F. Van Winden (1989), 'An empirical analysis of self-employment in the Netherlands', *Small Business Economics*, **1**, 263–72.

DiGregorio, D. and S. Shane (forthcoming), 'Why do some universities generate more start-ups than others?', *Research Policy*.

Dobbin, F. and T. Dowd (1997), 'How policy shapes competition: Early railroad foundings in Massachusetts', *Administrative Science Quarterly*, **42**, 501–29.

Dolton, P. and G. Makepeace (1990), 'Self employment among graduates', *Bulletin of Economic Research*, **42**(1), 35–53.

Dorfman, N. (1987), *Innovation and Market Structure: Lessons from the Computer and Semiconductor Industries*, Cambridge, MA, US: Ballinger Publishing Company.

Dosi, G. (1988), 'Sources, procedures and microeconomic effects of innovation', *Journal of Economic Literature*, **26**, 1120–71.

Douglas, E. (1999), 'Entrepreneurship as a career choice: Attitudes, entrepreneurial intentions, and utility maximization', in P. Reynolds, W. Bygrave, S. Manigart, C. Mason, C. Mason, G. Meyer, H. Sapienza and K. Shaver (eds), *Frontiers of Entrepreneurship Research*, Babson Park, US: Babson College, pp. 152–66.

Drucker, P. (1985), *Innovation and Entrepreneurship*, New York, US: Harper and Row.

Duchesneau, D. and W. Gartner (1990), 'A profile of new venture success and failure in an emerging industry', *Journal of Business Venturing*, **5**(5), 297–312.

Duncan, J. and D. Handler (1994), 'The misunderstood role of small business', *Business Economics*, **29**(3), 1–6.

Dunkelberg, W., A. Cooper, C. Woo and W. Denis (1987), 'New firm growth and performance', in N. Churchill, J. Hornaday, B. Kirchhoff, O. Krasner and K. Vesper, *Frontiers of Entrepreneurship Research*, Babson Park, US: Babson College, pp. 307–21.

Dunn, T. and D. Holtz-Eakin (1996), 'Financial capital, human capital, and the transition to self-employment: Evidence from intergenerational links', working paper, Syracuse University, US.

Dunne, T., E. Roberts and J. Samuelson (1988), 'Patterns of firm entry and exit in US manufacturing industries', *Rand Journal of Economics*, **19**(4), 495–515.

Durand, D. E. (1975), 'Effects of achievement motivation and skill training on the entrepreneurial behavior of black businessmen', *Organizational Behavior and Human Performance*, **14**, 76–90.

Durand, D. E. and D. Shea (1974), 'Entrepreneurial activity as a function of achievement motivation and reinforcement control', *The Journal of Psychology*, **88**, 57–63.

Earl, P. (1990), 'Economics and psychology: A survey', *The Economic Journal*, **100**, 718–55.

Eckhardt, J. (2003), 'Industry differences in entrepreneurial opportunities', Ph.D. Dissertation, University of Maryland, US.

Eckhardt, J. and S. Shane (2003), 'The importance of opportunities to entrepreneurship', *Journal of Management*.

Eckhardt, J., S. Shane and F. Delmar (2002), 'Multi-stage selection and the financing of new ventures', working paper, University of Maryland, US.

Eisenhardt, K. and K. Schoonhoven (1990), 'Organizational growth: Linking founding team, strategy, environment, and growth among US semiconductor ventures, 1978–1988', *Administrative Science Quarterly*, **35**, 504–29.

Eisenhardt, K. and K. Schoonhoven (1995), 'Failure of entrepreneurial firms: Ecological, upper echelons and strategic explanations in the US semiconductor industry', working paper, Stanford University, US.

Eisenhardt, K. and K. Schoonhoven (1996), 'Resource-based view of strategic alliance formation: Strategic and social effects in entrepreneurial firms', *Organization Science*, **7**(2), 136–51.

Eisenhauer, J. (1995), 'The entrepreneurial decision: Economic theory and empirical evidence', *Entrepreneurship Theory and Practice*, **19**(4), 67–79.

Ensley, M., J. Carland and J. Carland (2000), 'Investigating the existence of the lead entrepreneur', *Journal of Small Business Management*, **38**(4), 59–77.

Ensley, M., A. Pearson and A. Amason (2002), 'Understanding the dynamics of new venture top management teams: Cohesion, conflict and new venture performance', *Journal of Business Venturing*, **17**, 365–86.

Evans, D. (1987), 'The relationship between firm growth, size, and age: Estimates for 100 manufacturing industries', *Journal of Industrial Economics*, **35**(4), 567–81.

Evans, D. and L. Leighton (1989), 'Some empirical aspects of entrepreneurship', *American Economic Review*, **79**, 519–35.

Evans, M. (1984), 'Immigrant women in Australia: Resources, family and work', *International Migration Review*, **18**, 1063–90.

Evans, M. (1989), 'Immigrant entrepreneurship: Effects of ethnic market size and isolated labor pool', *American Sociological Review*, **54**, 950–62.

Fadahunsi, A. and P. Rosa (2002), 'Entrepreneurship and illegality: Insights from the Nigerian cross-border trade', *Journal of Business Venturing*, **17**(5), 397–430.

Fairlie, R. (1999), 'The absence of the African–American owned business: An analysis of the dynamics of self-employment', *Journal of Labor Economics*, **17**(1), 80–108.

Feeney, L., G. Haines and A. Riding (1999), 'Private investors' investment criteria: Insights from qualitative data', *Venture Capital*, **1**(2), 121–45.

Feeser, H. and K. Dugan (1989), 'Entrepreneurial motivation: A comparison of high and low growth high tech founders', in R. Brockhaus, N. Churchill, J. Katz, B. Kirchhoff, K. Vesper and W. Wetzel (eds), *Frontiers of Entrepreneurship Research*, Babson Park, US: Babson College, pp. 13–27.

Feldman, M. (2001), 'The entrepreneurial event revisited: Firm formation in a regional context', *Industrial and Corporate Change*, **10**(4), 861–91.

Fernandez, M. and K. Kim (1998), 'Self-employment rates of Asian immigrant groups: An analysis of intragroup and intergroup differences', *International Migration Review*, **32**(3), 654–81.

Fernandez, M. and N. Weinberg (1997), 'Sifting and sorting: Personal contacts and hiring in a retail bank', *American Sociological Review*, **62**, 883–902.

Fichman, M. and D. Levinthal (1991), 'Honeymoons and the liability of adolescence: A new perspective on duration dependence in social and organizational relationships', *Academy of Management Review*, **16**(2), 442–68.

Fisher, W. (1985), 'The narrative paradigm: An elaboration', *Communication Monographs*, **52**, 347–67.

Florida, R. and M. Kenney (1988), 'Venture capital financed innovation and technological change in the United States', *Research Policy*, **17**, 119–37.

Fonseca, R., P. Lopez-Garcia and C. Pissarides (2001), 'Entrepreneurship, start-up costs and employment', *European Economic Review*, **45**, 692–705.

Forlani, D. and J. Mullins (2000), 'Perceived risks and choices in entrepreneurs' new venture decisions', *Journal of Business Venturing*, **15**(4), 305–22.

Foster, R. (1986), *Innovation: The Attacker's Advantage*, New York, US: Summit Books.

Fotopoulos, G. and H. Louri (2000), 'Location and survival of new entry', *Small Business Economics*, **14**, 311–21.

Fraboni, M. and R. Saltstone (1990), 'First and second generation entrepreneur typologies: Dimensions of personality', *Journal of Social Behavior and Personality*, **5**(3), 105–13.

Francis, D. and W. Sandberg (2000), 'Friendship within entrepreneurial teams and its association with venture performance', *Entrepreneurship Theory and Practice*, **25**(2), 5–25.

Freeman, J. (1982), 'Organizational life cycles and natural selection processes', *Research in Organizational Behavior*, **4**, 1–32.

Freeman, J. (2000), 'Venture capital as an economy of time', working paper, University of California at Berkeley, US.

Freeman, J., G. Carroll and N. Hannan (1983), 'The liabilities of newness: Age dependence in organizational death rates', *American Sociological Review*, **48**, 692–710.

Fried, V. and R. Hisrich (1995), 'The venture capitalist: A relationship investor', *California Management Review*, **37**(2), 101–13.

Fry, F.L. (1993), *Entrepreneurship: A Planning Approach*, Minneapolis-St. Paul, MN, US: West Publishing.

Frye, T. and A. Schleifer (1997), 'The invisible hand and the grabbing hand', *American Economic Review Papers and Proceedings*, **87**(2), 354–58.

Gaglio, C. and J. Katz (2001), 'The psychological basis of opportunity identi-fication: Entrepreneurial alertness', *Small Business Economics*, **16**, 95–111.

Gans, J., D. Hsu and S. Stern (2000), 'When does start-up innovation spur the gale of creative destruction?', working paper, Massachusetts Institute of Technology, US.

Garofoli, G. (1994), 'New firm formation and regional development: The Italian case', *Regional Studies*, **28**(4), 381–93.

Gartner, W. (1985), 'A conceptual framework for describing the phenomenon of new venture creation', *Academy of Management Review*, **10**(4), 696–706.

Gartner, W. (1990), 'What are we talking about when we talk about entrepre-neurship?', *Journal of Business Venturing*, **5**(1), 15–29.

Gartner, W., B. Bird and J. Starr (1992), 'Acting as if: Differentiating entre-preneurial from organizational behavior', *Entrepreneurship Theory and Practice*, **16**(3), 13–32.

Gartner, W. and R. Thomas (1989), 'Factors which influence a new firm's ability to accurately forecast new product sales', in R. Brockhaus, N. Churchill, J. Katz, B. Kirchhoff, K. Vesper and W. Wetzel (eds), *Frontiers of Entrepreneurship Research*, Babson Park, US: Babson College, pp. 408–21.

Garvin, D. (1983), 'Spinoffs and the new firm formation process', *California Management Review*, **13**, 421–40.

Gentry, W. and R. Hubbard (2000), 'Tax policy and entrepreneurial entry', *American Economic Review Papers and Proceedings*, **90**(2), 283–92.

Georgellis, Y. and H. Wall (1999), 'What makes a region entrepreneurial? Evidence from Britain', *Annals of Regional Science*, **34**, 385–403.

Geroski, P. (1995), 'What do we know about entry?', *International Journal of Industrial Organization*, **13**, 421–40.

Geroski, P. (2001), 'Exploring the niche overlaps between organizational ecology and industrial economics', *Industrial and Corporate Change*, **10**(2), 507–40.

Gifford, S. (1992), 'Allocation of entrepreneurial attention', *Journal of Economic Behavior and Organization*, **19**, 265–84.

Gilad, B. (1982), 'On encouraging entrepreneurship: An interdisciplinary approach', *Journal of Behavioral Economics*, **11**(1), 132–63.

Gilad, B., S. Kaish and J. Ronen (1989), 'Information, search, and entrepreneurship: A pilot study', *The Journal of Behavioral Economics*, **18**(3), 217–35.

Gimeno, J., T. Folta, A. Cooper and C. Woo (1997), 'Survival of the fittest? Entrepreneurial human capital and the persistence of underperforming firms', *Administrative Science Quarterly*, **42**, 750–83.

Ginn, C. and D. Sexton (1990), 'A comparison of the personality type dimensions of the 1987 Inc. 500 Company Founders/CEOs with those of slower-growth firms', *Journal of Business Venturing*, **5**(5), 313–26.

Gioia, P. (1989), 'The prudence standard: Recent experience and future relevance', *Public Utilities Fortnightly*, **9**,11–17.

Girfalco, L. (1991), *Dynamics of Technological Change*, New York, US: Van Nostrand Reinhold.

Giudici, G. and S. Paleari (2000), 'The optimal staging of venture capital financing when entrepreneurs extract private benefits from their firms', *Enterprise and Innovation Management Studies*, **1**(2), 153–74.

Gnyawali, D. and D. Fogel (1994), 'Environments for entrepreneurship development: Key dimensions and research implications', *Entrepreneurship Theory and Practice*, **18**(4), 43–62.

Goldfarb, B. and M. Henrekson (forthcoming), 'Demand vs. supply-driven innovations: US and Swedish experiences in academic entrepreneurship', *Research Policy*.

Goldsmith, R. and J. Kerr (1991), 'Entrepreneurship and adaptation–innovation theory', *Technovation*, **11**(6), 373–82.

Gompers, P. (1995), 'Optimal investment, monitoring and the staging of venture capital', *The Journal of Finance*, **50**(5), 1461–89.

Gompers, P. (1997), 'An examination of convertible securities in venture capital investments', working paper, Harvard University, US.

Gompers, P. and J. Lerner (1999), *The Venture Capital Cycle*, Cambridge, MA, US: MIT Press.

Gorman, M. and W. Sahlman (1989), 'What do venture capitalists do?', *Journal of Business Venturing*, **4**(4), 231–48.

Granovetter, M. (1985), 'Economic action and social structure: The problem of embeddedness', *American Journal of Sociology*, **91**, 481–510.

Grant, D. (1996), 'The political economy of new business formation across the American States, 1970–1985', *Social Science Quarterly*, **77**(1), 28–42.

Greenberger, D. and D. Sexton (1987), 'A comparative analysis of the effects of the desire for personal control on new venture initiations', in N. Churchill, J. Hornaday, B. Kirchhoff, O. Krasner and K. Vesper (eds), *Frontiers of Entrepreneurship Research*, Babson Park, US: Babson College, pp. 239–53.

Guesnier, B. (1994), 'Regional variations in new firm formation in France', *Regional Studies*, **28**(4), 347–58.

Gulati, R. (1995), 'Does familiarity breed trust? The implications of repeated ties for contractual choice in alliances', *Academy of Management Journal*, **38**(1), 85–112.

Gulati, R. and M. Gargiulo (1999), 'Where do interorganizational networks come from?', *American Journal of Sociology*, **105**(5), 1439–94.

Gupta, A. and H. Sapienza (1988), 'The pursuit of diversity by venture capital firms: Antecedents and implications', in B. Kirchhoff, W. Long, W. McMullan, K. Vesper and W. Wetzel (eds), *Frontiers of Entrepreneurship Research*, Babson Park, US: Babson College, pp. 290–302.

Gupta, A. and H. Sapienza (1992), 'Determinants of venture capital firms' preferences regarding the industry diversity and geographic scope of their investments', *Journal of Business Venturing*, **7**(5), 347–62.

Haar, N., J. Starr and I. MacMillan (1988), 'Informal risk capital investors: Investment patterns on the east coast of the USA', *Journal of Business Venturing*, **3**(1), 11–29.

Hall, J. and C. Hofer (1993), 'Venture capitalists' decision criteria in new venture evaluation', *Journal of Business Venturing*, **8**(1), 25–42.

Halliday, T., M. Powell and M. Granfors (1987), 'Minimalist organizations: Vital events in state bar associations, 1870–1930', *American Sociological Review*, **52**(4), 456–71.

Hamilton, B. (2000), 'Does entrepreneurship pay? An empirical analysis of the returns to self-employment', *Journal of Political Economy*, **108**(3), 604–31.

Hamilton, R. and D. Harper (1994), 'The entrepreneur in theory and practice', *Journal of Economic Studies*, **21**(6), 3–18.

Hanks, S. and G. Chandler (1995), 'Patterns of formalization in emerging business ventures', in W. Bygrave, B. Bird, S. Birley, N. Churchill, M. Hay,

R. Keeley and W. Wetzel (eds), *Frontiers of Entrepreneurship Research*, Babson Park, US: Babson College, pp. 520–32.

Hannan, M. (1986), 'Competitive and institutional processes in organizational ecology', technical report 86–13, Department of Sociology, Cornell University, US.

Hannan, M.T. (1988), 'Social change, organizational diversity and individual careers', in M. Riley (ed.), *Social Change and the Life Course*, Newbury Park: Sage.

Hannan, M., J. Baron, G. Hsu and O. Kocak (2002), 'Staying the course: Early organization building and the success of high technology firms', working paper, Stanford University, US.

Hannan, M., D. Burton and D. Baron (1996), 'Inertia and change in the early years: Employment relations in young, high technology firms', *Industrial and Corporate Change*, **5**(2), 503–36.

Hannan, M. and G. Carroll (1992), *Dynamics of Organizational Populations: Density, Legitimation, and Competition*, New York, US: Oxford University Press.

Hannan, M., G. Carroll, E. Dundon and J. Torres (1995), 'Organizational evolution in a multinational context: Entries of automobile manufacturers in Belgium, Britain, France, Germany, and Italy', *American Sociological Review*, **60**, 509–28.

Hannan, M. and J. Freeman (1977), 'The population ecology of organizations', *American Journal of Sociology*, **82**, 929–64.

Hannan, M. and J. Freeman (1984), 'Structural inertia and organizational change', *American Sociological Review*, **49**, 149–64.

Hannan, M. and J. Freeman (1987), 'The ecology of organizational founding: American labor unions, 1836–1975', *American Journal of Sociology*, **92**(4), 910–43.

Hannan, M. and J. Freeman (1989), *Organizational Ecology*, Cambridge, MA, US: Harvard University Press.

Hansen, E. (1991), 'Structure and process in entrepreneurial networks as partial determinants of initial venture growth', in N. Churchill, W. Bygrave, J. Covin, D. Sexton, D. Slevin, K. Vesper and W. Wetzel (eds), *Frontiers of Entrepreneurship Research*, Babson Park, US: Babson College, pp. 320–34.

Hansen, E. (1995), 'Entrepreneurial networks and new organization growth', *Entrepreneurship Theory and Practice*, **19**(4), 7–19.

Hansen, E. and K. Allen (1992), 'The creation corridor: Environmental load and pre-organization information-processing ability', *Entrepreneurship Theory and Practice*, **17**(1), 57–65.

Harper, D. (1996), *Entrepreneurship and the Market Process*, London: Routledge.

Harper, D. (1997), 'Institutional conditions for entrepreneurship', working paper, New York University, US.

Harper, D. (1998), 'How entrepreneurs learn: A Popperian approach and its limitations', working paper, New York University, US.

Hart, M. and G. Gudgin (1994), 'Spatial variations in new firm formation in the Republic of Ireland, 1980–1990', *Regional Studies*, **38**(4), 367–80.

Haveman, H. (1992), 'Between a rock and a hard place: Organizational change and performance under conditions of fundamental environmental transformation', *Administrative Science Quarterly*, **37**, 48–75.

Hayek, F. (1945), 'The use of knowledge in society', *The American Economic Review*, **35**(4), 519–30.

Hebert, R. and A. Link (1988), *The Entrepreneur: Mainstream Views and Radical Critiques*, New York, US: Praeger.

Henderson, R. (1993), 'Underinvestment and incompetence as responses to radical innovation: Evidence from the photolithographic alignment equipment industry', *Rand Journal of Economics*, **24**(2), 243–66.

Henderson, R. and K. Clark (1990), 'Architectural innovation: the reconfiguration of existing product technologies and the failure of established firms', *Administrative Science Quarterly*, **35**(1), 9–30.

Highfield, R. and R. Smiley (1987), 'New business starts and economic activity', *International Journal of Industrial Organization*, **5**, 51–66.

Hills, G. and R. Shrader (1998), 'Successful entrepreneurs' insights into opportunity recognition', in P. Reynolds, W. Bygrave, N. Carter, S. Manigart, C. Mason, C. Mason, G. Meyer and K. Shaver (eds), *Frontiers of Entrepreneurship Research*, Babson Park, US: Babson College, pp. 30–43.

Hills, G., R. Shrader and T. Lumpkin (1999), 'Opportunity recognition as a creative process', in P. Reynolds, W. Bygrave, S. Manigart, C. Mason, C. Mason, G. Meyer, H. Sapienza and K. Shaver (eds), *Frontiers of Entrepreneurship Research*, Babson Park, US: Babson College, pp. 216–27.

Hills, G. and H. Welsch (1986), 'Entrepreneurship behavioral intentions and student independence, characteristics and experience', in R. Ronstadt, J. Hornaday, R. Peterson and K. Vesper (eds), *Frontiers of Entrepreneurship Research*, Babson Park, US: Babson College, pp. 173–86.

Hines, G. (1973), 'Achievement motivation, occupations and labor turnover in New Zealand', *Journal of Applied Psychology*, **58**(3), 313–17.

Hoffman, H. and J. Blakely (1987), 'You can negotiate with venture capitalists', *Harvard Business Review,* March–April, pp. 6–24.

Holmes, T. and J. Schmitz (1990), 'A theory of entrepreneurship and its application to the study of business transfers', *Journal of Political Economy*, **98**(2), 265–94.

Holmes, T. and J. Schmitz (1993), 'Specialization in entrepreneurship', *Advances in the Study of Entrepreneurship, Innovation and Economic Growth*, **6**, 85–108.

Holmes, T. and J. Schmitz (2001), 'A gain from trade: From unproductive to productive entrepreneurship', *Journal of Monetary Economics*, **47**, 417–46.

Holmstrom, B. (1989), 'Agency costs and innovation', *Journal of Economic Behavior and Organization*, **12**(3), 305–27.

Holtz-Eakin, D., D. Joulfaian and H. Rosen (1994a), 'Entrepreneurial decisions and liquidity constraints', *Rand Journal of Economics*, **25**(2), 334–47.

Holtz-Eakin, D., D. Joulfaian and H. Rosen (1994b), 'Sticking it out: Entrepreneurial survival and liquidity constraints', *Journal of Political Economy*, **102**(1), 53–75.

Honig, B. and P. Davidsson (2000), 'The role of social and human capital among nascent entrepreneurs', Academy of Management Proceedings, Washington, DC, US, B1–6.

Hornaday, J. and J. Aboud (1973), 'Characteristics of successful entrepreneurs', *Personnel Psychology*, **24**, 141–53.

Hornaday, J. and C. Bunker (1970), 'The nature of the entrepreneur', *Personnel Psychology*, **23**, 47–54.

Horvath, M., F. Schivardi and M. Woywode (2001), 'On industry life-cycles: Delay, entry, and shakeout in beer brewing', *International Journal of Industrial Organization*, **19**, 1023–52.

Hsu, D. and D. Bernstein (1997), 'Managing the university technology licensing process: Findings from case studies', *Journal of Association of University Technology Managers*, **9**, 1–33.

Hubbard, R. (1998), 'The golden goose? Understanding (and taxing) the saving of entrepreneurs', *Advances in Entrepreneurship, Innovation, and Economic Growth*, **10**, 43–69.

Hull, D., J. Bosley and G. Udell (1980), 'Renewing the hunt for heffalump: Identifying potential entrepreneurs by personality characteristics', *Journal of Small Business*, **18**, 11–18.

Hustedde, R. and G. Pulver (1992), 'Factors affecting equity capital acquisition: The demand side', *Journal of Business Venturing*, **7**(5), 363–74.

Hyrsky, K. and A. Kangasharju (1998), 'Adapters and innovators in non-urban environment', in P. Reynolds, W. Bygrave, N. Carter, S. Manigart, C. Mason, G. Meyer and K. Shaver (eds), *Frontiers of Entrepreneurship Research*, Babson Park, US: Babson College, pp. 216–27.

Ingram, P. (1993), 'Old, tired and ready to die: The age dependence of organizational mortality reconsidered', paper presented at the Academy of Management Meetings, Atlanta, GA, US.

Ingram, P. (1994), 'Endogenizing environmental change: The evolution of hotel chains, 1896–1980', working paper, Cornell University, US.

Ingram, P. (1998), 'Entrepreneurial capacity and the growth of chain organizations', *Advances in Strategic Management*, **15**, 19–35.

Jack, S. and A. Anderson (2002), 'The effects of embeddedness on the entrepreneurial process', *Journal of Business Venturing*, **17**(5), 467–88.

Jackson, J. and G. Rodney (1994), 'The attitudinal climate for entrepreneurial activity', *Public Opinion Quarterly*, **58**, 358–80.

Johannisson, B. (1988), 'Emerging female entrepreneurship: Network building characteristics', paper presented at the 18th European Small Business Seminar, Ghent.

Johansson, E. (2000), 'Self-employment and liquidity constraints: Evidence from Finland', *Scandinavian Journal of Economics*, **102**(1), 123–34.

Johnson, B. (1989), 'New and small venture performance: The interactive effects of entrepreneurial growth propensity, strategic management practices and industry growth', Ph.D. Dissertation, St. Louis University, US.

Johnson, B. (1990), 'Toward a multidimensional model of entrepreneurship: The case of achievement motivation and the entrepreneur', *Entrepreneurship Theory and Practice*, **14**(3), 39–54.

Johnson, P. (1986), *New Firms: An Economic Perspective*, London: Allen and Unwin.

Johnson, P. and D. Cathcart (1979), 'New manufacturing firms and regional development: Some evidence from the Northern region', *Regional Studies*, **13**, 269–80.

Johnson, S., J. McMillan and C. Woodruff (2002a), 'Courts and relational contracts', *Journal of Law, Economics and Organization*, **18**(1), 221–77.

Johnson, S., J. McMillan and C. Woodruff (forthcoming), 'Property rights and finance', *American Economic Review*.

Jones, G. and J. Butler (1992), 'Managing internal corporate entrepreneurship: An agency theory perspective', *Journal of Management*, **18**(4), 733–49.

Jovanovic, B. (1982), 'Selection and the evolution of industry', *Econometrica*, **50**(3), 649–70.

Jovanovic, B. (1984), 'Matching, turnover, and unemployment', *Journal of Political Economy*, **87**, 1246–60.

Judge, T., A. Erez, J. Bono and C. Thoreson (2002), 'Discriminant and incremental validity of personality measures', working paper, University of Florida, US.

Kahneman, D., P. Slovic and A. Tversky (1982), *Judgment under Uncertainty: Heuristics and Biases*, New York, US: Cambridge University Press.

Kaish, S. and B. Gilad (1991), 'Characteristics of opportunities search of entrepreneurs versus executives: Sources, interests, general alertness', *Journal of Business Venturing*, **6**(1), 45–61.

Kalleberg, A. (1986), 'Entrepreneurship in the 1980s: A study of small business in Indiana', *Advances in the Study of Entrepreneurship, Innovation and Growth*, **1**, 157–89.

Kalleberg, A. and K. Leight (1991), 'Gender and organizational performance: Determinants of small business survival and success', *Academy of Management Journal*, **34**(1), 136–61.

Kanbur, R. (1980), 'A note on risk taking, entrepreneurship, and Schumpeter', *History of Political Economy*, **12**, 489–98.

Kangasharju, A. (2000), 'Regional variations in firm formation: Panel and cross-section data evidence from Finland', *Papers in Regional Science*, **79**, 355–73.

Kaplan, J. (1994), *Startup: A Silicon Valley Adventure*, Boston, US: Houghton Mifflin.

Kaplan, S. and P. Stromberg (1999), 'Financial contracting meets the real world: An empirical analysis of venture capital contracts', working paper, University of Chicago, US.

Kaplan, S. and P. Stromberg (2001), 'Venture capitalists as principals: Contracting, screening, and monitoring', *American Economic Review Papers and Proceedings*, **91**(2), 426–30.

Katilla, R. and P. Mang (forthcoming), 'Exploiting technological opportunities: The timing of collaborations', *Research Policy*.

Katz, J. (1992), 'A psychosocial cognitive model of employment status choice', *Entrepreneurship Theory and Practice*, **17**(1), 29–37.

Katz, J. (1993), 'The dynamics of organizational emergence: A contemporary group formation perspective', *Entrepreneurship Theory and Practice*, **17**(2), 97–101.

Katz, J., H. Aldrich and T. Welbourne (2000), 'Special issue on human resource management and the SME: Toward a new synthesis', *Entrepreneurship Theory and Practice*, **25**(1), 7–10.

Katz, J. and W. Gartner (1988), 'Properties of emerging organizations', *Academy of Management Review*, **13**(3), 429–41.

Kaufmann, P. (1999), 'Franchising and the choice of self-employment', *Journal of Business Venturing*, **14**(4), 345–62.

Keeble, D. and S. Walker (1994), 'New firms, small firms, and dead firms: Spatial patterns and determinants in the United Kingdom', *Regional Studies*, **28**(4), 411–27.

Kelly, D. (1988), 'Organizational transformation and failure in the US airline industry, 1962–1985', Ph.D. Dissertation, Northwestern University, US.

Kelly, D. and T. Amburgey (1991), 'Organizational inertia and momentum: A dynamic model of strategic change', *Academy of Management Journal*, **34**(3), 591–612.

Kelly, P. (2000), 'Private investors and entrepreneurs: How context shapes their relationship', Ph.D. Dissertation, London Business School.

Kent, C., D. Sexton, P. Van Auken and D. Young (1982), 'Managers and entrepreneurs: Do lifetime experiences matter?', in K. Vesper (ed.), *Frontiers of Entrepreneurship Research*, Babson Park, US: Babson College, pp. 516–25.

Khilstrom, R. and J. Laffont (1979), 'A general equilibrium entrepreneurial theory of firm formation abased on risk aversion', *Journal of Political Economy*, **87**(4), 719–48.

Kirchhoff, B. (1994), *Entrepreneurship and Dynamic Capitalism*, Westport, CT, US: Praeger.

Kirchhoff, B. and B. Phillips (1989), 'Innovation and growth among new firms in the US economy', in R. Brockhaus, C. Churchill, J. Katz, B. Kirchhoff, K. Vesper and W. Wetzel (eds), *Frontiers of Entrepreneurship Research*, Babson Park, US: Babson College, pp. 173–88.

Kirilenko, A. (2001), 'Valuation and control in venture finance', *Journal of Finance*, **56**(2), 565–87.

Kirzner, I. (1973), *Competition and Entrepreneurship*, Chicago, IL, US: University of Chicago Press.

Kirzner, I. (1985), *Discovery and the Capitalist Process*, Chicago, IL, US: University of Chicago Press.

Kirzner, I. (1997), 'Entrepreneurial discovery and the competitive market process: An Austrian approach', *The Journal of Economic Literature*, **35**, 60–85.

Klepper, S. (2001), 'Employee start-ups in high industries', *Industrial and Corporate Change*, **10**(3), 639–74.

Klepper. S. (2002), 'The capabilities of new firms and the evolution of the US automobile industry', *Industrial and Corporate Change*, **11**(4), 645–65.

Klepper, S. and E. Graddy (1990), 'The evolution of new industries and the determinants of market structure', *Rand Journal of Economics*, **21**(1), 27–44.

Klepper, S. and S. Sleeper (2001), 'Entry by spinoffs', working paper, Carnegie Mellon University, US.

Klevorick, A., R. Levin, R. Nelson and S. Winter (1995), 'On the sources of significance of inter-industry differences in technological opportunities', *Research Policy*, **24**, 185–205.

Knight, F. (1921), *Risk, Uncertainty, and Profit*, New York, US: Augustus Kelly.

Koh, H. (1996), 'Testing hypotheses of entrepreneurial characteristics', *Journal of Managerial Psychology*, **11**, 12–25.

Koller, R. (1988), 'On the source of entrepreneurial ideas', in B. Kirchhoff, W. Long, W. McMullan, K. Vesper and W. Wetzel (eds), *Frontiers of Entrepreneurship Research*, Babson Park, US: Babson College, pp. 194–207.

Kourilsky, M. (1994), 'Predictors of entrepreneurship in a simulated economy', *Journal of Creative Behavior*, **14**(3), 175–98.

Krueger, N. and D. Brazeal (1994), 'Entrepreneurial potential and potential entrepreneurs', *Entrepreneurship Theory and Practice*, **18**(3), 91–104.

Krueger, N. and P. Dickson (1993a), 'How believing in ourselves increases risk taking: Perceived self-efficacy and opportunity recognition', *Decision Sciences*, **25**(3), 385–400.

Krueger, N. and P. Dickson (1993b), 'Perceived self efficacy and perceptions of opportunity and threat', *Psychological Reports*, **72**, 1235–40.

Kuratko, D., J. Hornsby and D. Naffziger (1997), 'An examination of owners' goals in sustaining entrepreneurship', *Journal of Small Business Management*, **35**(1), 24–33.

Lachman, R. (1980), 'Toward a measurement of entrepreneurial tendencies', *Management International Review*, **20**, 108–16.

Landry, R., R. Allard, B. McMillan and C. Essiembre (1992), 'A macroscopic model of the social and psychological determinants of entrepreneurial intent', in N. Churchill, S. Birley, W. Bygrave, D. Muzyka, C. Wahlbin and W. Wetzel (eds), *Frontiers of Entrepreneurship Research*, Babson Park, US: Babson College, pp. 591–605.

Landstrom, H., S. Manigart, C. Mason and H. Sapienza (1998), 'Contracts between entrepreneurs and investors: Terms and negotiation processes', in P. Reynolds, W. Bygrave, N. Carter, S. Manigart, C. Mason, C. Mason, G. Meyer and K. Shaver (eds), *Frontiers of Entrepreneurship Research*, Babson Park, US: Babson College, pp. 571–85.

Langer, A. and A. Applebee (1987), *How Writing Shapes Thinking*, Urbana, Il, US: National Council of Teachers of English.

Larson, A. (1991), '"Partner networks" Leveraging external ties to improve entrepreneurial performance', *Journal of Business Venturing*, **6**(3), 173–88.

Larson, A. (1992), 'Network dyads in entrepreneurial settings: A study of the governance exchange processes', *Administrative Science Quarterly*, **37**, 76–104.

Le, A. (1999), 'Empirical studies of self-employment', *Journal of Economic Surveys*, **13**(4), 381–416.

Lee, C., K. Lee and J. Pennings (2001), 'Internal capabilities, external networks, and performance: A study on technology-based ventures', *Strategic Management Journal*, **22**, 615–40.

Lee, D. and E. Tsang (2001), 'The effects of entrepreneurial personality, background and network activities on venture growth', *Journal of Management Studies*, **38**(4), 583–602.

Lehrman, W. (1994), 'Diversity in decline: Institutional and organizational failure in the American life insurance industry', *Social Forces*, **73**, 605–36.

Lentz, B. and D. Laband (1990), 'Entrepreneurial success and occupational inheritance among proprietors', *Canadian Journal of Economics*, **23**(3), 563–79.

Lerner, J. (1994), 'The syndication of venture capital investments', *Financial Management*, **23**(3), 16–27.

Lerner, J. (1995), 'Venture capitalists and the oversight of private firms', *Journal of Finance*, **50**(1), 301–18.

Lerner, J. (1999), 'The government as venture capitalist: The long run impact of the SBIR program', *Journal of Business*, **72**(3), 285–318.

Lerner, M., C. Brush and R. Hisrich (1995), 'Factors affecting performance of Israeli women entrepreneurs: An examination of alternative perspectives', in W. Bygrave, B. Bird, S. Birley, N. Churchill, M. Hay, R. Keeley and W. Wetzel (eds), *Frontiers of Entrepreneurship Research*, Babson Park, US: Babson College, pp. 308–22.

Lerner, M. and Y. Hendeles (1993), 'New entrepreneurs and entrepreneurial aspirations among immigrants from the former USSR in Israel', in N. Churchill, S. Birley, W. Bygrave, J. Doutriaux, E. Gatewood, F. Hoy and W. Wetzel (eds), *Frontiers of Entrepreneurship Research*, Babson Park, US: Babson College, pp. 562–75.

Levie, J. and J. Warhuus (1998), 'A four nation study of entrepreneur/banker interaction in young growing firms', in P. Reynolds, W. Bygrave, N. Carter, S. Manigart, C. Mason, C. Mason, G. Meyer and K. Shaver (eds), *Frontiers of Entrepreneurship Research*, Babson Park, US: Babson College, pp. 489–503.

Levin, R., A. Klevorick, R. Nelson and S. Winter (1987), 'Appropriating the returns from industrial research and development', *Brookings Papers on Economic Activity*, **3**, 783–832.

Libecap, G. (1993), 'Entrepreneurship, property rights and economic development', *Advances in the Study of Entrepreneurship, Innovation and Economic Growth*, **6**, 67–83.

Light, I. and A. Sanchez (1987), 'Immigrant entrepreneurs in 272 SMSAs', *Sociological Perspectives*, **30**(4), 373–99.

Lindh, T. and H. Ohlsson (1996), 'Self-employment and windfall gains: Evidence from the Swedish lottery', *Economic Journal*, **106**, 1515–26.

Littunen, H. (2000), 'Networks and local environmental characteristics in the survival of new firms', *Small Business Economics*, **15**, 59–71.

Locke, E. and G. Latham (1990), *A Theory of Goal Setting and Task Performance*, Englewood Cliffs, NJ, US: Prentice-Hall.

Lomi, A. (1995), 'The population ecology of organizational founding: Location dependence and unobserved heterogeneity', *Administrative Science Quarterly*, **40**, 111–44.

Long, J. (1982), 'The income tax and self-employment', *National Tax Journal*, **35**, 31–42.

Loree, D. (1993), 'Organizational mortality: The price paid for institutional linkages in the semiconductor industry', paper presented at the Academy of Management Meetings, Atlanta, GA, US.

Lorrain, J. and L. Dussault (1988), 'Relation between psychological characteristics, administrative behaviors and success of founder entrepreneurs at the start-up stage', in B. Kirchhoff, W. Long, W. McMullan, K. Vesper and W. Wetzel (eds), *Frontiers of Entrepreneurship Research*, Babson Park, US: Babson College, pp. 150–64.

Lounsbury, M. and M. Glynn (2001), 'Cultural entrepreneurship: Stories, legitimacy, and the acquisition of resources', *Strategic Management Journal*, **22**, 545–64.

Low, M. and E. Abrahamson (1997), 'Movements, bandwagons, and clones: Industry evolution and the entrepreneurial process', *Journal of Business Venturing*, **12**(6), 435–58.

Low, M. and V. Srivatsan (1994), 'What does it mean to trust an entrepreneur?', in S. Birley and I. MacMillan (eds), *International Entrepreneurship*, London: Routledge, pp. 59–78.

Lowe, R. (2001), 'Entrepreneurship and information asymmetry: Theory and evidence from the University of California', working paper, University of California at Berkeley, US.

Lu, D. (1994), 'The entrepreneurs who do both: Production and rent seeking', *Journal of Economic Behavior and Organization*, **23**, 93–8.

Macaulay, S. (1963), 'Noncontractual relations in business: A preliminary study', *American Sociological Review*, **28**, 55–67.

MacMillan, I. and P. Subba Narasimha (1987), 'Characteristics distinguishing funded from unfounded business plans evaluated by venture capitalists', *Strategic Management Journal*, **8**, 579–85.

Macpherson, D. (1988), 'Self-employment and married women', *Economic Letters*, **28**, 281–4.

Mahmood, T. (2000), 'Survival of newly founded businesses: A log-logistic model approach', *Small Business Economics*, **14**, 223–37.

Malerba, F. and L. Orsenigo (1996), 'The dynamics and evolution of industries', *Industrial and Corporate Change*, **5**(1), 51–87.

Malerba, F. and L. Orsenigo (2000), 'Knowledge, innovative activities and industrial evolution', *Industrial and Corporate Change*, **9**(2), 289–314.

Manigart, S. (1999), 'Post-investment evolution of Belgian venture capital backed companies: An empirical study', in P. Reynolds, W. Bygrave, S. Manigart, C. Mason, C. Mason, G. Meyer, H. Sapienza and K. Shaver (eds), *Frontiers of Entrepreneurship Research*, Babson Park, US: Babson College, pp. 419–32.

Marple, D. (1982), 'Technological innovation and organizational survival: A population ecology study of nineteenth century American railroads', *Sociological Quarterly*, **23**, 107–16.

Marsden, P. (1981), 'Introducing influence processes into a system of collective decisions', *American Journal of Sociology*, **86**, 1203–35.

Martin, J., S. Sitkin and M. Boehm (1985), 'Founders and the elusiveness of a cultural legacy', in P. Frost, L. Moore, M. Louis, C. Lundberg and J. Martin (eds), *Organizational Culture*, Newbury Park, CA, US: Sage, pp. 99–124.

Martin, R. (1988), 'Franchising and risk management', *American Economic Review*, **78**(5), 954–69.

Mason, C. and R. Harrison (1996), 'Informal venture capital: A study of the investment process, the post-investment experience and investment performance', *Entrepreneurship and Regional Development*, **8**(2), 105–25.

Mata, J. (1994), 'Firm growth during infancy', *Small Business Economics*, **6**, 27–39.

Mata, J. (1996), 'Markets, entrepreneurs, and the size of new firms', *Economic Letters*, **52**(1), 89–94.

Mata, J. and P. Portugal (1994), 'Life duration of new firms', *The Journal of Industrial Economics*, **42**(3), 227–43.

Mata, J., P. Portugal and P. Guimaraes (1995), 'The survival of new plans: Start-up conditions and post-entry evolution', *International Journal of Industrial Organization*, **13**, 459–89.

Mathews, C. and S. Moser (1995), 'Family background and gender: Implications for interest in small firm ownership', *Entrepreneurship and Regional Development*, **7**, 365–77.

Matusik, S. (1997), 'Motives, use patterns and effects of contingent resource use in entrepreneurial firms', in P. Reynolds, W. Bygrave, N. Carter, P. Davidsson, W. Gartner, C. Mason and P. McDougall (eds), *Frontiers of Entrepreneurship Research*, Babson Park, US: Babson College, pp. 359–72.

McCarthy, A., D. Krueger and T. Shoenecker (1989), 'Entrepreneurial time allocation patterns across early stages of development', in R. Brockhaus, N. Churchill, J. Katz, B. Kirchhoff, K. Vesper and W. Wetzel (eds), *Frontiers of Entrepreneurship Research*, Babson Park, US: Babson College, pp. 81–92.

McClelland, D.C. (1961), *The Achieving Society*, Princeton, NJ, US: Van Nostrand.

McMillan, J. and C. Woodruff (2002), 'The central role of entrepreneurs in transition economies', *Journal of Economic Perspectives*, **16**(3), 153–70.

McQueen, D. and J. Wallmark (1984), 'Innovation output and academic performance', in J. Hornaday, F. Tarpley, J. Timmons and K. Vesper (eds), *Frontiers of Entrepreneurship Research*, Babson Park, US: Babson College, pp. 171–95.

Megginson, W. and K. Weiss (1991), 'Venture capitalist certification in initial public offerings', *Journal of Finance*, **46**(3), 879–903.

Mesch, G. and D. Czamanski (1997), 'Occupational closure and immigrant entrepreneurship: Russian Jews in Israel', *Journal of Socio-Economics*, **26**(6), 597–611.

Mezias, J. and S. Mezias (2000), 'Resource partitioning, the founding of specialist firms, and innovation: The American feature film industry, 1912–1929', *Organization Science*, **11**(3), 306–22.

Michael, S. (1996), 'To franchise or not to franchise: An analysis of decision rights and organizational form shares', *Journal of Business Venturing*, **11**(1), 59–71.

Miller, D. and C. Drodge (1986), 'Psychological and traditional determinants of structure', *Administrative Science Quarterly*, **31**, 539–60.

Miner, A., T. Amburgey and T. Stearns (1990), 'Interorganizational linkages and population dynamics: Buffering and transformational shields', *Administrative Science Quarterly*, **35**, 689–713.

Miner, J. (2000), 'Testing a psychological typology of entrepreneurship using business founders', *The Journal of Applied Behavioral Science*, **36**(1), 43–69.

Miner, J., N. Smith and J. Bracker (1989), 'Role of entrepreneurial task motivation in the growth of technologically innovative firms: Interpretations from follow-up data', *Journal of Applied Psychology*, **79**(4), 627–30.

Miner, J., N. Smith and J. Bracker (1994), 'Role of entrepreneurial task motivation in the growth of technologically innovative firms', *Journal of Applied Psychology*, **74**(4), 554–60.

Minniti, M. (1999), 'Social environment and alternative patterns of entrepreneurial activity', working paper, Babson College, MA, US.

Mitchell, R., B. Smith, K. Seawright and E. Morse (2000), 'Cross-cultural cognitions and the venture creation decision', *Academy of Management Journal*, **43**(5), 974–93.

Mitchell, W. (1994), 'The dynamics of evolving markets: The effects of business sales and age on dissolutions and divestitures', *Administrative Science Quarterly*, **39**, 575–602.

Murmann, P. and M. Tushman (2001), 'From the technology cycle to the entrepreneurship dynamic', in K. Schoonhoven and E. Romanelli (eds), *The Entrepreneurial Dynamic*, Stanford, US: Stanford University Press, pp. 178–203.

Nahapiet, J. and S. Ghoshal (1998), 'Social capital, intellectual capital, and the organizational advantage', *Academy of Management Review*, **23**(2), 242–66.

Neher, D. (2000), 'Staged financing: An agency perspective', *Review of Economic Studies*, **66**, 255–74.

Neiswander, C., B. Bird and P. Young (1987), 'Entrepreneurial hiring and the management of early stage employees', in N. Churchill, J. Hornaday, B.

Kirchhoff, O. Krasner and K. Vesper (eds), *Frontiers of Entrepreneurship Research*, Babson Park, US: Babson College, pp. 204–19.

Nelson, R. and S. Winter (1982), *An Evolutionary Theory of Economic Change*, Cambridge, MA, US: Belknap Press.

Nohria, N. (1992), 'Information and search in the creation of new business ventures: The case of the 128 venture group', in B. Eccles and N. Nohria (eds), *Networks and Organizations*, Cambridge: Harvard University Press, pp. 241–61.

Norton, E. and B. Tenenbaum (1993), 'Specialization versus diversification as a venture capital investment strategy', *Journal of Business Venturing*, **8**, 431–42.

Norton, S. (1988), 'Franchising, brand name capital, and the entrepreneurial capacity problem', *Strategic Management Journal*, **9**, 105–14.

Olzak, S. and E. West (1991), 'Ethnic conflict and the rise and fall of ethnic newspapers', *American Sociological Review*, **56**, 458–74.

O'Reilly, C. and J. Anderson (1982), 'Personnel/human resource management in the US: Some evidence of change', *Journal of Irish Business and Administrative Research*, **4**(2), 3–12.

Oxenfeldt, A. (1943), *New Firms and Free Enterprise*, Washington, DC, US: American Council on Public Affairs.

Pandry, J. and N. Tewary (1979), 'Locus of control and the achievement value of entrepreneurs', *Journal of Occupational Psychology*, **52**, 107–11.

Pearce, W. (1992), *The MIT Dictionary of Modern Economics*, Cambridge MA, US: MIT Press.

Pennings, J. (1982a), 'Organizational birth frequencies: An empirical investigation', *Administrative Science Quarterly*, **27**, 120–44.

Pennings, J. (1982b), 'The urban quality of life and entrepreneurship', *Academy of Management Journal*, **25**(1), 63–79.

Pennings, J., I. MacMillan and A. Meshulach (1982), 'The urban quality of life and entrepreneurship', in K. Vesper (ed.), *Frontiers of Entrepreneurship Research*, Babson Park, US: Babson College, pp. 142–52.

Pisano, G. (1989), 'Using equity participation to support exchange evidence from the biotechnology industry', *Journal of Law, Economics, and Organization*, **5**(1), 109–26.

Pisano, G. (1991), 'The governance of innovation: Vertical integration and collaborative arrangements in the biotechnology industry', *Research Policy*, **20**, 237–49.

Podolny, J. (1994), 'Market uncertainty and the social character of economic exchange', *Administrative Science Quarterly*, **39**, 458–83.

Praag, C. and H. Pohem (1995), 'Determinants of willingness and opportunity to start as an entrepreneur', *Kyklos*, **48**(4), 513–40.

Ranger-Moore, J. (1991), 'Bigger may be better but is older wiser? Age dependence in organizational death rates', working paper, University of Arizona, US.

Ranger-Moore, J. (1997), 'If bigger is better, is older wiser? Organizational age and size in the New York life insurance industry', *American Sociological Review*, **58**, 901–20.

Ranger-Moore, J., J. Banaszak and M. Hannan (1991), 'Density dependent dynamics in regulated industries: Founding rates of banks and life insurance companies', *Administrative Science Quarterly*, **36**, 36–65.

Rao, H. (1994), 'The social construction of reputation: Certification contests, legitimation and the survival of organizations in the American automobile industry: 1895–1912', *Strategic Management Journal*, **13**, 29–44.

Rao, R. and L. Argote (1992), 'Collective learning and forgetting: The effects of turnover and group structure', paper presented at the Academy of Management Meetings, Las Vegas, US.

Raub, W. and J. Weesie (1990), 'Reputation and efficiency in social interactions: An example of network effects', *American Journal of Sociology*, **96**, 626–54.

Ravid, S. and M. Spiegel (1997), 'Optimal financial contracts for a start-up with unlimited operating discretion', *Journal of Financial and Quantitative Analysis*, **32**(3), 269–86.

Rea, R. (1989), 'Factors affecting success and failure of seed capital/start-up negotiations', *Journal of Business Venturing*, **4**, 149–58.

Rees, H. and A. Shah (1986), 'An empirical analysis of self-employment in the UK', *Journal of Applied Econometrics*, **1**, 95–108.

Reid, G. (1999), 'Complex actions and simple outcomes: How new entrepreneurs stay in business', *Small Business Economics*, **13**, 303–15.

Renzulli, L. (1998), 'Small business owners, their networks, and the process of resource acquisition', MA Thesis, University of North Carolina, US.

Renzulli, L., H. Aldrich and J. Moody (1998), 'Family matters: Gender, networks, and entrepreneurial outcomes', *Social Forces*, **79**(2), 523–47.

Reynolds, P. (1987), 'New firms: Societal contribution versus survival potential', *Journal of Business Venturing*, **2**, 231–46.

Reynolds, P. (1993), 'High performance entrepreneurship: What makes it different?', in N. Churchill, S. Birley, W. Bygrave, J. Doutriaux, E. Gatewood, F. Hoy and W. Wetzel (eds), *Frontiers of Entrepreneurship Research*, Babson Park, US: Babson College, pp. 88–101.

Reynolds, P. (1994a), 'Autonomous firm dynamics and economic growth in the United States, 1986–1990', *Regional Studies*, **28**(4), 429–42.

Reynolds, P. (1994b), 'Reducing barriers to understanding new firm gestation. Prevalence and success of nascent entrepreneurs', paper presented at the Academy of Management Meetings, Dallas, US.

Reynolds, P. (1997), 'Who starts new firms? Preliminary explorations of firms-in-gestation', *Small Business Economics*, **9**, 449–62.

Reynolds, P., D. Storey and P. Westhead (1994a), 'Cross-national variations in new firm formation rates', *Regional Studies*, **28**, 443–56.

Reynolds, P., D. Storey and P. Westhead (1994b), 'Regional characteristics affecting entrepreneurship: A cross-national comparison', in W. Bygrave, S. Birley, N. Churchill, E. Gatewood, F. Hoy, R. Keeley and W. Wetzel (eds), *Frontiers of Entrepreneurship Research*, Babson Park, US: Babson College, pp. 550–64.

Reynolds, P. and S. White (1997), *The Entrepreneurial Process: Economic Growth, Men, Women and Minorities*, Westport, CT, US: Quorum Books.

Ripsas, S. (1998), 'Towards an interdisciplinary theory of entrepreneurship', *Small Business Economics*, **10**, 103–15.

Ritsila, J. and H. Tervo (2002), 'Effects of unemployment on new firm formation: Micro-level panel data evidence from Finland', *Small Business Economics*, **19**, 31–40.

Roberts, E. (1991a), *Entrepreneurs in High Technology*, New York, US: Oxford University Press.

Roberts, E. (1991b), 'High stakes for high-tech entrepreneurs: Understanding venture capital decision making', *Sloan Management Review*, **32**(2), 9–20.

Roberts, E. and H. Wainer (1971), 'Some characteristics of technical entrepreneurship', *IEEE Transactions on Engineering Management*, **18**(3), 100–109.

Robichaud, Y., E. McGraw and A. Roger (2001), 'Toward the development of a measuring instrument for entrepreneurial motivation', *Journal of Developmental Entrepreneurship*, **6**(2), 189–202.

Robinson, P. and E. Sexton (1994), 'The effect of education and experience on self-employment success', *Journal of Business Venturing*, **9**(2), 141–56.

Robinson, P., D. Stimpson, J. Heufner and H. Hunt (1991), 'An attitude approach to the prediction of entrepreneurship', *Entrepreneurship Theory and Practice*, **15**(4), 13–31.

Robson, M. and C. Wren (1999), 'Marginal and average tax rates and the incentive for self-employment', *Southern Economic Journal*, **65**, 757–73.

Romanelli, E. (1989a), 'Environments and strategies of organization start-up: effects on early survival', *Administrative Science Quarterly*, **34**, 369–87.

Romanelli, E. (1989b), 'Organization birth and population variety: A community perspective on origins', in B. Staw and L. Cummings (eds), *Research in Organization Behavior*, 11, Greenwich, CT, US: JAI Press, pp. 211–46.

Romanelli, E. and K. Schoonhoven (2001), 'The local origins of new firms', in K. Schoonhoven and E. Romanelli (eds), *The Entrepreneurial Dynamic*, Stanford, US: Stanford University Press, pp. 40–67.

Rotter, J.B. (1966), 'Generalized expectancies for internal versus external control of reinforcement', *Psychological Monographs: General and Applied*, **80**(1).

Roure, J. and R. Keeley (1990), 'Predictors of success in new technology based ventures', *Journal of Business Venturing*, **5**(4), 201–20.

Roure, J. and M. Maidique (1986), 'Linking pre-funding factors and high-technology venture success: An exploratory study', *Journal of Business Venturing*, **1**(3), 295–306.

Rousseau, D.M. (1997), 'Organizational behavior in the new organizational era', *Annual Review of Psychology*, **48**, 515–46.

Rueber, A. and E. Fischer (1993), 'The learning experiences of entrepreneurs', in N. Churchill, S. Birley, W. Bygrave, J. Doutriaux, E. Gatewood, F. Hoy and W. Wetzel (eds), *Frontiers of Entrepreneurship Research*, Babson Park, US: Babson College, pp. 234–45.

Ruef, M. (2002), 'Strong ties, weak ties, and islands: Structural and cultural predictors of organizational innovation', *Industrial and Corporate Change*, **11**(3), 427–50.

Rumelt, R. (1987), 'Theory, strategy and entrepreneurship', in D. Teece (ed.), *The Competitive Challenge: Strategies for Industrial Innovation and Renewal*, Cambridge, MA, US: Ballinger, pp. 137–58.

Sagie, A. and D. Elizur (1999), 'Achievement motive and entrepreneurial orientation: A structural analysis', *Journal of Organizational Behavior*, **20**, 375–87.

Sahlman, W. (1990), 'The structure and governance of venture capital organizations', *Journal of Financial Economics*, **27**, 473–521.

Sahlman, W. (1994), 'Insights from the venture capital model of project governance', *Business Economics*, **29**(3), 35–8.

Sanders, J. and V. Nee (1996), 'Immigrant self employment: The family as social capital and the value of human capital', *American Sociological Review*, **61**, 231–49.

Sapienza, H. (1989), 'Variations in venture capitalist–entrepreneur relations: Antecedents and consequences', Ph.D. Dissertation, University of Maryland, US.

Sapienza, H. (1991), 'Comets and duds: Characteristics distinguishing high and low performing high potential ventures', in N. Churchill, W. Bygrave, J. Covin, D. Sexton, D. Slevin, K. Vesper and W. Wetzel (eds), *Frontiers of Entrepreneurship Research*, Babson Park, US: Babson College, pp. 111–27.

Sapienza, H. (1992), 'When do venture capitalists add value?', *Journal of Business Venturing*, **7**(1), 9–27.

Sapienza, H. and A. Gupta (1994), 'Impact of agency risks and task uncertainty on venture capitalist-CEO interaction', *Academy of Management Journal*, **37**(6), 1618–32.

Sarasvathy, S. (2001), 'Causation and effectuation: Toward a theoretical shift from economic inevitability to entrepreneurial contingency', *Academy of Management Review*, **26**(2), 243–63.

Sarasvathy, D., H. Simon and L. Lave (1998), 'Perceiving and managing business risks: Differences between entrepreneurs and bankers', *Journal of Economic Behavior and Organization*, **33**, 207–25.

Schefczyk, M. (2001), 'Determinants of success of German venture capital investments', *Interfaces*, **31**(5), 43–61.

Schell, D. and W. David (1981), 'The community infrastructure of entrepreneurship: A sociopolitical analysis', in K. Vesper (ed.), *Frontiers of Entrepreneurship Research*, Babson Park, US: Babson College, pp. 563–90

Schere, J. (1982), 'Tolerance of ambiguity as a discriminating variable between entrepreneurs and managers', *Academy of Management Best Paper Proceedings*, **42**, 404–8.

Schiller, B. and P. Crewson, (1997), 'Entrepreneurial origins: A longitudinal inquiry', *Economic Inquiry*, **35**, 523–31.

Schoonhoven, K., K. Eisenhardt and K. Lyman (1990), 'Speeding products to market: Waiting time to first product introduction in new firms', *Administrative Science Quarterly*, **35**, 177–207.

Schumpeter, J.A. (1934), *The Theory of Economic Development: An Inquiry Into Profits, Capital Credit, Interest, and the Business Cycle*, Cambridge, MA, US: Harvard University Press.

Schumpeter, J. (1942), *Capitalism, Socialism, and Democracy*, New York, US: Harper.

Schutgens, V. and E. Wever (2000), 'Determinants of new firm success', *Papers in Regional Science*, **79**, 135–59.

Schutz, A. (1967), *The Phenomenology of the Social World*, Evanston, IL, US: Northwestern University Press.

Scott, W. and J. Meyer (1983), 'The organization of societal sector', in J. Meyer and W. Scott (eds), *Organization Environments: Ritual and Rationality*, Beverly Hills, US: Sage, pp. 129–53.

Seth, S. and A. Sen (1995), 'Behavioral characteristics of woman entrepreneurs and executives vis-à-vis their male counterparts: An empirical study', *Social Science International*, **11**, 18–23.

Sexton, D. and B. Bowman (1983), 'Comparative entrepreneurship characteristics of students', in J. Hornaday, J. Timmons and K. Vesper (eds), *Frontiers of Entrepreneurship Research*, Babson Park, US: Babson College, pp. 213–32.

Sexton, D. and N. Bowman (1984), 'Personality inventory for potential entrepreneurs: Evaluation of a modified JPI/PRF-E test instrument', in J. Hornaday, F. Tarpley, J. Timmons and K. Vesper (eds), *Frontiers of Entrepreneurship Research*, Babson Park, US: Babson College, pp. 513–28.

Shackle, G. (1955), *Uncertainty in Economics and Other Reflections*, Cambridge: Cambridge University Press.

Shackle, G. (1982), *Imagination and the Nature of Choice*, Edinburgh, Scotland: Edinburgh University Press.

Shane, S. (1996), 'Hybrid organizational arrangements and their implications for firm growth and survival: A study of new franchisors', *Academy of Management Journal*, **39**(1), 216–34.

Shane, S. (1998), 'Making new franchise systems work', *Strategic Management Journal*, **19**(7), 697–707.

Shane, S. (2000), 'Prior knowledge and the discovery of entrepreneurial opportunities', *Organization Science*, **11**(4), 448–69.

Shane, S. (2001a), 'Technology opportunities and new firm creation', *Management Science*, **47**(2), 205–20.

Shane, S. (2001b), 'Technology regimes and new firm formation', *Management Science*, **47**(9), 1173–81.

Shane, S. (2002), 'Selling university technology: patterns from MIT', *Management Science*, **48**(1), 122–37.

Shane, S. and D. Cable (2002), 'Network ties, reputation, and the financing of new ventures', *Management Science*, **48**(3), 364–81.

Shane, S. and F. Delmar (2001), 'Planning for the survival of new ventures', working paper, University of Maryland, US.

Shane, S. and M. Foo (1999), 'New firm survival: Institutional explanations for new franchisor mortality', *Management Science*, **45**(2), 142–59.

Shane, S. and R. Khurana (2001), 'Career experiences and firm foundings', parper presented at the Academy of Management Meetings.

Shane, S. and T. Stuart (2002), 'Organizational endowments and the performance of university start-ups', *Management Science*, **48**(1), 154–70.

Shane, S. and S. Venkataraman (2000), 'The promise of entrepreneurship as a field of research', *Academy of Management Review*, **26**(1), 13–17.

Shane, S. and S. Venkataraman (2001), 'Entrepreneurship as a field of research: a response to Zahra and Dess, Singh and Erikson', *Academy of Management*, **26**(1), 13–16.

Shane, S., E. Locke and C. Collins (forthcoming), 'Entrepreneurial motivation', *Human Resource Management Review*.

Shapero, A. (1975), 'The displaced, uncomfortable entrepreneur', *Psychology Today*, **9**, 83–8.

Shepherd, D., E. Douglas and M. Shanley (2000), 'New venture survival: Ignorance, external shocks and risk reduction strategies', *Journal of Business Venturing*, **15**, 393–410.

Shuman, J., G. Sussman and J. Shaw (1985), 'Business plans and the start-up of rapid growth companies', in J. Hornaday, E. Shils, J. Timmons and K.

Vesper (eds), *Frontiers of Entrepreneurship Research*, Babson Park, US: Babson College, pp. 294–313.

Simon, H. (1955), 'A behavioral model of rational choice', *Quarterly Journal of Economics*, **69**, 99–118.

Simon, H. (1976), *Administrative Behavior*, New York, US: The Free Press.

Simon, M. and S. Zahra (1994), 'The strategy and performance of independent and corporate-sponsored new ventures', in W. Bygrave, S. Birley, N. Churchill, E. Gatewood, F. Hoy, R. Keeley and W. Wetzel (eds), *Frontiers of Entrepreneurship Research*, Babson Park, US: Babson College, pp. 278–89.

Sine, W. and R. David (forthcoming), 'Environmental jolts, institutional change, and the creation of entrepreneurial opportunity in the US electric power industry', *Research Policy*.

Sine, W., H. Haveman and P. Tolbert (2001), 'Institutional influences on founding variation in the emerging independent power industry', working paper, University of Maryland, US.

Sine, W., S. Shane and D. DiGregorio (2002), 'The halo effect and technology licensing: The influence of institutional prestige on the licensing of university inventions', working paper, University of Maryland, US.

Singh, J. and C. Lumsden (1990), 'Theory and research in organizational ecology', *Annual Review of Sociology*, **16**, 161–95.

Singh, J., D. Tucker and R. House (1986a), 'Organizational change and organizational mortality', *Administrative Science Quarterly*, **31**, 587–611.

Singh, J., D. Tucker and R. House (1986b), 'Organizational legitimacy and the liability of newness', Administrative Science Quarterly, **31**(2), 171–93.

Singh, J., D. Tucker and A. Meinhard (1991), 'Institutional change and ecological dynamics', in W. Powell and P. Dimaggio (eds), *The New Institutionalism in Organizational Analysis*, Chicago, US: University of Chicago Press, pp. 390–422.

Singh, R., G. Hills, R. Hybels and G. Lumpkin (1999), 'Opportunity recognition through social network characteristics of entrepreneurs', in P. Reynolds, W. Bygrave, S. Manigart, C. Mason, C. Mason, G. Meyer, H. Sapienza and K. Shaver (eds), *Frontiers of Entrepreneurship Research*, Babson Park, US: Babson College, pp. 228–41.

Sleeper, S. (1998), 'The role of firm capabilities in the evolution of the laser industry: The making of a high-tech market', Ph.D. Dissertation, Carnegie Mellon University, US.

Smith, A. (1992), 'Race, gender and entrepreneurial orientation', *National Journal of Sociology*, **12**(2), 141–55.

Smith, K., M. Gannon, C. Grimm and T. Mitchell (1988), 'Decision-making behavior in smaller entrepreneurial and larger professionally managed firms', *Journal of Business Venturing*, **3**(3), 223–32.

Sorenson, O. and P. Audia (2000), 'The social structure of entrepreneurial activity: Geographic concentration of footwear production in the United States, 1940–1989', *American Journal of Sociology*, **106**(2), 424–62.

Sorenson, O. and T. Stuart (2001), 'Syndication networks and the spatial distribution of venture capital investments', *American Journal of Sociology*, **106**(6), 1546–88.

Staber, U. (1989), 'Organizational foundings in the cooperative sector in Atlantic Canada: An ecological perspective', *Organization Studies*, **10**, 383–405.

Starr, J. and I. MacMillan (1990), 'Resource cooptation via social contracting: Resource acquisition strategies for new ventures', *Strategic Management Journal*, **11**, 79–92.

Stearns, T. (1996), 'Strategic alliances and the performance of high technology new firms', in P. Reynolds, S. Birley, J. Butler, W. Bygrave, P. Davidsson, W. Gartner and P. McDougall (eds), *Frontiers of Entrepreneurship Research*, Babson Park, US: Babson College, pp. 268–81.

Stearns, T., N. Carter, P. Reynolds and M. Williams (1995), 'New firm survival: Industry, strategy and location', *Journal of Business Venturing*, **10**(1), 23–42.

Steier, L. and R. Greenwood (1995), 'Venture capitalist relationships in the deal structuring and post-investment stages of new firm creation', *Journal of Management Studies*, **32**(3), 337–57.

Stewart, W. and P. Roth (2001), 'Risk taking propensity differences between entrepreneurs and managers: A meta-analytic review', *Journal of Applied Psychology*, **86**(1), 145–53.

Stewart, W., W. Watson, J. Carland and J. Carland (1999), 'A proclivity for entrepreneurship: A comparison of entrepreneurs, small business owners, and corporate managers', *Journal of Business Venturing*, **14**(2), 189–214. .

Storey, D. (1982), *Entrepreneurship and the New Firm*, London: Croom Helm.

Storey, D. (1994a), 'New firm growth and bank financing', *Small Business Economics*, 6, 139–50.

Storey, D. (1994b), *Understanding the Small Business Sector*, London: Routledge.

Storey, D. and A. Jones (1987), 'New firm formation – a labour market approach to industrial entry', *Scottish Journal of Political Economy*, **34**(1), 37–51.

Storey, D. and B. Tether (1998), 'New technology-based firms in the European Union: An introduction', *Research Policy*, **26**, 933–46.

Stuart, T., H. Huang and R. Hybels (1999), 'Interorganizational endorsements and the performance of entrepreneurial ventures', *Administrative Science Quarterly*, **44**, 315–49.

Stuart, T. and D. Robinson (2000), 'The emergence of interorganizational networks: Probation until reputation', working paper, University of Chicago, US.

Stuart, T. and O. Sorenson (2002), 'Liquidity events, noncompete covenants and the geographic distribution of entrepreneurial activity', working paper, University of Chicago, US.

Swaminathan, A. (1995), 'The proliferation of specialist organizations in the American wine industry, 1941–1990', *Administrative Science Quarterly*, **40**(4), 653–80.

Swaminathan, A. (1996), 'Environmental conditions at founding and organizational mortality: A trial-by-fire model', *Academy of Management Journal*, **39**(5): 1350–77.

Swanson, D. and L. Webster (1992), *Private Sector Manufacturing in the Czech and Slovac Republics: A Survey of Firms*, Washington, DC, US: The World Bank.

Taylor, M. (1996), 'Earnings, independence or unemployment: why become self-employed?', *Oxford Bulletin of Economics and Statistics*, **58**, 253–66.

Taylor, M. (1999), 'The survival of the fittest: An analysis of self-employment duration in Britain', *The Economic Journal*, **109**, C140-C155.

Taylor, M. (2001), 'Self-employment and windfall gains in Britain: Evidence from panel data', *Economica*, **68**, 539–65.

Teece, D. (1980), 'Economics of scope and the scope of the enterprise', *Journal of Economic Behavior and Organization*, **1**, 223–47.

Teece, D. (1981), 'The market for know-how and the efficient international transfer of technology', *The Annals of the American Academy*, **458**, 81–96.

Teece, D. and G. Pisano (1994), 'The dynamic capabilities of firms: An introduction', *Industrial and Corporate Change*, **3**(1), 537–56.

Thakur, S. (1999), 'Size of investment, opportunity choice and human resources in new venture growth: Some typologies', *Journal of Business Venturing*, **14**(3), 283–309.

Tolchinsky, P. and D. King (1980), 'Do goals mediate the effects of incentives on performance?', *Academy of Management Review*, **5**(3), 455–67.

Trow, D. (1961), 'Executive succession in small companies', *Administrative Science Quarterly*, **25**, 12–15.

Tucker, D., J. Singh, A. Meinhard and R. House (1988), 'Ecological and institutional sources of change in organizational populations', in G. Carroll (ed.), *Ecological Models of Organizations*, Cambridge: Ballinger, pp. 127–51.

Tucker, D., J. Singh and A. Meinhard (1990), 'Organizational form, population dynamics, and institutional change: The founding patterns of voluntary organizations', *Academy of Management Journal*, **33**, 151–78.

Tullar, W. (2001), 'Russian entrepreneurial motive patterns: A validation of the Miner sentence completion scale in Russia', *Applied Psychology: An International Review*, **50**(3), 422–35.

Tushman, M. and P. Anderson (1986), 'Technological discontinuities and organizational environments', *Administrative Science Quarterly*, **31**, 439–65.

Tyebjee, T. and A. Bruno (1981), 'Venture capital decision-making: Preliminary results from three empirical studies', in K. Vesper (ed.), *Frontiers of Entrepreneurship Research*, Babson Park, US: Babson College, pp. 281–320.

Tyebjee, T. and A. Bruno (1982), 'A comparative analysis of California start-ups from 1978 to 1980', in K. Vesper (ed.), *Frontiers of Entrepreneurship Research*, Babson Park, US: Babson College, pp. 163–76.

Tyson, L., T. Petrin and H. Rogers (1994), 'Promoting entrepreneurship in Eastern Europe', *Small Business Economics*, **6**, 165–84.

Utsch, A. and A. Rauch (2000), 'Innovativeness and initiative as mediators between achievement orientation and venture performance', *European Journal of Work and Organizational Psychology*, **9**(1), 45–62.

Utterback, J. (1994), *Mastering the Dynamics of Innovation*, Boston, US: Harvard Business School Press.

Uusitalo, R. (2001), 'Homo entreprenaurus?', *Applied Economics*, **33**, 1631–8.

Uzzi, B. (1996), 'The sources and consequences of embeddedness for the economic performance of organizations: The network effect', *American Sociological Review*, **61**, 674–98.

Van de Ven, A., R. Hudson and D. Schroeder (1984), 'Designing new business startups: Entrepreneurial, organizational, and ecological considerations', *Journal of Management*, **10**(1), 87–107.

Van Osnabrugge, M. (1998), 'Do serial and non-serial investors behave differently?: An empirical and theoretical analysis', *Entrepreneurship Theory and Practice*, **22**(4), 23–42.

Van Osnabrugge, M. (2000), 'A comparison of business angel and venture capitalist investment procedures: An agency theory-based analysis', *Venture Capital*, **2**(2), 91–109.

Van Praag, C. and J. Cramer (2001), 'The roots of entrepreneurship and labour demand: Individual ability and low risk aversion', *Economica*, **68**(269), 45–62.

Venkatapathy, R. (1984), 'Locus of control among entrepreneurs: A review', *Psychological Studies*, **29**(1), 97–100.

Venkataraman, S. (1997), 'The distinctive domain of entrepreneurship research: An editor's perspective', in J. Katz and R. Brockhaus (eds), *Advances in Entrepreneurship, Firm Emergence, and Growth*, **3**, Greenwich, CT, US: JAI Press, pp. 119–38.

Ventresca, M., M. Washington, D. Diadlin and R. Lacey (1999), 'Between traits and rates: Form entrepreneurship in online database services, 1972–1992', working paper, Northwestern University, US.

Verheul, I. and R. Thurik (2001), 'Start-up capital: Does gender matter?', *Small Business Economics*, **16**(4), 329–45.

Vesalainen, J. and T. Pihkala (1999), 'Motivation structure and entrepreneurial intentions', in P. Reynolds, W. Bygrave, S. Manigart, C. Mason, C. Mason, G. Meyer, Sapienza, H. and K. Shaver (eds), *Frontiers of Entrepreneurship Research*, Babson Park, US: Babson College, pp. 73–87.

Von Hippel, E. (1986), 'Lead users: A source of novel product concepts', *Management Science*, **32**, 791–805.

Von Hippel, E. (1988), *The Sources of Innovation*, New York, US: Oxford University Press.

Von Mises, L. (1949), *Human Action: A Treatise on Economics*, New Haven, US: Yale University Press.

Wade, J., A. Swaminathan and M. Saxon (1998), 'Normative and resource flow consequences of local regulations in the American brewing industry, 1845–1918', *Administrative Science Quarterly*, **43**, 905–35.

Wagner, J. (1994), 'The post-entry performance of new small firms in German manufacturing industries', *The Journal of Industrial Economics*, **42**(2), 141–54.

Wainer, H. and I. Rubin (1969), 'Motivation of research and development entrepreneurs: Determinants of company success', *Journal of Applied Psychology*, **53**(3), 178–84.

Walsh, J. and P. Anderson (1995), 'Owner–manager adaption/innovation preference and employment performance: A comparison of founders and non-founders in the Irish small firm sector', *Journal of Small Business Management*, **33**(3), 1–8.

Walsh, S., B. Kirchhoff and R. Boylan (1996), 'Founder backgrounds and entrepreneurial success: Implications for core competence strategy application to new ventures', in P. Reynolds, S. Birley, J. Butler, W. Bygrave, P. Davidsson, W. Gartner and P. McDougall (eds), *Frontiers of Entrepreneurship Research*, Babson Park, US: Babson College, pp. 146–54.

Walstad, W. and M. Kourilsky (1998), 'Entrepreneurial attitudes and knowledge of black youth', *Entrepreneurship Theory and Practice*, **23**(2), 5–18.

Ward, E. (1993), 'Motivation of expansion plans of entrepreneurs and small business managers', *Journal of Small Business Management*, **31**(1), 32–8.

Weber, M. (1947), *The Theory of Social and Economic Organization*, New York, US: Oxford University Press.

Weinberg, J. (1994), 'Private information and inventive activity', *Journal of Economic Behavior and Organization*, **24**, 71–90.

Welbourne, T. and A. Andrews (1996), 'Predicting the performance of initial public offerings: Should human resource management be in the equation?', *Academy of Management Journal*, **39**(4), 891–919.

Westhead, P. (1995), 'Survival and employment growth contrasts between types of owner-managed high-technology firms', *Entrepreneurship Theory and Practice*, **20**(1), 5–27.

Westhead, P. and D. Storey (1997), 'Financial constraints on the growth of high-tech small firms in the UK', *Applied Financial Economics*, **7**, 197–201.

White, S. and P. Reynolds (1996), 'Government programs and high growth new firms', in P. Reynolds, S. Birley, J. Butler, W. Bygrave, P. Davidsson, W. Gartner and P. McDougall (eds), *Frontiers of Entrepreneurship Research*, Babson Park, US: Babson College, pp. 621–35.

Wholey, D., J. Christianson and S. Sanchez (1992), 'Organization size and failure among health maintenance organizations', *American Sociological Review*, **57**, 829–42.

Wicker, A. and J. King (1989), 'Employment, ownership, and survival in microbusiness: A study of new retail and service establishments', *Small Business Economics*, **1**, 137–52.

Williams, D. (1999), 'Why do entrepreneurs become franchisees? An empirical analysis of organizational choice', *Journal of Business Venturing*, **14**(1), 103–24.

Williamson, I., D. Cable and H. Aldrich (2002), 'Smaller but not necessarily weaker: How small businesses can overcome barriers to recruitment', in J. Katz and T. Welbourne (eds), *Research in Entrepreneurship and Firm Growth*, **5**, Greenwich, CT, US: JAI Press, pp. 83–106.

Williamson, O. (1975), *Markets and Hierarchies: Analysis and Anti-Trust Implications*, New York, US: Free Press.

Williamson, O. (1985), *The Economic Institutions of Capitalism: Firms, Markets, Relational Contracting*, New York, US: Free Press.

Wilson, R. (1985), 'Reputations in games and markets', in A. Roth (ed.), *Game Theoretic Models of Bargaining*, New York, US: Cambridge University Press, pp. 65–84.

Winter, S. (1984), 'Schumpeterian competition in alternative technological regimes', *Journal of Economic Behavior and Organization*, **5** (3–4), 287–320.

Wong, Y. (1986). 'Entrepreneurship, marriage, and earnings', *Review of Economics and Statistics*, **68**(4), 693–9.

Woodruff, A. and T. Alexander (1958), *Success and Failure in Small Manufacturing*, Pittsburgh, US: University of Pittsburgh Press.

Wooten, K., T. Timmerman and R. Folger (1999), 'The use of personality and the five-factor model to predict new business ventures: From outplacement to start-up', *Journal of Vocational Behavior*, **54**, 82–101.

Wu, S. (1989), *Production, Entrepreneurship and Profit*, Cambridge, MA, US: Basil Blackwell.

Wyant R. (1977), *The Business Failure Record*, New York, US: Dun and Bradstreet.

Young, R. and J. Francis (1991), 'Entrepreneurship and innovation in small manufacturing firms', *Social Science Quarterly*, **72**(1), 149–62.

Yu, T. (2001), 'Entrepreneurial alertness and discovery', *The Review of Austrian Economics*, **14**(1), 47–63.

Zahra, S. and W. Bogner (2000), 'Technology strategy and software new ventures' performance: Exploring the moderating effect of the competitive environment', *Journal of Business Venturing*, **15**(2), 135–73.

Zahra, S. and G. Dess (2001), 'Entrepreneurship as a field of research: Encouraging dialogue and debate', *Academy of Management Review*, **26**(1), 8–11.

Zietsma, C. (1999), 'Opportunity knocks – or does it hide? An examination of the role of opportunity recognition in entrepreneurship', in P. Reynolds, W. Bygrave, S. Manigart, C. Mason, C. Mason, G. Meyer, H. Sapienza and K. Shaver (eds), *Frontiers of Entrepreneurship Research*, Babson Park, US: Babson College, pp. 242–56.

Zimmer, C. and H. Aldrich (1987), 'Resource mobilization through ethnic networks: Kinship and friendship ties of shopkeepers in England', *Sociological Perspectives*, **30**(4), 422–55.

Zimmerman, M. and G. Zeitz (2002), 'Beyond survival: Achieving new venture growth by building legitimacy', *Academy of Management Review*, **27**(3), 414–31.

Zucker, L., M. Darby and M. Brewer (1998), 'Intellectual human capital and the birth of US biotechnology enterprises', *American Economic Review*, **88**(1), 290–305.

Index

Aboud, J. 100, 106
Abrahamson, E. 190
absorptive capacity 13, 50–54, 253
achievement motivation 99–103, 254
acquisition 211, 224
Acs, Z. 3, 66, 122–3, 124, 127, 138, 141, 148, 151
actions 184–8, 257, 266
adaptability strategy 213
adverse selection 40, 166, 168, 172, 174, 175, 178, 233–4, 241
advertising 140–41, 203
age 89–91, 129–30, 207–9, 254
agreeableness 99, 254
Ahmed, S. 100, 104, 109
Alba-Ramirez, A. 65, 90
Aldrich, H. 1, 5, 7, 20, 22, 27, 33, 47, 49, 51, 53, 61, 79, 92–3, 113, 132–3, 145, 157, 161, 168–9, 178, 182–3, 185–7, 191, 197, 202, 207, 215–16, 219–22, 228, 241–6, 261
Alexander, J. 74
Alexander, T. 222
Allen, K. 237
alliances 213–15
Allinson, C. 115
Amburgey, T. 27, 208
Amit, R. 8, 63, 103, 113, 150, 152, 166, 186, 189, 196–8, 205, 226
Anand, B. 231
Anderson, A. 50
Anderson, J. 245
Anderson, P. 3, 57, 131, 226, 227
Andrews, A. 247
anti-dilution provisions 173
Anton, J. 128, 137, 211
Applebee, A. 222
appropriability conditions 135–8, 256
Arabsheibani, G. 114
Argote, L. 242
Arora, A. 231

Arrow, W. 7, 37, 39, 43, 136, 161, 167, 174, 220, 226, 231, 243, 244
asset specificity 179, 232
Audia, P. 31–2, 133
Audretsch, D. 3, 30, 32, 65–6, 71, 119, 122–4, 127, 138–41, 143, 148, 151, 201, 224–6, 228, 232
Azoulay, P. 15, 220, 221, 233

Babb, E. 98, 101
Babb, S. 98, 101
Baker, T. 215–16, 221, 222, 242
Baldwin, J. 141–2
Bamford, C. 163, 203, 212
Banaszak-Holl, J. 162, 202
Bandura, A. 111
Bania, N. 139
Barnes, M. 232
Barnett, W. 27, 29, 126, 130, 133–4, 152, 200, 202, 208
Barney, J. 113, 114, 115, 188, 197
Baron, J. 220
Baron, R. 56, 98–9, 111, 113, 115, 223
Barrick, M. 97, 99
Barron, D. 151
Barry, C. 174, 175
Barzel, Y. 166, 168, 180
Basu, A. 180
Bates, T. 67, 69–70, 72–3, 76–7, 80, 90–91, 119, 162, 164, 169, 180, 185, 189, 209, 211, 239–40
Baum, J. 27–8, 55, 81, 125, 127, 131–4, 138, 149, 151, 162, 196, 200, 202, 204, 209, 214–16, 222–3, 227, 239
Baumol, W. 39, 113, 145, 146, 265
Bayer, K. 81
Begley, T. 85, 100–101, 103–4, 105, 159
behaviours 184–8, 257, 266
Bellu, R. 57, 100
Bernardo, A. 21, 113
Bernhardt, I. 64, 68, 170